OHIO POLITICS

OHIO POLITICS

❖

Edited by Alexander P. Lamis

❖

with the assistance of
Mary Anne Sharkey

❖

The Kent State University Press

KENT, OHIO, & LONDON, ENGLAND

© 1994 by The Kent State University Press,
Kent, Ohio 44242
ALL RIGHTS RESERVED
Library of Congress Catalog Card Number 94-7637
ISBN 0-87338-507-1 (cloth)
ISBN 0-87338-509-8 (pbk).
Manufactured in the United States of America

03 02 01 00 99 98 97 96 95 94   5 4 3 2 1

All photos are reprinted with permission
from the *Columbus* (Ohio) *Dispatch.*

Library of Congress Cataloging-in-Publication Data

Ohio politics / edited by Alexander P. Lamis with the assistance of
    Mary Anne Sharkey.
        p.   cm.
    Includes bibliographical references and index.
    ISBN 0-87338-507-1 (alk. paper)∞
    ISBN 0-87338-509-8 (pbk. : alk. paper)∞
    1. Ohio—Politics and government—1951– 2. Ohio—Politics and
government—1865–1950. I. Lamis, Alexander P. II. Sharkey, Mary
Anne.
    F496.2.O37   1994
    320.9771—dc20   94-7637
                                                        CIP

British Library Cataloging-in-Publication data are available.

❖

This book is dedicated to the People of Ohio—

In hope that knowledge about our political system

will contribute to enlightened government

❖

Contents

❖

❖

Preface

❖

❖ This book began in a chance encounter I had in April 1991 at the annual meeting of the Organization of American Historians. The location was only a stone's throw from the Ohio River, but, I must confess, it occurred a little down river from the Buckeye State—in Louisville, Kentucky!

Making my rounds of the publishers' exhibits, I stopped at the Kent State University Press booth and picked up a copy of an appealing-looking, newly published Kent book entitled *Ohio and Its People* and written by the distinguished University of Akron historian George Knepper, who later became a friend of mine and the author of the first chapter of this volume. While thumbing through Knepper's book, I casually mentioned to the gentleman at the booth what a shame it was that no comprehensive book on Ohio politics existed. The gentleman, who turned out to be John Hubbell, director of the Kent State University Press and a noted Civil War historian, shot back the ominous reply "Why don't you do one?"

I thought it over quickly and responded that it might be possible to assemble a team of writers—journalists and academics—to tackle the job, and I said I would look into it when I returned to Cleveland, mentioning that my first task would be to recruit a veteran reporter who knew the Columbus political scene well. At the end of the spring semester I contacted Mary Anne Sharkey, then the editorial director and now the politics editor of the Cleveland *Plain Dealer*. If the genesis for this book began a hundred miles or so from the Ohio state line, there could not have been a more fitting Cleveland location for the initial planning lunch Mary Anne and I had in the summer of 1991: a Slovenian restaurant next to the Slovenian National Home on St. Clair Avenue in the old neighborhood of Frank J. Lausche, whose era in Ohio politics starts this book's gubernatorial chapters and who shares his ethnic origins with our current governor, George Voinovich.

From that planning session and several others at Case Western Reserve University, Mary Anne and I drew up a list of potential contributors and drafted an outline that, with the usual midstream modifications, yielded the present product. As senior editor, the bulk of the organizational, administrative, and editing tasks fell to me, although Mary Anne's role was pivotal in the selection of most of the journalist contributors and in the important decision to structure a major part of the book by key gubernatorial eras. Her intimate knowledge of Ohio politics, gained throughout a distinguished career of reporting, including a stint as the *Plain Dealer*'s Columbus bureau chief, influenced the book's direction at various turns. I very much appreciate the important editorial assistance she provided.

Whatever merit this book has is due in large measure to the hard work, skill, and insights of the diligent contributors. Although they are of two general backgrounds, journalism and academe, the chapter writers bring the best instincts of their respective fields to bear on the common problem—understanding contemporary Ohio politics. The journalists have at their command a richness of association with the heat of the political struggle, a close familiarity with the personalities involved, and a keen appreciation for the vagaries of political life, not to mention a facility with language. The political scientists bring to the assignment a mastery of the general workings of political institutions and processes that draws on a rich, venerable, and growing body of theoretical knowledge dating back at least to the writings of Aristotle. Employing the strengths of each set of writers was the challenge of this volume. In fact, in my letter of March 1992 to the contributors announcing the signing of the contract with Kent and the kickoff of the chapter writing, I referred to this goal: "Further, our combination of political journalists and academics holds out the promise that our different perspectives can complement each other and create a product greater than the sum of the parts." I am confident the reader will find that the mixture has been a beneficial one.

In roughly the first half of the book, the journalists present analytical narrative histories of the various gubernatorial eras from the end of

World War II to the present. In the latter part, the political scientists analyze the major components of Ohio's political system—the legislature, executive, judiciary, interest groups, and political parties and elections. There are two departures from this general scheme. First, the book opens with a historical overview by Professor Knepper. And, second, the transition from the narratives to the overtly analytical sections is accomplished in two chapters: one examining the role of the news media in Ohio politics (written, incidentally, by a journalism professor who is a former newspaper reporter) and the other covering a half century of Ohio politicians who operated mainly on the banks of the Potomac.

So much for the overall structure. What is there to learn in the chapters that follow? Much more, of course, than I can possibly cover here, but a preview of each chapter is in order.

In chapter 1 Knepper emphasizes Ohio's diversity of geography, population, and economic activity. For example, he notes that the state's many ethnocultural divisions encouraged compromise, stifled extremists, and drew "all factions toward the political center." Next, he takes us on a rapid historical tour of Ohio politics from the days of William McKinley and Marcus Hanna through the Progressive Era and the Great Depression to the six-year governorship of the conservative Republican John W. Bricker, which ended when Bricker joined the losing Republican national ticket in 1944 as Thomas Dewey's vice presidential running mate. This is an invaluable excursion, since the rest of the chapters plunge us into the midst of post-1944 politics and the reader is likely to be a little curious about what immediately preceded the main story. Knepper ends by summoning the image of the Roman god Janus, whose two faces looking in opposite directions encapsules for the dean of Ohio historians the up-and-down passage of our state since World War II. The use of this image is an apt one for what was perhaps an unintended reason: Janus, from whose name we derive January, signified beginnings, and Knepper provides a good one.

Brian Usher and Mike Curtin, two experienced journalists and longtime Columbus political observers, are too young to have covered the governors they write about in chapters 2 and 3, respectively, making them the exceptions among the writers of the gubernatorial chapters. But both men eagerly waded into the Ohio Historical Society's voluminous archives and produced accounts that make you think they were as close to the scene as their other colleagues. Usher demonstrates that Democrat Frank Lausche's ten years as governor, broken by two years under Republican governor Thomas J. Herbert, did not represent an era of Democratic dominance in Ohio. In fact, Lausche, "the quintessential ethnic politician," was so out of step with the mainstream of the Democratic party as it was transformed by the New Deal that he was actually given consideration for a spot on the Republican national ticket in 1956! Known for his frugality in government expenditure and his independence, especially from organized labor, Lausche was flexible enough to retreat on his "no new taxes" pledges a time or two when threatened by deficits. He won a U.S. Senate seat in 1956 and served two full terms before his "independence" caught up with him in the Democratic primary of 1968.

Curtin chronicles six generally bullish years when Ohio's population growth and economic prosperity appeared on a permanent upward path. Two major politicians—Republican C. William O'Neill of Marietta, a former House speaker, and Democrat Michael V. DiSalle, a former mayor of Toledo—dominated the period, starting with their face-off in the 1956 election for the state's last two-year gubernatorial term, which O'Neill won handily as President Eisenhower was coasting to reelection. Two years later DiSalle turned the tables in a sweeping Democratic victory aided by the monumental GOP miscalculation over the 1958 right-to-work initiative as well as the deep economic recession of that year. "DiSalle considered himself a reformer," Curtin writes, "and he was quick to argue that Ohio's social welfare obligations had gone largely unmet under penny-pinching administrations of both Democrats and Republicans of the previous two decades." To fund his ambitous programs, DiSalle proposed and the Democratic legislature adopted an increase in several state taxes. Republicans tagged him "Tax-Hike Mike" and recaptured the legislature in 1960. Two years later DiSalle was turned out of office by the man who would become Ohio's longest-serving governor, James A. Rhodes, the state auditor and a former mayor of Columbus. Curtin quotes DiSalle on the difficulty of campaigning against the skillful Rhodes: "[It] is like trying to play ping-pong on a pogo stick," no doubt a feeling more than a few other politicians experienced in the years to come.

The next five chapters, going from Rhodes's first two terms through the initial years of Voinovich's first term, were crafted by veteran journalists who covered every day of their respective administrations for their newspapers or wire service. (For the specifics concerning each writer's background, consult the biographical sketches of the contributors at the end of this book.) In these chapters they draw frequently from their own contemporary articles for facts and quotations. Collectively, they tell a fascinating first-hand story.

Looming large over the state's politics was Jim Rhodes, the Coalton, Ohio, native who methodically worked his way up the political ladder to the state's top job. In chapter 4, Richard G. Zimmerman depicts how this master politician launched massive capital building campaigns paid for by voter-approved bond issues that doubled the number of state-supported universities and dotted the countryside with branch campuses and community colleges. There were also highway projects, new state office buildings, expanded facilities at state parks, and a new prison. Rhodes's mastery of the press, his occasionally controversial steward-ship of the Ohio Republican party, the 1969 *Life* magazine article that temporarily put the governor on the defensive, the shootings at Kent State, Rhodes's defeat in 1970 for the U.S. Senate nomination—all are there. Zimmerman ends his chapter with a thoughtful, evenhanded as-sessment of what are generally agreed to have been the better of Rhodes's four terms.

Governor John J. Gilligan, the Cincinnati Democrat elected in 1970, came to office decrying the state's low-tax, low-service mentality, which he said had produced "a nearly bankrupt education system; de-caying cities; polluted air and filthy water," among other things. Hugh McDiarmid's chapter 5 captures the key events in Gilligan's drive to "do better," including his successful push in 1971 for Ohio's first corpo-rate and personal income tax. The governor's quick wit came with a confrontational style, and both are on display in several vivid episodes that McDiarmid recreates, such as the legendary 1972 Ohio State Fair "sheep shearing" tale. In the end, an overconfident Gilligan was nar-rowly defeated for reelection in the amazing 1974 political resurrection of former governor Jim Rhodes, who charged Gilligan with "taxing everything in Ohio that walks, crawls or flies."

In chapter 6, which is devoted to Rhodes's second two terms, Lee Leonard presents the most detailed of the gubernatorial chapters. In fact, Leonard's attention to all aspects of the ongoing governmental struggle makes the chapter a fine case study in the dynamics of Ohio's political institutions. Rhodes pushed immediately for a series of bond issues in 1975 to create jobs for Ohioans. "We will make the dirt fly on construc-tion jobs—this year," he declared, but the voters decisively rejected the issues. After this rebuff, Rhodes stayed remarkably quiet on the policy initiative front. However, the wily governor's considerable administrative talents remained on constant display—from organizing the state during the natural gas shortage of 1977 to his personal leadership of the response to the fierce blizzard of January 1978. The chapter ends with an account of the 1982 fiscal crisis that resulted in, among other things, a controversial "temporary" personal income tax surcharge. "Statehouse reporters," Leonard notes, "eager to hang Rhodes for his past hypocrisy on taxes, presented the surcharge as a fifty percent increase," which says something about the frustrations of reporters who had to deal with the veteran governor's "bob-and-weave political skills," to borrow another Leonard phrase.

Tim Miller admirably tackles in chapter 7 the difficult task of recreating and assessing the frenetic eight years of Richard F. Celeste, the first Democratic governor to win reelection since Lausche. Was Celeste's gubernatorial tenure one of "tremendous potential not realized," as a notable Republican state representative phrased it, or was Celeste "an innovative governor, perhaps the first 'global' governor at the end of the twentieth century," to quote the governor himself? The Celeste era is steeped in controversy not just because of its immediacy but more importantly because it raises issues that cut to the heart of the continuing political debate in Ohio, issues that remain just below the surface in the more placid Voinovich days.

After tracing Celeste's origins in an Italian family in the westside Cleveland suburb of Lakewood, his education, and steady rise to statewide prominence, Miller details the multifaceted 1982 campaign that brought the forty-five-year-old candidate to the governorship. A defining moment of his tenure, to use a more recent term, came early. Faced with a huge budget deficit in 1983, Celeste won approval of what was dubbed his "90 percent tax hike," which included the "temporary" Rhodes income tax increase plus other adjustments and which, Celeste's supporters argue, was much less than 90 percent. There followed reforms in mental health and in the budget process, the establishment of the Eminent Scholars and Edison programs, visible efforts to promote job creation, increased funding for schools, and the widely praised response to the Home State savings and loan crisis. The downside, in addition to higher taxes, involved charges of cronyism in appointments and in the awarding of state contracts, allegations of demands for campaign contributions in order to get state business, and a series of scandals involving gubernatorial appointees. In a Miller interview, Celeste says that "history will judge me better than my contemporaries," and, with the former governor still short of retirement age, more than a few observers think the judgment may come sooner—in a future election for high office.

Thomas Suddes, in chapter 8, carries the story of Ohio's post–World War II governors through the first three and a half years of the incumbent, Republican George Voinovich, the former Cleveland mayor who won the governorship in 1990 after over two decades in a series of elective positions. Promising to work "harder and smarter and do more with less," Voinovich engaged in a variety of budgetary battles with the legislature, culminating in a December 1992 agreement that raised taxes but avoided further cuts in education. Suddes adeptly explains the complexities of the fiscal conflicts of the Voinovich years, which are at the core of state government. Suddes also ranges widely across the Ohio political landscape, offering a fascinating profile of outgoing House speaker Vernal G. Riffe, Jr., unquestionably the most powerful Democrat in the state, until he chose to retire when his term expires on December 31, 1994, and touching on key recent developments, such as the bitterly contested 1992 legislative redistricting and the 1993 "reform" of Ohio's workers' compensation system. With the 1994 election season fast approaching, Suddes's panoramic overview provides an insightful preview of the campaign to come as Governor Voinovich seeks reelection later this year.

In chapter 9 Sharon Crook West scrutinizes the way the news media cover Ohio politics, focusing on the thirty-five or so reporters in Columbus who devote their full time to state government. For this chapter, she and a graduate research assistant, Peter F. O'Connell, conducted fourteen interviews with top journalists and political leaders, including a former governor. She weaves their responses into her own penetrating assessment of the strengths and failings of the Statehouse press corps, findings well worth pondering by all Buckeye State political spectators who are dependent on these reporters for their information about state government. Incidentally, the authors of several of this book's gubernatorial chapters were interviewed as part of West's study.

Tom Diemer's chapter 10 is a lively tour through nearly fifty years of Ohio's representation in Congress, starting with "Mr. Republican," Cincinnati's Robert A. Taft, the Senate majority leader and very nearly the Republican presidential standard-bearer in 1952. Included are the political stories of our current U.S. senators, Democrats John Glenn and Howard Metzenbaum, the former reelected to his fourth term in 1992 and the latter retiring this year after three terms. Among the tales told here is the amazing one about a powerful and infamous House Democrat, Congressman Wayne L. Hays of Belmont County, who was brought down by a sensational scandal. Diemer, who covers the Ohio congressional delegation for the Cleveland *Plain Dealer*, is ideally situated to sum up "Ohio in Washington," and he pulls no punches, concluding that the state's members of Congress have been "under-achievers" given the state's size and wealth and considering the clout amassed by delegations from lesser states. Diemer ends this half-century journey with an overview of the nineteen current U.S. House members from Ohio—ten Democrats and nine Republicans—who were elected in 1992 after the district lines were redrawn for the 1990s.

Next are the five chapters devoted to analyzing key Buckeye State political institutions and processes. All are written by political scientists at Ohio universities, although a lone journalist had a hand in the multi-authored final chapter.

In chapter 11 Samuel C. Patterson, one of America's foremost legislative scholars, begins his assessment of the Ohio General Assembly by pointing out a paradox not uncommon today among American legislative bodies: as the Ohio legislature has become more professional and effective, its standing with the public has declined, a sentiment demonstrated in 1992 in the overwhelming voter approval of term limits for legislators. By comparing a detailed 1988 survey of Ohio legislators with a survey done in 1957, Patterson is able to chart significant changes over the years. In 1957, for example, the legislature had only five women and one black, a situation markedly different today. After the 1992 elections, there were twenty-nine women legislators and fifteen African Americans, the latter, incidentally, organized in an important caucus—Black Elected Democrats of Ohio (BEDO). Close observers of the legislature will not be surprised to discover that considerable space is devoted to the role of the outgoing speaker Riffe, the longest-serving speaker in Ohio history and the single most powerful person in the legislature. Patterson carefully examines the sources of Riffe's power along with the role of other legislative leaders. The chapter also covers the backgrounds of legislators and their ideological orientations, the committee system, and the part political parties play in the legislature, among other key topics.

In chapter 12 John J. Gargan takes on the giant of state government—the executive branch. He begins with a discussion of the centrality of the governor, considering, among other items, the career paths followed by those who seek the governorship and the office's formal powers (Ohio falls into the "strong governor" category in comparative rankings). Gargan then surveys the important people surrounding the governor, beginning with the heads of the state's twenty-three cabinet departments and including the governor's immediate staff. He refers to high-level personnel difficulties that have bedeviled recent administrations and touches on the tensions that occasionally develop between department heads and the executive staff. The attorney general, secretary of state, treasurer, and auditor—the four other executive officials who are elected statewide but separately from the governor—are scrutinized, along with an important, if frequently obscure, component of state government, the several hundred state boards and commissions. Three useful tables pinpoint the parts of the executive branch that have the highest number of employees and where the most money is spent. The chapter ends with a sober assessment of the difficult fiscal reality a governor faces in the 1990s and calls for the exercise of political vision by the occupant of the state's top position.

Ohio's third branch of government, the judiciary, receives comprehensive treatment in chapter 13, written by Lawrence Baum and his graduate student Mark Kemper. After a brief overview of the state court structure, they devote considerable space to Ohio's method of judicial selection—nomination by partisan primary followed by a general election using a nonpartisan ballot. They contrast this system with the Missouri plan's "merit" selection scheme and discuss the overwhelming rejection of the "merit" alternative by Ohio voters in 1987. There is an interesting analysis of lower-court elections, revealing, among other things, how different these less-visible elections are in large urban counties compared to rural, small-town counties. Considerable attention is devoted to the state's highest court, the Ohio Supreme Court, elections to which are competitive, high-visibility affairs that are becoming increasingly expensive. The authors find that the majority of the Supreme Court's work falls into four areas: regulation of the legal profession, workers' compensation, taxation, and criminal law and procedure. In telling how the high court operates, they describe recent controversies that have surrounded several prominent justices as well as the highly publicized conflicts that have erupted on the court. Throughout the chapter the authors place the judiciary squarely in the midst of the state's political struggles, and, in their conclusion, they show that this political role is both legitimate and inevitable.

Lobbying the government to influence public policy is an accepted part of the democratic process, and in chapter 14 Charles Funderburk and Robert Adams explain how it is done in Columbus, by whom, and with what result. They stipulate in the beginning that "those who have less" are usually left out of the process, because only organized interest groups are players at the table of power. To get at how interest-group politics works in Ohio government, the authors interviewed ten lobbyists and seventeen legislators. They present tabulations of part of their findings in six important tables, which spotlight the interest groups that are perceived to have the most clout in the capital. Here are a few of the topics covered in the chapter: the "pay-to-play" system that is fueled by the rising cost of election campaigns; the proliferation of single-issue and "public interest" lobbying groups in Columbus; and, the recent ascendancy of so-called "hired-gun" lobbying firms that work on contract for a variety of clients and that are run by political insiders with close ties to leading legislators of both parties.

Finally, our attention turns exclusively to elections and political parties, subjects that have been present, of course, in one form or another in all of the preceding chapters. Written by David E. Sturrock, Michael Margolis, John C. Green, and Dick Kimmins, chapter 15's opening survey of recent elections makes clear that Ohio's status as a competitive two-party state is in no danger of erosion. The regularity with which the Republicans and Democrats have occupied the governorship, for example, is without parallel among the fifty states, the authors point out. In 1992 Ohio's pivotal role in presidential elections was again on display in, among other ways, the frequent number of visits to the state by the main candidates. Once more the winner that year—Democrat Bill Clinton—carried Ohio, as has happened in every presidential election in the twentieth century except two (1944 and 1960). Incidentally, no Republican has ever won the White House without carrying Ohio. A geographical illustration of the strongholds of the state's two parties is presented in a fascinating map that divides the state's eighty-eight counties into quartiles based on their percentages of the 1990 vote for Governor Voinovich. So stable is Ohio's two-party system that similar partisan patterns can be found in rough fashion in all other recent major statewide elections.

This chapter also surveys party organization in the state, offering nuts-and-bolts information not widely known about the intricacies of these partisan structures. In an era when political parties are generally viewed as in decline, partly as a result of the dominance of television in modern campaigning, the authors make clear that Ohio party leaders still make a difference. The point is driven home through the recreation of a 1990 episode so dramatic that it struck one of the authors as analogous to a scene from the sequel to the movie *The Godfather*. The story, best left to the chapter, concerned how it came to be that two prominent Republicans avoided a major primary battle to the benefit of the party's long-term strategy. That episode and much other data lead the authors to conclude that "Political parties still play a major role in the state's political life."

Upon completion of this long and multifarious journey through contemporary Ohio political life, one is likely to ponder what is in store for the state's political system in the years ahead. And this is a most propitious time for such speculation because, as a result of a momentous international event, the end of the cold war, Americans are giving more and more attention to the state of our own democracy. After fifty years of successfully carrying at great cost the burden of leadership of the free world, we are, I believe, at the beginning of a great new experiment in our own democratic development. The attention given to domestic matters both in the 1992 presidential election and in the first year of the Clinton administration is evidence of this renewed interest in our own problems, even though, of course, we are not about to abandon our vital role in world affairs. The topics at the top of the nation's political agenda today are primarily domestic in nature—health-care and welfare reform, education, job creation and economic development in an increasingly competitive global market, crime and drugs, environmental protection, rebuilding our neglected infrastructure.

Even at the height of the Great Society—that bold experiment in domestic reform so pilloried in the 1980s as big government run amok—President Lyndon Johnson called for the creation of a New Federalism, the first of every president since the 1960s to recognize the necessity of an innovative federal-state partnership in our far-flung, diverse nation. If we have learned anything by watching powerful interests milk the Washington system—many of them well-to-do Democratic lawyer-lobbyists adept at perverting for the benefit of their privileged clientele measures adopted with the best of motives—it is that the solutions to our domestic concerns cannot afford to wait on the cumbersome and malodorous political arena the nation's capital has become. If the best the federal government's politicians can do—and Republicans and Democrats share this shame about equally—is to increase the national debt from $1 trillion, where it stood in the late 1970s after 190 years of our history, to over $4 trillion a decade or so later, reliance on solutions from Washington is not sensible.

So, that leaves the states—and for us in Ohio, our state government. If my reading of the direction of national affairs is correct, more and more responsibility is going to flow to the state level. Therein lies a great challenge for Ohioans.

Self-government is no easy task. Democracy is not just a word to enshrine with reverence and place on an altar to be forgotten. It is an everyday opportunity for citizens to participate in guiding the destiny of the world around them. After over two centuries of experimentation, Americans have institutionalized the forms of democratic practice— free and fair elections, honest public accounting for the expenditure of public money, the rule of law and the protection of civil liberties, including the right of free expression, to name some of the basic elements. How hard these democratic mechanisms are to develop is displayed daily as we watch the people of the former Soviet Union and their once-captive satellite nations, not to mention the "expectant people" of what we used to call the Third World, struggle to establish what we take for granted.

Thus, with a fully functioning democratic process, one less than a decade away from celebrating the two-hundredth anniversary of statehood in 2003, how can Ohioans make the Ohio political system work better? This is a question, of course, that no book or writer can answer. Ohioans must seize the challenge the post–cold war era offers and provide the answer through hard work, daring, and sacrifice. It is the hope of this book, as reflected in the words of the dedication, that the knowledge contained here will be of assistance in such a worthy journey, a venture that one would like to see conducted with optimism and a modicum of joy, a quantity not so highly visible in our nation's political life since the passing of Hubert H. Humphrey, that great crusader for a better world.

Many people assisted during the preparation of this book, and I would like to acknowledge their assistance and express my sincere appreciation to all of them. If I have forgotten anyone in the listing that follows, it is inadvertent and I apologize in advance.

At Case Western Reserve University, my former dean, Suzanne Ferguson, and my current dean, John Bassett, of the College of Arts and Sciences, provided two small grants that helped cover editorial expenses, which I appreciate very much. My chairman, Vince McHale, of the CWRU Department of Political Science, was supportive throughout the project, going beyond the bounds of duty to provide me with the most up-to-date computer equipment and services as well as a little extra department money for expenses.

Mike Curtin of the *Columbus Dispatch* deserves special thanks for combing through decades of photographs in the *Dispatch*'s files to retrieve the ones that appear in this book. I would like also to thank Robert B. Smith, the editor of the *Dispatch*, for granting us permission to use his newspaper's photographs.

Jack Gargan deserves my appreciation on several counts. First, he and I collaborated to write the bibliographical essay at the end of the book, which was a pleasant working experience guided by both his extensive familiarity with the literature and his good humor. Second, he served as a sounding board for me throughout the editorial process, providing frank and valuable advice, plus encouragement from time to time. And, finally, he read the entire manuscript in final form.

Nearly all of the other contributors also assisted in various helpful ways apart from writing their chapters, and I am very thankful to have had their aid. In particular, Brian Usher was a constant source of encouragement and advice throughout the project and served ably and cheerfully as Columbus coordinator for the October 29, 1994, Ohio politics forums planned to mark this book's publication. Rick Zimmerman and Tom Suddes kindly assisted by reading and commenting on chapters written by their colleagues. And Lee Leonard provided me with one of the most memorable experiences of the editorial process when he took me along for a fascinating three-hour interview session with former governor Rhodes in November 1992.

Andrew Lucker, a Ph.D. candidate in my department, provided important assistance in translating the various contributors' computer disks into a master copy, a job that required him to put in countless hours grappling with more than a few exotic computer languages. Also, he kept me supplied with clean, laser-printed manuscript copies throughout the editing process and on several occasion made calls to authors to get corrections and updates. All this he did as a volunteer, and I am very thankful to have had his aid.

Margaret Rawa, Gail Taylor, Sharon Skowronski, William C. Daroff, Florencio Yuzon, Thomas Zeeb, Elsie Finley, and Susan Mohorcic helped in one task or another during the two years this book was in the making. I appreciate their assistance very much.

At the Kent State University Press, I am in the debt of John Hubbell for more than the idea for this book. He devoted considerable time to the project, guiding it along smoothly each step of the way. In particular, he proved that press directors can still edit copy, going over the manuscript line by line and offering scores of valuable suggestions.

Also, I would like to express my appreciation to the Kent State University Press's senior editor, Julia Morton, who skillfully supervised the editorial production, and to the book's copy editor, Joanna Hildebrand, whose fine work immeasurably improved the manuscript. Will Underwood, the Press's director of design and production, helped me in an important way apart from his excellent work on the book's design: he took charge of the logistics involved in copying and transporting the fine *Columbus Dispatch* photographs that add so much to the book's appearance.

Finally, I must mention again my special gratitude to all the chapter contributors for their long and hard labor in what must have seemed along the way like a quixotic, not to mention never-ending, project.

Alexander P. Lamis
January 1994, Cleveland

❖

CHAPTER ONE

Ohio Politics:

A Historical Perspective

❖

GEORGE W. KNEPPER

❖ Joseph Carter Brand, eager to escape the curse of slavery, moved north into Ohio from Bourbon County, Kentucky, early in the nineteenth century. He settled in Champaign County on a farm he called "Pretty Prairie" and was soon deep in Ohio politics, "as it seems the fate of most Ohioans to be." His abolitionist principles led him to the newly organized Republican party. His grandson, the distinguished author and progressive politician Brand Whitlock, would later write, "One became, in Urbana and in Ohio for many years, a Republican just as the Eskimo dons fur clothes." Whitlock's grandfather thought it "inconceivable" that any "self-respecting person should be a Democrat." After the Civil War, wrote Whitlock, the Republican party was a "synonym for patriotism, another name for the nation."[1]

Such intense party loyalty strikes us as a bit quaint, but it points up a condition of political life a century and a half ago. Party loyalty was often an inheritance, based on ethnocultural roots and passed from one generation to another. A vast literature has emerged from scholars trying to determine the bases of party loyalty and voter preference. And the task's complexity is suggested in the example of Joseph Carter Brand. One might assume that, as a Kentuckian, he would have been a Democrat, but he was a Kentucky Whig whose fierce adherence to antislavery principles caused him to migrate among like-minded people and to assume their Republican political coloration.

Joseph Carter Brand aside, there was indeed an ethnocultural base to early Ohio politics, and it was especially strong in the nineteenth and early twentieth centuries. But there was also a geographic base and an economic base to Ohio political behavior. They created an uncommon balance in the state between agriculture and industry, between rural and urban. Ethnoculturalism added diversity. Taken together, they shaped Ohio's essentially conservative political behavior.

OHIO'S EARLY POLITICAL LANDSCAPE

Few states, if any, can match Ohio's historic balance—a balance of interests that rested in large part on geography, which in turn helped determine economic development. And both geography and economic opportunity helped determine settlement patterns.

Eastern Ohio, dominated by a westward extension of the Allegheny Plateau, was a combination of glaciated, fertile lands to the north and unglaciated mineral-rich lands to the south. Its economic base and population mix suggested New England, New York, and Pennsylvania influences. Much of western Ohio comprised an eastward extension of the cornbelt whose economic base and population mix suggested those of its western neighbors. Ohio was also the meeting point of Northern and Southern influences. Northern Ohio's population mix and much of its economic activity complemented those of its northern neighbors. Southern Ohio drew its largest population cohorts from the Upland South— western Virginia, western Maryland, and Kentucky. Much of its trade was with Southern slaveholding states. The North-South dichotomy exists to this day in the eyes of some observers. They cite the old National Pike (U.S. Route 40) which bisects the state at its midpoint as the dividing line.

Geography also shaped the agricultural-industrial balance which developed in the late nineteenth and early twentieth centuries. While remaining among the most productive agricultural states, Ohio was also in the forefront of the industrial surge. The balance between farm and factory was reflected in a balance between rural dwellers and urban dwellers. By 1905, at least 50 percent of Ohioans lived in urban regions. Since that time, urbanites have dominated, but numbers alone did not determine political influence.

Political campaigners in any state must consider the interests of both rural and urban people, but those in Ohio have an especially tough assignment in the cities. Ohio had, and still has, an extraordinary number of industrial cities. Prior to World War II it had more cities with over 100,000 population than did any state, and they were widely distributed across its area, with only the southeast quadrant lacking a major city. Twenty smaller cities, in the 25,000 to 85,000 population range, were also widely distributed.

Ohio's major cities often cancelled each other out politically. Unlike Chicago-dominated Illinois or Michigan, overwhelmed by greater Detroit, Ohio had no overarching urban center. Cincinnati and Columbus were, and are, among America's more conservative big cities. Today they usually vote Republican. Cleveland and most northern cities have been dominated since the 1930s by the ethnic-labor-black vote that formed much of the old "Democratic coalition." Those involved in statewide campaigns must deal with this problem: what pleases Cleveland is almost certain to alienate Cincinnati, and Columbus is different still. Eight media markets serve Ohio, requiring campaigners to make their appeals broad enough to service most constituents. This in turn tempers ideological extremes, and the resulting compromises favor conservative postures, since it is easier to persuade voters to stay with the known rather than venture into something new. This blandness also contributes to what political scientist John Fenton called Ohio's "issueless politics."[2]

From its early settlement period, geographic and economic elements underlay distribution of the diverse population cohorts that have characterized the state. The Ohio River was the great avenue into the West following the Revolutionary War. Early settlement was most pronounced along the river and its tributaries. Upland Southerners, many of Scots-Irish background, used this river access, tending to settle in the so-called river counties close by the Ohio. Other Scots-Irish simply crossed the river from southwestern Pennsylvania and located in Ohio's eastern counties. Overwhelmingly they were farmers, although some engaged in commerce and in small-scale industrial activity.

The first New England enclave also used the Ohio River as its link to the outside world. Marietta and Washington County attracted what was undoubtedly the best supported migrant group to reach Ohio. A much larger New England infusion occurred in the Connecticut Western Reserve. This relatively inaccessible region of northeastern Ohio grew slowly, shut off as it was from easy access to markets. Canals brought growth to this region after 1827 when commerce, industry, and agricultural specialization (in dairy farming and cheese making) became feasible. Pennsylvanians of German background were prominent as well among early settlers. Many of them were associated with pietist religious groups like the Mennonites or the Brethren. Although enclaves of these people settled widely across the state's southern reaches, the largest concentration was in the "backbone counties," those stretching westward from Columbiana to Richland along the divide separating northward-from southward-flowing rivers. Here they could carry on the general farming that they had perfected in their former homes.

Early migrants also came from the Middle States. New Yorkers were especially prominent in the Western Reserve, and New Jersey and Delaware sent a few thousand citizens to the Miami Valley. Some New Jerseyites were Quakers who migrated in communites; other Quaker communities came from Pennsylvania, Maryland, Virginia, the Carolinas, and Georgia (escape from a slaveholding society helped motivate those from the South). The eastern counties received the largest number of Quakers, although they were well represented in the southwestern regions as well. Many of these people were farmers, but the Quaker merchant and miller were well-known figures in pioneer society.

Pioneer Ohio was further enriched by immigrants coming directly from overseas. Thousands of Catholic Irish first appeared as canal laborers after 1825. Eventually many clustered in growing towns and cities along the canals and later along the railroads they had helped build. Their numbers greatly increased with the new immigration surge after 1830. Germans also arrived in large numbers after 1830. Some practiced their craftmanship and their merchant proclivities in the growing urban centers, especially Cincinnati; others cleared and settled rural reaches of the state, frequently gathering in areas that were exclusively German Catholic or German Lutheran. Welsh communities were widely dispersed with the principal concentrations close by the mines and quarries in which they worked. English, Scots, French, and Swiss immigrants appeared in smaller numbers.

In 1850, Ohio was the nation's third most populous state and perhaps its most culturally diverse. Every migrant and immigrant group brought

along its cultural baggage—its religious practices, educational preferences, agricultural and architectural styles, and political persuasions.[3]
This ethnocultural diversity was not unique to Ohio, but Buckeye newcomers established enclaves that were large enough and enduring
enough that they could hold their own against others. But no single
group was powerful enough statewide to impose its will. Compromise
was the essence of political life. As was the case with the state's geographic and economic balance, ethnocultural compromise tended to
blunt extremes, drawing all factions toward the political center.

Ethnocultural voting patterns were readily visible in the early nineteenth century. Historian Stephen Fox studied 1830s and 1840s voting
records for twenty-seven Ohio communities and found a high correlation between a community's ethnocultural makeup and its voting behavior.[4] As the transportation and communication revolutions increased
mobility, however, the purity of the ethnocultural samples tended to di-
minish. After 1880, Ohio cities, especially in the booming industrial
reaches of the northern counties, attracted hundreds of thousands of
new European immigrants from many different ethnic origins. Their tendency to settle together simplified analysis of voting behavior. One
could readily predict the vote of an Irish ward, a Jewish ward, an Italian
ward. Mobility ultimately diffused these ethnic clusters, however, as
second and third generations moved out of the old neighborhoods and
merged with neighbors from quite different backgrounds.

OHIO POLITICS 1900 TO 1945

Ohio entered the twentieth century as a leader in nearly every important
field of endeavor except, perhaps, political reform. From the end of the
Civil War until McKinley's presidency, both Democrats and Republicans
showed strength in statewide and presidential elections. Republicans
controlled the statehouse for more years than the Democrats, but a cyclical pattern evolved whereby after about four years of Republican dominance, the voters would "turn the rascals out" in favor of Democrats, who
would prosper for two years only to be turned out for yet another
Republican go-round. The state's strong two-party character made it a
political barometer eagerly scrutinized for voter trends and preferences.[5]

By 1896, Republicans, increasingly identified with the support of big
business, became more dominant in Ohio and in the nation than at any

time since the Civil War era. While Democrats lacked effective statewide organization and suffered intraparty splits on money issues, two Republican "machines" were vying for supremacy in state politics. Marcus Hanna, a wealthy Cleveland industrialist and United States senator (1897–1904), is best known as the architect of William McKinley's successful campaigns for governor of Ohio and president of the United States. Hanna's political organization was especially effective in northern Ohio. Southern Ohio was dominated by Cincinnati's Republican machine led for thirty years by George "Boss" Cox, nominally a saloon keeper.⁶ Each of these machines hoped to control state government with its patronage and its coercive power over municipalities, a power exercised through the use of "ripper" bills which permitted the state legislature to intervene directly in city affairs. State legislation, designed to preempt patronage and reward friends, was used to override local ordinances.

Control of the state legislature was obviously of prime importance, made more so by the fact that until 1903 the governor had very limited veto powers. Republicans tried to assure control of the General Assembly in 1903 by sponsoring a successful constitutional amendment, often called the Hanna Amendment, that revised the apportionment formula to assure every one of Ohio's eighty-eight counties at least one seat in the Ohio House. Since Republicans came to dominate the most thinly populated rural counties, this measure enhanced the party's power for decades to come.⁷

This reinforcement of rural strength should not imply that Republicans were weak in the cities; they were in some, but not in others. Nor should one assume that Democrats were weak in rural areas; they were especially strong in those with a heavy German population. Nevertheless, few would challenge the assertion that the Hanna Amendment worked to the Republicans' advantage until Ohio was reapportioned under the "one man, one vote" mandate laid down by the United States Supreme Court in the 1962 *Baker v. Carr* decision. While Republicans consolidated their place in state government, the party was dominated by "stand patters," conservatives opposed to a growing call for political, economic, and social reform, and the party's progressive wing was not strong enough to have its way. Democrats also had a substantial conservative faction, but the party boasted a growing, influential progressive wing.

American historians characterize the first two decades of the twenti-eth century as the Progressive Era, a period of unparalleled interest in legislation designed to address the serious abuses and inequities that had proliferated as America evolved from a rural, agriculturally domi-nated society toward an urban-industrial society. Reform-minded Ohioans of both parties had their own personal agendas, but generally they hoped to create order and efficiency in business, reduce the influ-ence of rapacious monopolies, regulate banks and utilities, protect labor in the workplace, eliminate child labor, give the voters broader and more direct political powers, and remove city government from unwarranted state interference. Many hoped to secure the franchise for women, and some enthusiastically backed statewide prohibition. The latter two ob-jectives were reached independently through state statutes and federal constitutional amendments shortly after the conclusion of World War I.[8]

Meanwhile a state constitutional convention met in 1912. Dominated by young, pragmatic, reform-minded progressives (Democrats held a 2-to-1 majority), the delegates drafted forty-one proposed amendments to the Ohio Constitution, and the voters approved thirty-three. The new Democratic governor, James M. Cox, pressured the state legislature into enacting supportive statutes.[9] The new progressivism influenced the Buckeye State in many quarters, but none more so than in the political realm. Initiative and referendum were introduced to allow voters to by-pass an obstructive state legislature bent upon protecting its own inter-ests and those of its friends. The direct primary was extended to all elections, and home rule (charter government for cities) was enacted, promising the end to "ripper" bills.

The Progressive initiative cooled during World War I, except perhaps for the idealism that spurred the adoption of the women's franchise and prohibition. Women first exercised unrestricted votes in the 1920 presi-dential election, helping to give Ohio newspaper publisher Warren G. Harding (R) a resounding victory over Ohio newspaper publisher James M. Cox (D). By 1923 Ohio women occupied four seats in the Ohio House and two in the Ohio Senate. The presence of women in political office failed to grow, however, and they remained gravely underrepresented.[10]

As women adapted to new electoral roles, Ohio blacks were making a symbolic advance. Since the 1870 ratification of the Fifteenth Amend-ment to the United States Constitution (and to a limited extent even be-fore that), black males had voted in Ohio. In the last third of the nineteenth century a number of blacks served effectively in the Ohio Senate and the Ohio House, even though the Constitution of 1851 (still Ohio's basic law) had granted the franchise to white males only, and numerous Republican-led attempts to eliminate that restrictive language failed in the 1860s. By constitutional amendment, the task was finally accomplished in 1923, about the same time, incidentally, that American Indians were granted United States citizenship.[11]

Postwar reaction against World War I policies and President Woodrow Wilson's League of Nations contributed to Republican dominance in both state and national politics during the 1920s. Ohio strongly supported Harding's "return to normalcy" and the sentiment behind President Calvin Coolidge's assertion that "the business of America is business." The Harding-Coolidge-Hoover leadership in national affairs was matched in Ohio by Republican control of the state legislature, although, paradoxically, a popular Democrat, A. Victor Donahey, won three successive terms as governor (1923–29). Donahey was a conservative Democrat; and like Frank Lausche in the post–World War II era, he was almost as popular with Republicans as with Democrats, thanks to his tight grip on the state payroll and purse strings. On matters other than financial, enough strains developed between governor and legislators to warrant Donahey's nickname, "Veto Vic."[12]

The stock market crash of 1929 heralded a decade of economic malaise deeper and more prolonged than any in American history. The Great Depression brought radical shifts to the nation's political, economic, and social sectors. Starting in 1933, President Franklin D. Roosevelt and a strongly Democratic Congress enacted a New Deal agenda embracing an extraordinary number of palliative and reform measures. Support for the new administration came from a "Democratic coalition" consisting of labor, urban ethnics, blacks, and the Solid South.

The New Deal and the Democratic coalition helped polarize Ohio politics. Few who did not live through the New Deal era can appreciate the level of hero worship accorded FDR by his admirers, and the level of venom directed at him by his political enemies. Political rhetoric and feelings aside, Ohio suffered as much as any state from massive unemployment, especially in its industrial sector. Heavy, basic industry, once Ohio's glory, was now its millstone. In hard times people forego autos, tires, heavy machinery, and the basic manufactured goods that Ohio specialized in producing. Industrial unemployment reached astonishing levels in 1932–33, and the job picture improved only slowly. As late as

1938, Ohio had more persons on the Works Progress Administration (WPA) federal work relief program than any state save Pennsylvania. Perhaps as many as a million workers and their dependents, roughly one out of every seven Ohioans, were forced to rely on it. High unemployment was accompanied by underemployment; work hours were severely cut in many jobs. Akron's tire factories responded by instituting the six-hour shift in an effort to spread available work.

Reduced earnings in turn caused tax revenues to plummet, forcing schools and public offices to close early, cut back programs, and, in some cases, pay employees in scrip. In desperation, the legislature enacted Ohio's first state sales tax (3 percent), but only after overcoming great pressure against it from the Ohio Chamber of Commerce and the Ohio Manufacturers' Association. It took effect in 1935.[13]

That same year, Congress enacted the Wagner Act, sometimes called "labor's Magna Carta." By protecting unions, especially in their organizing activities, this federal law greatly stimulated labor union membership and militancy. After 1936, the newly formed Congress of Industrial Organizations (CIO) targeted basic Ohio industries, starting with rubber and moving to automobile and steel manufacturing. Despite management's bitter resistance, the CIO prevailed, and soon the United Auto Workers, United Rubber Workers, and United Steel Workers were among those unions seeking a place in Ohio's political life. Ohio has always ranked well above the national average in the percentage of its organized industrial workers, yet its various unions have had a hard time coming together in concerted action. No single union was clearly the lead dog, as in Michigan where the United Auto Workers held sway.[14]

New Deal social and economic policies, organized labor's new-found confidence and muscle, and tax resentment contributed to the firming of political lines. A combination of war weariness in the 1920s followed by the New Deal era made rural Ohio a "Republican stronghold." Historian Bernard Sternsher made the claim more specific by demonstrating that there was both a post–World War I Harding revolution and a postdepression John W. Bricker revolution in rural northwestern Ohio, both of these obviously benefiting the Republican party. Ohio Republicanism was identified with low-tax, small-government, probusiness positions.[15]

Many Ohio cities, meanwhile, conformed more and more to the stereotypical Democratic support profile. One must be cautious, however, in generalizing about Ohio cities' political complexion. In Cleveland and Youngstown the "Democratic coalition" was effective. Akron and Dayton largely conformed to the coalition profile, but their ethnic component was less eastern and southern European and more Southern, white Appalachian, a distinction that ultimately gave them a flavor somewhat different from cities dominated by European ethnics. Columbus and Cincinnati retained their conservative political population bases.[16]

The Great Depression hit Ohio cities with unequal force. Akron, overly concentrated in rubber, and Youngstown, almost totally beholden to steel, suffered from 60 percent industrial unemployment for a brief period in 1932–33. Toledo staggered along with the auto industry. Cleveland's industrial unemployment reached its nadir of 50 percent before starting a slow recovery. Cincinnati was an important manufacturing city that suffered its share of industrial unemployment, but it was also a major producer of household goods, processed foods, clothing, shoes and other products that people had to buy with whatever funds they could muster. Columbus claimed to be "recession proof" due to payrolls dominated by white collar, governmental, educational, and commercial workers.

During the great economic crisis, Ohioans who might ordinarily have voted their ethnocultural heritage voted their economic interests instead. Ethnic workers in Ohio's industrial cities probably would have voted Democratic for both economic and ethnocultural reasons. Akron's tire builders, disproportionately white, Protestant Appalachians, supported the New Deal about as enthusiastically as did their East European ethnic, largely Catholic neighbors in other northern Ohio cities.[17] Economic conditions were certainly important in swinging votes to the Democrats during the depression's early years, yet Ohio's large reservoir of conservative sentiment still packed plenty of punch. Franklin D. Roosevelt enjoyed but one overwhelming victory margin in Ohio out of four tries, and that came in 1936 when he defeated "Alf" Landon by 620,000 votes. He won by much more modest margins in 1932 and 1940, and in 1944 Ohio voters rejected him, giving Republican Thomas Dewey a 12,000-vote victory margin. The 1944 results were likely skewed by favorite son John W. Bricker's presence on the ballot as Dewey's running mate.

Gubernatorial politics during the 1930s also reveal Ohio's political caution. Moderate Democrat George White won the office in 1930 and again in 1932, but his administrations were hardly liberal given the acute needs of that time. His successor was Democrat Martin L. Davey, a Kent tree surgeon. To the consternation of his party, Davey not only failed to establish cordial relations with the national administration, but he actually alienated Washington bureaucrats who were funneling aid to the stricken Buckeye State. He challenged the Roosevelt administration's control of patronage in federal relief programs. Davey's intransigence revealed itself in other ways as well, and it was claimed, though never proved, that he profited personally from his position.[18]

Orthodox political wisdom would assert that a depressed industrial state should be relatively safe for the Democrats during a period when that party controlled federal programs essential to the state's well being. It was not to be. Ohio's cornbelt farmers, its strong, organized business interests, and its ethnocultural conservatives combined to keep the Republican party viable in statewide and presidential politics. Their opportunity came in 1938 when John W. Bricker defeated Davey for the governorship. Bricker, a conservative Republican, won reelection in 1940 and 1942 before landing on the national ballot in 1944 as candidate for the vice presidency of the United States. Supported by the legislature, Bricker's first move as governor was to trim the state payroll, always a popular move among Ohio voters. He also profited politically by presiding over the state as it experienced an economic renaissance brought on by World War II.[19]

JANUS-FACED OHIO, 1945–1990

Like the Roman deity Janus, Ohio faced in two different directions in the half century following World War II. For the first twenty-five years of that period, the state was prosperous, growing, optimistic. In the last twenty-five years, the mood changed as an economic malaise resulted in severe losses of well-paying industrial jobs, population stagnation, deterioration of central cities, chronic underfunding of state services, and a host of other problems. Ohioans turned away from rosy projections and wishful thinking, much of it emanating from Columbus. The boom and bust cycle was again on "bust."

Those citizens who came to maturity in the 1970s and 1980s had never experienced a vigorous, "can-do" Ohio. Having grown up in an age of high unemployment and "rust belt" psychology, they may have assumed this to be the natural order of things. The record is quite different.

World War II and the spending spree that followed it created new jobs on a grand scale, especially in the heavy, basic industries. Population figures illustrate the impact: Ohio gained 1,039,000 people in the 1940s, another 1,759,000 in the 1950s, and 951,000 more in the 1960s. During part of this period, Ohio had more new plant investment than any state. Its great industrial cities reached their peak populations in the 1950–70 period: Cleveland, 914,800; Cincinnati, 503,000; Toledo, 383,000; Akron, 290,000; and Dayton, 262,000. All have experienced dramatic population fall-off; only Columbus, home of America's great growth industry, government, and a host of white-collar service industries, continued to grow. This growth was enhanced by municipal leaders who had the foresight in the 1950s to annex surrounding rural land. When several other major cites tried to emulate Columbus, only Toledo found available rural lands contiguous to the city limits; the others were hopelessly choked by a necklace of incorporated communities and antagonistic townships.

Ohio's major cities were also hampered by underrepresentation in the state legislature. At the very moment population growth and industrial expansion were bringing increased tax takes into the treasury, the so-called "cornstalk brigade" was exerting a disproportionate influence on state spending. Urban representatives compounded their problems by competing with one another for state largess rather than cooperating to counter the claims of rural regions, one result being that Ohio lagged behind many of her sister states in urban redevelopment.

It would seem that the prosperous period 1945–65 was the right time for the state to use increased revenue to catch up in the funding of vital state services—education, mental health, children's services, penal facilities, environment—which it had underfunded in comparison to all but a handful of other states. The opportunity was lost, however, as the state legislature and Governors Frank Lausche, Thomas Herbert, and C. William O'Neill continued Ohio's penurious level of public support.[20]

The support issue was addressed in 1959 by Democratic governor Michael DiSalle, who pushed modest tax increases through the legislature. He paid dearly for his efforts, however, as Republican James A. Rhodes defeated him in 1962 by resurrecting the old Ohio war chant of "no new taxes." Super-salesman Rhodes persuaded Ohio voters (who apparently wanted to believe despite much evidence to the contrary) that they compared favorably with other states in funding essential state services. The enhanced revenues flowing from DiSalle's program, plus those resulting from economic growth, allowed Rhodes to cement his political position. Supported by a Republican legislature, he also addressed several urgent concerns, doing much to improve higher education, state parks, highway systems, airports, and state office facilities.[21]

These improvements, plus the rising cost of services such as social welfare programs, absorbed state revenues. And in 1971, when Democrat John J. Gilligan entered the governor's office, financial resources were again pinched. Gilligan had stated during his campaign that new revenue resources were needed and that the instrument for securing them was a state income tax. He expended much of his political leverage to secure this tax, designed to bring Ohio into line with progressive states. Nevertheless, Gilligan was confident of reelection in 1974. But he misplayed his hand, and Jim Rhodes defeated him by a narrow margin—a victory that rested in part on Rhodes pinning the "high tax" label on Gilligan.

Rhodes's proverbial political luck would run out in his second two terms. Before the end of the sixties, ominous clouds already shadowed some sectors of Ohio's economy, and in the seventies and eighties the state lost a considerable part of its industrial base. The reasons for this are numerous and complex, but two grand generalizations stand out: Ohio had become a costly place to make things, and foreign competition hit especially hard those industries that were the backbone of the state's economy—steel, automobiles, rubber, machine tools, heavy equipment, and the like. Unemployment skyrocketed as industries moved out of state or succumbed to the streamlining of their new owners; around 300,000 of the world's best-paying industrial jobs were lost. Ohio's unemployment rate exceeded the national average until the nineties.[22]

Leaders of state government had difficulty dealing with the resulting problems. Population growth nearly ceased; new job growth was in the service sector with wages and benefits far below those of the lost industrial jobs. Meanwhile, economically distressed people and an ever-increasing number of indigent, aged persons placed additional strains on government. The federal government added to the problem by shifting expenditures to state governments and by mandating costly services such as those relating to the environment. Stagnating state revenue was inadequate to meet state needs. But Governor Rhodes was locked in his old thinking and his pet formulas. While continuing to espouse the "no new taxes" theme, he sought money through proposed bond issues, most of which the electorate soundly defeated. He revived "Rhodes's Raiders," scouring the foreign and domestic landscape for industrial jobs. This time in office the governor was faced with an obstructive legislature, unwilling to take the initiative to secure new revenue resources. The governor and the General Assembly played out an unheroic struggle, both recognizing Ohio's needs but neither showing courage (they would have called it political suicide) in meeting them.

This was the climate in Columbus when a new Democratic governor moved to address the state's financial crisis. Richard Celeste asked the legislature to enact higher income-tax rates. Upon assuming office in 1983, he inherited a 50-percent surcharge rushed through in the last months of the Rhodes administration, but the increase was designed to expire shortly after Celeste assumed office. Celeste succeeded, however, in persuading the legislature to make that 50 percent permanent and to enhance it with an additional 40-percent increase. He then had to stand the flak from those belaboring Celeste's "90-percent tax hike." Ohioans overwhelmingly sustained the new rates in a referendum vote, but the salubrious effect of the increase was reduced when the governor and legislature succumbed to pressure and rescinded part of the increase.

It is a truism that demand for state services always exceeds revenues, and demand rises when hard times reduce tax flow. George Voinovich, Ohio's new Republican governor, felt the full force of these conditions upon assuming office in 1991. Although Ohio was coming through the recession of that period in somewhat better style than northeastern states and California, the Buckeye State still faced budget deficits that required cuts in state service areas already chronically underfunded compared with other industrial states. Social welfare services, the penal system, elementary and secondary education all escaped major cuts, while public higher education took the brunt of the budget slashing. To prevent further cuts, the governor and legislative leaders finally agreed on new taxes designed to make up budget deficits, but these taxes were not adequate to allow any substantial "catch-up" in the state's unfavorable ranking in per capita support of vital services.

OHIO'S POLITICAL ENVIRONMENT: A SUMMING UP

History serves as a guide to present understanding, and so it is with the evolution of Ohio's political culture. By having a sense of historic conditions, one can see more clearly the hows and whys of Ohio's current political life. One must be cautious, however, in trying to draw a straight line from earlier to more recent political attitudes and practices; the road to political understanding is filled with zig-zags. Consider a few of the important ones.

Residency requirements and voter registration have changed dramatically from the restrictive practices of old to the relative ease of today. Early in the nineteenth century, local election officials determined residency, commonly setting standards that withheld the franchise from new settlers whose ethnocultural background or economic status threatened the local power structure. Oral voting, where one stated aloud whom he was voting for, gave way to the secret ballot. The practice of straight-ticket voting, once encouraged by allowing the voter to cast his ballot for the entire party slate by making a single mark, was eliminated. The electorate was expanded over many years by adding eligible black males, then women, then persons eighteen and over. No broadly conceived study has yet shown the effect of this widening of the franchise.

Initiative and referendum, direct primaries, the direct election of senators, and adoption in some Ohio political units of the recall (by which an elected official can be voted out of office) wrought substantial change in the political process. Gerrymandering, an old practice brought to new levels of sophistication, has long undermined regional voting patterns by artificially changing districts to suit the party in power.

Campaigning has always been influenced by technological advances—the railroad, telegraph, telephone, movie camera, and a host of other developments. Since World War II even more dramatic change has occurred, as television, computerized data, market surveys, polling, and similar innovations have increased costs to a level that eliminates poor people from campaigning or makes candidates beholden to campaign contributors and political action committees, in short, to special, selfish interests. Efforts to secure campaign reform, as of 1993, have been stonewalled and allowed to die quietly. Public outrage, however, led to a successful initiative vote in 1992 that limited terms of Ohio General Assembly members, elected members of the executive branch, and Ohio's delegates in the U.S. Congress. Only time will tell whether the voters' hopes will be realized from this latest restructuring.

These changes have influenced political life, but they are perhaps less important than changes in the political preferences of voters. Ohio's geographic, ethnic, and economic diversity remain inordinately complex. Its traditional balance persists: candidates for statewide office must see the state as a whole. Republican strength remains effective despite the larger number of voters whose party identification is Democrat. A substantial pool of independents, not allied practically or emotionally with either party, has emerged and is particularly strong in the suburbs.[23] It is tempting to generalize about the current status of the major parties, but in doing so one realizes how shaky some long-accepted generalizations have become.

Republicans compensate for their lower numbers by remaining better organized and disciplined in statewide elections. Republicans seem to benefit from Ohio's underlying conservatism, especially in financial matters. Historically they were the better-funded party and garnered support from the Ohio Chamber of Commerce and the Ohio Manufacturers' Association. The entrepreneurial owners and publishers of the state's great newspapers were once disproportionately Republican, an advantage that has been lost as major papers, affiliated with national chains, make an effort to educate the public on all the candidates and issues. Some papers print their own preferred slate just before the election, which some claim unduly influences voters; but responsible papers "split the ticket" according to how they view the candidates' merits rather than their party affiliations. Compensating for the fall-off in the number of Ohioans living in strongly Republican rural areas, the party has held its own in the growing suburban and exurban regions. Ohio's fastest-growing counties are formerly rural counties now connected to major population centers by a modern highway system. Medina County and Portage County on Cleveland's distant outskirts exemplify this trend.

Ohio Democrats have shown signs of transcending their historic disadvantages. We have noted their superiority in voter preference, but the party still has its work cut out in exploiting that advantage. The ethnic worker base has not grown, and, as third- and fourth-generation ethnics amalgamate more thoroughly in the mainstream, they lose much of their ethnocultural identity. In suburbia, removed from old-time religious parishes, foreign-language newspapers, ward bosses, and social clubs, they have few ethnocultural and economic ties to their ancestral neighborhoods and the political behavior it espoused. Compensating somewhat for these conditions are improvements in statewide Democratic organization as illustrated by a recently retired leader of the state party turning a financial deficit into a modest surplus.[24] Democrats are still prone to party infighting, expending energy, goodwill, and resources on bitter primary struggles. Organized labor has improved its support for Democrats under the aegis of the combined AFL-CIO, but important unions like the Teamsters still pursue their own interests rather than endorse AFL-CIO leadership. Finally, in recent decades the party's liberal element has become more visible in statewide politics. To moderates like U.S. senator John Glenn or former attorney general Anthony Celebrezze, the unsuccessful gubernatorial candidate in 1992, one can add traditional Democratic liberals such as John Gilligan, Richard Celeste, and U.S. senator Howard Metzenbaum, the latter a classic Democratic liberal.

No effort to address and interpret the political life of a state will pass unchallenged . . . nor should it! It is clear, however, that Ohio remains a bellwether state. Its representative character and its strong two-party record attract prognosticators who hope to find therein clues to future political behavior, not just for Ohio, but for the nation. Politically, those who understand Ohio understand America.

❖

CHAPTER TWO

The Lausche Era,

1945–1957

❖

BRIAN USHER

❖ Late October 1952. It was the year of flying saucers, campus panty raids, and the breakdown of truce talks in Korea. It was also the year of Eisenhower. On this brisk fall day in Columbus, Ohio, the hero general of World War II and presidential nominee of the Republican party climbed out of an official car on Broad Street and inched his way through the "I Like Ike" buttons toward the steps of the Statehouse. Suddenly, a tall, bare-headed man with a trademark thatch of black hair pushed his way through the crowd to the side of the balding president-to-be. A grinning, tousled Frank J. Lausche grabbed Ike's hand and they exchanged pleasantries. Then the uninvited Democratic governor of Ohio plunged back into the crowd and made his way back to his Statehouse office to listen to Ike's campaign speech on the radio. "He's a great American and it was a great speech," Lausche said later.

"Lausche's simple act, perfectly timed, almost stole the show from the general," *Collier's* reported the following March.[1] Indeed, the Slovenian immigrants' son from Cleveland was the only statewide Democratic candidate to survive the Eisenhower landslide of 1952. He won an unprecedented fourth term (two years in those days) as governor by defeating a Taft—Charles P., son of President William Howard Taft and younger brother of Senator Robert "Mr. Republican" Taft of Ohio. As Ike carried the Buckeye State by a half million votes, Lausche beat Charles Taft by

450,052, becoming the first Ohioan ever to win two million votes—
2,019,029. But more astoundingly, an immigrant's son defeated an Ohio
president's son for governor.

The surprise welcome to Republican standard-bearer Ike and the
record-breaking victory in 1952 were quintessential Lausche perfor-
mances. To his admirers he was Lausche, the ethnic champion; Lausche,
the organized crime buster and guardian of the public purse; Lausche,
the maverick Democrat who stood up to party chairmen and union
bosses. Lausche broke all his own records in 1954 and won his fifth term
as governor by defeating James A. Rhodes, later a four-term and sixteen-
year governor. Fearing they would never get Lausche out of the Governor's Mansion, Republican legislators pushed through (with voter
approval) an Ohio constitutional amendment limiting future governors
to two consecutive, four-year terms. By the mid-1950s, Lausche had
made the covers of both *Newsweek* and *Time,* and the *Saturday Evening
Post* described him as "rumpled, rugged in a way that is often described
as Lincolnesque." He loved to quote Lincoln and resembled him somewhat in style and appearance. No less a GOP character witness than
President Ronald Reagan wrote to Lausche on his ninetieth birthday in
1985: "It has been customary to call you the Lincoln of Ohio. Anybody
who gives the matter a moment's thought will understand why: People
readily see how much you resemble Lincoln in homespun good sense
and rugged honesty."[2] And Ike himself, according to his later biographers, once seriously considered dumping Vice President Richard
Nixon for the Cleveland Democrat as a running mate in 1956.

Lausche's personal popularity, his independence of thought, and his
conservative ideological principles enabled him to cut across party lines
and attract Republicans election after election. In post–World War II
Ohio, statewide elections have turned on conservative, pocketbook issues. Moreover, the state's many unions have played a major role only
sporadically over the years. Labor, like other elements of the Democratic
coalition, was fragmented in Ohio's many population centers, often concerned more with local than statewide issues. Many political experts believe Lausche both contributed to and benefited from fragmented labor
and the weakened condition of the Ohio Democratic Party. Democratic
labor-based, issue-oriented party organizations flourished in Great
Lakes states with dominant urban centers—Illinois (Chicago), Michigan (Detroit), Minnesota (Twin Cities), and Wisconsin (Milwaukee).
But, politically, Ohio usually remains fragmented into separate urban

Democratic fiefdoms except when strong Democratic governors forge temporary alliances. Lausche was a strong Democratic governor but declined to build his party while in office for four decades. And in his later years, he often openly endorsed many Republicans for top offices, notably Jim Rhodes for governor and Ronald Reagan for president. Still, Lausche left a tremendous political legacy. He was the first ethnic trailblazer in a state whose roster of governors used to read like a Mayflower manifest. Clevelanders with names like Celebrezze, Locher, Celeste, Perk, Kucinich, and Voinovich followed him as Cleveland mayor and Ohio governor. For this, Lausche (rhymes with "now-she") was also known as the "George Washington of nationality politicians."[3]

On Lausche's ninetieth birthday, a retrospective article in the Cleveland *Plain Dealer* said, "For the better part of 40 years, Frank J. Lausche dominated politics in Ohio. No one before or since has come close to his record." And he had a big impact on every Ohio governor (and most other politicians) who followed him. In the fifty years since Lausche was first elected in 1944, Democratic and Republican governors have split the years in the Governor's Mansion about equally—thanks mainly to Lausche's one-man stand against Republican domination of the postwar years. His frugal spending, "no new taxes" policies, and independent politics shaped the actions and reactions of his GOP and Democratic successors in the executive branch as well as the Lausche-era legislators and their progeny.

A gritty, steel-mill neighborhood on Cleveland's southeast side, a settling place for Slovenian immigrants, was the birthplace and training ground for Frank J. Lausche. He was born in 1895 to Louis and Frances Lausche, who emigrated from Slovenia barely four years earlier. In 1900 the industrious couple erected on St. Clair Avenue near East Sixty-first a structure that became known as the Lausche Building. It housed their family of twelve and such family enterprises as a restaurant, bowling alley, the *Ameriska Domovina* Slovenian-language newspaper, and a wine shop for thirsty Slovenian immigrants. (It is not to be confused with the State of Ohio office building in downtown Cleveland, also known as the Lausche Building.) "The Lausche Building was the hub of neighborhood society, the local political forum and a sanctuary for new arrivals from the old country. The elder Lausches were passionately patriotic; they helped thousands of newly arrived Slovenians and other immigrants to put down roots."[4] This neighborhood was Lausche's political base, his lifelong anchor, and the site of his birth and death.

In his youth, Lausche was a lamplighter, a minor-league baseball player, an Army officer in World War I, and a graduate of Cleveland Marshall Law School. As a young lawyer, his first attempts at politics were fruitless, as he lost races for the General Assembly in 1922 and 1924. Discouraged, he dropped out of politics for several years and married Jane Sheal, a Scots-Irish Protestant. Although the Lausches moved in with Jane's father, and lived there for sixteen years, he never lost touch with his Slovenian, Catholic roots. Jumping back into politics, he supported a reform candidate named Ray T. Miller for Cleveland mayor in 1931. Lausche carried his home ward, the Twenty-third, a key ethnic area, for Miller. A year later, Miller appointed Lausche to a judgeship on the Municipal Court. He won election as a judge on the Cuyahoga County Common Pleas Court in 1936, his springboard for the Cleveland mayorship in 1941 and the governorship in 1944.

In Lausche's Cleveland political career of the 1930s and 1940s were sown the seeds of both his political success—his reputation as an organized gambling and crime crusher—and his ultimate political downfall at the hands of organized labor. Cleveland was wide open for organized crime and gambling in the 1930s, and Lausche used his bench to attack the racketeers. Lausche declared that gambling clubs would close and empaneled an aggressive crime-busting grand jury that dragged in witnesses, mayors, and police to gather evidence. Lausche ordered raids on the casinos and launched removal-from-office proceedings when the sheriff balked.[5] "Fearless Frank" became the darling of the *Cleveland Press* and its powerful and equally fearless editor, Louis B. Seltzer, who launched a "draft Lausche for mayor movement," which Lausche resisted for several years. Finally, though, in 1941, he was ready to run for mayor of Cleveland.

Cleveland was then considered a Republican stronghold, and Democrat Lausche launched his campaign with a typically "Fearless Frank" move: he quit his beloved bench. In his *Inside U.S.A.*, John Gunther recorded the action: "Lausche, a profoundly honest man, resigned from his judgeship, a twelve thousand dollar job—more than he got as governor—before he was nominated. He felt it would be morally wrong to run for an office while holding another, though the opposite example had been set by, let us say, a hundred thousand other politicians who hold onto whatever job they have for as long as possible."[6]

As the first "nationality" candidate in Cleveland, he won with landslide victories of 60 percent in 1941 and 71 percent in 1943. As mayor he began to buck the organizations that he ostensibly should be working with—the Democratic party and labor unions. The AFL sought a raise for municipal building trades employees, but Lausche vetoed it. The City Council overrode the veto and Lausche answered with a landslide reelection victory in 1943.

But, a more crucial test—and the chance to flamboyantly demonstrate his independence from "bosses"—came early in his first term as mayor. He had won in 1941 with the warm backing of his old friend and mentor, Democratic county chairman Ray Miller, who had appointed him to his first judgeship, and the Democratic organization, including local union leaders. Miller had promised labor leaders that Lausche would fire Elliot Ness, the Republican director of public safety, but Lausche felt that Ness had done a good job and should stay. Ness was later to be lionized as a fighter against mobs and gangsters in the 1950s TV series "The Untouchables." Miller and Lausche became bitter enemies, as Miller charged that Lausche had promised to fire Ness and Lausche denied it. *Time* recorded the incident in a 1956 article, "The Lonely One," and summarized its meaning: "From that time on, Lausche walked alone. The wrath of the organization Democrats and of labor rained on his shoulders. Despite new enemies, he was re-elected by an avalanche of votes in 1943, continued his crusade against gambling and provided Cleveland with clean government and inspirational leadership in World War II."[7]

Such independent actions in today's more sophisticated climate of media punditry might launch a debate as to whether Lausche was grandstanding with his populism—quitting the bench, vetoing pay raises for city employees in an election year, and keeping Republicans in office. But in World War II Ohio the electoral landslides and favorable local media coverage propelled him toward Columbus and the Statehouse.

LAUSCHE'S FIRST TERM

Lausche defied more than the party leaders of Cleveland and Ohio to run for governor in 1944. He defied the conventional wisdom of his day. Ohioans had never sent to the governor's mansion the son of an immigrant. Downstate voters wanted to know how to pronounce a candidate's name by simply reading it on the ballot. Ohio had never elected a Roman Catholic governor. Lausche was a lifelong member of the St. Vitus Catholic Church in his Slovene neighborhood. He had no money and precious little organized party support in an era of big-city machine politics. And the Ohio Republican party fielded an apparently invincible ticket—Mayor James Garfield Stewart of Cincinnati along with Ohio's incumbent governor John Bricker running for vice president on the GOP national ticket with Thomas Dewey.

Lausche's statewide campaigning style was unorthodox. He often traveled by bus and mingled with voters at county fairs and strawberry festivals—usually without platform appearances or introductions. While most historians and Ohio politicians regarded Lausche as an accomplished orator in most situations, a *Saturday Evening Post* writer, who traveled with him in 1944, wrote that "he appeared to be a poor campaigner. His speeches were usually short and almost always slightly ponderous. But on his principal issue—bossism—the state believed what he said—that he was unfettered."[8]

Lausche also set a campaign precedent in 1944. For every day on the campaign trail, he returned his pay as mayor of Cleveland. Also, his campaign manager, John Lokar, went off the city payroll and traveled the state on his own savings. He turned down money from party and union political action committees of the day and set up his own campaign committee. When his campaign headquarters ran out of stamps, a friendly newspaper story brought in an emergency stream of small-change offerings. He received some campaign donations from wealthy Republicans, including $1,000 from Marshall Field, his biggest contributor. Although always a strong FDR backer, Lausche got not one penny from the National Democratic Committee. When the national committee sent him $19.50 worth of Roosevelt posters, it sent a note that read, "Please remit check to cover." In all, he spent a paltry $27,162 in the 1944 race. His Republican opponent, Stewart, and the statewide party spent $988,000. While Roosevelt lost Ohio by 11,500 votes, Lausche beat Stewart by 108,000 votes. It was a sweet victory, and his Cleveland friends, including newspapers, celebrated. In an editorial the *Plain Dealer* gushed, "The election of Mayor Frank J. Lausche as governor of Ohio is as inspiring a demonstration of the true American spirit as it is a remarkable political performance."[9]

Basking in the statewide and national limelight, Lausche remained unorthodox and independent. Although his campaign was in debt by $3,700, he refused help offered after the election by the newly impressed Democratic National Committee. He also made an announcement that is as astounding today as it was then: "No contributions to campaign funds will be accepted, directly or indirectly, from anyone having business dealings with the state."[10]

Lausche and his wife, Jane, moved into the old executive mansion on East Broad Street, but he took a pay cut from $15,000 as Cleveland mayor to $10,000 as governor. He moved into the mansion with one suit and two pairs of shoes; Bricker moved out with ninety-two suits. In comparison to most lawyers and politicians, Lausche was a pauper. And he remained a penny-pincher. He squelched an unofficial move to increase his salary and opposed a bill to grant a retroactive pay raise to state employees.

As expected, Lausche's independence was the theme of his inaugural address on January 13, 1945. The *Columbus Dispatch* headlined "Gov. Lausche Spurns Partisanship in Speech." The *Cincinnati Enquirer* reported "New Governor Works Hard, Defies Politicians." Assuring continuity in the war effort was his main objective as governor; he would tolerate no relaxation in the effort to supply the military fronts, and he was not afraid to use executive power. A biographer, William C. Bittner, wrote, "Whenever there was a strike that defied the public interest, Governor Lausche acted lightening fast. . . . In one instance, he directed the Selective Service Board in Akron to induct into the armed forces striking employees at the Goodyear war material plant unless they returned to work. Never again was Lausche to get active support from any of the large labor unions."[11]

Reviews are mixed on his work style as governor. Gunther wrote that Lausche "works like an ox." He was at his desk early, seldom went to lunch, and saw visitors hour after hour—many of them "neighborhood folk," many of them "foreign-born," and few were ever turned away. Others noted that his "lone wolf" style made him weak in administrative ability in his first term as governor with an inability to delegate tasks well. The *Saturday Evening Post* observed, "Frank was usually behind with his scripts for radio addresses and some of his speeches were extemporaneous because he had not prepared them in time. He frequently mislays his brief case and glasses, and he loses more hats than anyone else in Ohio." The *Plain Dealer* and *Cleveland Press* usually touted Lausche, and their editors became his powerful allies in establishing his statewide political base. However, the *Cleveland News* had a different view: "The public sees him only on stage—the red, white and blue patriot, the independent dedicated to the cause of humanity. The common

man does not see behind the scenes [where] Lausche is shrewdly moving pieces on a political chessboard."[12] But Ohio voters appeared to love
him—until 1946.

THE HERBERT INTERLUDE

Nineteen forty-six was a Republican year—a reaction to four FDR elections and fourteen years of Democratic national rule. Returning GIs
launched the Baby Boom generation, and the United States launched
atomic bomb testing in the Pacific atolls. A national meat shortage was
blamed on Democratic president Harry S. Truman. The Republicans
took control of both houses of Congress. Soviet expansionism in eastern
Europe (including Slovenia) fueled the first stirrings of the cold war,
which in turn fueled growing suspicions of "commies" in powerful positions in the United States.

Ohio Republicans nominated one of their best for governor—
Thomas J. Herbert, a Clevelander, a World War I flying ace, and a three-
term attorney general who was not above a little "red-baiting" now and
then. Frank Lausche was in trouble. Trapped in Columbus as a freshman wartime governor, Lausche had missed the usual endless rounds
of marriages, wakes, and other ceremonial gatherings in the Cleveland
neighborhoods. He had alienated Democratic party and union leaders
around the state, including his home county.[13] It was not the best way to
get reelected governor. And he did not. Herbert defeated Lausche by
40,000 votes in the gigantic "Had Enough?" Republican landslide of
1946. Republicans captured all statewide offices and elected Bricker to
the U.S. Senate.

Tom Herbert, a white-haired, fifty-two-year-old widower, moved
into the Governor's Mansion with his three children. Herbert was
known mainly as a war hero and an energetic campaigner with a hearty
appetite for ice cream and corn-on-the-cob. Besides campaigning in all
eighty-eight counties and logging more than thirty-thousand miles, Herbert's reputation was enhanced by the fact that he declared his candidacy from his hospital bed in October 1945, a full six months before the
filing deadline. Generally, politicians of the era waited until the last
minute to tip their hands on running. Herbert had been in the University
Hospital in Columbus recovering from an operation on his leg due to a
complication from a wartime injury. A native of Cleveland, Herbert had

interrupted his study at Western Reserve University's law school in 1917 to enlist in officers training school. On August 8, 1918, he was wounded and shot down in aerial combat over France. In six dog fights, Herbert and other fighter pilots attacked eighteen German Fokker biplanes. Herbert, shot in the leg during the final skirmish, guided his damaged plane back to friendly lines and was decorated by both U.S. and British governments. Returning to Cleveland, he began his legal and political career in 1921 as assistant law director for the city. Losing for Ohio attorney general in the Roosevelt landslide of 1936, he rebounded to win three consecutive two-year terms as attorney general. He lost a primary battle for governor in 1944 to Cincinnati mayor Jim Stewart.[14]

In his 1946 campaign, he vigorously attacked Lausche from the start, linking him to Truman and the New Deal policies "that were a great detriment" to Ohio. Although Lausche was estranged from labor, Herbert adopted a favorite tactic of criticizing the CIO and its leaders. He charged that the CIO was an "organization held captive by those who admittedly want to overthrow our American form of government." Herbert said he was referring to the "CIO's defeat of a resolution to oust members affiliated with the Communists, Fascists, Nazis or any other subversive political group," according to the *Columbus Dispatch*.[15]

Such "red-baiting" language was not lost on the voters of 1946, nor on the newspapers. The Soviets had moved into both Yugoslavia and Slovenia. Lausche biographer Edward Gobetz recorded that the cold war stirrings of 1946 hurt the Ohio governor: "Indeed, the 1946 campaign against Lausche also capitalized, to a large extent, on prejudice. Although the accusation borders on ridiculous, Lausche, one of the most determined anticommunists, was accused of being a communist and of harboring communists in his administration. While born and educated in America and an ardent American patriot, he was on several occasions falsely pictured as being foreign-born and un-American." Latter-day Ohioans who heard Lausche's anticommunist tirades of the Vietnam era would find the 1946 campaign charges ludicrous. The *Cleveland Press*, in its editorial endorsement of Lausche for reelection, summarized the situation: "Actually, the campaign against Frank Lausche adds up to this— to smear him—to try to smear him with the meat shortage, with Communism, with every prejudice the Republicans can lay hands on in these times of heated prejudice."[16] Whether or not Herbert himself used the "Communist" charge against Lausche is not clear. But there is an interesting footnote. Years later in 1955, Herbert managed to get himself appointed by President Eisenhower to the Subversive Activities Control Board. The board, under a 1950 act of Congress, had the authority to determine whether organizations are subversive.

During his two years as governor, Herbert emphasized two accomplishments—tax reduction and veterans' benefits. At his urging, six bills reduced or eliminated certain taxes, saving taxpayers $86 million. Included was elimination of the sales tax on small purchases under 41 cents. The treasury surplus from the first Lausche administration was tapped for about $45 million in bonus compensation for World War II veterans.[17] In his own opinion, given to biographers, these were Herbert's favorite achievements—thus placing him among the less innovative of Ohio governors. Although some appropriations for education and other services were increased over prior administrations, Herbert, like Lausche, practiced the kind of hold-the-line politics and policy that set the stage for tougher fiscal decisions by later governors wrestling with the effects of the Baby Boom and economic hard times.

OHIO POLITICS IN THE EARLY POSTWAR YEARS

Postwar Ohio was a microcosm of postwar America. Thousands of Ohio men and women joined the twelve million Americans in finding their way back into the nation's mainstream and its job market. The GI Bill, the Baby Boom, suburban growth, and expanded peacetime industries all had their impact on the ballot box and state government. Unions picked up power in expanding memberships, although minorities and women faced barriers to obtaining or even keeping their old jobs with the return of war veterans.

Ohio's population surged by 1,760,000 people in the 1950s, recording the state's largest growth of the twentieth century. About 5.3 percent of Americans lived in Ohio throughout the 1950s, and Ohioans produced about 6 percent of the Gross National Product, ranking fourth or fifth in industrial production. One historian summed up the postwar years in Ohio this way: "Ohio just plowed through history, turning out immense amounts of manufactured goods, paying among the nation's highest wages to its factory workers but shortchanging others less fortunate, practicing a politics of indifference."[18]

For the most part, the Republican party dominated elections and politics of the era—except for Frank Lausche, of course. Although Lausche succeeded Republican John W. Bricker as governor, Bricker and Robert A. Taft—"Mr. Republican"—won most of the elections for the U.S. Senate in the postwar period. Bricker, a Columbus attorney, had kept Ohio in the Republican column in 1944 when he ran as Tom Dewey's vice presidential running mate against the victorious Roosevelt-Truman ticket. He then won Senate terms in 1946 and 1952. In the early 1950s, Bricker was Ohio's GOP apostle of anticommunism, as summed up in this hometown editorial about his 1952 reelection: "[Bricker] has set his face like flint against the socialization of the American economy. He has supported every move to ferret out Communist infiltration of government and to punish subversives when they have been exposed."[19] After the Korean conflict, Bricker was noted for his battle for an amendment to the Constitution: President Truman's commitment of American soldiers in Korea without congressional approval had alarmed many Republicans and peace groups, and Bricker's amendment would have limited the president's power to make unilateral executive agreements with foreign nations. It failed by one vote in the Senate.

Meanwhile, Robert A. Taft retained his Senate seat throughout the 1940s and through the postwar period until his death in 1953. The son of President William Howard Taft, he was a a dominant national voice for the GOP even though his presidential ambitions were thwarted first by Dewey and then Eisenhower in 1952. His leadership skills in the Republican policy committee made him a force in the nation's politics as well as Ohio's. He was best known for his caution in foreign affairs (he originally was a pre–World War II isolationist) and for his sponsorship of the Taft-Hartley Labor Management Act of 1947. Union leaders in Ohio and nationwide despised Taft and Republicans because the law outlawed the closed shop, provided for mandatory cooling-off periods during labor difficulties, and forced labor union officers to sign affidavits disavowing any Communist party connections.[20] Republican George Bender was elected in 1954 to fill Taft's unexpired term, defeating a temporary appointment of Governor Lausche's, Democrat Thomas A. Burke of Cuyahoga County. It took Frank Lausche himself to finally break the Republican hold on Ohio's U.S. Senate elections when he defeated Bender in 1956.

No fewer than four Ohioans served in President Eisenhower's cabinet during his two terms in office. They included Secretary of Defense Charles Wilson of Minerva, a former president of General Motors Corporation, and Treasury Secretary George M. Humphrey of Cleveland in

Eisenhower's first term and Secretary of Defense Neil McElroy of Cincinnati and Secretary of Health, Education and Welfare Arthur S. Flemming of Delaware, a former president of Ohio Wesleyan University, in the second term.[21]

Republicans also fared well in congressional and legislative elections in Ohio through the Lausche era. They maintained a majority in the congressional delegation, and the ancient Hanna Amendment, which guaranteed each county at least one representative in the Ohio House, helped them maintain control of the General Assembly through the 1950s. Since the GOP dominated most rural counties, this meant Republican control of at least the House (and often the Senate) and underrepresentation for the urban county (often Democratic) population in the legislature.[22] Therefore, this so-called Lausche era was actually one of Republican dominance, except for the remarkable ability of Frank Lausche to survive in the state's highest executive posts as a single politician who was hardly ever on very good terms with his own party leadership. But he was on good terms with rank-and-file voters as well as successful Ohioans who became national celebrities in a variety of professions.

Lausche and his powerful friends in the Ohio Newspaper Association launched the Governor's Award in 1949—the highest award a governor bestows to this day. The recipient roster during the Lausche years reads like a Who's Who of postwar America. And the list demonstrates the breadth of human talent Ohio gave to the nation in that era. From 1949 through 1956, they included novelist Louis Bromfield of Mansfield; entertainer Bob Hope of Cleveland; columnist-author Earl Wilson of Rockford; New York Yankee MVP Tommy Heinrich of Canton; General Motors president and inventor Charles Kettering of Loudonville; All-American Soap Box Derby founder Jim Schlemmer of Akron; actor William "Hopalong Cassidy" Boyd of Cambridge; war-hero aviator and chairman of the board of Eastern Airlines Captain Eddie Rickenbacker of Columbus; founder of Ohioana Library Martha Kinney Cooper of Cincinnati; U.S. senator and "Mr. Republican" Robert A. Taft of Cincinnati; national tennis champion Tony Trabert of Cincinnati; Secretary of Defense Charles Wilson of Minerva; entertainer Joe E. Brown of Holgate; U.S. Steel Corporation president Benjamin F. Fairless of Pigeon Run; World War II commander of the Strategic Air Command General Curtis LeMay of Columbus; *New York Times* editor Charles Merz of Sandusky; author-minister Norman Vincent Peale of Bowersville; all-American football player for Ohio State University

Howard "Hopalong" Cassady of Columbus; cartoonist Milton Caniff ("Steve Canyon") of Hillsboro; developer-sportsman John W. Galbreath of Mount Sterling; and OSU football coach and legend Wayne Woodrow "Woody" Hayes of Columbus.[23]

LAUSCHE RETURNS

The Lausche comeback of 1948—and the rest of the remarkable Lausche era—almost never happened. His defeat at Herbert's hands in 1946 had left him "heartbroken," in his own word, and he nearly quit active politics to become a railway lobbyist. But he changed his mind when he learned that his old mentor and nemesis Ray Miller, the Cuyahoga County Democratic boss, had declared his candidacy for governor in the 1948 primary. Lausche jumped in too. Miller lined up union and party leaders behind him, taking advantage of Lausche's past difficulties with them. Lausche's policy as governor of separating himself from the regular Democratic organization developed into almost open warfare during his losing bid for reelection against Herbert. He exercised an iron hand over platform writers at the 1946 state Democratic convention, ensuring that the platform positions on issues were to his liking. Then he continued to warn that he would be a "man free of any party dictates if elected to a second term." Newspapers published headlines like "Lone Wolf Lausche" and "Lausche Asserts Independence."

While he had lost with such tactics in 1946—a big Republican year nationally and in Ohio—1948 was a different story. Miller learned a harsh lesson about Lausche's ability to appeal over the heads of party leaders to grass roots Democrats. Lausche carried eighty-seven of eighty-eight counties in the primary, including Cuyahoga. Learning some lessons from his own defeat, he managed to close ranks with party leaders—especially the top party leader in the nation, President Truman. Truman was viewed as a sure loser in Ohio that year and a definite underdog against Dewey. But Lausche campaigned extensively with Truman throughout Ohio and is credited with helping Truman squeak by with a 7,100-vote victory in Ohio. "I didn't think he [Truman] had a chance," Lausche later told the *Plain Dealer*. "We took a train ride through the state near the end of the campaign and no one on the train thought he had a chance. Only Truman thought he had a chance." Lausche regarded Truman and Republican Ronald Reagan as the outstanding presidents he knew. "Truman and Reagan were the only ones with the guts to take on the spendthrifts," Lausche said in 1985.[24] Lausche beat Herbert with a landslide margin of 221,261 votes in 1948. He did it despite the fact that the AFL and the CIO both refused to endorse him (or Herbert). Both the "spendthrifts" and labor would have many more battles in the years ahead.

Nationally, 1992 may have been the "Year of the Woman," but in the Ohio Senate it was 1948. Senator Margaret Mahoney, a three-term Democratic senator from Cleveland, became the first woman to be elected Senate president pro tempore, Senate majority leader (in those days, the lieutenant governor still presided as Senate president). In 1992 some Ohio media incorrectly bestowed the honor of "first woman to head a legislative caucus" on Representative Jo Ann Davidson, a Reynoldsburg Republican who was elected House minority leader for the 1993 session. But more than forty years earlier, Senator Mahoney earned that distinction for one brief session. On her first day in office, the *Columbus Dispatch*—perhaps taken with the oddity of a woman legislative leader—devoted three pictures to Senator Mahoney at the top of page one. Featured prominently in the article was her shopping trip for lost earrings, including an interview with the jewelry store clerk.[25]

With apologies to George Bush, 1949 could also be called the "year of Lausche's lips"; the comeback governor forced the legislature to watch his lips carefully when he said "no new taxes." In April 1949, Governor Lausche submitted to Senator Mahoney and her legislative colleagues a biennial budget with a grand total of $649,461,445—barely a fraction of the $30-billion budgets Representative Davidson and her colleagues dealt with in the early 1990s. And, characteristically, Lausche submitted his budget with no new or increased taxes. Almost immediately, Lausche and Senator Mahoney faced open rebellion in Senate ranks on both sides of the aisle.

A bipartisan group of senators pushed through the Senate Rules Committee proposals that would add $47 million to the budget and require new taxes—proposals opposed by both Lausche and Senator Mahoney, who chaired the rebellious Rules Committee. One proposal would increase teacher salaries by $25 per month with a special appropriation of $27 million. Another proposal, called the Youngstown Plan, would earmark the state tax on intangible personal property for the Local Government Fund and increase that fund's receipts from the state sales tax by about $6 million annually. Lausche met personally—and unsuccessfully—with the rebel senators and then went public with a stinging attack. "When I submitted my budget, the opposition in the Legislature labeled it as an extravagant one. Yesterday, we had the revealing spectacle of one of the very men who vigorously attacked me setting into motion the machinery for the passage of bills that will spend $47.5 million of new tax money," Lausche said. The shot was directed mainly at Republican senator Roscoe Walcutt of Columbus, who was joined in the bipartisan uprising in the Rules Committee by Democratic senators Clingan Jackson of Youngstown and Emmett R. Guthrie of Coshocton and Republican senator Fred Adams of Bowling Green. Lausche charged that their package would disrupt his budget plans, unbalance the budget, and increase state taxes and that they knew it.[26] Eventually, the teachers would get their raises and the Youngstown Plan intangibles tax would be earmarked for the Local Government Fund. But Lausche won over the wayward senators and virtually set in stone the precedent of the executive branch initiating—or not initiating—major taxes in the Ohio budget process. Rarely would a future legislator initiate a major new tax in Ohio, especially if the governor was calling for no new or increased taxes, a frequent refrain in subsequent administrations, including Lausche's.

Ironically, although Lausche is credited with virtually inventing the "no new taxes" mantle for governors, he actually wore it exclusively for only one more biennium. In the 1950 elections, Republicans swept the General Assembly races and just about everything else in Ohio except Lausche's chair and that of Democratic lieutenant governor George D. Nye. In March 1951, Lausche greeted the new Republican-dominated legislature with a record budget (almost every new state budget is a "record") of $729,114,379—about 2 percent of the 1993 level. Lausche preached no new or increased taxes again and railed against "needless expenditures, waste and extravagance."[27]

Reelected for a fourth term in 1952, Lausche amended his old "no new taxes" position by advocating higher existing taxes on gasoline and race track operators; in the 1953 General Assembly session, he also threw his support to a Republican plan for an "axle-mile" tax on commercial trucks. After his record fifth-term victory over Republican auditor James A. Rhodes in 1954, Lausche—fresh from a 200,000-vote margin—used his mandate to jolt the Republican-dominated legislature. "New taxes will be required to meet the rising costs of government," he wrote in a "grimly-worded" letter—dated February 3, 1955—to House speaker Roger Cloud of Logan County and Senate majority leader C. Stanley

Mechem of Nelsonville. Both Republican leaders had already taken a "no new taxes" stand, and Lausche appeared to take a position firmly on the fence by saying that "new taxes are required," but in the next paragraph adding, "I am firmly of the belief that new taxes ought not to be imposed." Lausche said the state faced a $15-million deficit instead of a $40-million surplus as reported earlier by his director of finance. About $37 million was needed to fund the school foundation formula. Generally, Lausche and the legislative leaders of the era felt education was a "local matter" to be dealt with by local school boards with minimal interference or assistance from the state. In his letter to Cloud and Mechem, Lausche also appeared to duck responsibility for setting school aid levels: "The administration has no discretionary control over the funds that are provided for local schools. The amounts are fixed by the Legislature."[28] Lausche would leave it to future Ohio governors to exert activist leadership for new or increased sales and income taxes to aid schools and universities and to cover state services.

Besides his penchant for penny-pinching, Lausche had other ways of gaining popularity, notably by waging war against gamblers with both words and actions. "Fearless Frank" had risen to power in Cleveland closing gambling dens and fighting hoodlums. He found that the message also played well on the statewide stage. For example, shortly after returning to the Governor's Mansion in Columbus, he branded commercialized gambling as a major menace to Ohio and launched a campaign against "this multi-million racket." He pinpointed four deluxe gambling halls and sought power from the legislature to close them; he did not trust local law enforcement to do it. He sought legislative authority to removed sheriffs who were lax in enforcing gambling laws and the right to padlock gambling establishments if county prosecutors failed to act. As he ran into legislative reluctance to make him an antigambling czar as well as governor, he served notice that he would not backtrack. He began mapping plans with departments to exercise whatever executive authority he could muster. He renewed the effort in 1951 at Senate hearings in Cleveland on gambling and proposed a federal ban against betting wires.[29]

As the years wore on, Lausche found new ways of asserting his independence in the eyes of voters without continually bashing gamblers and other Democrats. Lobbyists became a favorite target, despite the fact he almost became a railway lobbyist in 1948 before staging his gubernatorial comeback. In his January 1953 message to the General Assembly, he issued a warning to legislators to beware of special-interest lobbyists. He said there "will be no registered spokesmen for the general public," and "unless you and I act as the people's spokesmen, the millions of Ohioans who placed their trust in us will be powerless and defenseless." He followed that with a nine-point program built around his "no new taxes" philosophy. Exceptions to that philosophy included taxes to "modernize highways and to compel certain business interests, such as race tracks, to carry their share of the burden."[30]

In 1954 Lausche escalated his rhetoric against the moneyed interests during his campaign for reelection against Rhodes. In an October speech to the Democratic state convention at the Deshler Hotel in Columbus, he told fellow Democrats and candidates to be careful of taking campaign contributions. "Try to keep yourself in a position where you will always be free. Don't allow anyone to get a lasso around your neck through campaign contributions and approaches by public utilities, railroad moguls, distillers, road builders and sellers of material."[31] In those days cash flowed freely, and loosely worded campaign finance laws required little reporting, according to many reformers twenty years later. Lausche himself could afford to practice his preaching and limit his campaign fundraising. By the time of his sixth statewide campaign for governor, he was highly popular in the general electorate and unchallenged in Democratic primaries. Still, there were few signs of Lausche hypocrisy on the special interests against which he railed. He fought the trucking lobby resistance to axle-mile taxes in an effort to keep the gasoline tax low for all Ohioans. He kept the pressure on race tracks to carry a fair share of the commercial tax burden. He campaigned hard, but in vain, for major utility rate-setting reform; throughout the early 1950s, he wanted to abandon Ohio's reconstruction cost new (RCN) formula in the utility rate-setting process, a reform opposed long and successfully by Ohio utilities. The RCN repeal and other utility-rate reform would not happen in the legislature for another twenty-five years.

Lausche's fiscal style led to minimal improvements in state services—mostly allowed by the natural growth of state revenue in an expanding postwar economy. Public welfare spending for 1952–53 was increased to a total of $97.4 million, a pittance by standards just a decade later. In 1993 the Ohio House cut three times that amount from the governor's $13.7-billion budget for the Human Services Department and still allowed for $2-billion growth in the welfare spending. During Lausche's terms, modest physical improvements were made at state hospitals for the mentally retarded. New buildings were constructed at Applecreek, Lima, and Tiffin state hospitals, but there was little appreciable progress in treatment.[32]

On Halloween in 1952 a serious prison riot erupted at the nineteenth-century Ohio State Penitentiary in Columbus. Faced with incredibly overcrowded penal institutions, Lausche appointed a task force to develop a plan for prison improvement. The 100th General Assembly appropriated $8.5 million for prison expansion, adding that to a $5-million program already under way. But Lausche's crowning glory in bricks and mortar was highway construction in general and the turnpike in particular. The legislature authorized construction of an Ohio turnpike to hook up with Pennsylvania's turnpike in 1949, and it was completed in 1955. The 242-mile highway was built and maintained with revenue bonds and paid off with tolls from motorists instead of the gasoline tax revenue that covered Ohio's conventional highway building boom of the 1950s. It was named the James W. Shocknessy Ohio Turnpike after the late Turnpike Commission chairman from Toledo, who jealously guarded the turnpike's financing system for decades from frequent attempts to combine it with the regular Ohio highway system. In 1951 Lausche called a special session of the legislature and appointed a highway commission to deal with the need for building an Ohio highway system to meet the postwar explosion in population, car travel, and suburban growth. In 1953 the first bond issue of $500 million for general highway construction was approved by Ohio voters.[33] Bonds were backed with a gasoline tax and weight-distance taxes on trucks and later with the axle-mile tax. This program was integrated with the federal interstate system, also launched in the 1950s. Both efforts would dramatically change the life-styles as well as the road maps of Ohio.

During the early 1950s at the height of the cold war and Korea, America was wracked with "red-baiting," McCarthyism, and the investigations of the House Un-American Activities Committee (HUAC). Ohio had its own Un-American Activities Commission, a joint House-Senate group created in 1951 by the 100th Ohio General Assembly. The commission was headed by Samuel Devine, an attorney and Republican House member from Columbus and a former FBI agent who investigated subversives during World War II. During its first three years of existence, the Ohio Un-American Activities Commission investigated forty Ohioans, asking each of them the question "Right now, are you an active member of the Communist Party?" All forty cited Fifth Amendment immunity from answering the question, and all were subsequently indicted by grand juries in counties where the hearings were held. At least fifteen were convicted.[34]

In 1953 Devine sponsored a package of bills extending the life and powers of the joint commission. Under tremendous cold war–era pressure in Ohio, Governor Lausche signed three of the bills into law, including a basic extension of the life of the Ohio Un-American Activities Commission. But, perhaps recalling his own troubles with "red-baiting" in his 1946 campaign for governor, Lausche vetoed the main Devine anti-Communist bill, which created jail terms and stiff fines for targets of commission investigations. Lausche issued a stinging rebuke in his veto message on July 30, 1953, nearly a year before the 1954 Army-McCarthy hearings were to grip the nation. In his message Lausche said he was in sympathy with the view that "Communism is a menace to our country," but he warned against smearing the reputations of innocent individuals: "I can see nothing but grave danger to the reputations of innocent people against whom accusations can be made on the basis of rumor and frequently rooted in malice." Lausche also criticized the Devine bill language that would make criminal any act that would constitute "a clear and present danger to the security of the country." The former Cleveland judge and crime fighter wrote that no judge or juror could clearly determine what constituted a "clear and present danger." He wrote, "Criminal laws ought to be clear and certain in their definition. . . . I can see the reputations of innocent persons actually ruined by rumors, doubts, innuendoes and guilt inferred through association."[35] Lausche's veto was overridden by Devine and his legislative colleagues, who extended the life of the commission for many years to come. But Lausche's veto message was remarkable in light of the cold war tension of the early 1950s and in light of Lausche's own later reputation as a conservative, anti-Communist U.S. senator in the Vietnam War era.

Lausche won his record fifth term as governor in 1954 by defeating state auditor James A. Rhodes of Columbus by a landslide. That election climaxed one political era in Ohio and sowed the seeds for another. Rhodes, a former Columbus mayor and the son of a Jackson County coal miner, was the only Republican to rival Frank Lausche as a governor and political figure in the latter half of the twentieth century. Rhodes broke Lausche's record for years of service as Ohio governor and set his own as the nation's first four-term (sixteen years) governor. He ran against every Democratic governor of the postwar period, winning four and losing two general elections. He defeated Governors DiSalle (1962), Gilligan (1974), and Celeste (1978) and lost to Lausche (1954) and Celeste (1986.) He also lost a Republican primary for governor to Don Ebright of Akron in 1950, who lost to Lausche.

But it was in his loss to Lausche in 1954 that Rhodes earned his "Ph.D. in politics" and got an education on how to run for governor. Rhodes lost by more than 200,000 votes and said later he knew he "didn't have a chance." But he appeared to pull out all the stops in his campaign. President Eisenhower campaigned with Rhodes in Cleveland in late October. Full-page advertisements in Ohio newspapers pictured Rhodes and Ike together and proclaimed that "The President Supports James A. Rhodes."[36] In campaign speeches Rhodes repeatedly attacked the Lausche record and rhetoric. He charged Lausche with tolerating "irregularities, improprieties and favoritism" in the state Liquor Department. He said he would "remove political influences" from the Welfare Department and lighten the "overpowering burden" of taxation by employing "businesslike and honest methods." Rhodes said he would "exterminate rather than preach about gambling and vice" in Ohio—a clear shot at an issue Lausche felt he "owned." Rhodes also criticized Lausche cabinet members and the organization of the state highway department.

One of Rhodes's favorite ploys, first used against Lausche in 1954, was to call on opponents to investigate scandal. Speaking to about six hundred people in a Painesville park on October 13, Rhodes said that Lausche should call in the attorney general or the legislature to investigate the "half million dollar liquor department scandal."[37] Rhodes said, "If Lausche doesn't know what's going on in his own liquor department, he doesn't deserve a fifth term. If he does know what's going on, he should ask the attorney general to conduct a sweeping investigation or call the legislature back into session to probe the scandal." Liquor agents were indicted in Cincinnati and Cleveland in connection with an alleged half-million-dollar shakedown of liquor-permit holders. Lausche, for the most part, ignored Rhodes's charges or generally dismissed them as "mudslinging." And after Rhodes's Painesville challenge, Lausche abandoned an earlier decision not to campaign and hit the trail later in October. Despite the hard-fought campaign, Lausche and Rhodes became good friends in later years, and Lausche often endorsed Rhodes in his later campaigns for governor.

On the night of Lausche's election for a record fifth term, Ohio voters made two other decisions that would have long- and short-term impact.

First, they approved a constitutional amendment limiting governors to two consecutive four-year terms. It was placed on the ballot by a Republican legislature determined that Democrat Lausche's five terms and ten years would never be duplicated. Ironically, the first governor ever to be affected by the amendment was Jim Rhodes, who was blocked from running for a third term in 1970. The further irony is that when he won his third and fourth four-year terms in the 1970s, Rhodes shattered Lausche's record of ten years in the Governor's Mansion. The second decision Ohioans made on election night 1954 was to elect Republican John W. Brown of Medina to the post of lieutenant governor. The short-term result was the shortest gubernatorial administration in Ohio history.

THE ELEVEN DAYS OF GOVERNOR JOHN BROWN

To almost everyone—except maybe John W. Brown—his eleven-day term as governor of Ohio in 1957 is just a historical footnote. It was the shortest administration in Ohio history and possibly the most bizarre.

Brown had been serving as lieutenant governor under Lausche in 1956 while Lausche ran successfully for the U.S. Senate and Brown lost the Republican primary for governor. Lausche resigned as governor on January 3, 1957, to take his new seat when the Senate convened. Republican attorney general C. William O Neill, the incoming governor, could not be sworn in until January 14 under the Ohio Constitution. That set the stage for an eleven-day interim administration for lame-duck Brown. And he made the most of it.[38]

To the surprise of O'Neill, Brown immediately moved into the Governor's Mansion—and always bragged later he was the last governor to live in that building (O'Neill later moved into the "new" mansion in Bexley, still in use today)—and then into Lausche's vacated office, replacing portraits of Democratic governors with portraits of Republicans. Brown called Lausche's lame-duck cabinet together and assured them that their jobs were safe. About midway through his eleven days, he called a joint session of the General Assembly and delivered a State of the State address.

O'Neill grew nervous early in Brown's term when Brown began trying to settle a telephone strike in Portsmouth, where there had been some violence. Then Brown announced he wanted to draw a governor's pay, instead of a lieutenant governor's salary, for eleven days. To bolster his case for a favorable court ruling later, he sought an official opinion

from Attorney General O'Neill and then started to appoint his own lieu-
tenant governor for the term. Now Brown was really starting to annoy
O'Neill. But O'Neill relented and issued an official opinion saying that
Brown could be paid at the rate of $25,000 a year instead of $6,000.

Brown later deposited with the Ohio Historical Society five boxes of
his gubernatorial papers, as was the custom. (Lausche deposited about
four hundred boxes.) Two strange documents can be found in Brown's
papers. One is a letter on the governor's letterhead asking Columbus
mayor M. E. Sensenbrenner to take care of an over-time parking ticket.
Another is an exchange of letters with Vice President Richard Nixon,
Brown seeking Nixon's help in finding a federal job after his eleven-day
term expired. Brown got a letter back from Nixon but no job.[39]

But Brown's unprecedented administration made the most news and
got into the most trouble when he commuted the sentences of five convicted murderers, two of them convicted in connection with the slaying
of a Cleveland police officer. All five were later paroled. Cleveland public officials and editorial writers were outraged at Brown's commuting
of sentences from first- to second-degree murder. Cleveland mayor
Anthony J. Celebrezze, Sr., called the action "an inexcusable error."
Cleveland Press editor Louis B. Seltzer, a Lausche backer, printed Brown's
picture with the word "irresponsible" under it and wrote that Brown
"was allowed to slither into office by a fluke."[40] Brown defended his actions, saying the men were model prisoners and had been recommended
for parole by their warden and approved by parole authority members.
They were among twenty-five appeals he considered. Interestingly,
Brown refused to act in two cases of note that later became widely
known: Dr. Sam Sheppard, whose plight became the basis for the TV series "The Fugitive," and Thomas "Yonnie" Licavoli of the Purple Gang
in Toledo. Sheppard won on appeal to the U.S. Supreme Court in a landmark decision about pretrial publicity. Licavoli's sentence was later
commuted by Governor Rhodes, who became the subject of a cover story
in *Life* magazine in 1969, headlined "The Governor and the Mobster."

POSTSCRIPTS ON GOVERNORS LAUSCHE, HERBERT, BROWN

After his eleven days, John W. Brown launched a comeback as a House
member from Medina County in 1960. He won three more terms as lieutenant governor (1962, 1966, 1970), matching Rhodes's sixteen-year

record as governor. Brown served in the number-two office under Governors Rhodes and Gilligan. Finally, in 1974, as Rhodes launched his gubernatorial comeback against Gilligan, Brown ran for a record fifth term as lieutenant governor. Brown's sixteen-year career was ended by a youthful state representative from Lakewood named Richard F. Celeste, who won the state's number-two office. Twelve years later Celeste also denied Rhodes his fifth term, ending his sixteen-year record as well. Brown died in 1993 at his home in Medina.

After his loss to Lausche in 1948, Tom Herbert practiced law in Cleveland for several years before President Eisenhower appointed him in 1953 to the Subversive Activities Control Board. He returned to the campaign trail in 1956 and was elected to one six-year term on the Ohio Supreme Court. After a stroke in 1961, Herbert decided to retire from politics and dropped almost totally from public sight. But in 1964 a Cleveland columnist reported that he found an "aging and ailing" Herbert spending most of his time in a wheelchair in his suburban home in Upper Arlington. "He watches television and reads, and frequently his friends, like Eddie Rickenbacker, come and take him for a ride," columnist Roelif Loveland wrote.[41] One of Herbert's three sons, John, was elected state treasurer and was running for attorney general in 1970 when he became embroiled in what became known as the Crofters loan scandal. Tom Herbert died in 1974 in a Grove City nursing home.

Before defeating U.S. senator George Bender in 1956, Frank Lausche flirted with notions of running for president or vice president in 1956. The labyrinthian corridors of the Ohio Statehouse were abuzz again with "Potomac fever." During the fifty years after the Civil War through to the Roaring Twenties, seven Ohio-born sons had made it to the White House. And in 1956, Ohio appeared to be pregnant again with expectations for a favorite son on the national ticket. Amazingly enough, Lausche was considered as a possibility on both Democratic and Republican tickets. Ohio newspapers and national media carried much speculation about Lausche as a possible Democratic nominee. But two historians in the 1980s recorded that Lausche was considered secretly as a possible running mate for Republican president Eisenhower in 1956. Edward Gobetz, who in his 1985 book tribute to Lausche, summarized the Ike-Lausche mutual admiration relationship this way: "While Eisenhower considered Lausche a natural for the U.S. presidency, Lausche in turn was convinced that Eisenhower was the best man for the highest and most demanding position in the nation." William Bragg Ewald, Jr., wrote that Ike speculated with top advisers James Hagerty and Len Hall about "dumping" Richard Nixon as vice president in 1956 and possibly replacing him with Democrat Lausche. Despite Lausche's labor-leader troubles, Ike particularly liked the idea of running with a Catholic Democrat, according to a reported conversation with Hall. "If the Republicans don't run a Catholic this time," Hall rejoined, "the Democrats would next time," and he mentioned John F. Kennedy as "an attractive guy." Gobetz and Ewald recorded that "Hall even took a poll" indicating that Lausche would run as well as anyone else in the number-two spot with Ike. When Hall carried the poll results and the Lausche speculation to Nixon, Hall recalled, "I never saw a scowl come so fast over a man's face. But beyond that we got no response at all." Ewald wrote that Hall's notion was that Nixon would be persuaded to step down as a "hero" and a "new realignment of parties would result." Eisenhower reportedly said, "It would just knock the props out of the opposition. I would love to run with a Catholic, if only to test it out." How serious Eisenhower was about Lausche is not clear. Gobetz reported that Lausche removed himself as a potential national ticket candidate for either party in 1956 and openly supported Eisenhower while running successfully for the U.S. Senate.[42] The "what if" question of an Ike-Lausche ticket in 1956 is a mind-boggling one when such giant figures as Nixon and Kennedy and the later tides of history are considered.

Lausche served two terms as U.S. senator and was finally defeated in the 1968 Democratic primary when John J. Gilligan, Ohio's union leaders, and the tumultuous 1960s finally caught up with him. After many years in Washington, he returned to his native Cleveland and died at the age of ninety-four on April 21, 1990, at the Slovene Home for the Aged, several miles east of the home of his youth.

Upon Lausche's death, old rival and friend Jim Rhodes said, "He was a man of immense intellect, of unquestioned integrity and of steadfast devotion to the highest principles of public service." Governor Celeste, who recalled tearing up as a Cleveland youth at Lausche speeches, said Lausche was "an eloquent voice for his state and country—a dedicated patriot who could bring tears to the eyes of audiences young and old. . . . Frank Lausche was the most significant figure in post–World War II Ohio."[43]

❖

CHAPTER THREE

The O'Neill-DiSalle Years, 1957–1963

❖

MIKE CURTIN

❖ In Ohio, the period from January 1957 to January 1963 represented an interregnum between the legendary gubernatorial reigns of Democrat Frank J. Lausche and Republican James A. Rhodes. The six-year span saw the rise and fall of two governors—Republican C. William O'Neill and Democrat Michael V. DiSalle. Although neither achieved star status or longevity in the governor's office, their combined tenure covered a period of dynamic change, progress, and political upheaval in the state. It was a time in which Ohio was reaching its peak in population growth, manufacturing strength, labor-union membership, and national electoral clout.

When Lausche decided to run for the U.S. Senate in 1956, there was no shortage of candidates to succeed him as governor. Seven men—two Republicans and five Democrats—sought their respective party nominations for governor in the May 8, 1956, primary. The Republicans were John W. Brown, a two-term lieutenant governor and former mayor of Medina, and O'Neill, the state's three-term attorney general and a former speaker of the Ohio House of Representatives. The Democrats were DiSalle, a former mayor of Toledo and former director of the federal Office of Price Stabilization under President Truman; Oscar L. Fleckner, a former state liquor director and former city manager of Springfield; Frank X. Kryzan, a two-term mayor of Youngstown; Robert W. Reider, a Port Clinton publisher and former state representative; and John E. Sweeney, a Cleveland municipal judge. Neither primary, however, was much of a contest.

O'Neill had built an extensive political organization during his eighteen years in elective office, especially in his six years as attorney general. During the primary campaign, Brown complained about the "well-heeled and well-oiled machine of my opposition" and compared it to New York's Tammany Hall.[1] O'Neill crushed Brown with machinelike efficiency, winning the Republican nomination by carrying eighty-four counties and capturing 72 percent of the vote.

In the Democratic primary, DiSalle and his twenty years of political experience were just as overpowering. DiSalle collected 57 percent of the Democratic vote in the five-man race. Sweeney finished a distant second, followed by Reider, Kryzan, and Fleckner.

The ensuing DiSalle-O'Neill battle pitted two men small of stature (O'Neill was five-feet-four; DiSalle was five-feet-five) but large in political ambition. Both candidates had impressive records in office, had won favorable newspaper reviews across the state, and were thought by some to harbor presidential aspirations. At age forty-eight, DiSalle already had served as a state representative, Toledo's assistant law director, city councilman, vice mayor, mayor, and federal price administrator. He also had statewide exposure from two losing campaigns, a 1950 bid against Joseph T. Ferguson for the Democratic nomination for the U.S. Senate and a 1952 challenge to Republican U.S. senator John W. Bricker. O'Neill, just forty, had been a state representative from Marietta at age twenty-two, speaker of the Ohio House at thirty, and attorney general at thirty-four. He had been Ohio's youngest state legislator, youngest House speaker, and youngest attorney general. Now he aimed to be its youngest governor.

DiSalle and O'Neill ran for the last two-year term in the Ohio governorship. In November 1954, the state's voters (a 57-percent majority) had approved a constitutional amendment establishing four-year terms for governor, lieutenant governor, attorney general, and secretary of state to take effect in January 1959.

The 1956 general election campaign was largely conducted on promises to meet the growing public service demands of a booming state. During the 1950s, Ohio's population grew by 22 percent and reached 9.7 million in the 1960 census. That was the fastest rate of growth in Ohio since the mid–nineteenth century, and it put tremendous pressure on state government to build highways, schools, mental health institutions, recreation facilities, and parklands. "Our population, industry, agriculture, small business and large—all are growing. Nine million people today, we will be 11 million strong by 1966," O'Neill declared in his remarks to the 1956 Republican state convention in Columbus. "Standing second in the nation in manufacturing and with a billion-dollar-a-year farm business, it is difficult to foresee where our expansion and progress will stop."[2]

The bullish forecasts for Ohio's population growth were typical of the time. The U.S. Bureau of the Census had predicted Ohio's population would reach 12 million by 1970, which would have made Ohio the nation's third-most-populous state behind New York and California. In 1960, a report on land needs, water management, and recreation issued by the Department of Natural Resources and the Legislative Service Commission predicted that Ohio's population would reach 20 million by the year 2000.[3] Perhaps no one could have predicted that by 1990 Ohio's population still would be under 11 million, but in the mid-1950s it seemed Ohio's growth would continue indefinitely.

It was a time to build, especially highways. Thanks to the Federal-Aid Highway Act of June 29, 1956, states could obtain 90 percent federal funding for interstate highway projects. "We are going to build highways starting in January 1957," O'Neill told members of the Cincinnati Transportation Club a few weeks before the November 1956 election. "We are going to build the 1,300-odd miles of the interstate defense system. There is no state problem more important to the ordinary citizen of Ohio than that of highways. Everywhere I go, everyone to whom I talk wants new roads, wide roads, safe roads." Indeed, Ohio's motor vehicle registrations were shooting up from 2.8 million in 1950 to 4.1 million by 1960, and the state's old road system was becoming choked with traffic.[4]

Prior to enactment of the Federal-Aid Highway Act, Ohioans had approved bond issues to finance highway projects. But there was much criticism that the state was constructing small stretches of highway here and there, attempting to spread the projects and jobs around the state rather than building long stretches connecting major population centers. "Three years ago the people by an overwhelming vote furnished half a billion dollars for better roads. Now, where are the highways? Where is a single modern highway running from North to South across Ohio?" O'Neill asked. "This kind of construction—a half-mile here, a half-mile there—does not give us what we want, a good road from here to there.

This does not result in a new good highway which connects centers of population." O'Neill pledged to ensure that "every construction project be designed to complete a good road between two or more population centers."[5] In 1955, completion of the Ohio Turnpike, a toll road across northern Ohio, had shown Buckeye State motorists how much of an improvement limited-access highways would be, and public demand for them was accelerating.

DiSalle also preached the gospel of progress. He spoke of road building, but he put more emphasis on improving Ohio's social welfare system—assistance to the aged and mentally retarded and efforts to rehabilitate criminals. "I hope to put forth a program that would be not only humanitarian, but one of social justice," he said.[6] DiSalle did not talk of tax increases, suggesting instead that natural growth in state revenues would supply the needed funds.

O'Neill and DiSalle both had been praised in Ohio newspapers for their records of achievement. As attorney general, O'Neill won plaudits for fighting Ohio's narcotics traffic and forcing the State Board of Education to abide by the U.S. Supreme Court's landmark 1954 school desegregation ruling. O'Neill's investigations of the narcotics business led to enactment of a 1955 law providing for prison sentences of forty to eighty years for drug trafficking. In his campaign, O'Neill credited that law for the reduction in Ohio narcotics arrests from 933 in 1954 to 171 in 1956. "Addicts and peddlers by the score have left Ohio and have gone to other states," he said. "We have been advised by the Federal Bureau of Narcotics that 75 percent of the narcotics peddlers have left Ohio." The narcotics law was the chief reason cited by the *Ohio State Journal* for its endorsement of O'Neill over DiSalle in the 1956 campaign.[7] Of Ohio's eighteen largest newspapers in 1956, O'Neill was endorsed for governor by all but three—the Toledo *Blade,* the *Dayton Daily News,* and the *Cincinnati Post.*

Another reason for O'Neill's strong standing with some editors was his 1956 attorney general's opinion telling the state schoolboard it had the authority to withhold money from school districts practicing segregation. Some southern Ohio school districts, most notably the Hillsboro system, were ignoring the Supreme Court's *Brown v. Board of Education* ruling and were continuing to operate separate schools designated for blacks. Charles P. Lucas of Cleveland, the first and only black member of the twenty-three-member State Board of Education, had argued that the board should withhold funds from the

Hillsboro system. But the board majority stalled on his request until O'Neill's opinion ended the controversy.

DiSalle had been widely praised for his directorship of the Office of Price Stabilization and for his efforts to bring labor peace and sound financial operations to Toledo. Appointed federal "price czar" in November 1950, DiSalle was charged with overseeing a temporary general freeze on prices. With the outbreak earlier that year of the Korean War, inflation was raging and consumer prices for moderate income families were rising by an annual average of 8.5 percent.[8] He held the office until February 1952 and was widely credited with a job well done. His other major claim to fame was the Toledo Plan, an industrial-relations program he initiated in 1945 while Toledo's vice mayor. With an eighteen-member labor-management-citizens committee as its centerpiece, the plan aimed to keep labor strife to a minimum in a city that had a sixty-year history of violent strikes. The plan was widely hailed as a success and attempts to copy it were made in cities across the country.

After his election as Toledo mayor in 1947, DiSalle was credited with paying off the city's debt and restoring financial soundness. That was possible largely through Toledo's enactment in 1946 of a 1-percent personal and business income tax. It was the first municipal income tax in Ohio, and the nation's second (Philadelphia was first in 1939). Toledo's income tax enabled the city to initiate many civic improvement programs. Within twenty years, 139 of Ohio's cities and villages would levy income taxes; by 1992, 512.[9]

O'Neill, who had never lost an election, proved to be too strong for DiSalle in 1956. O'Neill outraised and outspent DiSalle, making a series of televised campaign speeches, and was able to win support from some traditionally Democratic labor unions. O'Neill reported spending $235,847 on his campaign, compared to DiSalle's $82,179. The campaign marked the emergence of television advertising in Ohio gubernatorial contests: O'Neill spent $59,952 on TV; DiSalle spent $18,281.

So while Dwight D. Eisenhower was winning his reelection by a landslide over Democrat Adlai E. Stevenson, O'Neill won the Ohio governorship in impressive fashion, taking eighty-three counties and 56 percent of the vote. On January 14, 1957, O'Neill—son of an Irish American justice of the peace—was inaugurated as Ohio's fifty-ninth governor, his second stop on the way to becoming the only person to hold the top positions in the legislative, executive, and judicial branches of Ohio government. The O'Neill family was the first to occupy the new Governor's

Mansion in Bexley, built in 1925 as a private residence and donated to the state in 1955. Also in November 1956, Ohio voters approved, by a 57-percent majority, a constitutional amendment to increase the terms of state senators to four years from two years.

O'Neill entered the governor's office with fellow Republicans in control of both the Ohio Senate (22 R–12 D) and the House of Representatives (97 R–42 D). Except for the 1949–50 legislative session, Republicans had dominated both chambers since before World War II. The Republican and rural domination of the legislature was in no small way attributable to the Hanna Amendment of 1903, which had given each county at least one representative in the Ohio House. The transfer of power to urban areas would not begin until the mid-1960s, after a series of U.S. Supreme Court decisions ended in a landmark June 1964 ruling (*Reynolds v. Sims*) that required states to apportion both houses of their legislatures on the basis of population.

O'Neill's governorship got off to a rocky start even before his inauguration. As governor-elect, he supported salary hikes for department heads and board and commission members, got the legislature to approve them in January, then asked lawmakers in April to rescind the pay increases after witnessing widespread public criticism. Other early problems included three cabinet appointments challenged as illegal because of their failure to meet residency rules and other requirements. "It was one mistake after another," said Keith McNamara, a Columbus lawyer, admirer of O'Neill, and Republican activist who later served in the Ohio House. For the most part, O'Neill's organization was composed of lawyers in their twenties. "The enthusiasm of youth was there but experience was lacking," McNamara said. O'Neill "picked Charlie Noble [of New Jersey] for his highway director, then found out that Ohio law required that an Ohioan be chosen for highway director," McNamara added. The governor was forced to hire Noble as a consultant until the one-year residency requirement was fulfilled. The early missteps were compounded by a feeling that O'Neill was a man in a political hurry, McNamara said. "He had no more than been elected before people started talking about O'Neill for president. These were his own people; his insiders. It created a negative image very early."[10]

In proposing a $1.7-billion biennial budget to the General Assembly in February, O'Neill acknowledged that increasing demands on state government had spawned discussions of the need for a state income tax. Thirty-three states had individual income taxes by this time, although none of the industrial states of the Midwest had yet joined that group. "So long as I am governor I will oppose such a proposal," O'Neill told the legislature. "Our citizenry is already overtaxed."[11] He pledged to run state government for two years without any new or increased taxes. He did so, following in the footsteps of the parsimonious Lausche.

The O'Neill administration had suffered its share of mistakes, but those were nothing compared to its miscalculation on the right-to-work issue. By 1958 a total of nineteen states had right-to-work laws, which prohibit the adoption of labor contracts that establish union membership as a condition of employment. Indiana had just passed a right-to-work law in 1957, making Ohio's western neighbor the first northern state with such a law. Taking notice, big business interests in Ohio wanted the same. For several years, they had been unsuccessfully trying to push right-to-work legislation through the General Assembly.

Driven by the Ohio Chamber of Commerce and the Ohio Manufacturers' Association, an initiative petition committee calling itself Ohioans for Right to Work gathered signatures and qualified the issue for the November 1958 ballot. Despite the reservations of Ohio Republican chairman Ray C. Bliss and Senator Bricker, O'Neill agreed to campaign for passage of the right-to-work amendment, and it became the issue in his reelection campaign. Bliss's concern was evident by the absence of any reference to right-to-work in the Ohio Republican party's 1958 platform. The business groups behind the issue were largely the same interests that financed Republican campaigns in Ohio, and many political observers believed O'Neill felt he had little choice but to support the initiative.

In the years prior to 1958, organized labor had been divided in Ohio. The right-to-work proposal remedied that problem, energizing the labor movement as seldom before. The state's major labor organizations already had negotiated for union-shop clauses in a majority of labor contracts in Ohio; they saw the proposed amendment as a threat to their existence, and they joined to form United Organized Labor of Ohio to defeat it. "It galvanized labor like I never saw them galvanized before," said John C. Mahaney, Jr., who worked with Ohioans for the right-to-work issue. "Labor was at the zenith of its power," added Mahaney, who later became president of the Ohio Council of Retail Merchants.[12]

O'Neill clearly saw the peril of his position on the amendment. "There are only two issues in this campaign. One of them is the right-to-work issue. And the other is the implications of the loss of that issue in Ohio,"

O'Neill told business leaders in a September speech, in which he scolded them for not doing enough to pass the issue. "All the work is being done against it, and no work is being done for it. The unions outregistered the Republicans and the business people, and they are now preparing to get their vote out," O'Neill said. "If it's defeated then they will run Ohio, believe me, gentlemen."[13] Indeed, the labor movement had been so active (and so intimidating, by some accounts) in organizing opposition to the amendment that some business leaders shied away from their earlier support of the proposal. Besides labor, other groups that joined to oppose the amendment were Ohio's Catholic bishops, the Ohio Council of Churches, the NAACP, and many veterans' organizations.

O'Neill took his appeal to television, making a series of addresses on the issue. "What is the real issue of the 1958 campaign? It is: 'Shall the corrupt labor bosses be permitted to take over Ohio?' This is simply and frankly the decision which the people of Ohio will make on Nov. 4," O'Neill said in an October televised speech. "Their goal is to build Ohio in the image of Michigan where the labor bosses dominate the state." O'Neill received a great volume of mail on the issue. Typical of the pro-amendment side of the debate was a letter from Roger C. Brown of Waynesville: "I have been a member of organized labor for over 18 years, and if our union continues to be the kind of organization it has been, I expect to remain a member of it. But in the last three years our contract with General Motors has contained a union-shop (I call it a compulsory membership) clause. And I have resented every minute of it. Along with most union members, I disagree with the ones who have been called 'free riders.' But I still think they should have a choice in the matter." Representative of the antiamendment side was a letter from Robert L. Kelley of Cincinnati, recording secretary of Local 5684 of the United Steelworkers of America: "If politics is going to be influenced by big men of industry then it is my opinion that little men of labor better have a union! It appears to me, governor, that step by step, someone is trying to put the working class or factory worker back where he was in the 1820s where it took the wages of everyone in the family to obtain the bare necessities of life."[14]

The right-to-work amendment turned out to be a much greater foe than O'Neill's actual election opponent—once again Michael V. DiSalle, who had won the Democratic nomination in May over six opponents: Cleveland mayor Anthony J. Celebrezze; Cuyahoga County engineer Albert S. Porter; Cincinnati attorney Robert N. Gorman; Columbus mayor M. E. Sensenbrenner; Youngstown newspaperman Clingan Jackson, and little-known Vivienne L. Suarez of Columbus. O'Neill had been challenged in the Republican primary by Charles P. Taft, a Cincinnati councilman. A son of William Howard Taft, the twenty-seventh president, and younger brother of Senator Robert A. Taft, Charles was a self-styled "standby" candidate in 1958, in case O'Neill's health forced him to drop out of the race. O'Neill had suffered a heart attack during his first year in office. O'Neill won renomination with 64 percent of the vote.

In the general election, the right-to-work issue probably would have been enough by itself to defeat O'Neill. But if that was not enough of an obstacle, Ohio and the nation were suffering from an unemployment rate of near 7 percent, a post–Great Depression high. In Ohio, manufacturing employment had fallen 11 percent from 1957.[15] For his part, DiSalle opposed the right-to-work amendment but stayed out of that debate as much as possible. His campaign concentrated on hammering O'Neill as being indecisive and a do-nothing governor while engaging in deficit spending and juggling the financial books to cover it up.

In the election, O'Neill and the right-to-work amendment went down together. DiSalle captured 57 percent of the vote by carrying all the large counties and piling up big margins in the heavily industrialized ones. The amendment was defeated more soundly, by 63 percent of the vote. It was approved in only eighteen counties, all primarily agricultural. Outside Ohio, right-to-work proposals were voted down the same day in California, Colorado, Idaho, and Washington. Only Kansas went against the tide and approved a right-to-work law. Afterward, right-to-work faded from the stage as an important national issue.

Democrats scored their biggest gains in twenty years in the 1958 election. In Ohio, Republicans lost a U.S. Senate seat (Bricker's), the Ohio House, the Ohio Senate, and every statewide office except secretary of state. Nationally, Democrats won twenty-two of thirty-two gubernatorial contests and picked up 49 seats in the U.S. House of Representatives.

In correspondence after the election, O'Neill wrote that he would not change his mind on the right-to-work issue. "I never felt so completely right on any issue in my life," he wrote.[16] He left the governor's office in January 1959 saying that he had upheld his promise of no new taxes and kept the budget balanced. It was O'Neill's only defeat in what became a forty-year political career. He went on to win election to the Ohio Supreme Court in 1960, where he served with distinction until his death in 1978. For eight of those years, he was chief justice.

Ohio's sixtieth governor and first to have a four-year term, DiSalle was the son of Italian immigrants. He was the son of a union worker described as a militant fighter for union rights and a son of Toledo's Irish Hill neighborhood. DiSalle was the first Toledoan to become the state's chief executive. He entered office with the advantage of fellow Democrats in control of both the Ohio Senate (20 D–13 R) and the House (78 D–61 R), and he wasted little time in laying out an ambitious and expensive program for improvements in state services.

DiSalle considered himself a reformer, and he was quick to argue that Ohio's social welfare obligations had gone largely unmet under penny-pinching administrations of both Democrats and Republicans of the previous two decades. For most of the twentieth century, Ohio had the reputation of being a low-tax, low-spending state. In 1957, Ohio's state government spent $106.20 per capita, compared to the national average of $136.64. In spending on primary and secondary education, Ohio ranked seventh among the twelve Great Lakes and Plains states and below its big industrial neighbors of Michigan, Pennsylvania, and Illinois.[17]

In his State of the State message on January 27, DiSalle left little doubt that he soon would send the General Assembly a budget proposal designed to address these shortcomings. "We face a new era of governmental finance in Ohio," DiSalle said, hinting strongly of the need for new taxes.[18] He laid out plans for a Department of Industrial and Economic Development, an Ohio Scholarship Endowment Fund for college scholarships, a Civil Rights Commission, and higher payments in public welfare, education assistance, unemployment compensation, workers' compensation, and aid for the aged. He also recommended repeal of Ohio's death penalty, his first gubernatorial shot in what would become a lengthy battle against capital punishment.

The following month, DiSalle received support for his contention that the state had been living beyond its means by relying on surpluses accumulated during World War II in a study released by the Legislative Service Commission showing that state spending from 1947–58 increased by an annual rate of 9 percent, while revenues rose by an annual rate of 4.3 percent. (During World War II, Ohio built a surplus in its treasury largely because the national war effort prevented much construction of roads, buildings and other capital improvements.) In March, DiSalle submitted a proposed budget calling for some $337 million in new taxes to help finance $2.1 billion in spending over the coming biennium. "The recommendations I have given you here are not easy and are not pleasant, but they are necessary if our state is to respond to the needs of our society and our economy," DiSalle said.[19]

With final enactment in June, DiSalle's tax package included a 2-cent increase in the gasoline tax (to 7 cents); a 2-cent increase in the cigarette tax (to 5 cents a pack); a wine and mixed-beverage sales tax; an increase in the horse racing tax; an increase in the corporate franchise tax from 1 mill to 3 mills on the value of capital stock in Ohio; a decrease in the amount exempted from the sales tax from 41 cents to 31 cents. In all, DiSalle was able to boost state spending by nearly a half-billion dollars over the previous biennium.

The Republican attacks on DiSalle's tax plan began immediately, with arguments that the higher taxes would drive businesses out of state. The debate served as a preview for the 1960 legislative campaigns and the 1962 gubernatorial campaign. Feeling the political heat from his tax increases, DiSalle decided to tour the state and explain their necessity. He stopped at state institutions and facilities and tried to show the services and benefits derived from the revenues. He also pointed out that twenty-eight other cash-strapped states were forced to enact tax hikes in 1959.

In August, DiSalle signed into law a measure creating the Department of Industrial and Economic Development. He said it would play a dominant role in his adminstration with its primary mission to attract new business and industry into the state. Also enacted in the first year of DiSalle's term were a civil rights law and the Ohio Civil Rights Commission to enforce it. The legislature also voted to amend Ohio's Sunday-closing law (the so-called Blue Law) to permit operation of state and county fairs on Sundays. Attempts to repeal the entire Blue Law, which dated back to 1831, were unsuccessful.

As the 1960 presidential campaign approached, the state Democratic organization sent petitions to all eighty-eight county Democratic chairmen, asking them to support DiSalle as a favorite-son candidate. But after Massachusetts senator John F. Kennedy paid him a visit, DiSalle aligned himself with Kennedy and delivered the state's Democratic convention delegates to the senator. Ohio become the first big state outside Massachusetts to line up with Kennedy. However, though Kennedy narrowly won the presidency, Republican Richard M. Nixon carried Ohio with relative ease, 53 percent to 47 percent, and DiSalle was given much of the blame by Ohio Democrats. Throughout the fall campaign, Republicans had hammered DiSalle and his tax program for driving jobs out of state. In central Ohio, for example, Republicans pointed to the Kilgore Manufacturing Company of Westerville, a Columbus suburb. In business in Westerville since 1923, this manufacturer of toys and flares announced its move to Tennessee, partly because of Ohio's higher tax burden. The move eliminated about four hundred central Ohio jobs. Besides failing to carry the state for Kennedy, DiSalle suffered another political setback in Ohio's 1960 state legislative elections: Republicans regained both the Senate (20 R–18 D) and the House (84 R–55 D).

DiSalle's political problems stemmed largely from the tax increases, but he also received considerable editorial and public criticism for his strong opposition to capital punishment. DiSalle made repeated attempts to persuade the legislature to abolish the death penalty, only to have the bills killed in committee. He also commuted the sentences of five men and one woman from death to life in prison. It was the case of the woman, Edythe Klumpp of Cincinnati, which caused a statewide sensation.

In July 1959 Klumpp had been found guilty of first-degree murder in the 1958 shooting death of Louise Bergen. Klumpp, a divorcee who was romantically involved with the victim's husband, William Bergen, at first said the shooting was accidental, with the gun going off as she struggled with Louise Bergen. But after a judge sentenced Klumpp to die in the electric chair, and an execution date was set for December 13, 1960, Klumpp changed her story and claimed that William Bergen actually did the killing.

DiSalle reviewed the case in detail, interviewed Klumpp himself, and then took the unusual step of directing that Klumpp be interviewed again by a doctor after being given an injection of a sedative, or "truth serum." DiSalle concluded that Klumpp was telling the truth and was not the guilty party in the slaying. He granted a commutation in January 1961. The decision caused an uproar in the newspapers. "No other governor in our recollection has done more to negate the conscientious labor of juries, police and prosecuting attorneys in carrying out the law against capital offenses," thundered the *Cincinnati Enquirer*. "Governor DiSalle has developed a penchant for retrying cases."[20] Even the Toledo *Blade*, DiSalle's usually supportive, hometown newspaper blasted the governor over his commutations.

In a letter of response, DiSalle wrote: "During the past two years I have had nine clemency cases before me. Four were executed; five received commutations. The four executions were little publicized. The five commutations received a great deal of attention." He said that he had "a deep-seated antipathy towards capital punishment, but the fact that four people have been executed does not indicate that it has become an obsession which interferes with what I feel is a duty on my part. I might wish that the law would be otherwise but, until it is changed under the due process of our democratic system, I have no alternative except to permit those who are sentenced to death to be executed unless there is justifiable reason to halt the execution." As governor, DiSalle continued, "I feel that I am entitled to the same prerogative of reasonable doubt in arriving at my decision as is a court or a jury; the right of clemency is a constitutional responsibility which is a part of our system of justice."[21]

During DiSalle's four years as governor, six men were executed in the Ohio Penitentiary's electric chair. Seven men had been electrocuted during O'Neill's two-year term. After his defeat in November 1962, but before leaving the governor's office, DiSalle issued seven commutations to convicted murderers who had been employed at the Governor's Mansion.

Once out of office, DiSalle took an opportunity to more fully explain his opposition to capital punishment by coauthoring a book published in 1965, *The Power of Life or Death*. "During my term as governor, I came to dread the days leading to an execution," he wrote. "Even when I was convinced of the man's guilt, doubt haunted my unconscious long after the warden had notified me that the prisoner was dead. The men in death row in the Ohio State Penitentiary today, as during my administration, have one thing in common: they are penniless. I have never seen a person of means go to the chair. It is the poor, the illiterate, the underprivileged, the member of the minority group—the man who because he is without means is defended by a court-appointed attorney—who becomes society's blood sacrifice."[22]

Besides opposing capital punishment, DiSalle wanted as governor to close the Ohio Penitentiary, the state's maximum-security prison that had opened in 1834 in Columbus. DiSalle considered it medieval and in 1960 pledged to shut down the old penitentiary within six years. It stayed in operation until 1984.

The 1959 tax hike and the clemency cases were not the only political injuries to hobble DiSalle. Unlike in the first two years of his term, DiSalle faced a Republican-controlled legislature in the 1961–62 session.

In 1961, DiSalle proposed a budget calling for almost $150 million in new spending for the biennium, although he did not propose any new taxes. He insisted the state needed more money for vital services but wanted to force the Republican-controlled legislature to figure out how to raise it. The legislature responded by reducing many of the governor's budget requests, so in July 1961 DiSalle took the unprecedented step of vetoing all legislative appropriations for the second year of the biennium, forcing a budgetary stalemate that would be resolved in January 1962 when a pared-down budget became law without DiSalle's signature. While some newspapers called DiSalle's veto ingenious and daring, others had begun wondering if his political epitaph was already inscribed.

Throughout 1961, political speculation had been mounting that Democrats might encourage another candidate, perhaps Cleveland mayor Anthony J. Celebrezze, to run in the 1962 governor's race. Acknowledging his predicament, DiSalle announced in October 1961 that he would not seek reelection so that he could fight for his programs without the burden of a candidacy. The following month, supporters organized a "draft DiSalle" movement to convince him to change his mind. In January 1962 DiSalle got back in the race, although by that time Attorney General Mark McElroy already had announced he would seek the Democratic nomination.

The DiSalle committee began extolling the virtues of his administration, citing improvements in mental hygiene, better programs for the mentally retarded, the authorization of community colleges and university branches, programs for the academically gifted, continued highway improvements, increased minimum teacher salaries, and creation of an educational television commission. The state's Democratic party also began an offensive against the Republican-controlled General Assembly, faulting it for failure to regulate lobbying activities, failure to redistrict Ohio's congressional boundaries, failure to obtain $27 million in available federal funds for children of unemployed parents, and other alleged shortcomings.

But the major state government debate of 1961–62, as in previous administrations and those to come, was over the level of public services and the willingness to pay for them. Among the conservative voices was the Canton *Repository*, which mocked DiSalle for continually citing statistics "to show how bad off the state of Ohio is—42nd in state tax collections per $1,000 of personal income. That's wonderful. Calls for congratulations all around. Maybe if we all try hard we can get to be 50th—best in the Union!" Summing up the opposing argument, the *Troy Daily News* editorialized, "This is an essentially conservative state, after all. One observer has remarked: 'It should be noted that the average citizen of Ohio is very strongly in favor of progress. All he is opposed to is paying for that progress.' And Mike DiSalle, thanks to his enemies, is firmly associated in the mind of John and Jane Buckeye with the idea of paying for that progress."[23]

DiSalle clearly was in political trouble. The Cuyahoga County Democratic Party, the state's largest local Democratic organization, endorsed McElroy for the Democratic nomination in the May primary. DiSalle survived the primary, but unimpressively: DiSalle received just 50 percent of the vote; McElroy received 45 percent, and the remainder went to Alexander G. Metrakos of Cleveland, a gadfly who ran on a platform of legalizing gambling. In the Republican primary, State Auditor James A. Rhodes secured his party's nomination by winning 90 percent of the vote against William L. White, an engineer and conservationist from Mount Vernon.

Besides the DiSalle-Rhodes battle, the 1962 fall campaign featured a spirited conflict over whether to amend the Ohio Constitution to liberalize the state's 131-year-old Sunday-closing law. For several years, the Lawson Milk Company of Cuyahoga Falls had attempted unsuccessfully to get the law changed. Lawson's had operated seven-days-a-week stores in Ohio for twenty-three years and was upset about being the victim of overzealous enforcement of the Sunday-closing law in some communities. The old law, amended a few times over the years, allowed the sale of specified necessities but outlawed the sale of general merchandise. Yet by the 1960s, Sunday merchandising had become common. The problem was that in many Ohio communities law enforcement authorities ignored the Blue Law; but some enforced it.

Lawson's led an initiative petition drive to place the issue on the November 1962 ballot. If approved, it would have added "milk, milk products, (and) any food item or food product for human or animal consumption" to the list of Sunday necessities. The state's retail establishment vigorously fought the proposal. "We didn't want to be open on Sunday. Our employees didn't want to work. The unions were against it and the churches were against it," recalled John C. Mahaney, Jr., who led the campaign against the issue for the Ohio Council of Retail Merchants.[24] The pro-amendment campaign distributed literature urging

Ohioans to, "Vote yes for honest Sundays—Legalize Sunday Necessities!" The Mahaney-led forces countered that passage would mean "it would only be a matter of time until Sunday as we know it would be a thing of the past. Maintain Sunday as the traditional day of rest. Let's keep Sunday—Sunday!" ·

The retail establishment won handily, with 57 percent of voters rejecting the proposal. "We won this Pyrrhic victory," Mahaney said. "People were still looking to shop on Sunday, especially at these cut-rate stores. Nobody enforced the law after we won," and Sunday merchandising became evermore commonplace.

In the governor's race, DiSalle was constantly on the defensive, bombarded by charges of being "Tax-Hike Mike," antagonized by the *Columbus Evening Dispatch* and kept off balance by Rhodes's skillful campaign tactics. Campaigning against Rhodes, DiSalle remarked to reporters, "is like trying to play ping-pong on a pogo stick." DiSalle attempted to show that he was moving Ohio forward in education, mental health, financial accountability, and many other areas, while the Ohio Republican platform assailed him for running "a government whose sole solution to public problems is to spend and spend and tax and tax." DiSalle was unable to make his case effectively, and on November 6 he was buried in a landslide as Rhodes captured 59 percent of the vote.

In his morning-after press conference, a disappointed DiSalle said, "Let me say to one and all that Ohio is a better state today than it was when I assumed office. . . . My reward comes in the many expressions of thanks from the parents of the retarded, the relatives of the mentally ill, the neglected teachers of our public schools and the professors of our colleges and universities." He asserted, "Ohio will have to meet its obligations to the aged, the young, the sick and the needy. Ohio will have to bolster its educational program. It has been cheap, backward and neglected. Ohio has shortchanged our children at a time when education is our most important need." And he was unable to repress his animosity toward Rhodes. "I have never had an opponent for whom I have less respect and whom I feel is less qualified to serve the people of this state. I would not trade places with him or his conscience."[25]

After leaving the governor's office, DiSalle set up a private law practice in Washington. In March 1963 he became chief administrator of the model city project of Reston, Virginia, although he resigned that position in November 1963. He maintained his Washington law practice until his death in September 1981.

DiSalle would be remembered as a governor who struggled mightily to challenge Ohio's tradition of tight-fisted public spending. He was a liberal Democrat who espoused a greatly expanded role for state government in meeting societal needs. His successes and failures would be closely studied by future Democratic governors John J. Gilligan and Richard F. Celeste, who shared DiSalle's vision of government but had seen the political risks associated with it.

❖

CHAPTER FOUR

Rhodes's First Eight Years, 1963–1971

❖

RICHARD G. ZIMMERMAN

❖ James Allen Rhodes's inauguration as Ohio's sixty-first governor on a bitterly cold January 14, 1963, marked the realization of a dream, a goal, an ultimate ambition he is said to have harbored since he was a schoolboy.

Rhodes's single-minded pursuit of his native state's highest executive office had begun formally twenty-nine years before with his election as a Columbus Republican ward committeeman, and it never seems to have flagged. His election as governor was the result of his fourteenth political campaign, a record marred by only two defeats. Lacking the college education and law degree that promoted and accelerated the careers of his last five predecessors, Rhodes had made his way to the top in a very traditional way: step by careful, tedious step from ward committeeman to school board to city auditor to mayor to state auditor to become perhaps the most active, influential, and, to date, by far the longest-serving governor in Ohio's history.

While Rhodes liked to emphasize his humble beginnings, he actually was born into a middle-class environment (middle-class at least by Jackson County standards of the time) on September 13, 1909, in a small but comfortable clapboard house in Coalton, a village in the midst of Ohio's south-central coal fields. Like many of their neighbors, his parents, James and Susan Howe Rhodes, were mainly of Welsh ancestry. His mother had a high school degree, and his father had attended business college, working his way up from the deep shafts to become a mine superintendent. The elder James also was a Republican precinct committeeman. Rhodes recalled the origin of his Republican roots as being based on his recollection that John L. Lewis, who was rising through the ranks of the United Mine Workers, ultimately to become the union's president, was a family hero, " . . . and Lewis was a Republican. So my parents followed him."[1]

Rhodes was nine when his father died. "We had a different status in life. We were on the giving end before, helping a lot of people, and then we were on the receiving end," Rhodes recalled.[2] But he also insisted that his proud mother refused any help from government agencies and moved her family (James and two sisters) north to Springfield when it appeared authorities were prepared to place the Rhodes children in a county home.

"Dusty" Rhodes, as he is remembered by his high school classmates and teachers, made a lasting impression, if not always academically. He was a "very popular, active school citizen . . . he was a real promoter, a pretty good [basketball] guard, booked bands, always hustling some way to make a buck," recalled Charles Fox, his principal. It was Fox who claimed that Rhodes announced his intention to become governor of Ohio while attending Springfield High. No one recalls Rhodes ever expressing much interest in college, but when he secured a very modest basketball scholarship to The Ohio State University in 1932, the family picked up and moved the forty-three miles to Columbus, settling in close by the OSU campus. According to Rhodes, he immediately began playing basketball while also holding down several jobs, including booking bands, selling blotters, running an employment agency, and distributing magazines.[3]

Rhodes lasted only one quarter, although his official biographies usually state "student at Ohio State" without saying when or for how long. His official version for leaving the university is that his mother, whom he absolutely adored, was diagnosed as having cancer and young Rhodes had to drop out to care for her (she lived for seventeen more years). An additional reason, revealed only years later, may have been that Rhodes was on academic probation, having received "Ds" in English and geography and flunking hygiene, physical education, and military science, a course load totaling only thirteen hours.[4]

Rhodes immediately turned to his entrepreneurial skills both to make a living and to set the stage for his first venture into politics. Among other OSU-related endeavors, he opened Jim's Place on North High Street opposite the campus, where patrons could buy homemade donuts, reasonably priced hamburgers, book a band, talk politics, and, it has been alleged by some contemporaries, rent a stag film and place a bet on the numbers. Jim Rhodes became a well-known character both on and off campus and claims to have monitored a few classes without credit—and without paying tuition.[5]

In 1934, with a few dollars worth of campaign cards and a door-to-door, flesh-pressing style that would characterize his campaigns throughout his political life, Rhodes beat the incumbent veteran ward committeeman. He was twenty-five and on his way. In 1938 he won a five-way race for the Columbus school board, but he served only a year before being elected city auditor. He was reelected auditor in 1941, the same year he married Helen Rawlins. He was now ready to move to the next rung on the ladder: mayor of Ohio's capital city.

Rhodes's opponent was Franklin County sheriff Jacob Sandusky. To what degree Sandusky was directly involved in the area's vice epidemic remains unclear, but Rhodes seldom missed an opportunity to suggest that his opponent was part of the problem. He also campaigned on positive themes that he would orchestrate into a crashing, endless symphony during his successful gubernatorial campaign nineteen years later: more jobs through economic growth and fiscal responsibility.

But one favorite Rhodes theme of the 1960s—no new taxes—was missing when he ran for reelection as mayor in 1947. Faced with a nearly empty treasury and a zero credit rating, Rhodes dragged conservative Columbus voters into the mid–twentieth century by successfully promoting a city income tax. The tax was supported by an amazing 67 percent of voters, a testament to Rhodes's own popularity, powers of persuasion, and the pragmatism that would mark his career. Another of Rhodes's major accomplishments and legacies as mayor was enviously described by former state representative and later Cleveland mayor Carl Stokes: "Rhodes saw that the suburbs had to be forced to incorporate as part of Columbus if the central city was to survive. Whenever a newly developed area decided it wanted waterlines, Rhodes laid down his hard line. The suburbs either submitted to annexation or it got no water. As a result Columbus today has the largest land area of any city in the state."[6]

Three other aspects of Rhodes's three terms as Columbus mayor are worth noting. First, he honed his talent for indefatigably promoting his city (later his state) and, in the process, promoting himself. From this time on those describing Rhodes seldom failed to use the terms "promoter," "showman," "pitchman," and "huckster," not always in a wholly flattering way. Also, as mayor Rhodes forged a permanent alliance with Columbus's powerful Wolfe family, whose fortune grew from their banking empire and whose influence came from their ownership of the *Columbus Dispatch,* the capital's largest newspaper. The *Dispatch* may not have always lived up to its claim to be "Ohio's Greatest Home Newspaper," but there was never any doubt where the paper stood on issues and politicians, both on its editorial page and in its news columns. Rhodes and the Wolfes supped well at each other's tables for decades to come. But Rhodes learned a lesson in party protocol in the midst of his terms as mayor when he made his first run for governor as an unendorsed upstart and was trounced in the 1950 GOP primary by Don Ebright, the veteran Ohio treasurer who had his party's endorsement. (Ebright was handily defeated by incumbent Democratic governor Frank Lausche in the general election.) It was the last time Rhodes would ever run out of turn, without the blessing of the provincial barons of his party.

It is generally acknowledged that Rhodes was a good mayor. But was he an honest one? Despite the usual charges and rumors of uncontrolled patronage, payroll padding, employee kickbacks, campaign fund skimming, and backroom deals with the Columbus establishment, none of Rhodes's enemies, including Michael DiSalle, his 1962 gubernatorial opponent, was able to prove any charge serious and specific enough to hurt him. He emerged clean enough from his stint as a big-city mayor to make his next move.

It is conventional wisdom in Ohio politics that the best paths to the governor's office evolve from attorney general and state auditor. Both positions offer the incumbents the opportunity of almost unlimited statewide exposure, a ready-made statewide patronage network of loyal employees and informers in the form of assistant attorneys general or auditor's inspectors, and the power to embarrass, hassle, and punish enemies and to protect and reward friends. Not being a lawyer, the obvious post for Rhodes to seek in 1952 was auditor. He was fond of calling the office the "catbird-seat" of the Statehouse, since the auditor's resident field inspectors were responsible for monitoring every aspect of state and local government, from city halls to public libraries.

With the blessing of his party he took on incumbent Democratic auditor Joseph Ferguson. If Rhodes was the circus barker of Ohio Republicans, "Jumpin' Joe" Ferguson (a nickname derived from his habit of bouncing up and down, especially when talking to anyone taller than he, which was most of the world), was the clown of Ohio Democrats. In 1950 Ferguson had had the effrontery to run against Robert A. Taft, the icon of Ohio Republicans and elder statesman of the United States Senate, and had made somewhat a fool of himself. A story Rhodes delighted in telling and retelling was that when Ferguson was asked by a reporter during his senatorial campaign to comment on the issue of Quemoy and Matsu (the Chinese Nationalist–held islands being bombarded by mainland Communists), he confidently predicted, "I will carry them both in this election."[7] Emphasizing his own record, focusing on Ferguson's alleged incompetence and reputation as a lackey of organized labor, and receiving Dwight Eisenhower's help at the head of the national Republican ticket in 1952, Rhodes buried Ferguson. He was forty-two when his term began in January 1953 and was now making $12,000 a year.

Rhodes set about organizing the auditor's office in typical fashion: he installed a retinue of totally loyal retainers, many brought from Columbus city hall, to head various departments, usually making sure they were backed up by a competent, apolitical bureaucrat. This was true in his own case, as well, for he was much too busy making "Rhodes" a household word throughout Ohio to be totaling debit and credit columns. He would make a speech anywhere on any topic suggested, from a dry recitation of what the auditor of state does to much more interesting talks concerning the three short historical novels he published while auditor (with much help from Dean Jauchius, his press aide and resident writer, and from a researcher on the auditor's payroll). Rhodes also was attracted to county fairs like Winnie-the-Pooh to honey and appeared truly to enjoy munching soggy hotdogs and admiring well-scrubbed hogs. These non-election-year political forays around the state were financed in large part by a semisecret "flower fund," which Rhodes, like many Ohio politicians of both parties, maintained and which was supported largely by employee contributions.[8] Rhodes's flower fund was to play a role both in his 1962 campaign for governor and in his 1970 primary campaign for the U.S. Senate, but unfortunately for him not just as a source of campaign funds.

Rhodes made only one major miscalculation during his ten years as auditor: he took on Democratic incumbent Frank Lausche for governor in 1954. If protocol were followed, it was Attorney General C. William O'Neill's turn to run for governor, having been in state government longer than Rhodes. But O'Neill was up for reelection as attorney general that year while Rhodes was in the middle of a four-year term (at that time only the auditor among state officials served a four-year term) and did not have to put his career on the line. So O'Neill ran again for attorney general and Rhodes took on maverick Democrat Lausche, one of Ohio's most successful vote-getters. Rhodes conducted an unusually negative campaign and lost—but he learned. "I liked Frank Lausche, and I didn't like my campaign," Rhodes said in retrospect. "It wasn't like me. The things people want is answers. They already know the questions."[9]

Lausche moved on to the U.S. Senate in 1956 and the same year O'Neill beat Toledo mayor Michael DiSalle to serve out the last two-year term as governor. In 1954 voters approved a state constitutional amendment giving the governor a four-year term but limiting any one person to two consecutive terms as governor. Rhodes easily beat Ferguson again for a second four-year term as auditor.

In 1958 DiSalle came back to beat O'Neill, thanks mainly to the right-to-work issue, to become Ohio's first four-year governor. Two years later Rhodes successfully won a two-year "short term" as auditor, devised to bring the auditor's term in line with other state officials' new four-year terms.

So as 1962 dawned, Rhodes had a choice: run once again for auditor or claim what was now rightly his—the chance to face DiSalle for the office of governor. There was never any doubt what he would do.

On Labor Day 1962, the traditional start of statewide campaigns in Ohio, Rhodes was a few days shy of fifty-three years old. It had been thirty years since he arrived in Columbus. Physically, he looked the part of a gubernatorial candidate. Carl Stokes, who made history in his own right in 1962 to become the first African American Democrat to be elected to the Ohio legislature, recalls Rhodes's appearance: "He stands over six feet tall and looks like a football player turned mortician. His gray hair is combed up in a small pompadour and then swept back. Although his clothes style has changed now, back in the 1960s he wore almost a uniform—blue suit, blue shirt, blue tie. He must have had a dozen suits, all the same cut and color. Yet somehow, on him, it didn't look as plain as it sounds. He managed to look natty."[10] While a bit jowly and widening a little in the midsection, and despite a constant diet of cheese, bologna, and snack food, he appeared to be in excellent health, keeping in shape by frequent rounds of golf. His peripatetic sweeps through county fairgrounds often left trailing reporters, many half his age, out of breath.

Rhodes was a devoted family man, now the father of three daughters. As officeholder and campaigner he was constantly on the road, but his practice always was to return home to sleep in his own bed whenever practical. His wife, Helen, shy and never what might be called a political wife, nevertheless did her duty, appearing by his side when protocol called for her presence. There was never a hint of scandal concerning his family life.

But some patrician Republicans found his personal style a bit too rustic, too unpolished, too "good ol' boy." At times he butchered English grammar, and he was a master of wonderful malapropisms (for example, he misquoted John Donne to the effect that "no man is an Ireland" and called Ohio University "this venereal [venerable] institution"). His accent was distinctly small-town southern Ohio: he pronounced Ohio as "O-hi-ah," push as "poosh," fish as "feesh." And except for his claim to have authored three historical novels and the brief biographical reference to his attendance at Ohio State, Rhodes never downplayed his proletarian, untutored background. On the contrary, he reveled in his Jackson County roots. A favorite Rhodes one-liner was to recall that "a seven course dinner down there [Jackson County] is a possum and a six-pack." Between campaign stops while on the road, Rhodes often played gin rummy, which he called "Jackson County bridge," and his favorite off-color joke featured a fabled oversexed Jackson County coon hound named Old Blue.

Yet even the most scornful Republican gentry had to concede that Rhodes's shrewdly crafted, self-made-man populist image appealed to rank-and-file Republicans and independents. He bounced from the 1962 Republican primary unscathed, beating a token maverick opponent by a margin of 90 percent. DiSalle, on the other hand, staggered from a hotly contested, three-way Democratic primary badly mauled, winning only about 50 percent of his own party's support.

At the onset, the 1962 general election campaign was predictable, even routine. True, these two former mayors had known each other for years and sincerely did not like one another, which added extra spice to the contest. But their basic roles at the start were as set and cast as the protagonists in a classical Greek drama.

As controversial incumbent, DiSalle was mostly on the defensive, justifying his tax increases, defending the sluggish progress of Ohio's interstate highway program, and blaming the legislature for not passing his liberal programs. DiSalle's public agonizing over and retrial of each capital punishment case he reviewed had alienated much of the law enforcement and judicial establishments. He had an uncanny way of becoming embroiled in controversies he could have avoided, such as declaring that he did not like to wear seat belts at a time when most highway safety officials were urging their use. And DiSalle, while the son of immigrants, was somewhat of an urbane aristocrat and definitely was not comfortable sampling sweet-corn relish at a county fair.

Rhodes's campaign was built largely around the positive theme of "Jobs and Progress," augmented with the slogan "Profit is not a dirty word in Ohio." Ohio historian George Knepper summed up Rhodesian philosophy: "[Rhodes] insisted all would be well if the state increased jobs, which he claimed would reduce crime, divorce, delinquency, mental illness and similar problems." Knepper dryly observed that this catch-all solution "seemed simplistic to professionals in the field" but apparently not to voters.[11]

But Rhodes's campaign was not without its negative thrusts. Noting that DiSalle's agency for creating jobs was the Department of Industrial and Economic Development, with the acronym DIED, Rhodes would repeatedly squawk, "DIED is dead, dead as a dodo." He also was not above using gimmicks, most of which he thought up himself. He staged press conferences at deserted, dusty construction sites at the end of uncompleted interstate highway segments to dramatize his charge that despite DiSalle's two-cent-a-gallon gasoline tax increase, road construction was behind schedule—at least behind Rhodes's schedule.

While all candidates tend to repeat themselves during a long campaign, Rhodes did so to an extraordinary degree. His campaign staff produced a series of detailed position papers on other topics, but Rhodes himself seldom wavered from the Gospel of Jobs. To pass the time while listening to the same speech over and over, reporters formed pools as to how many times Rhodes would use the word "jobs." Once, excusing himself from dinner, Rhodes said he had to go "make my 300th speech." Helen Rhodes put in, "No, Jim, you're going to make the same speech for the 300th time."[12] But while "no new taxes" became a familiar Rhodes chant later in his first term as governor, it was not emphasized during the 1962 campaign. Rather than pinning himself down, he shrewdly suggested that better management might preclude new taxes.

In late September the campaign turned nasty. The *Cleveland Press* and papers subscribing to the related Scripps-Howard statewide wire service reported that Joseph Mackler, the president of Waterfill and Frazier Distilling Company of Chicago, was claiming that "he had to pay 'influence peddlers' so he could do business in Ohio" and get his minor-league bourbon listed by state-monopoly liquor stores. Further, Mackler claimed, his bourbon was delisted when he failed to keep up his shakedown payments.[13] As political scandals go, this one was pretty thin. No state official was named as directly taking part in the alleged shakedown. Mackler conveniently disappeared after the original story appeared and remained incommunicado until after the election. But the *Press* and Ohio Scripps-Howard, presided over by *Press* editor Louis Seltzer, an avid DiSalle baiter, kept the story alive, creating the impression that the "DiSalle Liquor Department" was a hotbed of corruption.

Next it was DiSalle's turn. For several weeks he had been coyly suggesting that reporters should ask Rhodes "the $54,000 question." No one knew what he was talking about until Democratic state chairman William Coleman alleged in early October that in 1958 the Internal Revenue Service had charged Rhodes with diverting $18,000 in campaign funds to personal use and that he had "borrowed" $36,000 from his campaign committee. Rhodes released a statement saying, "I categorically deny I owe the government of the United States any money," and he charged DiSalle with attacking "me with globs of slime and vicious fictions." But as the Cleveland *Plain Dealer* noted, "There was no denial in the statement that he had diverted campaign funds in other years to his personal use."[14] Later, Rhodes maintained that the $18,000 was reimbursement for travel and other expenses and the $36,000 loan was covered by an interest-bearing note that he had repaid. On October 17 DiSalle asked that a grand jury investigating the alleged liquor scandal expand its inquiry to include claimed irregularities in the auditor's office, including the charging of local governments for rental of auditor inspectors' adding machines under a lease-purchase agreement, when in fact the machines had already been paid for by the state. DiSalle spread tales of these rentals being collected in cash, stuffed into the proverbial "plain white envelopes."

Legally, nothing came of the mud slinging, and it probably had only a marginal effect on the outcome of the election. But both candidates agreed during their Cleveland City Club debate the weekend before the election that it was " 'the most vicious campaign' [of] the Ohio governorship."[15]

On Tuesday, November 6, 1962, Ohio voters overwhelmingly elected Rhodes by a 59-percent margin in a state where any win over 55 percent is considered a landslide. He carried with him every Republican state candidate except Lausche's Senate opponent and, more importantly, helped elect comfortable Republican majorities to both houses of the Ohio General Assembly.

Upon assuming office, Rhodes immediately added several words and phrases to his simple and basic lexicon of practical politics: to jobs, profit, and promotion he appended austerity, no new taxes (at least for the time being), delegation of detail, and avoidance of public controversy.

At his simple, austere inaugural ("I do not want to have an elaborate inauguration at the expense of taxpayers"), held in the rotunda of the Statehouse because of the near-zero weather, Rhodes pledged the "institution of rigid economies and prudent spending." A few days later about 3,500 state employees were fired as part of a pledged 9.1-percent across-the-board cut in state spending, made necessary by what Rhodes claimed was an $83-million deficit left by DiSalle. As Democrats charged "jungle politics," the new administration also prepared legislation to remove as many as 19,000 state employees from civil service protection and admitted that "all employees are to be screened to determine their loyalties to the administration."[16]

Rhodes's minister of austerity and lord high executioner of civil servants was finance director Richard Krabach, a craggy, appropriately cadaverous, Cincinnati-born lawyer and former comptroller of the Virgin Islands in the Eisenhower administration. He, along with John McElroy, Rhodes's chief of staff, was recruited from outside Rhodes's cortege of hangers-on from his days as mayor and state auditor, and he became one of the most visible members of the new administration. In March Rhodes presented to the legislature Krabach's biennial budget, a record $1.3 billion, balanced with no new taxes, and containing no provision for capital improvements (both would come later). Rhodes pledged that there would be no increase in consumer taxes for at least two years and no new taxes on business and industry for four years. Having presented the budget, Rhodes left the details of passage to Krabach and hoisted the finance director to serve as a lightning rod to deflect the thunderous demands for more from special interest groups, especially the Ohio Education Association and welfare and mental health lobbies.

McElroy, a bookish, articulate lawyer, a protégé of former governor and U.S. senator John Bricker and a former minority counsel of the U.S. Senate Commerce Committee, was described by Rhodes as "the closest any one can get to being a deputy or assistant governor." His modest, cluttered office adjoined Rhodes's, and he had constant access to the governor whenever he could catch him sitting still. "I approach him like a newspaperman," McElroy explained. "I begin by telling him the important things first . . . so no matter when he gets away from me he always had, at least, the who, what, where, when and why."[17]

McElroy's handling of the mandated gubernatorial review of all capital punishment cases serves as an example of how Rhodes's "desire to avoid controversy appears to be almost an obsession," in the words of a contemporary political columnist.[18] While DiSalle, an avowed opponent of the death penalty, publicly wrung his hands over each capital case, he nevertheless allowed six out of twelve first-degree murderers to be executed during his four years. During Rhodes's first eight years in office not a single person "rode Old Sparky," thanks to McElroy's quiet, judicious delays and recommended commutations. To this day, few know Rhodes's personal views on capital punishment, which is exactly the way he wanted it. Such controversial side issues simply were not a part of his agenda.

McElroy, Krabach, the cabinet, and his personal staff (most of whom were from his old retinue) usually surrounded Rhodes when he held a rare press conference, and the wary governor expertly tossed to them questions that were too detailed or too contentious. For Rhodes had other matters to attend to, mostly promotion of everything and anything Buckeye. There was the annual state fair, which he attended daily, personally arranging top-flight entertainment. Ohioans responded by attending the fair in record numbers. He turned a dreary Department of Highways publication into a slick, colorful tourist magazine and called it *The Wonderful World of Ohio*. He announced plans to build a bridge across Lake Erie to link Ohio and Ontario, not bothering to ask Canada if they would pay half. (They wouldn't.) And there was Ohio tomato juice: "If every Ohioan would drink an extra 16-ounce can of [Ohio] tomato juice a year, 2,000 jobs would be created in Ohio," Rhodes crowed, and installed a tomato juice–laden merry-go-round in the Statehouse rotunda.[19]

But there were more serious promotions as well. Early in his first administration Rhodes organized a road show of state and local development officials, legislators, and industrial moguls, collectively-known as "Rhodes Raiders," to roam the country and the world to tout Ohio's favorable, low-tax industrial climate. Once, in China, bragging about Ohio's contribution to aviation and space exploration, he wildly flapped his arms and crowed "Wright brothers!" as Chinese officials tried to fathom this supersalesman from Ohio. "These promotional efforts . . . resulted in some success," observes historian Knepper. "Huge new investments were made in Ohio, especially by the automotive industry. . . . The Lordstown complex, opened by General Motors in 1966 in Mahoning County, dramatically illustrates the kind of development that made Ohio second only to Michigan in the automotive industry."[20]

A governor can administer and promote by himself, but to truly govern he must have the cooperation of the legislature. Rhodes usually did, especially during his first two years in office, when the Senate was split twenty Republicans to thirteen Democrats, the House eighty-eight Republicans to forty-nine Democrats. With the exception of 1965–66, when the Senate was evenly split as a result of the 1964 Lyndon Johnson landslide, the Republicans enjoyed comfortable legislative margins throughout Rhodes's first two terms. Rhodes also was blessed with generally cooperative and able Republican leaders in both houses.

Rhodes began winning the hearts of many Republican legislators even before they were elected, tirelessly campaigning for General Assembly candidates as he criss-crossed Ohio promoting himself and his own projects. But avoiding great controversy as usual, he was careful not to alienate the Democratic candidate too much, especially if the outcome of the local election was at all in doubt. Never can tell when a Democratic vote might be needed.

Theodore Gray of Piqua, Republican leader of the Senate for six of Rhodes's initial eight years, recalls that once the legislature assembled Rhodes imposed a cardinal rule on himself and members of his administration: "Don't screw with the legislature!" He meant, of course, do not feud and bicker with legislators of either party in public, as did DiSalle, constantly and usually to no avail. Rhodes and his advisors were quite capable of using both the carrot and the stick to get what they wanted, but it was all done privately. "He never, never went public," Gray said admiringly. Charles Kurfess of Bowling Green, Republican House speaker during Rhodes's second term, pointed out another reason for Rhodes's success with the legislature. "Of all the governors, the one who did not make the mistake of overloading his staff with so-called 'bright young people' was Jim Rhodes," Kurfess believes. "He took with him his old crowd [from the auditor's and mayor's office] or got [seasoned] people like Krabach and McElroy. There were no young bucks who offended old timers, who felt allegiance only to the governor, who forgot they were dealing with a lot of egos [in the legislature]."[21]

Given the huge amounts of capital improvements funds Rhodes was able to raise, the source of the carrots he was able to dangle in front of legislators was obvious. There is nothing an egocentric politician loves more than a hometown ground breaking or the dedication of a new facility, and Rhodes made sure local legislators of either or both parties shared the spotlight with him whenever a spade was turned or a ribbon cut. Thus, with the promise of a branch campus or community college in a district, Rhodes effectively stroked and controlled even the likes of Ross Pepple of Lima, the cantankerous, penny-pinching, ultraconservative chairman of the Senate Finance Committee. Lima got both a branch university and a tech school.

As for the stick, Carl Stokes relates a revealing tale in his book *Promises of Power*. Stokes won passage of a pet bill guaranteeing the right of a person under arrest to see a lawyer promptly. As bills go, it was not major legislation, but for Stokes, a freshman and a member of the minority party, passage was important to him and to his mostly black constituency. Stokes got the word that Rhodes planned to veto the bill, even though the governor did not especially like to use the veto because it meant confrontation. He usually was able to head off legislation he disliked in advance of passage. So a bemused Stokes went to Rhodes's office to find out what the problem was. His version:

"John," [Rhodes] called out to McElroy, "go get Carl's file."

McElroy came in with a folder full of newspaper clippings. Rhodes sat there and rattled off the headlines: Stokes Assails Rhodes; Stokes Slams Rhodes on Education; Stokes Says Rhodes Programs Ruining the State. The list went on and on. "There it is, Carl. You know, you've been giving me hell all over this state. And you never heard me say anything, did you?" "No, governor, I never did," I replied.

"Well, now it's my turn," he said. "I've been laying in the weeds for you."

There was never a public disclosure of this meeting at the time. But as Stokes observed after his exchange with Rhodes, "My political education took a great leap forward . . . the Republican governor and the second-term black Democrat from Cleveland began to find areas they could agree upon."[22]

Working out such basic agreement on his programs in private prior to public hearings and floor votes was a constant Rhodes goal. Gray recalls that during meetings with legislative leaders Rhodes would toss out an idea and "then he'd read your eyes. If you didn't respond positively, he'd move on to someone else until he'd find someone interested in the idea. He learned people, he could read people." Kurfess recalled that Rhodes could be blunt, too, as he was with Stokes. "I remember Rhodes used to say often that you don't try to sit down at dad's [Rhodes's] table after you've kicked him in the ass."[23]

There also were times when Rhodes was able to grease the way for legislation even before it reached the General Assembly. During his first campaign Rhodes had produced a position paper titled "Blue Print for Brain Power," in which he called for the creation of a nine-member Board of Regents to oversee the operation of both Ohio's six state-supported universities and of an anemic, underfunded network of municipal universities and lesser post–high school institutions. The six presidents of the major universities were not amused. As unseemly and unruly as the process was, these proud princes of academe preferred their independence, preferred to appear individually before the legislature to battle one another for funds. Shortly after his inauguration, Rhodes quietly called the six presidents together and laid it out. He was prepared to back a $250-million bond issue, he confided, of which $175 million would be set aside for higher education capital improvements. But unless the presidents at the very least agreed not to oppose the creation of the Board of Regents, the deal would be off. Starved for capital funds, the presidents got the message and, to the amazement of most, including many in the legislature, they bit their tongues and kept their peace as the Board of Regents bill sailed through the legislature and became law in June 1963. And so the college drop-out effectively took control of Ohio's system of higher education. And what a system it was soon to become.

If Rhodes is to be long remembered, as he surely will, it will be mainly for the massive capital building programs he undertook during his first eight years in office. It involved four voter-approved bond issues raising almost $1.8 billion for higher education, highways, industrial development, parks and recreation, and other projects. While many of the projects were sorely needed, even former finance director Krabach now admits, "We may have made mistakes on the side of quantity."[24] And because this bonded indebtedness was not directly tied to new taxes, but rather to extending existing taxes or obligating general revenue funds to pay off principle and interest over decades, Rhodes preordained that massive new taxes, including a state income tax, would be needed down the road to operate and maintain the facilities. But, oh, did Jim Rhodes have a splendid time building them!

Much of the money went for expanding Ohio's lagging system of higher education. When Rhodes came to the governorship, there were six state universities; at the end of his first eight-year tenure, there were twelve. New medical schools were planned; branch universities, community colleges, and tech and vocational schools sprang up across the state as part of Rhodes's goal of having some sort of state-supported institution of advanced education located within thirty miles of every Ohioan. Also, highway projects were expedited, a new forty-story office building was to be built across the street from the capitol (and eventually was named for Rhodes, as were many new campus buildings), a new maximum-security prison was constructed, and new lodges and cabins went up at state parks.

Rhodes made one major miscalculation in the area of capital improvements. In May 1967, buoyed both by approval of his first three bond issues and by winning a second term by a stunning margin (he beat a nominal Democratic opponent, state senator Frazier Reams of Toledo, by a majority of 62 percent), Rhodes asked voters to approve a permanent, ongoing bonding program. It would authorize an Ohio Bond Commission (OBC) to obligate up to 6 percent of general revenue monies for capital improvements within eight-year cycles. He was essentially asking the people to change the state constitution and hand over to a powerful, nonelected board their historic right to vote on individual bond issues for specified amounts and purposes. Rhodes called the OBC consitutional amendment "the most important piece of legislation I've ever known of since I've been in public life" and campaigned mightily for it, ending his hard-sell pitch with an election-eve fly-in to fifteen cities.[25] For a variety of reasons—opposition to it by Democrats and organized labor, its complexity, the power and lengthy terms it proposed giving to a non-elected commission—voters rejected the OBC amendment by a two-to-one margin. The very next year voters approved a fourth bond issue that also contained provisions for permanent financing of capital construction but without a special commission. But Rhodes never quite got over the loss of his OBC proposal. His confidence in his own political infallibility seemed shaken. He had pressured the legislature to put the fourth bond issue on the ballot, but he did not openly campaign for it. After OBC's defeat, he began vaguely to support tax increases, allowing a $300-million increase in sales and corporate franchise taxes to pass in late 1967. In 1969 he came up with a confusing, poorly drafted tax and education bill which seemed to require that counties pass an income tax, but he practically left the measure on the legislature's doorstep rather than actively introducing and pushing it. According to one observer, his ardent campaign for the OBC also "marked a turning point in the rapport between Rhodes and the working press which thereafter took the view that his 1966 election success had been used to try to 'put one over' on the public."[26]

In discussing Rhodes's relations with the print and television media, a clear distinction should be made between publishers, top editors and station owners, and the beat reporters who daily trudged to the grubby, crowded Statehouse press room. For most of his first eight years as governor, Rhodes enjoyed excellent relations with those at the top of the media heap, often for exactly the same reasons he got along so well with the legislature: he had goodies to pass around. What publisher or local editor would care to take on a governor who promised their community a new university or branch campus or state park lodge? His close and friendly relationship with the Wolfe family, owners of the *Columbus Dispatch*, already has been noted. Under *Cleveland Press* editor Louis Seltzer, the Scripps-Howard Columbus bureau practically became an adjunct of Rhodes's own humming publicity machine. Thomas Vail, the young publisher and editor of the *Plain Dealer*, who was trying to assume the title "Mr. Cleveland" from the aging Seltzer, also was won over by Rhodes's promises of great and good public works projects for Cleveland, including the establishment of Cleveland State University. Paul Block, the autocratic owner of the Toledo *Blade*, was seduced by the promise of a new medical school at Toledo. And the *Cincinnati Enquirer* remained as it always had been: staunchly Republican. Only the top layer at the traditionally Democratic *Dayton Daily News* and the relatively liberal *Akron Beacon Journal,* among major Ohio dailies, remained somewhat dubious about Rhodes's blandishments. In some cases, the beat reporters assigned to Columbus faithfully reflected the views of their bosses, but to Rhodes's general dismay and genuine bewilderment not all did.

As mayor and state auditor, Rhodes had enjoyed the company of mostly old-school reporters, who usually accepted his press releases and story tips as uncritically as they accepted his Christmas hams. But when he announced his campaign for governor, Rhodes faced an influx of younger, better educated, more critical (some would say more cynical), and generally more analytical beat reporters. It was not that they disliked Rhodes. His earthy good humor and constant flow of pungent, rustic homilies made him personally popular and quotable, at least on unsubstantial matters. But when it came to serious issues of government, Rhodes's almost obsessive aversion to public controversy, which of necessity involved subterfuge, secrecy, double-speak, and sometimes downright lying ("that's not my bill," he'd say of a piece of controversial legislation that had just come directly from his office), often frustrated and angered reporters. Journalists thrive on controversy and confrontation and Rhodes gave them very little of either, at least openly. "An interview with James Allen Rhodes is like trying to tow a lumbering old barge into a harbor on the end of a kite string," Abe Zaidan, *Beacon Journal* politics writer, said of Rhodes's evasive tactics. "You are usually left holding just the string."[27]

Whether the break with the working press came abruptly at the time of his OBC campaign is debatable. But while most major newspapers editorially supported the OBC amendment, many reporters remained skeptical and critically analyzed the proposal. They were not reluctant to air opponents' charges that it was a raw power grab. Rhodes wanted cheerleaders; he got hardballers. He began to really believe the description of the press he was fond of quoting to aides: "The press are like dogs in heat. If you stand still, you get screwed. If you run away, they chase after you and bite you in the ass."[28]

After OBC's defeat, Rhodes did in fact "head for the weeds," as his new finance director Howard Collier predicted he would. He became more reclusive and held fewer and fewer press conferences. Automatic buzzer-operated locks were installed on doors in the executive office suite and his secretaries became more protective of him. More and more often John McElroy became the reporters' main source in the executive suite. But there were times when even Rhodes could not avoid the harsh searchlight of press scrutiny, times when he had to emerge from the weed patch. Among those times were when he had to assume the mantle of party leader, especially during presidential election years.

There are two quite different views of Rhodes's stewardship of the Ohio Republican party during his first two terms as governor. A benevolent assessment comes from former Ohio Republican chairman John Andrews, the Lucas County chairman chosen by Rhodes to take over the state party machinery when the legendary Ray Bliss was called to Washington to reassemble the national Republican party in the wake of the Goldwater debacle of 1964. A second, darker view is held by former House speaker Kurfess, who eventually was to challenge Rhodes unsuccessfully in the 1978 Republican gubernatorial primary.

Andrews dismisses those who say Rhodes tried to take over the party as his own. "I never tried to run the state and he never tried to run the party," Andrews insists. "He was very sensitive to the role and needs of the party." Andrews recalled that he and Rhodes privately hammered out new legislative apportionment and congressional redistricting plans to meet the Supreme Court's "one man, one vote" dictum, after which Rhodes said, "Now, I'll [publicly] support this, or I'll oppose it—whatever will do you [the party] the most good." Andrews pointed out that in 1966, only two years after LBJ's mammoth triumph, Rhodes led the Ohio Republican ticket to its greatest victory ever. Not only did Rhodes carry eighty-seven counties, the Republicans also won 18 of 23 congressional seats. "He was out campaigning for everyone else," Andrews said. He added that Jim and Helen Rhodes constantly entertained county-level Republican stalwarts, especially women, at the mansion.[29]

Kurfess disagrees as to the motives and results of Rhodes's party activities. "He patterned himself after Frank Lausche," who never ran as a regular Democrat but always as a maverick Lausche Democrat and who paid little attention to the established party structure, Kurfess believes. "In his first term, Rhodes supported all Republican candidates. But after that [1966], it was all Rhodes's game. He built up his own cadre of support apart from the Republican party. I always had a certain disdain for Lausche, and Rhodes ended up doing the same thing. We [the party] had lost everything by the time Rhodes lost."[30]

Both Kurfess and Andrews are probably right. Rhodes was never quite the maverick that Lausche was, and publicly, at least, he appeared to maintain proper relations with the party's state committee. But he never won over some elements of the state party and so had good reason to create a cadre of his own loyalists outside the party apparatus. That Rhodes was not in total control of the party was made clear at both the 1964 and 1968 Republican national conventions.

By the time of the 1964 National Governors Conference, held in early June in Cleveland (thanks to Rhodes's promotion the year before), the Goldwater wing of the national party seemed unstoppable. Several efforts hesitatingly launched during the conference by moderate Republicans to "stop Goldwater" fell flat. Host Rhodes, preferring to tout the glories of Cleveland and Ohio, appeared to have taken little or no part in the eleventh-hour maneuvering. But he headed the Ohio delegation to the convention as favorite son, and the state's fifty-eight votes were pledged to him on the first ballot. State chairman Bliss desperately wanted Ohio to remain neutral as long as possible. His surveys showed that Goldwater would do badly in Ohio, so badly that he might bring down the entire state ticket, led by Robert Taft, Jr., who was running to follow his father to the U.S. Senate.

But as the July convention date approached, the right wing of the Ohio party, led by former senator and governor John Bricker (once described as "a white-maned war horse of reaction") and a young congressman from Johnstown named John Ashbrook, began seriously to pressure Rhodes to release the delegates, most of whom by this time were itching to join the Goldwater juggernaut. On a stopover in Chicago on his way to the convention in San Francisco, Rhodes was met by a bevy of out-of-state reporters demanding to know what Ohio was going to do on the first ballot. Reacting typically to reporters he saw as trying to drag him into controversy, Rhodes made a muddled, vague reference to the fact that the Ohio delegation would caucus on the Monday before the first roll call. Reporters interpreted whatever he did say to mean Rhodes was releasing the delegation, and this news was flashed to San Francisco. The *San Francisco Chronicle* reported that Rhodes's action "presumably guarantees Barry Goldwater the Republican nomination on the first ballot."[31]

Whether Rhodes meant to release the delegation or was just trying to fend off reporters in Chicago remains unclear. But by the time he reached San Francisco the damage had been done, and he was forced to state clearly that he would not pressure Ohio delegates to vote for him on the first ballot. In practical terms, the delegate release probably meant absolutely nothing to the outcome of the convention. But psychologically it administered the coup de grace to the already moribund "stop Goldwater" movement: Ohio cast fifty-seven votes for the Arizona senator on the first ballot.

During the 1964 campaign that followed, Rhodes avoided Goldwater as often as he decently could, diverting most of his energies to Taft's cause. Goldwater lost Ohio by more than a million votes and Taft lost by 17,000. Doctrinaire conservative Republicans had never fully trusted Rhodes because of his undoctrinaire pragmatism and his open admiration for liberal New York governor Nelson Rockefeller. They considered his treatment of Goldwater shabby, and suspicion turned to a certain disenchantment, which was to grow four years later.

In 1968 Rhodes again took control of the Ohio delegation to the national convention. Believing that his friend Rockefeller had a chance to side track front-runner Richard Nixon for the nomination, Rhodes this time did withhold Ohio's votes on the first roll call. Reporters noted that many in the Ohio delegation were visibly distraught as Nixon rolled to a first-ballot nomination as Ohio sat impotently on its fifty-five useless votes. Relations between Nixon and Rhodes remained proper but chilly thereafter.[32]

By early 1969 it was clear that Rhodes, constitutionally prohibited from seeking a third consecutive gubernatorial term, was preparing to run for the United States Senate. Most who knew him wondered if, at age sixty-two, he would have the temperament to accept the traditional restrictions imposed on a freshman senator or the patience to handle the snail's pace of the Senate's deliberative process. But he was a compulsive campaigner and simply had nowhere else to run.

About the same time Statehouse reporters became aware that an investigative reporter from *Life* magazine had been nosing around Ohio asking questions about Rhodes. Losing circulation and ad revenue and in its death throes as a weekly, the magazine had turned in desperation to muckraking to save itself. Reporters—and Rhodes—held their collective breath.

The edition of *Life* that became available in late April 1969 featured a picture of Rhodes on its cover along with the headline "The Governor and the Mobster."[33] The story inside was essentially in two parts. The "mobster" referred to was Thomas "Yonnie" Licavoli, an aging, nearly blind former member of the notorious Prohibition-era "Purple Gang," formed in Detroit but with a branch in Toledo. In 1934 he had been convicted of masterminding four gangland slayings as a rising young Mafia star and sentenced to life in prison. Rhodes had recently signed papers commuting Licavoli's first-degree murder sentence to second degree, making him eligible for immediate parole. *Life* repeated a hoary legend that the mob had a long-standing offer of $250,000 to anyone who could spring Yonnie. The article then claimed that Licavoli's brother Pete still was one of the five ruling dons of the Detroit Mafia, that Yonnie himself maintained mob ties all the while he was incarcerated in various Ohio prisons, and that Rhodes did know or should have known all this. The magazine offered absolutely no proof in the body of the story that a bribe had been paid to Rhodes or anyone else. But pictures, layout, headlines and promotion of the article in full-page newspaper ads certainly left the impression of payoffs at the highest levels.

The second part of the article was an updating of DiSalle's 1962 "$54,000 Question." DiSalle's charge involved a settlement Rhodes allegedly made with the IRS in 1958. *Life* maintained that Rhodes's tax problems extended to 1966 and that eventually he had to settle for more than $100,000 in back taxes, interest and penalties for converting political funds to personal use.

Rhodes categorically denied that he had been offered or accepted a bribe to commute Licavoli's sentence. John McElroy took full responsibility for recommending the Licavoli commutation. Those who were aware of how Rhodes operated his office, of McElroy's compassion, and of *Life*'s total lack of evidence and who carefully and critically read the article were satisfied with this part of Rhodes's denial. But as in 1962, Rhodes's answer to the tax charge was hedged and, to many, unsatisfactory. He denied only having to pay a "penalty" and said that *Life*'s figures were "exaggerated."

The *Life* issue faded. What lasting effect it had on voters' perceptions of Rhodes, if any, is unclear. But Rhodes became convinced that had it not been for the *Life* article, Congressman Robert Taft, Jr., would have been content to run for governor, probably unopposed in the primary, as many in the party were urging him to do. Instead, Taft announced he would oppose Rhodes in the 1970 Republican primary for the U.S. Senate.

The pitting of an immensely successful and popular up-from-the-wards pol against the ruling prince of one of Ohio's oldest and most distinguished political dynasties should have been the primary campaign of the decade. As it turned out, it was a fairly tame, predictable affair.

Both candidates were moderate Republicans, so there were few substantive national issues on which they disagreed. Early in the campaign
Rhodes vaguely brought up a conflict-of-interest issue, mentioning neither names nor details. What he was talking about was answered the
very next day when the faithful *Columbus Dispatch* took Taft to task for
voting as a congressman on issues that involved many corporations in
which the Taft family held substantial financial interest. This and Taft's
fairly poor congressional attendance record remained the two major issues Rhodes used against the Cincinnati brahmin. Taft, a quiet, retiring,
fifty-three-year-old, pledged early in the campaign not to use the *Life* article against Rhodes, yet he continually emphasized the issue of "integrity." And voters knew what he was referring to. Taft also hired
Roger Ailes, a pioneer in the growing business of campaign and media
consulting, to brighten his rather dull image.

Rhodes suffered a blow at the height of the campaign when it was
found that Lake Erie fish contained unacceptable levels of mercury.
Rhodes long had been accused of neglecting environmental issues in favor of promoting industrial growth. He promptly blamed Canada for the
lake's condition. Taft said Lake Erie was turning into a polluted swamp
thanks to Rhodes's inattention.

The two Republicans conducted four debates, the final held in
Cleveland the Saturday before the primary. Rhodes again defended
his hardline approach to putting down continuing campus upheavals
and again suggested that Taft would not be nearly as tough. "My
opponent's soft attitude on campus violence is not surprising since in
1968 he voted against an amendment . . . requiring colleges to deny federal funds to students who participate in serious campus disorders,"
Rhodes charged.[34] Then, on Sunday, May 3, 1970, the morning after the
Cleveland debate, on the same front page it reported the final Taft-
Rhodes exchange, the *Plain Dealer* carried an ominous headline: "Kent
ROTC Office Ablaze."

By one count, Rhodes had called out the Ohio National Guard forty-
four times as the result of a variety of civil disturbances or to aid local
authorities in the wake of natural disasters prior to his adjutant general
ordering troops to Kent, a small university town thirty-five miles southeast of Cleveland, on Saturday, May 2. Roving bands of antiwar students
and nonstudents alike were smashing merchants' windows and confronting city police. The next day, Sunday, after the Kent ROTC building
had been torched the night before, Rhodes ordered troops to the campus

without consulting university officials, ignoring the county prosecutor's advice simply to shut down the university. On the scene, Rhodes, red-faced, dramatically pounded the table at the Kent firehouse and vowed he would not cave in to this kind of disorder, emotionally calling the students "worse than the brown shirt and the Communist element and also the night riders and the vigilantes. They're the worst kind of people we harbor in America."[35]

On Monday, May 4, at about noon, guardsmen confronted a small band of jeering, rock-throwing students as a larger group, gathering for an antiwar rally, looked on peacefully. The troops began retreating up a hill and then, without warning or apparent specific provocation (and probably without orders), turned and began firing. The volley of M-1 rifle rounds lasted an awful thirteen seconds. Four students were killed. Nine were wounded, two very seriously.

The next morning, the *Plain Dealer* editorially voiced a concern of many: "Tough talk by Governor Rhodes over the weekend certainly did nothing to pacify the students."[36] That same day, Rhodes lost the primary by 5,270 votes, one-half of 1 percent of 940,000 cast.

Did the Kent State tragedy beat Rhodes? Polls indicate the opposite. Three polls conducted about a week prior to the primary showed Rhodes losing by from 7 to 8 percent. Yet he lost by less than 1 percent. It is worth recalling that Ohio had been the scene of an unusually high number of campus uprisings, and citizen resentment against campus demonstrators was running high. Moreover, older, more conservative voters tend to turn out for primary elections, especially Republican primaries. Many Ohioans openly approved of the action by the guard at Kent State. Many more did not. But there is no question that Rhodes's give-no-quarter stance generally enjoyed wide support at the time.

But why was Rhodes running so far behind in the polls just a week prior to Kent State that he was unable to catch up? *Life*'s article may have played a role, but probably only in this sense: it was among many factors contributing to voter perception that, while a wheeling-dealing, hard-sell promoter may be perfectly acceptable as governor, he is not exactly the type that more sophisticated voters prefer to send to the United States Senate, especially given the choice they had in Ohio in 1970.

It is the view of John Andrews, as well as Charles Kurfess, that voters view candidates differently at different levels. There are numerous examples of candidates who successfully run for lesser offices time and time again but who are soundly beaten when their reach seems to voters to be exceeding their grasp. "With Rhodes and Taft, voters looked at the names in a different frame of reference, it was a matter of level of expectation," Kurfess believes.[37] That Rhodes was able to return and twice be reelected governor tends to bear out this theory of voter perception and expectation: governor yes, senator no.

Delivering his first inaugural address, Rhodes ended with a quote from Robert Frost: "I have promises to keep, and miles to go before I sleep." Did Rhodes keep his promises, especially his repeated pledge to be "governor of all the people"?

If you were a welfare mother from Cleveland, caught in the grip of unending poverty, he was not your governor.

If you were a forty-year-old child restrained in a crib in a roach-infested ward at Orient State Institution for the mentally retarded, he was not your governor.

If you were an environmentalist, wondering where all the magnificent Lake Erie walleye had gone, or were concerned about the yellow haze that hung like a shroud over the little towns clinging to the steep banks of the Ohio River, he was not your governor.

If you were a beleaguered public school administrator watching per-pupil state support for public education dwindle from 40 percent to less than 30 percent, watching as some local systems even temporarily shut down for lack of funds, he was not your governor.

But if you were the average Ohioan who wanted the security of a job, who wanted an education or a skill without having to drive halfway across the state over half-completed highways, he was your governor. Or tried to be.

If you were a commuter weary of endless urban traffic jams or the head of a family of modest means who wanted a comfortable place to spend a vacation close to home, he was your governor. Or tried to be.

If you were an industrialist or businessman who appreciated low taxes and a favorable climate in which to prosper, he was your governor. Or tried very hard to be.[38]

Compared to the five postwar governors who preceded him, Rhodes for eight years was a governor the likes of whom Ohio had not seen, and may not see soon again. Bricker, Lausche, Thomas Herbert, and O'Neill were essentially men of limited vision. They also were skinflints. DiSalle had the vision, but lacked the political skill to implement it. Rhodes not only had the vision for the state he truly loved, he had both the skill and the tenacity to get most of what he wanted from Ohio for Ohio. Even most of his critics concede that when he briefly exited the scene in 1971, he left Ohio a very different, and in many respects, a far, far better place than it had ever been.

James Allen Rhodes was approaching his eighty-third birthday when this chapter was being prepared. He still reports to his industrial development firm on the thirteenth floor of a Columbus high rise at about 11 A.M. most days. He plays golf about twice a week, but no longer claims his old, low handicap. He is a widower and grandfather to nine. He says he cannot recall any major mistakes he made as governor. He remains semiactive in politics, having just returned from the 1992 Republican National Convention in Houston. He is by most reports a well-to-do elder statesman.

❖

CHAPTER FIVE

The Gilligan Interlude,

1971–1975

❖

HUGH C. MCDIARMID

❖ It was on the afternoon of September 1, 1972, midway through his first and only term as Ohio's sixty-second governor, that John Joyce Gilligan strolled into the Ohio State Fair on the north side of Columbus, visited the radio booth broadcasting live from the fairgrounds, and engaged in this exchange:

> Announcer: "Where you headed, governor?"
> Gilligan: "To the sheep shearing."
> Announcer: "Gonna shear a sheep?"
> Gilligan: "Nope. I shear taxpayers, not sheep."[1]

Oof! There in five quick words, Gilligan, who was fifty-one years old and one of the few quick-witted, genuinely intellectual governors in recent Ohio history—but also a controversial one—summarized what would be the essence of his administration: taxes.

Specifically, they were the state's first-ever corporate and personal income taxes. And, they proved to be not only his most significant accomplishment as governor but also a running political sore that, as much as any other single factor, would bring a wholly unexpected end to his tenure and promising career in politics that was poised to go national as early as 1976, quite possibly for president.

The irony, of course, was that Gilligan—and, yes, the controversial income taxes that took him nearly a year to push through a hostile, suspicious legislature—were the key factors that enabled relatively affluent Ohio to begin escaping the low-tax, low-service stigma that had settled on the state following the post–World War II boom, a stigma more commonly associated with states such as Arkansas or Mississippi. Gilligan, in fact, was only the third genuinely liberal (in a social-welfare, activist sense) governor of Ohio in the century.[2] And his efforts, which produced substantial reforms in education, welfare, mental health, the environment, consumer protection, and governmental ethics, marked the first successfully progressive administration in more than fifty years, since the first term of Governor James M. Cox in 1913–14.

None of this came easily. Gilligan was widely, though not always accurately, perceived as aloof and arrogant. And his quick, often acerbic tongue—which in some ways was almost a foreign language to Ohioans long accustomed to the more prosaic, blustery, and usually less responsive offerings of a John Bricker or a Frank Lausche or a Jim Rhodes—often got him in trouble and provided all sorts of openings for political enemies, who took to labeling him "the fastest lip in the West."[3] He faced near-continuous, knee-jerk resistance from conservative, largely rural, mostly Republican naysayers who made up what was known as Ohio's "cornstalk brigade," which had ruled local and state government since the mid-1940s. And, finally, there was regular (and, as it turned out, more justified) opposition from business interests, some economists, and more thoughtful Republican politicians worried that once Ohio's booming but cyclical economy slowed, as it surely would, the high costs of some of Gilligan's "reforms" would put major strains on the state budget. And, beginning in the late 1970s, they did.

All this turmoil, of course, made Gilligan highly vulnerable to the "tax and spend" mantra that had served Ohio Republicans so well for years and would be played so effectively in 1974 by the party's improbable candidate for governor, the sixty-five-year-old, scandal-scarred—but, as it turned out, still durable and v-e-r-y popular—former governor James A. Rhodes. Rhodes, in fact, set the tone for his comeback on primary election day, May 5, referring to the incumbent administration as "the Gilligan gougers" and accusing Gilligan of having "taxed everything in Ohio that walks, crawls or flies."[4] It was vintage Rhodes hyperbole, of course, but Ohioans had bought it in the 1960s and, shortly, would do so again at Gilligan's expense.

Yet Gilligan and the top people in his largely progressive administration had managed to lead Ohio out of its long, reactionary torpor. And, by the time they departed, the state had plainly become a more enlightened, more humane, far more responsible place in which to live. And for those souls, including one-term governors, who measure their lives or their immortality by such accomplishments, Jack Gilligan was a success.

And it was all so improbable.

Gilligan, a politician who easily qualified as a liberal Democrat, came from—some might say "survived"—staunchly Republican Cincinnati, known through most of the 1940s and 1950s as "Taft country," after the influential U.S. Senate conservative Robert A. Taft, the son of Cincinnati's only president, William Howard Taft. Gilligan was the fourth generation of an Irish family that settled in Cincinnati in the 1840s. His great-grandfather founded a funeral business, which prospered, remained in the family, and made the Gilligans very prominent and reasonably well-off members of the city's Catholic community for most of this century.

Jack—never "John"—who had a twin sister and two younger, twin brothers, had mostly pleasant memories of his childhood. In a 1974 interview, for example, he summarized it this way: "Our family, when I was growing up, was a kind of irreverent group. They razzed each other a lot. I remember growing up in a house full of people laughing pretty hard and most of the time it was at each other or at ourselves . . . one of the things we learned to feel most strongly about was pomposity. It was a little hard to take yourself very seriously in that crowd."[5]

Gilligan attended the private, Catholic Summit Country Day School and St. Xavier High School, both in Cincinnati, and then Notre Dame University. Pearl Harbor was bombed in his junior year, 1941, so he finished his course of study in an accelerated V-7 program, getting his A.B. degree in December 1942. He joined the navy and was commissioned in the spring of 1943. He spent the rest of the war as a gunnery officer aboard ship, mainly in the Pacific, where he won a Silver Star for valor off Okinawa.

By war's end, Gilligan had given up thoughts—spawned by an influential literature professor at Notre Dame—of entering the Jesuit order and becoming a priest. Instead, after being released from the navy, he taught literature for six years (until 1952) at Xavier University in Cincinnati and married long-time schoolmate Mary Kathryn Dixon, the daughter of a prominent Cincinnati lawyer. During that time he got an M.A. in English at the University of Cincinnati. Jack and Katie had five children in those years and made it financially with help from both sets of parents.[6]

Gilligan also dabbled in the family funeral home business in the 1950s and early 1960s, but never full time. He sold his share to his two brothers after he surprised almost everyone in Cincinnati, including himself, by getting elected to Congress in 1964, some years after he first got involved in politics. He had been influenced by the 1952 presidential campaign of the witty, urbane Illinois governor Adlai Stevenson, whom Gilligan much admired. Later, when he, too, was a governor, Gilligan reflected on the Stevenson influence: "I thought, holy smoke, this is the first man I ever heard speaking on matters political who isn't talking to me like I was a 6-year-old at the candy counter." Based largely on the standing of his father, Harry, in the community, he was recruited in 1953 by the Charterites, then the main opposition to Cincinnati's Republicans, to run for city council. He won, though narrowly, and spent the next eleven years, first as a Charterite and later as a Democrat, as an outspoken, sometimes controversial leader of local government progressives. That led to an unsuccessful 1962 campaign for an Ohio congressman-at-large seat and then in 1964, benefiting hugely from Lyndon Johnson's rout of Barry Goldwater, his upset win over incumbent Republican U.S. representative Carl Rich, a former Cincinnati mayor. The following year he explained to political reporter David S. Broder, "I come from an area where it is customary for Republicans to retire to Congress. Things like me just aren't supposed to happen."[7]

Indeed, until Gilligan took office, Cincinnati's First Congressional District had been held by conservative Republicans for sixty of the prior sixty-five years. And it offered the ambitious newcomer, who became an enthusiastic supporter of President Johnson's Great Society legislation, a fine forum for expressing his decidedly nontraditional views (by Cincinnati standards) on the importance of the federal government—views, incidentally, that may have betrayed Gilligan's long-range desire to make Washington, not Cincinnati or Columbus, a permanent home. He told Broder, "If I have one consuming interest, it is to get through to the people of this community that the federal government is our government, not an alien force. That it is, or can be, far more responsive to the needs of our people than even the state or local government. And that it has much greater capacity and power than either of those other two to meet our needs, to add dimensions of freedom and opportunity to our lives."[8]

But Gilligan's congressional days were short lived. A combination of Republican controlled redistricting and a formidable opponent, Robert Taft, Jr., conspired to limit him to a single two-year term. The loss prompted a furious response from the quick-tempered Gilligan. He bought newspaper ads and billboards in Cincinnati that redid his slogan "the congressman 'who gets things done'" to read "who got undone" and added, "Would like to express to those who supported him, his appreciation; To those who opposed him, his sympathy." Copies of the ad, which included the words "au revoir!" at the end, became a staple in later, anti-Gilligan campaign arsenals that sought, among other things, to brand him as arrogant. Or, as the *Wall Street Journal* put it two years later, the Gilligan style stemmed "in part from philosophic conviction, in part from an intellectual arrogance that often seems to force him to make enemies."[9]

But the wounds healed, and by mid-1967 Gilligan, now a partner in a Cincinnati insurance firm, had joined the successful fight to block Rhodes's ambitious ballot proposal—one Gilligan referred to as a "cock-eyed scheme"—for a five-member Ohio Bond Commission to oversee a massive state public works program. Gilligan's role in the defeat of the bond proposal led him into the 1968 U.S. Senate race with another surprising success, the defeat in the primary of conservative Democrat, Frank J. Lausche.

It was some struggle. Lausche had been a major figure in Ohio politics since the mid-1940s, serving as governor for ten years and as senator for twelve and establishing a record that was, even by conservative Ohio standards, far more Republican than Democratic. But Gilligan, with solid primary backing from Ohio's labor chiefs and the national AFL-CIO hierarchy, beat him by more than 100,000 votes, 55 to 45 percent. The general election was a different story, however. Due in part to Gilligan's antiwar position on Vietnam (anathema to the AFL-CIO's national president George Meany), labor took a walk, and Gilligan lost to William B. Saxbe, Ohio's popular Republican attorney general, by 114,812 votes, or 52 to 48 percent.

Undeterred, Gilligan first considered a 1970 U.S. Senate race against his old adversary, Bob Taft, who had moved up from the

U.S. House, but decided instead to run for governor. That, as it turned out, was quite a year for Ohio Democrats!

For openers, Rhodes was constitutionally barred from running for a third consecutive term, depriving Republicans of the advantage of a popular incumbent. Then, after a bruising primary, the Republican party nominated state auditor Roger W. Cloud, a well-liked but awesomely bland former speaker of the Ohio House who proved to be an inept choice for many reasons. For example, he chose his politically naive son, Clifford, to manage his campaign. And then he hired a press secretary who, in an embarrassing (but prophetic) lapse of judgment, described his boss to nationally syndicated columnist Joseph Kraft in these words: "To know Roger Cloud is to forget Roger Cloud."[10] Also, Cloud was forced to grapple throughout the fall campaign with what became known as the "Republican loan scandal." It resulted in an embarrassing, seemingly endless unfolding of headline-grabbing revelations documenting millions of dollars worth of illegal loans made during Rhodes's second term as governor from state retirement systems controlled by the Republican state treasurer, John D. Herbert. The loans were arranged by Republican insiders who, in return, received fat finders' fees and contributed significantly to GOP coffers.

Meanwhile, a highly skilled Gilligan campaign team, headed by Mark Shields (later to become a syndicated columnist and network TV commentator), was up and running and benefiting hugely from the loan scandal's fallout and from Cloud's political ineptness. And by early fall, Gilligan seemed assured of winning. On November 3 he trounced Cloud, 1,725,560 to 1,382,659, or 56 to 44 percent.

Not only that, but Gilligan coattails plus the loan scandal legacy combined to elect all sorts of Democrats in Ohio in 1970, including a new state auditor, treasurer, and state attorney general.

Gilligan then set out to make good on his campaign promise that "we can do better." The promise depended on the new governor's ability to shepherd new programs and appropriations—and, of course, new taxes to pay for them—through a balky legislature controlled largely by anti-Gilligan Republicans and conservative Democrats. It would not be easy.

During the campaign, Gilligan had spoken boldly and often, though mostly without specifics about the need for a new state income tax. "It may take six months or it may take six years," he told one Dayton audience, "but the state will have to have it."[11] Once elected, he zeroed in on the issue. In January, buoyed by his big win over Cloud and the mandate it implied, he established a broad-based Citizens Task Force on Tax Reform, headed by Jacob Davis, the Kroger Company chairman from Cincinnati. And, almost immediately, it was clear that the task force would recommend new taxes on both business and individual income.

On March 1, in his first State of the State address, the new governor began lobbying in earnest, describing the results of years of low taxes and low spending: "A nearly bankrupt educational system; decaying cities; polluted air and filthy water; totally unnecessary suffering for thousands of people who need our help—the aged, the blind, the disabled, the mentally retarded child, the injured or unemployed workman." One of the most obvious needs was more money in K–12 education where the state's share of support had slipped from 40 to 29 percent in the eight years under Rhodes. In fact, in 1968 the Youngstown school system had been forced to shut down temporarily; and in 1969, ten other districts had, for varying periods, also been forced to close. State finances were so thinly stretched that even prominent Republicans, including Rhodes's most recent director of finance, Howard Collier, conceded the need for additional revenues and began supporting Gilligan's call for new taxes.

But not the legislature. Both the House and Senate were controlled by Republicans, most of them conservatives and many of them appalled by the presence of an aggressively liberal Democrat in the Governor's Mansion talking nonstop about the need for taxes, spending, and reform. Legislators in both parties remembered vividly how Mike DiSalle, the last liberal Democratic governor to try for new taxes, had been branded "Tax-Hike" Mike and unceremoniously broomed from office after his first and only term, 1959–63. And, particularly among the old-timers, there was a tendency to reminisce about how Rhodes, seemingly without raising taxes (although some were, indeed, raised while he quietly stood by), had managed to stretch the state budget while maintaining both vital services and his own popularity. Surely, they suggested, Gilligan could do the same if he tried—sentiments that ignored both Rhodes's reliance on state borrowing and his good fortune in holding office during the healthy economy of the 1960s.

Finally, there was the Frank W. King problem. King, the hot-tempered president of the state's AFL-CIO and a former Ohio Senate Democratic leader, was dead set against any fiscal plan that did not tax business first and foremost. And his trump card was his protege, the colorful but crude senator Anthony O. Calabrese, of Cleveland, who had succeeded him as

Democratic leader and, like King, had no use for the professorial, reform-minded Gilligan. Through the summer Calabrese lobbied successfully not only against a House-passed plan that was more or less acceptable to Gilligan but also anything that did not please King (which, in turn, was anything acceptable to Gilligan or to cautiously procompromise legislators). Eventually, with the assistance of pro-Gilligan elements in the AFL-CIO and from Ohio's passionately pro-Gilligan United Auto Workers union, King was neutralized.[12] And by September, as state government hobbled along on month-to-month continuation budgets, the pressure for a resolution to the legislative impasse became enormous.

Then came the park-closing flap. Gilligan, whose style was confrontational, had decided to turn the screws further by ordering up an austerity program that, among other things, closed state parks. It was a move that, even though it dramatized the legislative gridlock (and even though Gilligan quickly rescinded it), infuriated the public and provided fodder for Republican campaign ads two years later.

At the same time, aggressive Gilligan aides, led by chief of staff James Friedman, the young Cleveland lawyer who had been the 1970 campaign's finance director, began stalking the legislative halls day and night lobbying furiously for an acceptable tax bill. This was an escalation of a lobbying campaign that had been underway for months, ruffling more than a few feathers along the way.

In May, for example, state representative Gertrude Polcar, a Parma Republican, denounced "Democratic orangutans and their gorilla tactics." In midsummer, Representative David Albritton, a Republican from Dayton, referred to an earlier encounter and told reporters, "They turned my guts. They were trying to intimidate old Dave and I don't like that." In September, several other Republican legislators responded to Gilligan's austerity program by mowing the Statehouse lawn on their own (a gimmick Gilligan labeled "childish"). And in November, Calabrese denounced Gilligan, his fellow Democrat, in front of reporters as "a son of a bitch" for rejecting an antibusiness tax compromise that King favored.[13]

Finally, however, with a good deal of quiet, eleventh-hour prodding from progressive Republicans, including House speaker Charles Kurfess, a Perrysburg Republican, the legislature capitulated. And in December, Gilligan signed into law Ohio's first-ever income tax legislation, setting the stage for what turned out to be his best and most productive year as governor.

It was very easy to get distracted by the noisy, but less-than-cosmic dramas of 1972: the huge public row over Gilligan's use of the state plane for weekend travel to his Michigan cottage; a bloody, internal purge in his front office; awkward involvement in Ed Muskie's up-and-down campaign for president. First, however, it must be said that a host of important, lasting changes took place in Ohio that year under Gilligan's aggressive leadership. The structure of state government underwent wholesale reform: new appropriations began repairing years of damage to critical programs, especially in education, mental health, welfare, and the environment; and, on the political front, a Gilligan-controlled state reapportionment plan made it possible for Democrats in 1972 to win control of the Ohio House, 58 to 41, and narrow the Republican hold on the Senate to a single vote, 17 to 16, thus dampening at least some of the noisy partisanship of the previous year.

The governmental restructuring included creation of a new Ohio Environmental Protection Agency and new, separate departments for transportation and for economic development as well as the breakup of the old Department of Mental Health and Corrections into separate agencies.

And legislatively, in addition to new appropriations, the administration proposed and won enactment of reforms in consumer protection, occupational safety and health, and, after a bloody struggle with the clumsy but well-funded Ohio Reclamation Association, desperately needed strip-mine reform. The strip-mine controversy was triggered by years of virtually unregulated "strip it and leave it" practices across vast tracts of coal-rich eastern and southern Ohio, a rape that left huge, ugly, erosion-prone scars on millions of acres of hilly terrain and, through acid runoff, thousands of nearby lakes and streams sterile. The issue came to a head in March and produced some vintage Gilligan. When, in midlegislative debate, the president of Ohio's huge Hanna Coal Company threatened to close his strip mines, Gilligan responded that such talk was "an outrage," "a direct affront" to the legislature, and "a brazen and brutal attempt . . . to blackmail this government" and dared him to do it.[14] He didn't. The legislation was approved, and Ohio finally moved into the twentieth century on yet another front.

The year also was not without lingering tax controversy. A small group of legislators, whom Gilligan labeled "the prehistoric wing of the Republican party," succeeded in a petition drive to put an income tax repealer on the fall ballot. The initiative campaign jangled nerves in the administration and touched off a major counteroffensive. But with little financing or organized support, it lost by more than 2 to 1.[15]

Noisier but lesser 1972 dramas included:

• The replacement, amid much front-office turmoil, of Chief of Staff Friedman and a number of pro-Friedman staffers in what Gilligan later conceded had been a "bloody coup d'etat." Friedman's successor, the calmer, better organized, but politically tone-deaf John H. Hansan, a long-time Gilligan ally from Cincinnati who had been serving as state welfare director, proved highly competent in shepherding governmental restructuring and refereeing traditional state budget infighting, but he proved less adept as Gilligan's de facto campaign manager during the 1974 reelection year.[16]

• Gilligan's endorsement of Maine senator Edmund Muskie as the Democratic candidate most likely to defeat President Richard Nixon in the fall. Muskie, as it turned out, bombed, leaving Gilligan—who, like many ambitious governors, lusted for national attention—no role whatsoever at that year's Democratic National Convention in Miami Beach, where George McGovern was nominated for president. Gilligan, in fact, at first told reporters he wasn't going to the convention because "I'd just wander around the halls like Banquo's ghost," but he went anyway. And there was even a brief flurry of speculation about Gilligan for vice president. But the job was never offered.[17]

• The state plane controversy, one that had been inflamed by a drumbeat of criticism from anti-Gilligan newspapers (principally the *Columbus Dispatch*) because of Gilligan's frequent flights to Traverse City, Michigan, so he could spend weekends at his spacious family cottage on nearby Lake Leelanau. The matter came to a noisy head at a post–Labor Day press conference in Columbus where Gilligan snapped, "Yes, I use the state plane. I use the state telephones to make calls that have political overtones. I use the state automobile. I live in a state-owned house. I entertain political figures, including Vice President Spiro Agnew and Senator George McGovern in the state-owned house. They drank state water. Make whatever of it you will!" Interestingly, the state plane—a DC-3 manufactured in 1942 for the old Army Air Corps—had been purchased in 1964 for $80,000 at the insistence of Governor Rhodes, who also took heat from critics when he used it. Later, Rhodes's director of aviation, Norman Crabtree, using one of Rhodes's favorite and oft-quoted (in various contexts) lines, related this story: "Jim Rhodes pulled me aside and said to ignore them. He said it's like a dog in heat. If you run from 'em, they'll bite you in the ass, and if you stand still, they'll screw you."[18]

Nineteen seventy-three was supposed to be the year of preparation for a big, professional, well-oiled campaign machine for Gilligan's re-election in 1974, which everybody took for granted. Those preparations, however, got badly interrupted by, among others, John Glenn, although, as we shall see, it wasn't really Glenn's fault.

First, however, it should be said that the state government ran fairly smoothly. The administration fine-tuned its new programs and managed, after much jawboning, to win legislative approval of new ethics and campaign finance reforms and a batch of prolabor legislation. The ethics package was a Gilligan pet. In 1972 he had issued an executive order requiring full disclosure of personal worth by key state employees and setting up prohibitions against conflicts of interest by members of his administration. And, since 1970, he had been voluntarily disclosing his own finances. The 1973 package went further, calling for a new state Ethics Commission, public disclosure of sources of personal income by elected officials and full public disclosure of campaign contributions. The enactment of these reforms prompted Christopher Lydon to write later in the *New York Times* that "Ohio, not heretofore noted for puritanism, is quickly becoming a state where it is the rule that candidates must walk financially naked into the political arena."[19]

At the same time, enactment of new labor legislation provided Ohio with its first comprehensive, state-level minimum wage law and improvements to its existing unemployment and worker's compensation laws. The year also saw creation of the Ohio Commission on Aging, which Gilligan backed, and an Ohio state lottery, which he did not.

Meanwhile, there were continuing, often rancorous, internal discussions over who would lead the reelection campaign. Shields and Friedman, the two pros who had engineered the 1970 win, were the obvious choices, but Shields, who was in Washington, was ambivalent and Friedman, who had returned to Cleveland, was still feuding with Hansan, his successor as chief of staff. Gilligan, caught in the middle, searched for an outsider to head the campaign but came up short, finally installing Eugene P. O'Grady, a member of his cabinet and former state Democratic chairman, making it clear that Hansan was effectively in charge. This was a fateful decision. As it turned out, neither O'Grady nor Hansan proved flexible or imaginative enough when late in the campaign Rhodes began slashing into Gilligan's once-comfortable lead. By then Shields and Friedman, who might have been able to salvage things for Gilligan, were long gone.

Gilligan also got himself in a simply awful political jam with John Glenn. Glenn, having retired from the Marine Corps, and space travel, found it tough-going trying to pursue his political dream of becoming a U.S. senator from Ohio. An inner-ear injury forced him to quit the 1964 primary campaign, and in 1970 he suffered a humiliating primary upset at the hands of Howard Metzenbaum (who had gone on to lose that November to Taft, Jr.). In 1973 he was still at it, doggedly preparing for another try in 1974, this time for the seat held by Republican William Saxbe. Gilligan had watched Glenn's senatorial quests with a mixture of bemusement and scorn, but by 1973 he had begun thinking of Glenn as his running mate in 1974. Gilligan and his advisers felt that Glenn, a warm, friendly, well-liked figure, might neutralize the public's perception of Gilligan as abrasive and arrogant. Also, there was Gilligan's desire to avoid another disruptive Glenn-Metzenbaum primary in 1974, a potentially no-win situation for the governor, who sooner or later would have to choose sides. But during the summer, Glenn systematically rejected overtures from Gilligan and others, insisting his only interest was in the Senate.

Things came to a head on the night of September 18 at a meeting of the state party's executive committee, which had been staged expressly to pressure Glenn to sign up as Gilligan's running mate. Glenn showed up in person to deliver a blistering statement that accused Gilligan and other party leaders of "bossism" and "blackmail" and continued: "This would be a hoax, a sham and a fraud on the voters because I'm not interested in that office. This is pure political blackmail and a stab in the back after all my support for the party and the governor."[20]

Gilligan tried lamely to downplay the split and was waiting for things to cool down when, in a surprise, President Richard Nixon—then in the midst of the Watergate crisis—put the governor on the spot again by appointing Saxbe to be U.S. attorney general and creating an immediate Senate vacancy. That was in December, leaving Gilligan with the unpleasant chore—as his first order of business in the 1974 reelection year—of choosing between Glenn and Metzenbaum (or turning to someone else) to fill Saxbe's seat.

On January 4, Gilligan bowed to organized labor and appointed Metzenbaum to the Senate seat and further alienated Glenn. That meant that when Glenn, almost surely the best-known, best-liked public figure in Ohio, became a factor in the 1974 elections by defeating Metzenbaum in the Senate primary, he would be under no obligation to lift a finger on Gilligan's behalf. And, in fact, he did not.[21]

At the same time, there was awkward, politically premature, but unavoidable talk about what Gilligan would be doing come 1976. Some of it came from outsiders, such as the substitute chaplain—a Catholic priest and Gilligan admirer—who opened a January session of the Ohio House by asking God to make it possible for Gilligan, who was to deliver the State of the State address there that night, "to someday soon be delivering the State of the Union Message." (Republicans, who raised hell about the priest's partisanship, got an apology.) But a lot of it was from insiders. Gilligan's twenty-six-year-old daughter, Kathleen, who was on the campaign trail that year, remarked casually during a southeastern Ohio stop that "he'd probably like to be president." And when she was asked if her father might consider the vice presidency, she responded dryly, "No, his ego is too big to be vice president."[22]

There was also frequent, open speculation among party leaders and others in the administration about what office Gilligan might seek in 1976. The U.S. Senate (Taft's seat) was mentioned and so were vice president and president. According to David R. Larson, a former Ohio Historical Society division chief who sat in on some private Gilligan staff meetings and later wrote about the Gilligan years for his Ph.D dissertation, Gilligan even talked about it himself.

> During the summer of 1974, reporters started asking Gilligan about the mounting speculation that, after his probable reelection in November, he would run for the Democratic nomination for president. Gilligan fueled this notion earlier in the year when he stated his belief that the governor of a major state had a better chance of winning the presidency in 1976 than at any time since the last state governor, Adlai Stevenson of Illinois, ran for the office in 1952. Privately, Gilligan confided to a few insiders his desire to run in 1976. He felt that the three governors with the best chance of winning the Democratic nomination were Reubin Askew of Florida, Jimmy Carter of Georgia and himself. Gilligan felt he had the superior position because Ohio was a northern state.[23]

What was most significant about such speculation was not what it said about Gilligan's ambitions for 1976 but what it said about 1974, that Gilligan and his inner circle believed reelection to be certain. And they evidently were counting on a majority of Ohio voters sharing their view that the sixty-five-year-old Rhodes was an Ohio antique, a throwback to a bygone era. And when little-known state senator Charles Fry, a Springfield conservative and one of two challengers to Rhodes in the Republican primary, pulled 30 percent of the vote, Gilligan's people were convinced that they were correct (oddly unimpressed, however, by news that an even-lesser-known Democrat, James Nolan, had done almost as well against Gilligan in the Democratic primary).

It was, in short, a classic case of overconfidence. And it resulted in the reelection game plan that Gilligan would run on his record and ignore Rhodes as much as possible. As two of Rhodes's campaign operatives later wrote, "Gilligan's effort was resting upon a campaign threshold locked in a time and space warp, featuring a doorsill still firmly implanted a year in the past."[24]

Interestingly, according to David Larson, Gilligan grew restive at one point in August and "proposed making Rhodes's lack of integrity in his personal and campaign finances the central issue of the fall campaign." But staff, particularly Hansan, talked him out of it. There were other problems as well. With Glenn off and running in the Senate primary, Gilligan had to round up an acceptable lieutenant governor alternative and ensure that his choice was nominated (Ohio candidates for governor and lieutenant governor ran separately in both primary and general elections prior to 1978). The process ignited fresh unpleasantness with Senator Calabrese of Cleveland, who had been the unsuccessful 1970 nominee and wanted the nomination again. Gilligan ignored him and tapped an upstart Cleveland state representative and former Rhodes scholar, Richard F. Celeste. Calabrese vented his disappointment with this scornful assessment of Celeste: "He's not an Italian; he's a Methodist."[25]

Next, there were persistent claims by legislative Republicans of a prospective $60 million surplus in the state budget once the books closed on June 30, the end of the fiscal year. This would have been a relatively minor event had not Gilligan, in late June, denounced the reports as untrue and, at one of his "beeper" sessions, where he would respond to questions phoned in from radio and TV reporters, said that anyone who believed otherwise was "chasing moonbeams." But on July 1 the surplus materialized. And it was a whopping $80.5 million—more fodder for the Republican ad campaign. Somewhat later, Gilligan acknowledged that the controversy had undermined the administration's credibility and "was just about the worst thing that has happened to this administration and to me personally since I closed the parks in 1971."[26]

At about the same time, reports leaked out that Gilligan had discussed with cabinet members the need for additional revenues in the next administration and, indeed, would be seeking increases in both income and gasoline taxes once the election was over.[27] The campaign staff, horrified, convinced Gilligan to backtrack and adopt a "no new taxes" strategy for the rest of the campaign, but the governor's new stance was less than convincing. The damage had been done.

That was the backdrop for a fall campaign that included its share of hyperbole: Rhodes, by innuendo, blamed Gilligan for damage done by a disastrous Xenia tornado; Gilligan accused Rhodes of operating mental hospitals "like charnel houses or dog kennels."[28] But everything else seemed to be going according to script.

Until the final weeks, in fact, Gilligan's emphasis was almost entirely on his accomplishments and how he had brought Ohio back from the dead. He seldom mentioned Rhodes, who seemed content to campaign through the smaller towns, sniping away at Gilligan but seemingly preparing himself for defeat. Near the end, however, the script ran out. Rhodes, who until then had spent campaign money sparingly and had barely been heard from on TV, unleashed a barrage of slick ads, saturating the volatile Cleveland market and portraying Gilligan as an arrogant, uncaring, dangerously antibusiness liberal. Peter Hart, who was doing Gilligan's polling, warned that Rhodes was suddenly and rapidly closing the gap.

Yet for the most part the Gilligan team stood pat, convinced that its well-financed juggernaut of a campaign would prove a winner against Rhodes, who, except for the TV blitz, had been campaigning on a shoestring. Even late on election night, when returns showed the race much, much closer than anticipated, the Gilligan team was still confident. After all, two networks, ABC and NBC, had called it early for Gilligan, and Rhodes had impulsively (and, as it turned out, prematurely) conceded the election at a postmidnight press conference at the old Neil House Hotel, where he thanked his supporters, graciously wished Gilligan well in a second term, declared that "we lost the election and that's it," and went to bed.[29]

Governor Frank J. Lausche (*right*) met with former president Harry Truman at the Blackstone Hotel in Chicago during the 1956 Democratic National Convention for what the governor called a purely social call. Lausche, a conservative Democrat, had figured in speculation for the vice presidential nomination of both parties that year.

Republican Thomas J. Herbert defeated Governor Lausche in the GOP "Had Enough?" landslide of 1946 and served a two-year term before Lausche turned the tables on him to reclaim the governorship in 1948.

Governor C. William O'Neill, a Marietta Republican and a former speaker of the Ohio House of Representatives, was the state's chief executive from 1957 to 1959. He later became chief justice of the Ohio Supreme Court and the only person—so far—to head all three branches of state government.

Lieutenant Governor John W. Brown suddenly found himself governor in January 1957 when Governor Lausche resigned a week and a half early to take his seat in the U.S. Senate. Brown, a Republican, made the most of his eleven-day tenure, moving into the Governor's Mansion and making several controversial executive decisions. He is shown in a 1978 photo.

Governor Michael V. DiSalle (*left*) and Senator John F. Kennedy met in the Governor's Mansion in Columbus in June 1959. DiSalle's early endorsement of Kennedy for the 1960 presidential nomination gave the youthful Massachusetts politician his first big state support outside of New England.

Governor James A. Rhodes (*left*) confers with Ray C. Bliss, the Ohio Republican party chairman, at a Columbus luncheon shortly after Rhodes began his first term in January 1963. Rhodes, who went on to win the state's top office three more times and serve a record sixteen years as governor, stressed job creation throughout his career.

Rhodes awoke the next morning a winner. He had pulled a narrow but spectacular upset, winning by 11,488 votes out of nearly 3 million cast, or 50.2 percent to 49.8 percent. The geographical explanation for Rhodes's win was fairly simple. In 1970, Gilligan had carried thirty-five counties against Roger Cloud. But in 1974 against Rhodes he carried only nineteen. And in heavily Democratic Cuyahoga County, Gilligan's margin had shrunk from 102,000 in 1970 to 87,000 in 1974.[30]

But the political explanation was more complex. Gilligan was hardly the victim of a partisan landslide. Other Democrats, including Celeste, the anointed lieutenant governor candidate, and Glenn, the decidedly unanointed U.S. Senate candidate, won handily (Glenn by more than a million votes), triggering an emotional *mea culpa* five days later from Gilligan. It came in the form of a private memo to selected staffers as he was licking his wounds in Florida: "It was MY FAULT."[31] After thanking his campaign staff, he continued, "Thousands of people who voted for other Democrats running for high office declined to mark their ballot for me. Even Jim Celebrezze running down in the Supreme Court slot got almost as many votes as I did. That is truly a humbling experience." At one point in the memo, Gilligan conceded that "[I had] persuaded myself that I could run this campaign in a defensive crouch and that, in fact, it would be far safer to do so than to run the risk of 'losing my temper' or making some rash statement. So, in fact, I said nothing."

Later and less emotionally, Gilligan told Brad Tillson of the *Dayton Daily News* that, while the outcome was indeed a personal repudiation by voters and, personally, a "wrenching, harrowing shock," he had also been victimized by Rhodes's "super saturation lie" campaign. "It wasn't so much a campaign to elect him as it was a campaign to defeat me," Gilligan said. Still later, Gilligan declared himself "the victim of a television media assassination. . . . I was destroyed by a media campaign on television, radio and in the newspapers as if a rifle shot me."[32]

Some of this was probably true; but two other factors were decisive in Gilligan's defeat. First, there was the essentially conservative Ohio voting public's traditional, almost visceral dislike of taxes and politicians who support them, a reflex that Gilligan and his people sensed but never fully understood. And second, there was the public's perception of Gilligan as aloof and arrogant. In short, too many Ohioans never really liked him. Gilligan was aware of this perception, and even though he thought it unfair and inaccurate, he never was able to overcome it. Nor, to his credit, did he attempt political disguise in order to mask it. He even discussed it candidly in a 1974 interview several months before his crushing defeat:

> I have tried to take the rough, abrasive edges off. I've come to realize there are certain times when that kind of wit or repartee or whatever is unbecoming as governor. . . . But I'm not going to transform myself into something that I'm not. You know, become the plastic man, the painted candidate with the rouge and wig in place.
>
> I have this deep-seated revulsion against pomposity, against the fatuous phrase, against the mouthing of bromides. To subject myself to that would take all the fun out of it. It would take all the zest out of it. So, to hell with it. Who needs it?[33]

Gilligan considered running for the U.S. Senate in 1976, even telling the *Plain Dealer*'s Joe Rice that "the probability is quite strong I will declare."[34] But he reconsidered and, after dabbling again in insurance, accepted a fellowship at the Woodrow Wilson International Center for Scholars in Washington. In January 1977 he joined the Carter administration as head of the Agency for International Development. Two years later he moved to South Bend, Indiana, as a professor at the Notre Dame Law School and as founding director of the Institute of International Peace Studies. He retired in 1991 from the Notre Dame faculty and resettled in his hometown, where he is lecturing at the College of Law at the University of Cincinnati and serving as founder and director of the Civic Forum, essentially a community action group working on such problems as race and poverty.

A nonlawyer, Gilligan not long ago observed as follows about his law school work at Notre Dame and the University of Cincinnati and his continuing civic activism: "A degree in law is required in order to practice, but not to preach."[35]

Amen.

❖

CHAPTER SIX

Rhodes's Second Eight Years, 1975–1983

❖

LEE LEONARD

❖ When James A. Rhodes returned to the Statehouse in 1975 after a four-year absence, the rules of the game had changed and, to a certain extent, Rhodes had changed with them. Despite his sixty-five years, the governor dressed in the modern style of the day, and he recognized the heightened influence of nightly television news that evolved during the Vietnam War finale and the Watergate scandal. Having had some narrow escapes during his first eight years, Rhodes took extra pains in the post-Watergate era to avoid anything that might smell of scandal, and he insulated himself against spontaneous interviews on television.

Not everything was different. Returning with Rhodes were his bob-and-weave political skills. He still gravitated toward grandiose schemes. And there was the same philosophy of government: find out what the people want and give it to them—employment, low taxes, good roads, and a scandal-free government. Rhodes's political traffic cop, patronage chief Roy Martin, was back, along with many of the same tried-and-true staffers and cabinet members who were loyal to the governor and not out to advance their own careers at his expense.

Greeting Rhodes upon his arrival were a national energy shortage, which was to plague him for the rest of the decade, and a hostile Democrat-controlled legislature replacing the friendly Republican one he enjoyed in the 1960s. The boom of the 1960s was past, and so was Rhodes's dominance as a builder. Much of his second eight years was spent marking time, trying to keep the state afloat. There were few new programs. Most tax dollars were spent to keep up with inflation. Social programs took a back seat to the bread-and-butter issues of jobs, taxes, and education.

Rhodes's harshest critics said he gave up after his first two years, put the state on autopilot, headed for the golf course, and practiced the politics of blame. In fairness, he had some successes in industrial development, and some of his programs took root years later.

Jim Rhodes was lucky to be back for a third term at all. His Democratic predecessor, John J. Gilligan, had a huge lead early in the 1974 campaign and squandered all of it, losing by 11,488 votes (0.4 percent). "He gave the election away," Rhodes said. "Jim Rhodes became governor because of the losing tactics of the Gilligan campaign," agreed Eugene P. O'Grady, the chairman of that campaign. "We lost the governorship, Jim Rhodes didn't win it. There were a lot of personality conflicts, a lot of ill will. It was never really a happy campaign." O'Grady recalled infighting in the Gilligan camp. He said Gilligan's chief of staff, John E. Hansan, shielded the governor from wise political advice because he wanted to control the direction for the campaign himself. Appointing Howard M. Metzenbaum to a vacant Senate seat over John Glenn "played a monumental part in eroding the base of Democrats for Gilligan," O'Grady said. In addition, this former state Democratic chairman recalled that the ethics-conscious Gilligan discouraged his legions of state employees, particularly highway workers, from being active in the campaign. Two weeks before the election, O'Grady met with other cabinet members and "literally begged them to forget what Jack [Gilligan] had said . . . and to do what was necessary to get the campaign back on track, otherwise the campaign was going to go down the tube."[1]

Labor was a key cog in the Gilligan machine, and the governor got the support of the Ohio Conference of Teamsters on the condition that he would not aid a national boycott of California produce spearheaded by farmworkers' leader Cesar Chavez. Like a moth flying too close to the flame, Gilligan appeared on a Dayton speaking platform with Chavez and was spotted by Ohio union members. Jackie Presser of the Ohio Conference of Teamsters called O'Grady and gave official notice that he was turning his support to Rhodes. "Tell your boss to ——— himself," Presser shouted through the phone. Rhodes had been having trouble raising money to air a series of television advertisements he had in the can. "Jackie opened the door," recalled O'Grady. "That was the beginning of the unraveling of the campaign." Once Rhodes got his ads on the air, they were devastating, blaming Gilligan for closing the state parks and for "taxing everything that walks, crawls or flies." "We had very impressive ads," Rhodes recalled, "and Gilligan's attitude made friends for us."[2]

At approximately 3:30 A.M. the day after the election, a campaign aide had Rhodes's daughter wake him up to give him the good news so that he could appear at an early morning press conference as the winner, not the loser he had been when he went to bed. Asked why he conceded to Gilligan so prematurely the night before, Rhodes responded with a wry grin. "Concession," he said, "is good for the soul." Was that a slip of the tongue, he was asked years later, or a well-planned pun? "It came out, just off the top of my head," he replied.[3]

Before Rhodes even took office in January 1975, the stage was set for at least two years of partisan bickering by one of the strangest political dramas in the annals of the Ohio General Assembly. Democrats won control of the legislature for the first time in fourteen years, and they swiftly passed a package of six highly partisan bills, hoping to get them enacted before Gilligan left office. They spotted their chance: through a quirk in the Ohio Constitution, the General Assembly convened on January 6, but the new Republican governor would not be sworn in until January 13.

One bill realigned congressional boundaries to create Democratic districts in Cincinnati and Columbus. Others provided for house-to-house voter registration and liberalized unemployment compensation rules. Still others reduced the power of Republican secretary of state Ted W. Brown and preserved Democratic control of state consumer protection and tax collection jobs. As the bills cleared the House, powerless Republicans played over the speaker system a tape recording of a railroad train chugging and whistling, and shouted "All Aboard!" as the roll was taken. The bills also cleared the Senate within two days and were headed toward Gilligan's office and certain enactment.

Nevertheless, the Democrats had not counted on one obstacle. Republican lieutenant governor John W. Brown, who like Gilligan had been defeated in November, was obligated under the Ohio Constitution to sign the bills, attesting as presiding officer that the Senate indeed had passed them in proper form. The Democrats, afraid Brown would keep the bills and stall until Rhodes arrived, offered the lieutenant governor only copies of the bills; he demanded the originals. This standoff took a strange turn the evening of January 10, the Friday before Rhodes was to be inaugurated.

Brown settled in for the weekend at his office so that the Democrats could not bypass him in favor of the Senate's president pro tempore, Oliver Ocasek, a Democrat from Northfield, by claiming the lieutenant governor was absent from the Statehouse. A United Press International dispatch captured the spirit of the moment:

> For Lt. Gov. John W. Brown, happiness Friday night was a TV set, some refreshments, good Republican company and a couch in his Statehouse office.
>
> The TV set, refreshments and company were for celebrating. The Republicans had just literally forced Democrats to enact six partisan bills over John Brown's body.
>
> The couch was for sleeping, which Brown will have to do in his office each night until Monday, when he leaves office, to prevent the Democrats from bypassing him to enact their bills.[4]

The Republicans, making a record of protests throughout the process, had already filed a lawsuit contesting enactment of the bills. On Saturday afternoon, five Democratic senators made their point by visiting Brown in his office with copies of the bills. They said the originals were locked safely away but available to Brown any time he wanted to sign them. He refused. As time ran out, the Democrats blinked. Gilligan signed the bills Saturday night at the home of a friend, but they were authenticated only by House speaker Vernal G. Riffe, Jr., a Democrat, and not by anyone from the Senate. The bills were filed with the secretary of state's office for certification as laws, but Ted Brown merely saved them for Rhodes when he took office Monday, and they were put in a desk drawer. Fourteen months later, the bills were invalidated by the Republican-dominated Ohio Supreme Court on the grounds that they were unconstitutionally enacted.

Rhodes established the tone for his third term in his brief but straightforward inaugural address delivered in freezing weather on the west steps of the Statehouse. He left no doubt that his mission was still to bring jobs to Ohio and that he still favored bond issues, the bigger the better. His goal was to make Ohio "Depression-proof." There were few details, but the governor recommended bonds for construction of port facilities at ten sites on the Ohio River, including Cincinnati, and improvements to Cleveland's harbor. He proposed a massive effort to develop energy resources, especially coal—an effort that was to last for eight years with minimal results. He outlined his ideas for an immense push for center-city revitalization, housing development, transportation, and public construction—the colossal bond issues on which he would stake the success of his third term. "We can become the greatest state in the United States of America," he told the shivering faithful at his inaugural. "With God all things are possible. We're going to get jobs for all the people of Ohio regardless of race, color, creed or sex." The only words he uttered about social programs were two paragraphs calling for expanded pension benefits for widows of police officers, firefighters and prison guards killed in the line of duty.

The bond issues to save Ohio cities, build roads, and create housing constituted the largest such package of debt in Ohio history. The governor also proposed long-term tax abatement for new and expanding industries, especially those locating in inner cities. "Today Ohio ranks at the top of the list of states in taxes on industry," Rhodes claimed in his State of the State message to the General Assembly on March 12, 1975. "We might as well hang signs at the state borders that say 'Industry Not Welcome Here.' " The bond issues were unveiled in February. The governor presented a constitutional amendment allowing the state to sell up to $500 million worth of mortgage revenue bonds for low- and middle-income housing. A $1.64-billion transportation bond issue, funded by a penny hike in the gasoline tax, would provide $1 billion worth of highway construction over the next four years, and 100,000 construction jobs a year, Rhodes said.

The centerpiece of this mammoth package was a $2.5-billion public construction bond issue that came to be known as the "Christmas Tree" because it had something for everyone. It required raising the sales tax from 4 cents to 4.7 cents on the dollar, but Rhodes added sugarplums for almost every corner of the state, promising to clean up and revitalize downtown urban areas. He offered recreational facilities, senior citizen activity centers, and industrial parks to replace decaying homes and businesses and vacant lots. There would be a World Trade Center in Cleveland, he said, a state office tower in Cincinnati, and a minidome on the site of the rundown Ohio Penitentiary in downtown Columbus. Rhodes envisioned open-heart surgery clinics around Ohio and cancer centers for treatment and research in Cincinnati, Columbus, Cleveland,

and Toledo. "Give me the tools to fight crime, unemployment and welfare," said Rhodes, introducing his package in the House on February 19.
"We will make the dirt fly on construction jobs—this year."

Democratic legislative leaders were cautious, however. The governor
had given them only three weeks to get the issues ratified for the May
primary ballot. Legislative activity ran right up to the midnight deadline
for sending the proposals to the secretary of state's office, but none of the
issues got there.

Undaunted, Rhodes said he would collect 300,000 signatures and
place the proposals on the November ballot by popular demand. Meanwhile, he kept trying the legislative route. In his State of the State address, the governor told lawmakers he would compromise on parts of
the package, but only if they would place all four on the ballot as a unit.
"I am dead serious about these programs because they create 250,000
jobs," said Rhodes. "I will compromise on any constructive plan that recognizes that these four programs are dependent on each other. But I will
not compromise on the basic goal—creating jobs for Ohioans." He
claimed that 284,000 Ohioans were drawing unemployment benefits—a
figure that increased by 10,000 with each passing week. "Let us begin
now," said Rhodes, adding some advice that lawmakers would hear
about again the following year after they failed to heed it. "The best thing
you can do is to be able to return to the voters of your district and say, 'I
have done my job.' "

In June, Rhodes added $250 million to the public improvements pro-
gram and $110 million to the transportation bond issues, bringing the to-
tal to $4.5 billion. He also changed the housing program to allow direct
loans to home builders and trimmed the tax abatement for Ohio industries expanding within the state. Rhodes said his package would result
in 500,000 jobs in five years.

The governor promised to "go anyplace anybody invites me to talk
about the issues. I'll even go to a Democratic meeting." Yet he quickly
clammed up after being challenged to a debate by Lieutenant Governor
Richard Celeste, the Democrats' point man opposing the bond issues.
"My mind is made up. I don't need to debate anybody," said Rhodes.
"I'm for the bond issues. I'm for jobs. He's an obstructionist who's
against jobs and for unemployment, crime and welfare. He ought to be
coming up with an alternative."

The Democrats said they already had alternatives—long-term assistance for low-rent housing projects, the state's normal $600 million cap-

ital construction appropriation, and legislation allowing the state to finance energy development projects. Ocasek, the Senate Democratic leader, said Rhodes's bond issues would cost the state $5.1 billion in interest over the next thirty years, making Ohio the national leader in bonded debt. "I'm not against jobs and progress," Ocasek said. "I'm against fiscal irresponsibility."

What followed was a high-powered $1 million campaign for the bond issues designed by the Washington consulting firm of Bailey Deardourff and Eyre and paid for by Ohio contractors, building trades, and the manufacturing community. Rhodes said his "Blueprint for Ohio" would create 310,000 new jobs a year and cost the average worker only $30 per year. The price of failure, he said, would be an extra $2 billion in welfare costs. To the Democrats, the bond issues were a "Blueprint for Bankruptcy" and "Unfair Taxes for Unnecessary Buildings." The League of Women Voters, the Ohio Education Association, the United Auto Workers, and the Ohio Council of Churches also opposed the issues.

By election day, Rhodes had ballooned the jobs estimate to one million over five years. He said the projects would attract $5.4 billion in Federal funds to defray interest costs. And he accused his foes of using "scare tactics" to carry out a personal vendetta against him. But on election day the voters spoke loud and clear. The bond issues failed by an average of 4 to 1 and by up to 8 to 1 in some counties. It was the most convincing defeat of a bond issue in Ohio history. "The people made up their minds that this was a boondoggle," said Warren J. Smith, secretary-treasurer of the Ohio AFL-CIO. "Once they saw they were misled, they totally rejected what they saw as the grand swindle of the century."

Rhodes blamed the defeat on adverse publicity over New York City's huge debt and then sat back to see what the Democrats and labor unions would do to help put Ohioans to work. For months afterward, whenever he was asked what he was doing, the governor would fold his arms, smile, and reply, "We're waiting." But Rhodes was stung by the defeat of the bond issues and the editorial drumbeat that helped sink them. Reporters were puzzled by the governor's erratic behavior. During the bond issue campaign, he ducked interviews, posted no daily itinerary, and took off for Florida without notice. Then, in December 1975, he called eight press conferences within seven working days. At one of them he treated reporters to Wendy's hamburgers and chili and playfully tossed popcorn balls at them. William Payer, president of the Statehouse electronic news media association, said Rhodes had discovered the power of television during the 1974 campaign "and that made him wary of television he could not control—that is, news reporting instead of campaign ads." "Gov. Rhodes won't answer hard questions if it doesn't suit his purposes," said the author of this chapter, then president of the Ohio Legislative Correspondents Association. "The new guys are beginning to get frustrated with the problems of covering him. He may be wearing flare-bottom trousers and wide lapels, but it's still the same old Jim Rhodes." "He has extremely serious doubts about the objectivity of the press and you have doubts about his candor and veracity," said John Deardourff, the Washington consultant who had managed the bond issue campaign. "That creates some problems for him and for the press in coverage. There is a certain souring of the relationship, but I don't know that there is much at this stage of his career that he can do about it."[5]

Still, Jim Rhodes had few peers when it came to administration, and there were only a couple of soft spots during his second eight years. The state lottery, less than a year old when Rhodes returned, was a chronic problem with political activity, irregularities in awarding contracts, and poor cash, ticket, and license controls. Rhodes appointed seven successive directors of the lottery, including two of his best troubleshooters—Robert M. Chiaramonte, his retired Ohio Highway Patrol superintendent, and Richard L. Krabach—but nothing seemed to help. Chiaramonte was scarcely there a week before he quit because he could not get the firing and hiring power he needed to run the operation.

The only other time Rhodes allowed things to get out of hand was in 1976 when two of his cronies got into a catfight over turf. The combatants were Donald D. Cook, a former FBI man whose ties with Rhodes dated back to the 1940s, and Curtis Andrews, a major campaign fundraiser for Rhodes in 1974. Cook was director of the Ohio Department of Highway Safety and Andrews headed the Bureau of Motor Vehicles in that department. While Rhodes was in Florida on Thanksgiving vacation, Cook suspended Andrews for insubordination. When the governor found out, he was furious and immediately ordered Andrews reinstated. In a drama that played out over two weeks, Rhodes refused to deal personally with Cook and reassigned both men—Andrews to a higher-paying deputy director's post in the Department of Transportation and Cook to the noncabinet position of director for Operation Crime Alert. Unless he got a personal audience with Rhodes, Cook said he would quit and go public with the details of wrongdoing in the BMV. Rhodes agreed to meet with Cook, and afterwards Cook said he and the governor had reached an understanding: he would leave state employment, quietly. (Rhodes said later he fired Cook.⁶) For years reporters tried to get Cook to tell what he knew; but while he would criticize Rhodes to a point, Cook always stopped before revealing any damaging facts.

Rhodes's way of dealing with scandals was to preempt them. At the first breath, before the media got the scent, the governor would make his own headline, loudly blowing the whistle and turning matters over to the universally trusted Ohio Highway Patrol. If any wrongdoing was discovered, he would unashamedly claim that he caught the crooks.

The echoes from the 1975 bond issue fiasco had hardly subsided before Rhodes was off on his next crusade. Responding to disgruntled northeastern Ohio property owners threatening a tax revolt, he called for a freeze on all unvoted real estate taxes. He claimed that homeowners had been unfairly burdened with taxes totaling $1.25 billion during the preceding six-year property reappraisal period, solely because of inflation. The state Board of Tax Appeals discussed Rhodes's proposal and decided it would require a constitutional amendment. Rhodes was in no mood to wait for any more constitutional amendments: "We must act now to control these increases which are occurring without any vote by taxpayers." He wanted it done by administrative rule, so a hearing was scheduled for late January before the Board of Tax Appeals.

At the same time, the legislature was attempting to freeze unvoted real estate taxes without costing school districts and local governments any money. There were suspicions that Rhodes mounted his own offensive only after he discovered what the Democrats were doing in the legislature. Riffe and Ocasek, the Democratic legislative leaders, were so upset that they issued a joint statement saying Rhodes's plan was "irresponsible" and exceeded his authority. They said he was contradicting the uniform rule of property taxation established by the Ohio Supreme Court after ten painstaking years of judicial consideration. "In an effort to grab headlines, and we readily concede the executive's superior ability to do that, the governor has turned the serious question of property taxes into a device to restore his political credibility," said Ocasek and Riffe.

The Board of Tax Appeals held its hearing, as promised, on January 23, 1976. An angry group of Trumbull County residents testified and then went to the governor's office seeking a tax rollback. Rhodes met with them for about an hour but told them there was nothing more he could do; that property reappraisals are set by law, and the taxes could not be rolled back. In typical Rhodes fashion, he told them to go see their legislators.

Five days later, the Board of Tax Appeals froze unvoted property taxes for the next two years, affecting property owners in thirty counties undergoing reappraisals. "Everybody will be a winner," said board chairman Charles S. "Sam" Lopeman, who carried the proposal for Rhodes. But Ocasek, a long-standing champion of education, contended the property tax freeze would impair the ability of school districts to collect badly needed funds.

Two weeks later, the House passed its own property tax relief bill, the infamous House Bill 920 that education advocates would spend the next eighteen years trying to reverse. And Senate Democrats continued to pitch battle against Rhodes and Lopeman. On February 26, 1976, they rejected the governor's appointment of Lopeman as BTA chairman, saying he refused to answer questions about the rationale and timing of the tax freeze. "Charles Lopeman's crime was helping the Ohio taxpayers," Rhodes said. "He is guilty of taking strong, decisive steps to help Ohio property taxpayers. He caught the Democrat majority asleep and now they have gotten even."

And so they had. Yet the fighting over tax relief was not finished. The House and Senate quarreled over the size of the tax relief package and when it would take effect. In June they sent a compromise to the governor, freezing land values at January 1975 levels but delaying tax credits to property owners until 1977. They also decelerated the annual land value updates to every three years and reduced the tax on business equipment and inventory over a five-year period. Rhodes liked the latter part, but he chose to let the bill become law without his signature, saying it "falls far short of providing meaningful and effective tax relief." He stated that a veto would be futile because of the overwhelming support in both chambers of the legislature, something that seldom stopped him from vetoing other bills.

Amid the sparring over the bond issues and real estate tax relief in 1975, Rhodes and the legislature struggled with the state's two-year budget. It had been four years since the enactment of the personal income tax, but already revenues were less than expenditures. Rhodes submitted a $12.2 billion budget in March, slightly less than the "farewell" spending plan offered by Gilligan but higher than the $11.5-billion proposal of the House Democrats. Rhodes showed he was more than willing to spend the fruits of Gilligan's despised income tax; his recommendation was a whopping 18.4 percent above the existing appropriation of $10.3 billion.

Howard L. Collier, the trusted budget officer whom Rhodes had rehired, recommended a speed-up of corporate tax payments to help balance the budget. Rhodes, sticking with his corporate friends, ignored his budget director's advice. He said it was up to the legislature to balance the budget.

The House Democrats rearranged $400 million worth of Rhodes's spending priorities and inserted some of the strongest legislative spending controls in Ohio history, but their budget was about the same size as the governor's. Senate Democrats trimmed $94 million from the House version and took Collier's approach, accelerating the corporate tax payments to keep the budget in balance. Republicans insisted that both the House and Senate versions were underfunded; nevertheless, the $10.6 billion budget was passed by June 18, the earliest in eighteen years.

But Rhodes was far from satisfied with the budget. He made seventy-one item vetoes, mainly of language restricting the ability of state agencies to spend money as they saw fit. He also removed $345 million held in a contingency fund and told the Democratic lawmakers to reappropriate it directly to the agencies for which it was intended. To balance the budget, the governor ordered a 2-percent cut in spending by all agencies.

The vetoes were certain to be overridden in the Senate, so the House tried first with nine selected items. Jubilant minority Republicans sustained the governor. "What it shows," said Republican whip Alan E. Norris of Westerville, "is that the Republicans are going to be a part of this state government, and the Democrats had better quit trying to ride roughshod over us." But their happy days would be few and far between for the rest of Rhodes's tenure. In a classic power play by the Democrat-controlled General Assembly, a legislative committee was established to review rules written by state agencies in the executive branch. Rhodes vetoed the bill setting up the Joint Committee on Agency Rule Review; this time, however, he was overridden by the Senate and House.

Another Rhodes veto was more successful. The Democrats had been trying to enact a collective bargaining bill for public employees for ten years, but never got one through either chamber. By September 1975, the bill repealing Ohio's twenty-eight-year-old no-strike law for public workers had cleared both the Senate and the House. Rhodes said upon receiving the bill that he had a "very open mind" on it and would not buckle to pressure. Twenty-four hours later, he vetoed the bill, saying it would have given labor unions unprecedented control over public money and placed a heavy burden on taxpayers. He quoted Franklin Roosevelt as saying strikes by public employees would be "unthinkable and intolerable." The Senate overrode Rhodes's veto, but the House fell four votes short of an override. It would be another eight years before the Democrats, enjoying control of both chambers and the governor's office, would enact a collective bargaining law for public employees.

The General Assembly adopted a new "equal yield" school subsidy formula designed to minimize the differences between rich and poor Ohio school districts, but Rhodes made seven item vetoes, and the formula was never fully funded. The result was that Ohio schools continued to rely on a distribution formula emphasizing local wealth and taxing effort, and officials were still groping for a fair system as late as 1994.

In 1976, Rhodes and the legislature continued their fighting. The governor vetoed more than two dozen Democratic bills that he said cost the taxpayers too much money and placed too much of a burden on local governments. On a few occasions, the vetoes were overridden.

The clash between Rhodes and Democratic legislative leaders climaxed during a belated State of the State message in the House chamber on June 10, 1976. The governor accused the legislature of underfunding Medicaid, the state's health-care program for the indigent, by $77 million. He said he would have to cut other programs to offset the shortage. "Ohio law imposes upon me as governor the duty to balance the budget," Rhodes said. "I will uphold the law. I will stand between the taxpayers and the tax spenders."

The governor accused the Democrats of trying to "sweep the welfare crisis under the legislative rug until after the November election," and he complained that they had fought his efforts to induce industry to expand operations and hire additional workers. Abandoning his text, Rhodes looked out at the lawmakers. "Don't go back to your districts and say you've done everything you can," he scolded. "You've done nothing!" Lieutenant Governor Celeste and Speaker Riffe, flanking Rhodes, stared straight ahead, expressionless. Democratic legislators withheld applause. Afterward an angry Riffe told reporters that the legislature had "done much more than the governor has done" to encourage industry to provide jobs. He termed the governor's address "strictly political." The outburst triggered the battle of the year over Medicaid and poisoned relations for months between the executive and legislative branches.

Egged on by welfare demonstrators at the Statehouse, Senate Democrats fired Ray McKenna, the state welfare director who proposed the cuts, by rejecting his appointment by the governor. They said Rhodes's 2-percent general budget reductions caused the Medicaid crisis. Rhodes countered by installing McKenna as a policy-making deputy director and called the legislature into special session on July 27 to balance the Medicaid budget. He said it was $127 million short and that federal funding was jeopardized. Before the legislature could reconvene, Rhodes proposed another 2-percent cut from the Medicaid budget, and his new welfare director, Kwegyir Aggrey, proposed a 2-percent reduction in federally subsidized welfare payments. A joint legislative committee recommended cost-saving measures and budgetary transfers worth $114.6 million, but Aggrey said that would only solve half the problem.

This led to some of the more absurd theatrics in Rhodes's two-year war with the legislative leaders. The governor asked on August 13 to address a joint session of the General Assembly scheduled for September 14 on Medicaid and the inner-city crisis. Riffe and Ocasek were slow to reply, and they did not say yes.

At the same time the governor, who had vetoed a bill setting up a nursing home study commission and then had it overriden, suddenly staffed the panel with appointees and turned it into a Medicaid study commission. He called an organizational meeting and set an agenda. The duly elected chairman, House majority leader William L. Mallory of Cincinnati, walked out in protest. Rhodes's handpicked chairman proceeded. "These ringleaders are holding up the investigation of the Medicaid crisis, and we're going to go ahead with it, we don't care what they say," Rhodes said. "I'm trying to do something. They're doing nothing. They don't have a program."

Within a week the House and Senate Democrats came up with their own combination of cost savings and surplus funds to replace $116 million of the Medicaid shortage. They scrapped Rhodes's proposals and ended the special session. Aggrey threatened to cut Medicaid and welfare benefits by 12 percent on October 1.

As September 14 drew near, Ocasek and Riffe asked the governor to meet with them, but he knew he had them on the ropes. "We're not going to meet with anybody who wants to practice some kind of medieval censorship of the governor," said Rhodes. "They can censor the members of their own party if they want, but not me." Riffe and Ocasek, recalling Rhodes's June performance, said they did not want any more "political tirades" by the governor. "We don't go down to the cabinet room and deliver a tirade against him," Ocasek said. "When he comes into our house, we don't expect to be subjected to a political tirade." Rhodes retorted, "They have done nothing to solve the Medicaid crisis. They want me to tell them only what they want to hear. They don't want to hear the truth."

Denied access to the House chamber, Rhodes took to the Statehouse rotunda on September 14 and generated even more of a fuss. Speaking to about 250 people, most of them Republican legislators, lobbyists, and cabinet members and staffers, the governor blasted the legislature for acting "out of political fear rather than what is good for the state of Ohio." Demonstrators opposing cuts in welfare benefits chanted during the twelve-minute speech, but Rhodes outshouted them, his words echoing in the cavernous rotunda. Democratic senator Marigene Valiquette of Toledo, incensed by Rhodes's inflexibility, spoke for many when she observed: "The governor's approach to resolving problems appears to be a 'do-nothing' period followed by a flurry of press statements followed by another period of neglect."

Four days later, shortly before midnight, the legislature sent Rhodes a compromise $161.5 million appropriation. The governor called it a "halfway" solution; nevertheless, he signed it after knocking out $13 million and vetoing some agency spending controls. He also canceled the 12-percent cut in Medicaid and welfare benefits but instituted his own 1-percent cut in agency funds. Rhodes also vetoed a proposal calling for zero-based budgeting by the Department of Public Welfare, a curious stance for a governor who campaigned against skyrocketing costs of welfare and bureaucracy.

After a fourteen-month battle between consumer-oriented legislators and utilities, Ohio's sixty-three-year-old utility rate–making law was rewritten with an eye toward holding down utility rates. Key to the legislation was a compromise on charging customers for utilities' investments in costly new generating plants. Rhodes signed the bill but warned it would not reduce utility rates. The new law provided for Ohio's first "people's counsel" to advocate for consumers in utility rate setting. Ohio's first consumers' counsel, William A. Spratley, was in office until 1993.

Legislative Democrats solidified their position against Rhodes in the 1976 elections by taking a veto-proof majority in the House: 62 to 37. Now, it seemed, they could work their will because Rhodes could no longer preserve his vetoes of their bills. Rhodes also lost an ally in the White House; his old golfing buddy, Gerald Ford of Michigan, was replaced by southern Democrat Jimmy Carter, with whom Rhodes would feud for four years. In fact, Carter was scarcely sworn in before Rhodes began testing him on the federal response to a fuel crisis in Ohio.

The Arab oil embargo of 1973 had left the United States, particularly Ohio, in a precarious position. There were not enough natural gas transmission lines and oil storage facilities, and although Ohio had a rich supply of coal, federal air pollution standards prevented electric utilities and industries from burning high-sulfur coal without removing the contaminants. Rhodes's crusade for Ohio coal would pit him against environmentalists and the federal government for the balance of his tenure as governor.

As soon as he took office in 1975, Rhodes called for an Ohio Energy Development Authority to issue bonds (what else?) and make loans for developing fuel resources. He also forecast a natural gas shortage for the following winter and called for the extraction of natural gas and oil from Ohio's enormous field of shale deposits, at an initial cost of $50 million to $75 million. He proposed opening more coal mines and converting gas-fired boilers to coal. In addition, he called on the federal government to reduce the wellhead price of oil to encourage drilling and open more gas transmission pipelines.

Warning that a cold winter in 1975–76 could mean a 75-percent curtailment of industry in Ohio, Rhodes beseeched Vice President Nelson Rockefeller and the Appalachian Regional Commission for help with his ideas. By May 1975 he was threatening to go to court to force the opening of gas pipelines, and $250 million of his massive bond issue was earmarked to increase production of gas in Ohio. He summoned a special session of the legislature on May 21 to push for approval of the Energy Development Authority within a month. "Ohio, the greatest industrial state in the nation, faces an unprecedented crisis," he told the lawmakers. "It is urgent that we begin today to keep this crisis from becoming a full-blown disaster."

The majority of Democrats wanted separate energy planning and financing agencies. They proposed an Ohio Energy Resource Development Agency (ERDA) using the Ohio Development Center, which was already engaged in energy research and development. The jockeying continued for three months over the Democrats' ERDA bill and Rhodes's own proposal for long-term tax exemptions for coal gasification facilities.

In July, Rhodes vetoed the Democrats' ERDA bill, but the Senate overrode it—the first time in fourteen years the Senate had overridden a gubernatorial veto. Senator Harry Meshel, the Democrat from Youngstown who sponsored the ERDA bill, said that Rhodes had "effectively speechified progress on energy to zero." Republicans said the Democrats were jeopardizing the location of a federally financed coal gasification facility in southeastern Ohio. At the end of the month, Meshel and the Republicans compromised when the House Democrats were unable to override the veto. They gave Rhodes his single Energy Development Authority with bonding powers and the ability to plan for energy emergencies, and they accepted his proposals for tax abatement and financing for coal gasification facilities, which had been blocked in the Senate. Nevertheless, in November Illinois was awarded the $250 million Coalcon Corporation gasification plant with its six hundred jobs.

In January 1977, Rhodes began his eleventh year as governor, surpassing Frank J. Lausche's Ohio record of 3,650 days in office. At the age of sixty-seven, he was the oldest governor in the country.

Rhodes's prediction of a gas shortage came true in January 1977, giving him his first "crisis" to manage. The governor was attending President Carter's inauguration in Washington when his advisors had him declare an "energy emergency" under the terms of the new energy law. Subzero temperatures and dwindling natural gas supplies for Dayton Power and Light customers convinced state energy czar Robert Ryan and Luther Heckman, chairman of the Public Utilities Commission, to "close Dayton." Schools were ordered to shut for thirty days and retail establishments were directed to limit their hours of operation. Ryan warned that within a week the emergency would be extended through the entire state. Dayton citizens and business owners were furious.

The following day Attorney General William J. Brown, a Democrat, advised Rhodes that under the law he had no authority to take such a drastic step. If he wanted such powers, Brown said, the governor should have declared an "energy crisis." After returning from Washington, Rhodes conceded that Heckman and Ryan had overstepped their authority. "Everything is voluntary at this point," said Rhodes, referring to Dayton's energy conservation measures. "I don't think we can mandate."

Here was a demonstration of Rhodes's legendary political instinct. Despite badgering from state legislators to use his powers under the new energy emergency law, the governor refused to declare an "energy crisis" so he could use those powers. He knew that fuel conservation orders could not be enforced and that he would only be criticized if he tried. Employing his time-tested method of problem solving, the governor called together all legislative leaders, state energy officials, school officials, gas company officials, and representatives of business and labor. "Before I take any action, we're all going to agree on one program," Rhodes told those assembled. "These are the worst days in the history of Ohio as far as an energy shortage is concerned. We are on a narrow path of self-destruction in this state."

While declining to declare a "crisis," on Sunday, January 24, 1977, Rhodes called the next-lower priority, a statewide energy "emergency" and requested voluntary conservation of natural gas, especially by large industrial users. The governor also ordered an Energy Emergency Center set up in the Department of Development to deal with local problems and monitor the success of voluntary gas conservation. He called the legislature into special session and asked residents of Ohio to turn their thermostats back to sixty-five degrees during the day and fifty-five at night. He kept his own office at sixty degrees and turned off the heat in vacant state offices. Corridors in the state office buildings were darkened.

By now Rhodes was in his favorite role—ringmaster of a three-ring circus. He wired "President James Earl Carter Jr.," asking for help in obtaining natural gas for Ohio. And he met with spokesmen for the one thousand angry coal-mine operators and miners who jammed the rotunda in protest of federal clean air standards that threatened their livelihoods. Federal standards be damned: Rhodes authorized Ohio industries to burn Ohio's high-sulfur coal until the emergency was over. "We're going to burn coal or there's going to be 700,000 people out of work," he said, promising to risk federal arrest to make his order stick. An EPA official minimized Rhodes's defiance, saying only a few small companies were able to burn the high-sulfur coal and that the EPA was not going to crack down during an emergency anyway. "He hasn't really done anything," said Frank Corrado of the agency's Midwest office in Chicago. Liberal Democrats in the Ohio House had the same reaction. They criticized Rhodes for "almost total unpreparedness" for the energy situation and said he should be concerned with a true long-range program of energy conservation and incentives for developing alternative energy sources.

Rhodes was deaf to the criticism. Ever a step ahead of the game, he was already thinking about the potential for flooding when the weather warmed. He contacted governors of states along the Ohio River and announced that a contingency plan was being prepared. "The Ohio River can have the most devastating floods in our history," he said.

On Thursday, January 27, 1977, Rhodes finally declared an energy crisis and presented a seven-point plan for expediting the availability of natural gas, fuel oil, and propane for families enduring another round of subzero temperatures. "What we are talking about tonight is the survival of Ohio," he said. But he still refused to shut schools and businesses despite pleas from four gas companies.

That night a fierce snowstorm struck Ohio, and the coldest weekend of the winter was forecast. Rhodes placed the National Guard on alert and asked that all businesses except grocery and drug stores close by noon Friday. On Saturday Rhodes led a prayer service in the Statehouse rotunda. "We're not praying for ourselves," he said. "We're praying for those who have to make a sacrifice in this hour."

He did not let up. Rhodes closed seven state agencies the following Monday to save gas. He pestered President Carter with one telegram after another, each time requesting a more serious declaration of disaster than the last. So quick was Rhodes that he asked the president for help under the Emergency Natural Gas Act only twenty minutes after it was passed by Congress.

Rhodes claimed that Thursday night's storm had "immobilized virtually the entire state of Ohio." His agencies put out a blizzard of press releases about their activities. The governor's office command center limited access to personnel wearing special badges. A cynical Statehouse press corps made its own crude badges out of cardboard for entry to the Press Room. They read "Energy Panic!!"

Nevertheless, Rhodes's state of alarm worked. The president pledged federal relief and recovery assistance; within five hours the legislature passed the governor's bill to expedite unemployment compensation benefits for those thrown out of work (during the weekend) by the energy crisis; the Ohio Department of Education ordered Ohio public schools closed for the entire month of February. Still, Rhodes kept the pressure on. He and the legislative leaders began bullying the gas companies about their supplies and what plans they had for distributing their fuel. They also demanded that Ohio consumers not be charged higher rates for gas piped in during the crisis. By late February, Rhodes had visited Canada and Texas and had secured extra fuel shipments to ease the shortage. He viewed a new coal-fired boiler design at Battelle Memorial Institute in Columbus, one that engineers said would take six more years of research to perfect the burning of high-sulfur coal cleanly. Rhodes said it should be pressed into service at once. "We'll work the bugs out on the job."

In frustration, the governor convened twenty-five manufacturers, coal company executives, and mine union officials on March 25 and told them to investigate the latest research and recommend a way to burn high-sulfur coal. "You look at it," he told them. "Evaluate it. Look at the cost. Give us a report and we'll follow it. We've been drifting individually. Collectively we can solve the problem. We need two to three weeks of concentrated effort." Seventeen years later, despite countless meetings of those same interested parties, the problem had not been solved. Patience was never part of Jim Rhodes's makeup. Bluster and hyperbole were.

Rhodes refused to lift the energy crisis, even during an April heat wave, because it gave him an excuse to avoid the federal clean-air standards, to continue pressure on the gas companies, and to keep the situation in the public eye. He ridiculed the federal government for its attitude. "Oranges freezing in Florida and oyster beds endangered in Chesapeake Bay constitute a crisis but not 1.2 million Ohioans out of work and three-fourths of our schools closed," he said. And when President Carter finally outlined a national energy policy, Rhodes attacked it, saying it would cost Ohioans $30 billion over the next eight years in new taxes and energy-related expenses. He said Carter's plan contained nothing to increase energy supplies for Ohio.

At the end of May 1977, Rhodes relented and reinstated the federal clean-air standards. He announced demonstration projects for the "fluidized bed" method of removing sulfur from coal by combining it with limestone, the technology recommended by his special task force back in April. "We are going to prove to Ohio that the fluidized bed method is the answer to our problems," said a confident Rhodes. Three years later, however, in a test at the Central Ohio Psychiatric Hospital in Columbus, the boiler operated for sixty seconds and then quit.

Late in 1977, the legislature passed a bill creating a cabinet-level Department of Energy to replace the Energy Resource Development Agency. Rhodes would not sign the bill, saying it was full of "complications and duplications," but it became law without his signature. The new agency budget was $17.7 million—more than half of it for coal research—and it was funded by a graduated tax on coal, higher on low-sulfur coal. Rhodes still had not declared an end to the energy crisis, although officials said there was no gas shortage. A calamity of another sort was just around the corner.

Apart from energy matters, Rhodes was much more conciliatory toward the veto-proof legislature in 1977, and he met with considerable success. He vetoed only six bills out of 238 sent to him, and let twenty-seven others become law without his signature. Cooperation led to programs in the areas of consumer protection and industrial development tax incentives. The legislature wrested more control from the executive branch and the Democrats won major voter registration reform. Nevertheless, they again lost a big one for organized labor when a collective bargaining bill for public employees was vetoed by Rhodes and a few House Democrats helped sustain the veto.

Returning as the Democratic legislative leaders were Riffe, a small-town southern Ohio insurance man, and Ocasek, a liberal college professor from Akron. Riffe, whose political instincts would later equal or surpass Rhodes's, became legendary and had major impact on the nature of legislative operations in Ohio. The Republican leaders were Senator Michael J. Maloney, a moderate from Cincinnati, and former House speaker Charles F. Kurfess, a Bowling Green attorney who was active and highly respected in national "good government" groups. During the first six months of 1977, the Democrats in the legislature passed a $15.1 billion budget, hiking spending by 20 percent without a tax increase. What happened along the way represented the major fireworks of the year.

Rhodes had cut spending by 1 percent for the first half of 1977 to balance the existing budget, and he told affected students and school officials to complain "directly and loudly" to Democratic legislators. Yet the governor was still able to propose a new $14.5 billion budget for the next two years based on a projected $1.4 billion growth in state revenues. Little was new in the budget; most of the money was to keep up with increased costs of existing programs, and educators complained that their 13-percent increase would be the smallest in ten years.

The legislative Democrats trimmed some of Rhodes's appropriations and added to the education lines, but their major surgery divided the budget in two to thwart a repeat of Rhodes's seventy-one item vetoes two years earlier. In one bill was the money; but in the other four-hundred-page bill were the spending directives and controls, including the school aid distribution formula and the first Medicaid reimbursement schedule for nursing homes. A governor may only make item vetoes in appropriations bills. The so-called "language bill" contained no money, so Rhodes would have to take or leave the entire bill. The governor decided to accept it "in the spirit of cooperation with the General Assembly," though he said it was unconstitutional because bills are limited to a single subject. This one contained at least fifteen to twenty.

Budget deliberations were punctuated by a squabble among House Democrats two days before the deadline for passage. A conference committee had come up with a final version, but ten African American House members, disturbed by strings attached to a $9.7 million allocation for Central State University, walked out of the chamber and refused to vote. The budget was defeated by one vote. An angry Speaker Riffe met privately with black leaders, got them to back off, and the budget passed the next day, 64 to 33.

By May of 1977 the legislative Democrats pushed through a major voter registration reform bill they had sought for four years and had tried to pass without success during the "Six-Day War." It contained registration by postcard, door-to-door sign-ups, and registration at designated county offices and deputy motor vehicle registrars' offices. The cornerstone of the bill was election-day registration at the polls, a procedure Republicans said would lead to massive voter fraud. Since the bill contained an appropriation, Rhodes was able to veto the election day feature, permanent registration, and sign-ups at deputy registrars' offices, but he allowed the other registration opportunities. It took the Democrats only two days to override the governor's vetoes in the House and Senate.

A Republican-backed group was not about to give up, however. Fighting other Democratic officeholders, including the Ohio Supreme Court, Ohioans for the Preservation of Honest Elections managed to get a repealer on the November 1977 ballot and it passed by almost 2 to 1 despite opposition from Democrats and organized labor. It was the first time in twenty-eight years that Ohio voters had approved a constitutional amendment initiated by the people. The five-month-old instant voter registration program was history.[7]

A fierce January 1978 blizzard, complicated by a nationwide coal strike, renewed the state government's concern about keeping Ohio's people warm and safe and its industries percolating. Governor Rhodes reverted with gusto to his old role of commander in chief, activating more than 2,500 national guardsmen to dig more than 5,000 trapped motorists out of snowbanks and take food and medical supplies to the snowbound.

Dick Kimmins, then a Statehouse reporter for United Press International, told firsthand the story of how Rhodes took charge.

The morning of January 27, 1978, was UGLY. Snow was two feet deep in downtown Columbus and the power was off. I left home at 6 A.M. to get my wife, a registered nurse, to work by 7:30 A.M. It took that long to fight the blizzard and get downtown, but by 8 A.M. I was in the parking lot beneath the state Capitol.

There were no lights, forcing me to feel my way to a door and up the stairs to the hall outside the blacked-out office of the governor. The beam from a flashlight danced inside the office. Rhodes opened the door. "Come on in," he said, "we've got work to do."

The Patrol bodyguard had procured a four-wheel drive truck to get Rhodes from his suburban Columbus home to the office that morning. He was working at the long table in the cabinet room, a twelve-volt lantern and a telephone at his side. He said he was declaring a "statewide emergency" and would order all state employees to stay home that day.

"Now, you go tell everybody that and come back down here and we'll do something else," he said. As a wire service reporter, I could spot a scoop, especially when it fell in my lap. I went upstairs to find my computer terminal operating. A series of bulletins flew from the machine to the rest of the state. Word quickly spread that although nothing else was moving that day, Rhodes was at work trying to bring some order to Mother Nature's display of power.

"We're going through something today that we wouldn't want anybody to go through," Rhodes said later that day at one of the many news briefings he would hold. "I'm afraid we are going to lose some people tonight."[8]

Ohio did lose some people. Thirty to thirty-five deaths were attributed to the storm, which dumped record snowfalls in all sectors of the state and produced winds of more than one hundred miles per hour. Property damage reached $192 million and an estimated 175,000 families were left without heat or electricity in near-zero temperatures for up to four days. Rhodes was genuinely alarmed by the severity of the storm and touched by the stories of misery it brought. "This is a killer blizzard looking for victims," he said with tears in his eyes. "There are 150,000 people out of electric power through no fault of their own. They're helpless. They're victims. They want mercy. They want help and we can't get to them. They're going through something tonight that none of us would want to go through if that was our mother and father."

He may not have thought about it at the time, but the Great Blizzard of '78, Ohio's worst snowstorm in sixty-eight years, gave Rhodes the campaign issue he badly needed for reelection later that year. He set up a command post, ordered state services performed as he had during the gas shortage a year earlier, and conducted military-style briefings to spread the word across the state. He would make his leadership a campaign issue. He also began badgering President Carter, asking for federal help in snow removal and requesting an agricultural disaster declaration. "What we have is an economic disaster, impacting on state and local governments," he said. Carter responded with federal reimbursement of 75 percent of the cost of snow removal.

The United Mine Workers had been on strike for eight weeks, and Ohio's coal supplies were dwindling. Rhodes again asked Carter to step in. "If you pound the table, both sides will listen," Rhodes said. "I say bring them in [to the White House], set them down and say, 'Gentlemen, we are going to settle this strike.' " The strike would last for two more months.

A week after the blizzard the National Guard was still clearing roads in Ohio. And Rhodes was still moving. On February 8 he flew to the small Belmont County community of Goosetown to inspect flooding brought about by an ice-jammed creek. His National Guard helicopter landed in a shopping center parking lot, and as Rhodes exited the chopper, trailed by two bodyguards, two cabinet members and a dozen reporters, he was greeted by camera-wielding shoppers. "Everything these poor people have is wrapped up in their homes," said the governor after viewing the damage. "This is a little town with a big headache." Upon his return to Columbus, he wired the president for federal assistance to Goosetown.

The next day, Rhodes declared an energy "emergency," giving him the authority to seek voluntary fuel conservation and to ask utilities to cooperate in distributing fuel where it was needed. Legislators from both parties complained that the governor failed to use his authority after he declared the emergency. Later in February 1978, Rhodes met with governors of other nearby coal-producing states and tried to negotiate a separate coal contract for the miners in District 6, including eastern Ohio. The proposal was rejected by the union leadership. Lieutenant Governor Celeste, who would be Rhodes's opponent in the fall election, attacked the governor for a lack of leadership, saying Rhodes was "scrambling to get back on top of a situation over which he has lost control. Since Jim Rhodes began his third term of office, Ohio has experienced crisis after crisis," Celeste said. But few others dared quarrel with Rhodes's crisis leadership, and this one ended when the coal strike was settled and spring came in April.

With the strike over, Rhodes returned his attention to the onerous federal EPA regulations on air pollution. They had been imposed eight months earlier after a five-year fight because Ohio would not adopt its own clean-air standards. Now Rhodes wanted a three-year moratorium while the state developed an economical method of burning Ohio coal. He said stack gas scrubbers were an unacceptable alternative because they would raise electric rates by 10 to 15 percent. The EPA said scrubbers would cost users only eighty-eight cents a month. "A lot of industry avoids coming into Ohio because of the reputation Rhodes is giving the state," said George Alexander, Jr., regional administrator of the U.S. EPA. "If you're going to lay blame, just as well to put it where it is, on Rhodes. . . . The law is the law and Rhodes feels, I guess, that he is above the law."[9]

Rhodes claimed that his state EPA director, Ned Williams, said the scrubbers worked only 30 percent of the time and that Ohio had already cleaned up its air more than any other state. Williams and Rhodes said the federal government used computer models to project pollution levels unsupported by actual emissions readings. "The federal EPA wants us to install billions of dollars of controls and operate them 365 days a year to solve a pollution problem that exists for fewer than six days a year," said Rhodes. "That's like making every American put armor plate on his roof to protect him from falling meteors. This kind of bureaucratic thinking must be stopped."

As his fight with the EPA grew more intense, Rhodes's rhetoric grew more colorful. "Blaming Ohio for acid rain is like blaming Florida for hurricanes," he said. The governor was convinced that "Mother Nature," and not factory smoke, was responsible for the sulfur-laden precipitation falling on eastern states, killing fish, defoliating forests, and corroding monuments. He cited the blue haze over the Blue Ridge Mountains of Virginia. "They didn't name those for the Blues Brothers," he said. He was sure that the dangers of acid rain were overblown and that jobs of Ohioans were far more important. "We never found anybody who died from sulfur dioxide." If anyone dared challenge his assertion, Rhodes would resort to his time-honored defense: "Name one."

In the summer of 1978, Rhodes's remarkable political career seemed doomed. A *Columbus Monthly* article later summed up the situation: "Only months before the election, schools closed, public employees struck, industries fled, the state lottery reeked like a month-old egg in the noonday sun and a trail of unkept promises dangled from Rhodes like the fuse of a time bomb ready to explode."[10] Ready to light the fuse was Richard Celeste—young, energetic, and able to match Rhodes's eighteen-hour campaign days. Celeste had been handed the Democratic nomination because other pretenders to the governor's office were too timid to run against Rhodes. "If the trumpet sounds a broken note," Celeste cried repeatedly, "who shall lead?" At campaign rallies, Celeste would shout "James A. Rhodes!" and his hip supporters would reply: "Pack Your Bags!"

Only Rhodes's political guile would save him. Late in August he pre-empted Celeste on what he knew would be the Democrat's major issue in the campaign—school financing. He figured revenue growth would be at least $1.1 billion during the next four years, and he promised it all to the schools. "The education crisis is over!" Rhodes proclaimed. For the next five weeks, Celeste strung everyone along, promising a solid edu-cation plan. There was speculation he would call for an increase in the in-come tax to fund schools. Finally, on September 30, Celeste unveiled his long-awaited proposal to save the schools. It was a dud—a series of goals for primary and secondary education to be implemented by a special cit-izens' commission, the Ohio General Assembly, and the voters at large.

Rhodes initially was stunned, because he had been prepared to "nail Celeste to the wall" over a tax hike. Nevertheless, he wasted little time in working himself up into a combative frame of mind. "The young lion opened his mouth to speak, and out came a whine of indecision," chided Rhodes. "He has no plan. He has nothing. He is incapable of leading this state. He knows nothing about being governor. I wouldn't mind getting beat by somebody who's qualified, but not him." "He says education is a crisis," Rhodes continued. "So was the blizzard. And we did not have to appoint a commission to solve the blizzard. When you elect a governor, you elect management and not a commission."

On election night, Rhodes squeaked past his Democratic rival by 49,000 votes—a "landslide" compared with his win four years earlier. Part of the margin could have been attributed to antiabortionists, who distributed 700,000 leaflets, paid for by the Rhodes campaign, in shopping centers, neighborhoods, and Catholic church parking lots the week before the election. The governor was not hurt either, especially in Cleveland, by his running mate, popular Cuyahoga County commissioner George V. Voinovich. It was the first election in which the candidates for governor and lieutenant governor ran in tandem on the Ohio ballot.

Rhodes's reelection was not welcome news for the Statehouse press corps, which was weary of playing hide-and-seek with him and defending against his usually successful attempts to manage the news. The morning after the election, there appeared on the Ohio Legislative Correspondents Association bulletin board a note framed in black, reading, "OLCA, Pack Your Bags. JAR." One reporter lamented the death of his nine-year-old dog the day after the election, venturing, "Maybe he didn't want four more years of James A. Rhodes." And a long-frustrated Democrat spoke for many: "Look at the bright side of things. At least we're done with him in 1982. [Long pause.] I think."

Rhodes's final four years in the governor's office would be spent battling for Ohio coal, harping at the EPA, and blaming Jimmy Carter for the recession that forced Rhodes to ask for more taxes yet still left Ohio facing a $528 million deficit when his term was up. In the General Assembly, Ocasek was elevated to Senate president by the constitutional change that removed the lieutenant governor as presiding officer. Senator Paul E. Gillmor, an attorney from the Sandusky area, became the Senate Republican leader when Maloney resigned to take a local political office in Cincinnati. Kurfess, the House GOP leader, had challenged Rhodes in the Republican primary for governor and lost convincingly. He was replaced as leader by eight-term representative Corwin M. Nixon, a sixty-five-year-old southwestern Ohio harness race track operator who would work closely with Speaker Riffe for the next fourteen years despite their opposite party labels. Both talked Rhodes's language and shared his shrewd and practical ways.

Rhodes proposed a $17.7 billion budget in his 1979 State of the State address to the General Assembly, increasing spending by 17 percent without new taxes. Schools were to receive a 21-percent hike in state aid.

"We had some schools that closed that gave us a black eye in Ohio," he conceded. "No schools must be permitted to close in Ohio." Rhodes warned for the first time, however, that local citizens must support their schools or the state or federal government could take them over. "We have a golden opportunity to do some of the things that have been stuck under the rug all these years," Rhodes told the legislators. Following a series of summit meetings with legislative leaders from both parties, it was agreed that primary and secondary schools would receive even more than Rhodes recommended—$3.5 billion, an increase of $784 million over the prior two years—to ensure that the schools remained open.

Most disappointing to educators and Democratic legislators was the Ohio Supreme Court decision upholding Ohio's school funding system as constitutional, thereby killing any chance of reform because of the voters' reluctance to increase their own real estate taxes. "Equal yield" was abandoned as a concept for distributing state funds. Instead, poor and miserly districts were propped up by a "no-loss guarantee" because legislators refused to vote for a formula that would reduce aid to any of their school districts.

Further damage would be done the following year, when the legislators, in another case of tax revolt fever, placed on the ballot a proposal locking into the Ohio Constitution the four-year-old tax-reduction factors on inflationary values of residential and agricultural property. Naturally it passed, barring school districts from ever collecting taxes on any unvoted inflationary increases in land values. Lawmakers were still trying in 1994 to undo the effects of that give-back. They also were exploring ways to make the school funding formula equitable, but they had not found a satisfactory one.

The governor was frantic to end school closings, which had almost cost him the election. In 1978 the legislature had begun offering state loans for school districts in trouble. Cleveland schools immediately borrowed $20.7 million and went under direct state supervision. But Rhodes wanted a law forcing the schools to stay open by borrowing from banks or the state loan fund. House Bill 44 did. "I've never seen him put so much heat on for anything," said one insider. "He really wanted that one. Not even for the bond issues did he exert so much pressure."

Late in 1979 schools were threatening to close after the loss of levies on the November ballot. "Rhodes wanted in the worst way not to give the Cincinnati schools a chance to close," said the insider. The governor lined up Republican votes by giving a liquor permit here, a pet project there: "He said he'd give anybody that voted for [House Bill] 44 whatever they wanted and not give anybody that voted against it anything," reported one Republican leader. The bill passed, but before it could take effect, voters in Cincinnati rejected a 12-mill operating levy, the seventh failure in two years. Facing a $7.7-million deficit in six months, the school board closed the schools. "We're not in it," Rhodes said, denying any responsibility. "This is between the Cincinnati schools and the state Board of Education." (In the 1980s, the state school loan fund was abolished because the state could no longer afford to maintain it. Yet schools had to borrow from banks to remain open.)

After the governor and the legislative leaders agreed upon the extra school money, the 1979 budget deliberations went smoothly, or so it seemed. But on June 29, the day before the end of the fiscal year, the Senate defeated the final budget version, sixteen to seventeen, as two Democrats joined the Republicans in protest. To block the Democrats' budget, the Senate Republicans enlisted Ferald Ritchie, a seventy-two-year-old insurance salesman and Republican county chairman from Wapakoneta, to fill a vacancy. The vacancy was created by the appointment of Republican senator Walter L. White from Lima, who was appointed to the Board of Tax Appeals. Ritchie became a footnote in Ohio history by serving the shortest term of any senator—seventeen days.

Rhodes was headed on a seventeen-day Ohio trade mission to China and Japan, and he was trying to get the Republicans to vote for the budget, assuring them he would veto objectionable language. Democrats had added provisions on governmental reorganization and changes in permanent law, including how judges would be elected in Hamilton County. On Saturday, June 30, the Republicans again held up the budget, this time with Rhodes's blessing. "We must hang together or they [Democrats] will know all they have to do is wait us out," counseled the assistant minority leader from Ashland, Thomas A. Van Meter. "If we fold now, we look foolish." "Do what you have to do," Rhodes told the Republicans in a private meeting. "Stick to your position." While Rhodes flew to Chicago to catch up with the trade mission, leaving steamed Democratic legislative leaders in his wake, the Senate met before a packed gallery and enacted a thirty-day interim budget.

While in China, Rhodes behaved typically. Waving a dollar bill at Xiao Fan, vice chair of the Chinese Council for the Promotion of International Trade, the Ohio governor exclaimed, "We're here to make China green!" At another point, he told Chinese officials they ought to build their tourism by installing an escalator on the Great Wall of the People and by establishing a Disney World at the Peking Airport.[11]

When Rhodes returned from China, he got the Republican votes to pass the budget, later vetoing twenty-seven items that he said were encroachments on the executive's powers. By August 1979 there already was a projected revenue shortage of $75 million, and in November the state's bond rating was lowered to AA+, a harbinger of hard times to come in the early 1980s.

To the end of the year, Rhodes was playing his old game of professing to fight taxes while permitting them to be raised through the back door. He had his transportation director, David Weir, front for a badly needed gasoline tax hike that would pass in 1980. In the ultimate political maneuver, Rhodes sent to the secretary of state's office at 9:30 P.M. on a Friday night a bill passed by the legislature doubling the state's motor vehicle registration fees, hoping to conceal his part in it.

By June 1980 it was evident that dwindling revenues would not support appropriations, and the governor cut spending by 3 percent and imposed a 5-percent liquor price hike. A budget-balancing bill cleared in September, and Rhodes cut spending by another 3 percent, blaming Arab oil prices and the Carter administration. Finally, the governor went before a joint session of the General Assembly promising to cut spending by $101 million and asking for $395 million in higher taxes, including the sales tax and additional levies on business, utilities, industrial packaging, cigarettes, beer, and wine. Lawmakers gave him what he wanted in a little more than forty-eight hours, but his fiscal problems grew worse in the next two years.

The legislature and the governor placed on the November 1980 ballot a $500 million, five-year highway construction bond issue program. The voters defeated it, and the Ohio Department of Transportation was limited to maintaining existing roads. There would be no new construction or improvements. Voters also rejected for the third time state financial assistance for low- and middle-income housing. Losing at the polls as well was an initiative sponsored by the Ohio Public Interest Campaign that would have shifted massive amounts of individual taxes to corporations. The legislature did, however, nick corporations for a small tax surcharge to fund litter clean-up—a response to the voters' 1979 defeat of a mandatory 10-cent deposit on beer and soft-drink cans and bottles.

There was good news for Rhodes and the Republicans at the polls in November 1980. Not only did they recapture the Ohio Senate, eighteen to fifteen, but they reduced Speaker Riffe's working majority in the House to fifty-six Democrats, forty-three Republicans. Rhodes helped drive his nemesis, Carter, from the White House by personally schooling Ronald Reagan in how to carry Ohio and the industrial Midwest. He had Reagan campaign (and shoot a highly effective television commercial) outside a mammoth, rusting shell of the Campbell Works of the Youngstown Sheet and Tube, which had employed five thousand workers before it closed during Carter's watch. Rhodes also edited Reagan's Ohio campaign speeches, inserting inflammatory criticism of the EPA and replacing the word "recession" with "depression" to describe the state's economic condition. Reagan carried Ohio by 450,000 votes and became president, but that did not stop Rhodes from continuing to bash the federal government, especially the EPA. He was highly critical of air emission controls on automobiles, saying that cars were "designed in Washington and built in Detroit." After leading the Senate Democrats for three terms, Ocasek was ousted by Senator Meshel of Youngstown—his punishment for allowing the Republicans to take over. Meshel would ascend to the Senate presidency following the Democratic sweep of 1982.

The 1980 budget crunch left Rhodes undaunted. In his State of the State message on February 4, 1981, he called for a new $21 billion spending plan. Not only was this to be accomplished without additional taxes, but the "temporary" taxes enacted in December would expire on schedule, the governor said. As always, Rhodes had more programs to expand industry and create jobs. One was a bond issue for highways financed by a penny increase in the gasoline tax. He said it would build $2 billion worth of roads and bridges in five years and provide 12,000 jobs a year. That proposal later fell by the wayside, as key lawmakers persuaded Rhodes to give tacit approval to an outright 3.3-cent increase in the gasoline tax, the first such increase in twenty-two years. Included was an escalator clause permitting the tax to rise automatically, depending on gasoline use and highway construction.

Only Rhodes's continuing dollar-pinching kept the state in the black by June 30, 1981, in the face of slumping automobile sales, dwindling federal aid, and growing welfare caseloads. Legislators were so jumpy over the changing economic climate that neither the House nor the Senate would pass a full two-year budget. They each passed their own one-year spending plans at roughly half the normal amount. There followed two interim budgets as the lawmakers waited for better economic news and sought to forestall another tax increase.

After ten months of skirmishing, and four-and-a-half months late, the legislature finally adopted a $20.8-billion two-year budget requiring $1.3 billion in new taxes, including an increase in the state sales tax from 4 to 5.1 percent. Passage came just two days before the expiration of the second interim budget. Spending was increased by 22 percent over the old budget. There was an extra $750 million for public schools, an increase of 33 percent in basic aid from the state.

Rhodes signed the budget November 14, 1981, and called for belt-tightening. He said he would reduce the size of the state payroll. "No one in Ohio wants to increase taxes," the governor said. "But we are passing through one of the worst economic periods in our state's history. We cannot shut the state down. . . . I want to reaffirm my belief that Ohio's economic troubles are temporary and . . . any tax increases should also be temporary." It was wishful thinking on Rhodes's part. The worst was yet to come.

Meanwhile, Ohio's death penalty was reenacted in a carefully worded statute replacing the one struck down by the U.S. Supreme Court in 1978. Since then, more than one hundred people have been placed on Ohio's "Death Row." The law imposed death for seven specific crimes: murder for hire; mass murder; the killing of a prison guard, police officer, or high government official; or murder during a felony such as rape, kidnapping, aggravated burglary, robbery, or arson. Mitigating circumstances would have to be considered, and there would be a separate sentencing hearing after conviction. Opponents said that it was still cruel and unusual punishment and would be applied unfairly to minorities and the poor. Shortly after the new law took effect, Leonard Jenkins of Cleveland was convicted of killing a police officer and sentenced to death. Thirteen years later, the first execution had yet to take place under the new law. The last execution had been carried out in 1963, before Rhodes stopped the practice.

Late in 1981, the legislature gave Rhodes something he had been seeking for almost seven years—long-term tax abatements for industries locating or expanding in areas of chronic high unemployment. The state also started using $15 million worth of liquor profits each year to leverage low-interest loans for expanding businesses.

Political speculation had Rhodes running for the United States Senate against Senator Howard M. Metzenbaum because he was forbidden by the Ohio Constitution to seek a third straight term as governor. But Rhodes took himself out of the running in January 1982, saying he long

ago gave up any yearning to travel the "glory road" and by now had dis-
qualified himself because of his Washington-bashing. For a few more
weeks, the governor fueled speculation that he would run for state auditor against his long-time nemesis, Democratic auditor Thomas E. Ferguson. In the end he decided to retreat to private business—for awhile.

But no sooner had the budget, with its huge tax increase, been enacted in November 1981 than revenues began to go sour again. Rhodes
recalled his trusted lieutenant, Howard L. Collier, to be the state budget
director for the third time. A UPI dispatch captured the tenor of the fiscal crisis:

> As soon as he reappeared at the Statehouse—this jovial Santa
> Claus without a beard and a voice that sounds like he's three feet un-
> derwater—you had to know the state was in a pickle again.
>
> It was Collier who piloted the financial ship of state for Rhodes in
> the late 1960s, avoiding any huge surpluses or deficits. It was Collier
> whom Rhodes called upon to get him off on the right track again in
> 1975. When the administration needed mirrors to balance the budget
> in the late 1970s, Collier furnished them. When "temporary" taxes
> were finally required in 1980, Collier got the call for advice.
>
> Collier arrived at the State Office Tower for the New Year and sur-
> veyed the premises for his old bag of tricks to take the pressure off. It
> was gone.
>
> All the gimmicks had been exhausted from years of overwork.
> There was, as one lobbyist put it, "not one speck of grease" built into
> the budget.
>
> "I knew it was bad," said Collier, "but I didn't think it was this bad.
> If I had known, I would have been here six months earlier."
>
> How bad was it? Bad enough, Collier figured out, so that if the
> economy continued to stagnate, Ohio revenues would fall almost $1
> billion short of appropriations by June 1983.
>
> Rhodes, who had made it for ten years without a major tax increase
> and won election twice on "no new taxes," had just put his hand to a
> tax hike in November. Another one in 1982 would destroy any polit-
> ical credibility he had left. Nobody could survive the handle of "Two-
> Tax Jim" in an election campaign.[12]

Rhodes threatened spending cuts of up to 29 percent if more taxes
were not enacted by the General Assembly. Collier said it was Ohio's

worst fiscal calamity in forty-seven years. After five months of negotia-
tion, the legislature produced a bipartisan package of $411 million in
spending cuts and $591 million in new taxes, including small increases
on businesses and utilities. Key to the package was a 25-percent "temporary" surcharge on the personal income tax and a boost in the rate for
wealthy individuals. Since an entire budget year had gone by, the
income tax had to be withheld from paychecks at twice the surcharge
rate, or 50 percent, in order to produce the desired amount of revenue
for the two-year budget period. Statehouse reporters, eager to hang
Rhodes for his past hypocrisy on taxes, presented the surcharge as a 50-
percent increase to make it look as large as possible. When the next governor, Democrat Richard Celeste, proposed making the Rhodes
surcharge permanent and adding another 40 percent on his own, he became saddled with a "90 percent income tax hike," although in reality it
was far less.

When Rhodes and the legislators were finished, general government spending had been cut by 10 percent from the 1981 appropriation
level, but education and welfare were cut by only 4 percent. The first
statewide workfare program, in which able-bodied welfare recipients
would work for their benefits, was enacted, but phased in slowly by the
next administration.

In July 1982, Rhodes became the longest-serving governor in the history of the United States (later tied by Governor George C. Wallace of Alabama), easing past Arthur Fenner, Rhode Island's second governor,
who died in office in 1805 after fifteen and a half consecutive years.[13] As
Rhodes's record four-year term drew to a close, he held a cabinet reunion
to swap yarns about the old days and was feted and roasted by admirers. One group put up $70,000 for a larger-than-life statue of the gover-
nor carrying his briefcase, and a provision in the prison construction
bond issue bill stipulated that the statue be placed on the northeast quadrant of the Statehouse lawn. The provision was delivered to legislative
leaders by an aide to the governor because, Rhodes figured, if the monument was not in place when he left, it might never get there. The *Akron
Beacon Journal* referred to the statue as "a tribute in bronze to his brass."

Toward the end, Rhodes enjoyed teasing reporters who wanted to
know what he was going to do as a private businessman. He said he was
seeking a patent on a product, which he declined to identify, saying only
that "everyone will want one." That product became known as "the widget," and it was widely speculated that Rhodes was developing some

form of stored energy, such as a king-size battery for electric-powered cars. The widget turned out to be the "Environment City," where people could breathe 95-percent pure air and never have to go outside. Rhodes happened upon the idea when he took several of his grandchildren to Detroit in January 1981 to see the Cincinnati Bengals play in the Super Bowl. As the kids cavorted on the floor of the Pontiac Silverdome hours before the game, they became enchanted with the huge domed play-house. "Po," one asked his grandfather, "wouldn't it be great if we could live here?" The light bulb went on in Rhodes's head, as it had so many times before. He would adapt the dome to homes, office buildings, and recreation centers. There would be a system to recycle the air every fif-teen minutes so it would be purged of contaminants. Life would be pro-longed. Eventually there would be domed cities. By 1992 he had a patent on an airlock and purifying system, had one installed on his own home, and was planning a prototype to market.

No one could ever accuse James A. Rhodes of lacking vision. His 1975 issues—highway construction, housing and industrial tax abatement— eventually became reality, although on a more limited scale. In 1987 Ohio voters approved a $1.2 billion, ten-year public construction bond issue. Rhodes was responsible for convincing Honda to build motor-cycle and automobile assembly plants near Marysville, employing 12,500 people, and for the Ford transmission plant site near Batavia, pro-viding 1,600 jobs. He was instrumental in keeping the International Harvester truck plant from moving to Fort Wayne, Indiana, from Spring-field, and for the expansion of the Jeep plant at Toledo.

Although the Ohio Department of Energy faded into the Department of Development, much of the energy legislation enacted in the 1970s is still on the books, including thermal efficiency standards for home con-struction, fuel forecasting requirements for utilities, and discounts on winter heating bills for low-income and disabled homeowners over sixty-five. Rhodes's pride and joy, the Golden Buckeye Card program, continues to offer discounts to more than one million senior citizens at participating retail outlets. But he believed his finest accomplishments for Ohio were developing a top-notch educational system, bringing jobs to the state, and creating "the greatest park and recreational system in the world."

James A. Rhodes's days as governor ended amid yet another bizarre controversy in the General Assembly, but this time it was his fellow Re-publicans who attempted the power play. Democrats had won control of the Ohio Senate by one seat in the 1982 election, but Republicans were not quite ready to yield. At their December caucus reorganization meeting, veteran senator Theodore M. Gray of Columbus electrified onlookers with these words: "Mr. Chairman, I nominate Senator Morris Jackson for president of the Senate." The words were startling because Senator M. Morris Jackson of Cleveland, the state's senior black senator, was a Democrat. Republicans had persuaded him to join their caucus to give them the majority, promising that he could preside. Jackson felt he had been snubbed by Senate Democratic leader Harry Meshel of Youngstown, and he agreed to side with the Republican party. After three weeks of intense pressure by state and local Democratic leaders and black civic and religious leaders in the Cleveland community, however, Jackson relented and assured the Democrats of their majority in the Senate.

❖

CHAPTER SEVEN

The Celeste Era,

1983–1991

❖

TIM MILLER

❖ Tears welled in his eyes as he gazed across the ornate chamber that is home to the Ohio House of Representatives nearly twenty years to the day after he had launched his political career here as one of Ohio's ninety-nine state representatives. Now he was bidding farewell.

For twenty-five minutes his oratory held the legislators spellbound. He pleaded for an end to poverty, racism, and violence. He thanked them and "the people of Ohio for their confidence" in him. He spoke of "disappointments" in "myself and others" and asked them to share something he had learned: "Good people can do bad things. It's not a lesson I've wanted to learn, I guess. I've always wanted to believe the best about people."

Clasping his hands firmly in front of him, the volume of his voice rising and then falling almost to a whisper, he ended his remarks paraphrasing an African village chief he befriended years before while in the Peace Corps:

My prayer for you and for all of us—me included—is for the courage to reach out and grasp those toughest challenges that face us. For all of us, the strength not to point fingers of blame, but to reach out and join hands. I know now it's possible for people from all around the world—from all around Ohio—to join hands and make a better life.

May the God with whom all things are possible bless us all in this work.[1]

To thunderous applause, Richard F. Celeste, the sixty-fourth governor of Ohio, left the political stage he had once dominated.

Nearly seventy years prior to that January 1991 speech, a civics teacher in the mill town of Monessen, Pennsylvania, chose a student, Francesco Palme Celeste, to make a point. "Frankie Celeste," she said, mistakenly pronouncing the silent "e" in his name, "can never be President because he was born in Italy." The young Celeste did not let the issue pass. "Yes," he shot back, "but my son can be—because he will be born in America." On November 11, 1937, the son for whom Frank Celeste held such high hopes was born in the Cleveland suburb of Lakewood. Frank Celeste had left Pennsylvania to attend college in Ohio, where over time he became a successful lawyer, businessman, and the mayor of Lakewood. While he would prove unsuccessful in pursuing higher political office himself, he imparted invaluable political lessons to young Richard. "They practiced rough-and-tumble ethnic politics in Cleveland," Richard Celeste recalled years later. "You learned to go door-to-door, to listen to people, to find ways to make government work. And you learned to have a thick skin."

Young Dick Celeste earned a reputation in his neighborhood as a bright, determined young man who wanted to lead and who hated to lose. His determination was evidenced in junior high when doctors discovered two growths on his larynx. He was given two options: undergo a risky operation or remain silent for two months. He chose not to speak. For the next eight weeks he communicated using a child's "magic slate."

He attended public schools, as did his younger brother, Ted, and their sister, Patricia. After graduating fourth in a class of 360 at Lakewood High School, he went to Yale University, graduating magna cum laude and becoming a Cecil J. Rhodes scholar at Oxford University in England. But while obviously an intellectual, he disdained much of the social snobbery associated with the Ivy League and the elite of English society. At Yale he turned down an offer to join the exclusive "skull and bones" society. "I felt I was going to be the token public high school student," he said. "To me, it was elitist and I was happy to be on the fringe—a high school guy working to get something out of Yale academically."[2]

At Oxford, Celeste continued an interest in world peace. He received the "Hatch Prize" as the Yale graduate "most likely to contribute to peace." At a party he met Dagmar Braun, an Austrian student who was studying English at an academy in Oxford. For several hours they discussed nuclear disarmament. Three months later they were married.

The newlyweds returned to the United States in August 1962 and Celeste enrolled in graduate school at Yale and worked for the New Haven board of education. But he was not excited about the job. When a school friend, Sally Bowles, administrator for the newly formed Peace Corps, called, he accepted her suggestion to come to Washington. A few months after beginning his job as a staff member assigned to Latin America, he was invited to the office of Sally's father, Chester Bowles, President John F. Kennedy's ambassador to India. Celeste accepted Bowles's offer to become his executive assistant and, at age twenty-five, left for India in July 1963. Celeste later called his four years in India an "extremely important learning experience," and he cites Ambassador Bowles and his father as the two most influential people of his youth. Years later, Bowles recalled being greatly impressed with his young aide. When Celeste left India, Bowles gave him a personal check for $1,000 and urged him to "involve himself deeply in political affairs."[3]

Celeste returned to Ohio in 1967 to find his father involved in a tough Democratic primary for mayor of Cleveland. When Frank Celeste lost, he and his son turned their attentions to Frank's successful real estate business, in which Dick became a vice president. But in 1970, encouraged by his father and Dagmar, Celeste decided to seek his first political office—state representative. He won the contest easily in a district based in Mayor Celeste's Lakewood, and later he candidly admitted, "A lot of people thought they were still voting for Frank Celeste." In Columbus, he kept the traditional rookie legislator's low profile that first term. He spent some time in the Neil House bar listening to rising Democratic politicians such as southern Ohio's Vern Riffe and Toledo's Art Wilkowski.

In 1972 he easily won his second term, and the Democrats took control of the Ohio House. Celeste immediately went to work organizing the young liberals and African American members of the Cuyahoga County delegation. With their support, he defeated veteran representative James Celebrezze as delegation leader and then gained the newly created

House majority whip post for himself. There was little power with the position, but by carrying bills and doing other legislative chores for the House leadership and Democratic governor John J. Gilligan, he earned political favors. Among the bills he shepherded for Gilligan were ethics regulations, financial disclosure for candidates, and campaign finance reform.

In 1973 he decided to run the next year for lieutenant governor, an obvious stepping-stone to seeking the governor's office. His first chore was to get "one vote"—Gilligan's. After campaigning among party leaders around the state and within the Gilligan administration, Celeste received the endorsement of the governor. He had the backing of most of the party organization but established his own team in each of the eighty-eight counties. Celeste won a nine-person primary. He was ready to take on the incumbent lieutenant governor, John W. Brown, who had held the office for most of three decades. A fall victory, Celeste reasoned, would position him to take over the governor's chair after Gilligan completed his second term, or earlier if Gilligan sought national office in 1976, as many suspected.

But in November, Celeste and Gilligan were shocked. Republican James A. Rhodes scored a stunning upset over Gilligan. Celeste, however, outspent and outorganized an overly confident Brown. He suddenly found himself not only lieutenant governor–elect, but also, with Gilligan's ouster, in the top tier of Democratic leaders in the state.

Like many young Democrats of his era, Celeste's political and spiritual hero was President John F. Kennedy. Like Kennedy, Celeste's campaign rhetoric spoke of dreams for a better America, an America free of racism and dedicated to peace. Like Kennedy, Celeste expressed pride in his ethnic heritage. His stories of family, including a grandmother who could not read or write English, spoke of the American dream. Like Kennedy, he reveled in his youth, inviting one and all to touch football games featuring the older of his six children at his rented Delaware County farm. Like Kennedy, his father stood in the shadows encouraging him and helping him financially.

And, like Kennedy, his campaigns attracted young people—young people who were convinced they could make a difference in society. The youthful troops were eventually nicknamed "Celestials" because of their starry-eyed worship of their candidate. They were called much worse by party regulars who deemed them and Celeste too liberal for Ohio politics. "Dick needed to reassure party regulars that he wasn't a dreamy-eyed liberal who was going to lead the party to ruin," said Eugene "Pete" O'Grady, a former state party chairman and member of Gilligan's cabinet. "And he did reassure them. Dick has always been very persuasive in person. He convinced them he could lead the entire party."[4]

The upset of Brown cheered the young troops. But the euphoria was soon tempered by the first statewide negative publicity for the young lieutenant governor, which involved several of his Celestials. After Gilligan's defeat, officials in his administration had placed some campaign workers on the payroll of state agencies. Some failed to report for work at all; others held dubious jobs. A state highway patrol investigation called by Rhodes led to a grand jury, and several employees pleaded guilty to minor theft charges. Five of Celeste's employees had been placed on department payrolls but were working in a "transition" office Celeste had set up. There is little transition work for a lieutenant governor, and some of the employees admitted engaging in post-campaign political work.

At a press conference to deal with the "phantom employee" issue, Celeste argued that there was a difference between reporting and not reporting for work, as some Gilligan staffers had failed to do. But the state auditor ruled there was no authority in state law for "transition" expenses, and he ordered repayment of $7,000, which Celeste paid. "I made a bad judgment in transition," Celeste said later. "I accepted bad advice. What happened was wrong, and I took responsibility. I've learned from that to be more careful when you are in the public arena."[5] As the publicity over the "phantom employees" waned, Celeste turned his attention full-time to the next task—defeating Rhodes in the 1978 gubernatorial election.

The lieutenant governor's job offered little power—but it also made few demands. Celeste became a self-proclaimed ombudsman, helping citizens deal with government, and he quickly learned he had a role as the party's primary dissenter to the Rhodes administration. He was the leading opposition spokesman to Rhodes's 1975 bond proposals, which were soundly defeated, and he became a popular speaker at his party's favorite annual event—county Jefferson-Jackson Day dinners.

In 1976, Celeste gathered his volunteers and headed to the Democratic National Convention in New York City determined to have an impact. He did, but not quite as intended. The Celestials were highly visible, leading rules fights on the floor, throwing parties at the delegation's hotel, fueling a "draft John Glenn for vice president" move-ment, and making contacts for future use among other delegations. But the biggest fallout from the activity was an unflattering portrayal of a highly ambitious Celeste by author Richard Reeves in his book *Conven-tion*. He concluded that Celeste was "definitely running for President in 1984." Celeste laughingly called Reeves a "political novelist," but did not deny the prediction.

Celeste returned to Ohio with his eyes on the 1978 governor's race. Given the luxury of a statewide office with few duties—and no doubt helped by other potential candidates who believed Rhodes was unbeat-able—Celeste was virtually handed the Democratic gubernatorial nom-ination. The Celestials looked to the fall with great anticipation. Some could barely hide their disdain for Rhodes. To them the aging warhorse of the Republican party represented the worst of the politics of the past. "James A. Rhodes, Pack Your Bags!" Celeste would shout at the end of campaign appearances. The partisan crowds roared their approval.

In the early stages of the campaign, Rhodes virtually ignored the young upstart—hiding "in the weeds," Rhodes liked to say. Many Ohioans who liked Rhodes's position on taxes and his philosophy that government should be as unobtrusive as possible, were not ready to see him "pack his bags," and at the end of the campaign, Celeste was hit on two fronts. First, Rhodes charged that Celeste was itching to raise taxes if elected. Celeste, who had talked about the need for more money for education, did not deflect the charge well. Secondly, those opposed to abortion rights and opposed to Celeste mounted a last-minute grass-roots campaign, including the leafleting of most Catholic churches in the state the Sunday before the election.

Celeste's loss by 47,536 votes out of 2.7 million ballots cast was a bit-ter pill. But it was also a learning experience. "That election helped me become a 'Rhodes' scholar," he would say later. For the first time in eight years, Celeste was out of office. He briefly returned to the family busi-ness in Cleveland but soon accepted an offer from President Carter to be-come director of the Peace Corps.

Since Rhodes was prohibited from seeking a third consecutive term, politicians in both parties were eyeing the governor's race in 1982. After a tough spring primary, Congressman Clarence J. "Bud" Brown of Urbana emerged as the Republican nominee. But unlike 1974, the Democrats were not ready to hand Celeste the nomination. Veteran attorney general William J. Brown believed it was his turn to run at the top of the ticket. And the party also saw a "wild card" entry: Cincinnati city councilman Jerry Springer, whose previous statewide publicity was generated by his payment for services at a Kentucky brothel with a personal check.

Celeste resigned his Peace Corps post and returned to Ohio. He found that "Billy Joe" Brown had earned the support of most of the county chairs around the state. Many had always viewed Celeste as too liberal for their tastes, and the diminutive Brown, a native of coalfield-rich eastern Ohio, had positioned himself as a moderate-to-conservative politician who understood the concerns of blue-collar Ohio.

The party pros reasoned that running for governor as a private citizen, as Celeste would be doing, would be very, very difficult. "The candidates who are in office have the first call" on loyalties, said Cuyahoga County chairman Tim Hagan, who had been a Celeste supporter in earlier campaigns.[6] But Celeste drew upon his experience in the 1974 campaign for lieutenant governor. In that race his Celestials had fanned out across the state and set up offices dedicated to his candidacy. This time he established Celeste coordinators in all eighty-eight counties.

The lone county party chairman to support him, Jim Ruvolo of Toledo, became a key campaign operative. Another young activist, Jerry Austin, who, like Ruvolo, had been active in the McGovern presidential campaign in 1972, assumed a top strategy role. Celeste's brother, Ted, who had directed his 1978 effort, was moved aside; David Milenthal, a Columbus advertising executive, was itching to try his hand at a major statewide TV campaign.

While Celeste and Brown were circling each other, another top Democrat was seriously considering entering the fray. Like Celeste, Vernal G. Riffe, Jr., learned politics at the knee of his father-mayor, though the town ruled by the elder Riffe—New Boston—is about as distant in miles and political style as one could get from Cleveland and still be in Ohio.

Riffe (whose name rhymes with "life" and who is known as "June" to his neighbors) used his considerable political skills to earn what would become the longest serving tenure as speaker of the House in Ohio history. In addition to his powerful legislative position, Riffe had a political "sugar daddy"—Cincinnati financier Marvin Warner. They discussed putting together a ticket, even debating who would be "on top" and who would run for lieutenant governor. But when the pair began their statewide polling, they received some grim news: few people outside of New Boston had ever heard of Vern "Riffy," the common mispronunciation of his name. It would take millions of dollars in advertising just to move his name identification above a blip on the political radar.

But if he could not be king, Riffe concluded, he would be kingmaker. Even before Riffe made his decision not to run, he was targeted by Celeste. "My father had prepared a list of people I should talk to, people whose support he thought could be crucial to our success," Celeste recalled. Riffe was at the top.[7] Celeste had already made a good impression with the speaker by choosing state representative Myrl Shoemaker as his running mate for lieutenant governor. Shoemaker, from Bourneville in rural Ross County, was Riffe's right-hand man in the legislature. His folksy manner and down-home humor spiced the ticket and brought key support from the state's southern "Bible belt."

Another politician near the top of Frank Celeste's list was state representative C. J. McLin of Dayton. A leader in the early days of the civil rights movement, McLin, a trusted Riffe lieutenant, helped create and was the first president of the Black Elected Democrats of Ohio, the most powerful black political organization in the state. Celeste had always been popular among African American political leaders. "Dick had a very good record on civil rights and we felt we could get along pretty well," McLin said.[8]

Three months prior to the June primary, Celeste received the endorsements of Riffe, Warner, McLin, and another key component for victory—organized labor. The support of Warner and labor was critical to Celeste's success for one major reason: they provided prime sources of money to pay for TV advertising. If Brown had an advantage over Celeste, it was his ability to position himself as the moderate in the campaign. That advantage did not last long.

Although political campaign ads on TV were certainly not new in 1982, most previous spots had been standard fare: a well-dressed candidate talking about an issue or snippets showing a candidate mingling with voters. Austin and Milenthal had a different idea. "Dick Celeste is at his best talking off-the-cuff, directly with voters," Austin said. "We decided to sit him at his kitchen table and toss questions and issues at him and tape his response."

Austin said "we knew we had hit paydirt" when Celeste was asked about recent break-ins at his Cleveland home. "He talked about how he could sympathize with the victims of crime and how he would get tough with criminals if elected. He was great. And we knew it."[9] The resultant TV ad caught Brown off-guard and scored a direct hit on one of the attorney general's main themes: "I'm the crime-fighter." Milenthal and Austin produced another spot in which Celeste stood between an American-made car and a foreign one and talked about alleged unfair trade practices and the need to protect American jobs. "They didn't expect Celeste the moderate," Austin said. "Our polls were looking much better."

A month before the primary, Celeste received the editorial endorsements of both of his hometown newspapers, the *Plain Dealer* and the *Cleveland Press,* and in the final days he concentrated on getting out the vote in northern Ohio. On primary day, Celeste got 42 percent of the vote, with Brown trailing at 37 percent and Springer receiving 21 percent.

After the heated, hard-fought primary, the general election seemed almost anticlimatic. The Republican candidate, Congressman Clarence J. "Bud" Brown, had spent almost all his adult life inside Washington's Beltway. He was relatively unknown to Ohio voters and the political reporters covering the campaign, many of whom had covered Celeste for years. Brown's lack of in-depth knowledge about state government was becoming well documented, and Republicans worried about his ability to effectively attack the veteran campaigner Celeste. And while Brown was well aware of the adage that in Ohio a candidate had to run statewide once and lose before being successful in a gubernatorial or Senate campaign, he still did not begin campaigning hard until late summer, while Celeste was raising money and gathering endorsements.

Celeste repeated over and over again that he had become "a different kind of Rhodes scholar," after his 1978 campaign. The blue sportcoat, Oxford shirt, and penny loafers were replaced by a gray business suit and wing tips. Celeste knew that if the state's business community lined up behind Brown, he could have difficulty in November; so he set about persuading them that they should not fear a Celeste administration. "I made it clear that I recognized their importance to the state's economy and that they were going to have a seat at the table in deciding how to put people back to work."[10] He argued that the state's business leaders suffered from the haphazard budgeting processes of state government and said they could even benefit from increased taxes if the money was used to pay for better schools and provide better workers. Whether the business community liked what it heard from Celeste or sensed that Brown was a loser was not clear, but the Democratic candidate received unusually strong support from that quarter.

As Ohio's economy continued to slide midway through President Reagan's first term, Celeste stepped up his attack on the Republicans as the foes of working people. Keeping the offensive in their only statewide televised debate, a ninety-minute forum sponsored by Dayton Newspapers, Inc., just two weeks before the election, Celeste said the choice "is between someone who has a Washington perspective and someone who understands state issues and knows how to make state government work."[11]

In the final days of the campaign, Brown wandered through familiar but sparsely populated southern Ohio, while Celeste pounded home his themes in the vote-rich northern counties, primarily his home of Cleveland. On election day, Celeste won nearly 61 percent of the vote. When asked what suggestions he had for his successor, Governor Rhodes said, "Anybody that wins by 600,000 or 700,000 votes doesn't need my advice." The Celestials were ecstatic. State government, which had been James A. Rhodes's fiefdom for sixteen of the previous twenty years, was finally in their hands. Their governor, forty-five-year-old Richard F. Celeste, had promised "no more business as usual."

Even before his swearing-in, Celeste set about trying to meet that pledge. When Rhodes convened his cabinet after returning to office in 1975, it included twenty men and one woman, only two of the men African Americans. Celeste's cabinet had what he called "a more representative appearance" with his appointment of a half dozen women and four African Americans. The average age of Celeste's top staff and cabinet was thirty-five years, compared with fifty-one under Rhodes. Celeste announced that excess proceeds from his inauguration gala would go to the Hunger Task Force. And Dagmar Celeste declared that the Governor's Mansion, which Rhodes had left vacant in favor of his suburban Columbus home, would be called "the Residence" after a refurbishing and the Celestes moved in.

Celeste proclaimed an "action agenda." State government, which under Rhodes had reacted to problems, would now be "pro-active," offering solutions to problems before a crisis developed. Before he could launch any new programs, however, Celeste had a potential disaster on his hands: a projected $540 million deficit in the state budget. To deal with the state's budget problem during the national recession, Rhodes had convinced the legislature to pass a temporary 50-percent increase in the state income tax. That increase was to expire June 30. Celeste labeled the temporary taxes a gimmick that failed to seriously address the financial situation. "Those who have said 'temporary, temporary,' have fallen short every time," he said.[12]

Like its "rust belt" sister states, Ohio had seen its industrial base continue to decline during the 1970s and into the 1980s. Manufacturing, which had supplied half of the jobs in the state in the 1950s and 1960s, now accounted for less than a quarter of the employment. Many of the replacement jobs were in service industries that paid less and generally supplied fewer benefits. Celeste's first task was to get the state on firm financial footing. True to his word during the campaign, he consulted closely with the business community and eventually proposed a tax package that called for keeping Rhodes's 50-percent surcharge and increasing the income tax an additional 40 percent.

The outcry was immediate. Minority Republicans in the Senate blasted Celeste for not consulting with them about the plan. Statehouse tradition called for both parties to be involved in highly sensitive proposals, such as pay raises for legislative members and major tax increases. Celeste replied that he had tried but was rebuffed by the Republicans who wanted him to take the heat for a tax increase they knew was inevitable.

More damaging to the new governor was his failure to prepare the public for the breadth of his proposal. Statehouse reporters had simply added his 40-percent proposal to the temporary 50-percent surcharge for a total tax hike of 90 percent. Because Celeste's proposal also included other tax adjustments, such as an increase in exemption allowances, the administration would later argue that the actual hike was only 27 percent. But the damage was done, the headlines had been printed. "We should have stated the case better before the proposal was made," Jerry Austin admitted later. "If we had labelled it '50 percent Rhodes and 40 percent Reagan' early in the game, it might have helped."[13]

Riffe held a large majority in the House, which easily passed the proposal, but the Democrats held only a one-vote majority in the Senate, and the Republicans were holding firm in opposition. In one of the most dramatic moments ever in the Senate chamber, Senator Oliver Ocasek was flown from Florida, where his wife lay seriously injured from an auto accident, to cast his vote. A hush fell over the proceedings as a stoop-shouldered Ocasek whispered his "yes" and the tax package passed by one vote. But the Republicans almost immediately began an effort to repeal the tax. The vote was to become the defining moment in the legislature in the 1980s and even into the 1990s. The Republicans used it as the primary issue to take control of the Senate a year later, and the Democratic minority continued to decline until it gained one seat in the 1992 election.

Along with the tax increase, Celeste promised a change in the methods used in adopting the state's biennial budgets. Historically, the legislature had relied on its own Legislative Budget Office to forecast economic trends and predict how much money state taxes would bring in and how much state programs would cost. The governor's Office of Budget and Management did the same. Often during budget proceedings, the two projections would clash and the governor and the legislature would simply choose numbers most to their liking. The state had also been operating on an outdated accounting method that made forecasting less reliable. Under the direction of state tax commissioner Joanne Limbach and state budget director William Shkurti, two highly praised members of Celeste's cabinet, the state set up the Council of Economic Advisors to remove as much political maneuvering as possible from the process. The new process brought praise from national fiscal experts and even Celeste's Republican critics admitted the changes were for the best.

During the campaign, Celeste had said that government needed to be an "agent for change," improving the lives of citizens, particularly those who had trouble looking out for themselves. He proposed boosting money for Head Start, reforming the welfare system, and making it easier for citizens to access state government.

During the 1970s, Ohio had gained an unwanted national reputation in the area of mental health. The state ranked among the worst in mental health care due in part to an overdependence on state-run facilities, several of which could not meet certification standards. Under the direction of Pamela Hyde, a former executive director of the Ohio Legal Rights Service, the department moved steadily toward community-based care. With passage of the Mental Health Act in 1988, the state completed a long process of transferring responsibility for care to local community boards, a move highly praised among mental health professionals.

While Rhodes had created a separate commission on aging, Celeste went a step further and established the agency as a cabinet-level post and boosted funding considerably. The department was charged with developing innovative programs, such as PASSPORT, which used state and federal dollars to provide services when possible to the elderly in their homes rather than in expensive nursing homes. The emphasis on such programs not only provided better care to the elderly, most experts argued, it also helped combat the growing Medicaid drain on the state budget.

Perhaps no area of government was more appreciative of the tax increase than the education community. During the 1970s, state support for primary and secondary education had been cut to deal with state budget problems. At one point, as more and more schools struggled, a frustrated Rhodes and the legislature approved a bill simply prohibiting schools from closing. An underfunded emergency loan fund was created to help the poorest districts. Passage of the tax hike allowed an increase in state aid to schools. Colleges and universities benefited as well by being able to reduce large increases in tuition. The administration also created new progams such as "Eminent Scholars," which attracted top research professors to universities, and the "Edison program," which established nationally praised research centers jointly operated by schools, private business, and the development department.

Early in Celeste's first term, the state was also under increasing pressure to deal more effectively with its mentally retarded population. Legal action had resulted in the courts ordering the closing of state-run facilities that had been little more than warehouses for the severely retarded.

Although Celeste had chosen effective directors to reorganize the mental health and aging departments, some cabinet appointees were to be the source of his farewell address lament that "good people can do bad things."

During the campaign Celeste had said his election would signal an end to the cronyism that had surfaced during the Rhodes years and that state government would be accessible to the working men and women of Ohio.[14] Questions, however, were raised almost immediately about his ability to make good on that pledge.

Like any new governor upon taking office Celeste began repaying some political debts. Michael Del Bane, an old crony of Riffe's, was reappointed to the Public Utilities Commission of Ohio, despite a campaign pledge by Celeste to fire the commissioners and make the rate-making body more consumer oriented. Labor leader Warren Smith became the first nonengineer ever to head the state highway department. Organized labor was particularly pleased when Celeste signed a bill granting collective bargaining rights to public employees, a long-sought measure that Rhodes had vetoed. He rewarded campaign manager Austin with a lucrative deputy registrar's office in Columbus, and David Milenthal, his campaign media director, won a million-dollar unbid state travel and tourism advertising contract. At the urging of Cleveland African American leaders, James Rogers was named the head of the Department of Youth Services. State representative C. J. McLin persuaded Celeste to appoint Montgomery County's Minnie Fells Johnson director of Mental Retardation and Developmental Disabilities. Marvin Warner was named chairman of the Ohio Building Authority, the agency that oversees state buildings and leases, and Celeste's favorite county party chairman, Jim Ruvolo, was selected as the new chairman of the state's Democratic party.

Celeste was undaunted by newspaper editorials around the state questioning some of these appointments. His press secretary, Paul Costello, dismissed stories printed in March 1984 by the Horvitz Newspapers chain alleging that some vendors doing business with the state were advised to give money to the Democratic party or lose their contracts. The governor, Costello said, "just wants to make it very clear that any employee of this state should know that this type of conduct will not be tolerated."[15]

Attention from personnel matters was deflected when a sudden crisis arose that would prove to be one of Celeste's finest moments in office. During the evening of March 6, 1985, Robert Schmitz sat on the other side of the arena from Dick Celeste in Ohio State University's St. John Arena watching the Buckeyes battle Michigan in basketball. "I could tell from seeing how he was engrossed in the game that he couldn't know what was about to hit him," Schmitz, a vice president of the Ohio Savings and Loan League, would recall later. Schmitz had dashed to the phones all evening gathering information on the collapse of a little-known brokerage house in Florida—E.S.M. Government Securities Inc. The next day Schmitz drove to Dayton and found a long line of people downtown. "I said to myself, 'Schmitz, those folks aren't waitin' for the bus.' " Indeed, they were waiting for the opening of the Home State Savings Bank branch, a scene being repeated throughout central and southern Ohio.

What Schmitz knew that Celeste did not was that E.S.M. had a complex—and eventually proven to be illegal—financial arrangement with Home State. So when E.S.M. collapsed, Home State and Ohio's entire system of state-insured savings and loans would collapse with it. And in the middle of it all was Marvin Warner.

Ohio was one of the few states that operated a private insurance fund for savings and loans that did not have federal insurance. Most of the institutions were small and many were located in Cincinnati, where they had started as offshoots of German social organizations. Most were sound financially. But in the 1980s, Warner's Home State expanded rapidly through a risky series of deals until it dwarfed the other institutions. And when it collapsed, the entire Ohio Deposit Guarantee Fund toppled.

As the gravity of the situation became apparent to Celeste—88,443 Home State depositors faced the loss of $1 billion in deposits—he asked his old friend, Milenthal, to visit the Governor's Mansion for a beer. "I was very, very frustrated," he said.[16] Soon Celeste and his advisers reached several decisions that would guide him throughout the crisis: the state would stand behind the depositors so no one would lose a dime; if proven guilty of a crime, Warner would be punished to the fullest extent; and the savings and loans would reopen with federal insurance. Celeste faced several roadblocks to realizing those goals, however. The Republican-controlled Ohio Senate initally opposed guaranteeing all of the depositors' money. And buyers for Home State and some other troubled S&Ls were not readily apparent.

Senate president Paul Gillmor of Port Clinton initially denounced Celeste's executive order that shuttered the seventy state-chartered S&Ls. He also opposed the original bill that would use a state development program to provide funds to depositors so that the institutions could be slowly reopened. But Celeste, with considerable help from conservative Republican state representative William Batchelder of Medina, assembled a bipartisan team to work on reopening legislation, which eventually passed the Senate by one vote, thanks to strong lobbying from Cincinnati legislators, who were under intense pressure from constituents to deal with the problem.

Eventually, all of the institutions either reopened or were merged with existing financial organizations. When court cases showed fraud to be involved in the financial activities of E.S.M. and Home State, Warner was indeed imprisoned, and the state recovered its funds through legal action.

The largest bank holiday in the United States since the Great Depression, Celeste would say later, proved to be his proudest moment. "When you look at what was to happen later in other states and on the federal level with savings and loans, you have to be proud of the

action that we took in Ohio and the manner in which we acted to protect our citizens and punish those responsible," he said.[17]

Even as the Home State crisis was easing, Celeste was hit with revelations of financial irregularities and, even worse, patient abuse at group
homes for the mentally retarded. The reports first surfaced in Cincinnati
but were soon coming from other parts of the state, and the Senate
launched an investigation into the matter. The anger of families with relatives in the homes was directed squarely at department director Minnie Fells Johnson, who was being charged with awarding contracts to
operate the homes without properly investigating the owners.

Celeste was in a quandary. Two other African Americans had recently
been forced out of his administration: James Rogers resigned as head of
the Department of Youth Service after the *Plain Dealer* raised questions
about the hiring of convicted drug dealers to work with troubled youths
(he would later be convicted for misdeeds in his previous job in Cleveland) and Arnold Pinkney left the Ohio Building Authority after criminal charges were filed against him for non–state related activity (he was
convicted of a fourth-degree felony but was pardoned by Celeste in
1989). Celeste wanted to stand by Johnson, but as the Senate committee
investigation continued to raise troubling questions about the department, she resigned while Celeste was overseas on a trade mission. David
Hobson, a state senator from Springfield who later was elected to Congress, received praise from both political parties for his role in chairing
the investigation. "I went into the governor's office early and told them
'this is getting bad, it's getting out of hand,' but their response was they
needed to 'ride this one out,' " he said.[18]

No sooner had Johnson left than Celeste was hit with a nine-part series of articles in the now-defunct *Columbus Citizen-Journal* that greatly
expanding upon the earlier Horvitz Newspapers allegations. The articles
painted a picture of an administration in which campaign contributions
were expected in order to do business with the state and individuals had
to contribute to keep jobs or gain promotions. The article said that Celeste has used the county coordinators he had set up for the campaign to
"screen" contracts and employees through Ruvolo and the state party.

Celeste responded by sending forth his troubleshooter, Joseph Som-
mer, a former Riffe aide, to dispute the allegations point-by-point. But he
also issued an executive order telling agencies to ignore voting records
in hiring and to destroy any paper shredders, which the *Citizen-Journal*
said had been used on incriminating documents. A Franklin County

grand jury later indicted the state party's financial officer, Pam Conrad, but her conviction was overturned on appeal. Celeste's patronage chief, Larry McCartney, pleaded guilty to a misdemeanor charge. The governor charged that the Statehouse news media focused too much on the political intrigue. He said he took the allegations seriously, but "I'm not going to let us get 'Columbus-itis.' I urge you to try, if you can, to step back and put these things in perspective."

But one Ohioan was carefully cataloging all of the governor's missteps—James A. Rhodes. From the day Celeste took office, speculation abounded that Rhodes would try to return for a fifth term as governor. As the 1986 campaign neared, his aides kept in close contact with political reporters. And when Rhodes announced officially he would run again, few were surprised. But few Republican party leaders were happy.

The Republican brain trust that had taken control of the state Senate, the GOP's only position of power in the capitol, believed that Celeste could be beaten—but only by someone who could take advantage of the allegations of wrongdoing. Rhodes was not the man. "Jim Rhodes has served his party well," said state senator Paul Pfeifer of Bucyrus, who entered the Republican gubernatorial primary. "But he is not the answer that Ohioans are looking for." Rhodes had suffered through his own allegations of cronyism and favoritism during his four terms, and the legislative investigation into the Home State matter had shown that Rhodes's administration had been less than stellar in its oversight of Marvin Warner's financial activities. Senate president Paul Gillmor entered the primary and drew most of the support of his legislative colleagues. But Rhodes had tremendous name identification in the state and, thanks to his years of services, was able to tap most of the party's financial resources. Rhodes rather easily won the party's primary.

From beginning to end, the 1986 gubernatorial campaign was nasty. The seventy-six-year-old Rhodes almost daily attacked Celeste's ethics. Celeste tried to focus on the highlights of his administration—increased funding for schools, job creation, more minorities and women in state government, and an improving state infrastructure—but he was also mindful of the advice of former governor John Gilligan, who lost his reelection bid to Rhodes in 1974. Gilligan publicly suggested that Celeste "throw everything at him. Throw the kitchen sink. Throw dead fish."[19]

Celeste first had to choose a lieutenant governor running mate to replace Myrl Shoemaker, who had died of cancer the year before. He selected youthful Paul Leonard, the "rock and roll" mayor of Dayton, which served to highlight the contrasts in the tickets: the elderly Rhodes campaigned by bus, cajoling reporters with Statehouse tales; Celeste and Leonard flew to all parts of the state vigorously defending the governor's record.

With the approach of Labor Day, the unofficial campaign kick-off date, many Republicans' fears were realized. Independent polls showed voters viewed Rhodes as no better than Celeste on the ethics issue. "A Contest of Unpopularity" read the *Akron Beacon Journal* headline. "Voters Less than Enthused about Governor's Race," headlined the *Columbus Dispatch*.[20] Rhodes never was able to close in on Celeste, who outspent Rhodes two-to-one, getting even more contributions from the business community than he had in 1982.

In the final days of the campaign, in a move reminiscent of the anti-abortion campaign against Celeste in 1978, a group supporting Rhodes launched an attack upon Celeste as a supporter of "gay rights." The group suggested that the homosexual community had a hidden agenda in support of Celeste. The print ads were so vicious that even Rhodes's running mate, Hamilton County commissioner Robert A. Taft II, denounced them. Further, with the polls showing him trailing badly, Rhodes, who had suspended day-to-day campaigning when his wife, Helen, was hospitalized, agreed to the campaign's only debate, a statewide telecast from Cincinnati. Rhodes, who had begun his public career when TV was in its infancy, proved no match for Celeste, who focused primarily on the issues of jobs and education while Rhodes tried unsuccessfully to raise the corruption issue.

On election night, Celeste finally vanquished his old nemesis, winning 61 percent to 39 percent. As an exclamation point to a bitter battle, campaign manager Austin made a caustic reference to the 1970 tragedy at Kent State University, saying four families would "sleep better" that night knowing Rhodes would not be governor again. Celeste had become the first Democrat to win reelection since Frank Lausche and the first ever since the state went to four-year terms.

As Celeste began his second term, speculation began almost immediately that he would seek the Democratic presidential nomination in 1988. Although he dismissed such rumors, he had helped fuel them by giving several speeches on national issues across the country and involving himself in a dispute about sending Ohio National Guard troops to Nicaragua at the request of the Reagan administration. His advisers thought he had a natural national constituency among the liberal "peace" wing of the Democratic party and African Americans. They also thought that his handling of the savings and loan crisis as well as Ohio's fiscal stability would make him a viable candidate.

But whatever plans Celeste harbored about a presidential bid were dashed in June 1987 when the *Plain Dealer* published an article alleging that he had engaged in several extramarital affairs. Former Colorado senator Gary Hart had already seen his candidacy doomed just months earlier following newspaper articles about his private life. The *Plain Dealer* published its story several days after Celeste was asked at a press conference if he had any "Hart-like" problems that might prevent him from running. Rather than respond that his private life would remain just that, as aides had advised him, he answered "no."

Celeste and his family were outraged by the story, which touched off a vigorous debate in the media about what constituted proper reporting on a public official's private life. While the Celeste family never directly addressed the specifics of the story, Dagmar Celeste and her oldest children authored separate articles published in many of the state's newspapers defending the governor as a good husband and father. That summer Celeste made a trip to Iowa, the site of the first presidential caucuses, but it was clear any potential candidacy was doomed. In August he officially said he would not run for president.

That fall he again found his administration the focus of another ethics investigation as questions were raised about unbid state telephone contracts and reports of sexual harassment and questionable job training grants within the Ohio Bureau of Employment Services. Celeste vowed to move quickly on these reports. OBES chief Roberta Steinbacher soon resigned. Steinbacher, a close friend of Dagmar Celeste, had been one of three people on Celeste's original transition team in 1983. The other two were Larry McCartney and James Rogers. For the remainder of his term, Celeste tried to focus his administration and reporters back on favorite topics: education and job creation.

After the income tax hike of 1983, Celeste had rather reluctantly gone along with Republican-led efforts to repeal portions of it. The lowering of the taxes proved to be a good political move, but Celeste feared that the gains the state had made in the area of education would be eroded if additional funding was not found. Particularly troublesome was the deteriorating condition of school buildings across the state. He proposed an increase in the state sales tax to fund education, but it was quickly rebuffed by legislative leaders in both political parties who were not anxious to again face the wrath of voters over a large tax hike. Celeste had named Lieutenant Governor Leonard director of the state development department, and his final budget contained provisions designed to help small businesses and to benefit firms engaged in the growing area of high technology.

As attention turned to the 1990 campaign and to picking his successor, Celeste traveled around the state pointing with pride to projects and programs created in his administration. On May 4, 1990, the twentieth anniversary of the Kent State University shootings, he spoke on the campus and issued a formal apology from the state to the families of those who were killed and those wounded during the antiwar demonstration, a statement Rhodes had declined to make.

Near the very end of his term, he signed a law creating the office of state inspector general with broad authority to investigate allegations of misconduct by state officials and employees. Also in his final days, he again sparked considerable controversy. First, he issued pardons to twenty-five "battered" women. He said if the women had been allowed to raise the issue of abuse in their court cases, as state law later allowed, they likely would not have been convicted. A life-long opponent of the death penalty, he also used his gubernatorial authority to commute the sentences of Death Row inmates. That move touched off a storm of criticism. An old friend and political ally, Lee Fisher, the new state attorney general, took the issue to court, arguing that Celeste had failed to follow proper commutation procedures.[21]

Most observers believe the chief legacy of the Celeste years was the 1983 income tax increase not only because it stabilized state spending but also because the manner in which it was approved set the political tone for the decade. "His largest accomplishment was to impose a tax that was controversial and then make it stick," said Republican Stanley Aronoff of Cincinnati, who became Senate president in Celeste's second term.[22]

Former campaign manager Gerald Austin admits that Celeste came in "as the 800-pound gorilla and was knocking everybody down in his path." He said the administration might have fared better if the Democrats had not controlled both legislative chambers in 1983. State representative William Batchelder, a Republican from Medina, said Celeste succumbed to "partisanship, and 99 times out of 100 that will cause problems. . . . He was a very gifted individual. I would have hoped it would have been better for him. There was a tremendous potential not realized," he said.[23]

Celeste himself believes that "history will judge me better than my contemporaries" and that the Eminent Scholars, the Edison program, mental health reform, management of the savings and loan crisis, and his peace-making efforts will be the enduring legacy. "I believe I will be viewed as an innovative governor, perhaps the first 'global' governor at the end of the twentieth century," he said. "We tried to be creative and we tried to address major problems during difficult times." His biggest regrets were the hiring of James Rogers and his inability to deal more swiftly with other personnel problems: "People expected the highest standards of me, and I paid a price when I chose a crook [Rogers] for my cabinet." His greatest accomplishment, he said, was "putting people back to work." "The obituary for the Rust Belt was being written when I took over and I believe we turned that around in Ohio, better than any other Midwest state."[24]

After leaving office, Celeste opened a business consulting firm in Columbus, but he remained much in the minds of politicians in both political parties. Some cite his reputation as a historian and predict he will challenge Rhodes's record of four terms as governor. Others believe he may seek a seat in the U.S. Senate. Still others believe he has left public life. Celeste would not comment on future plans. In 1993 there was much speculation that he would again run for governor, but in midyear he announced he would not seek public office in 1994. Later in the year, President Clinton tapped him as one of his national speakers for the administration's health-care reform. The appointment kept Celeste in the public eye and encouraged his Celestials that someday he would return to the political arena.

❖

CHAPTER EIGHT

Panorama of Ohio Politics
in the Voinovich Era, 1991–

❖

THOMAS SUDDES

❖ George Victor Voinovich, the mayor who said he man-
aged Cleveland into solvency, became Ohio's sixty-fifth governor on
January 14, 1991, after the most expensive gubernatorial campaign in
Ohio history.[1]

The inauguration day was both a homecoming and a comeback for
Voinovich. He won his first public office, state representative, in November 1966 and took his seat in the very building that loomed just east
of the 1991 inaugural platform. Slightly twenty-six months before he formally became Ohio's governor, Voinovich had run a controversial—and
badly losing—campaign for the U.S. Senate, aiming to deny reelection
in 1988 to veteran Democrat Howard M. Metzenbaum. But the 1988 Senate campaign—so misdirected that Metzenbaum actually managed to
carry bedrock Republican Hamilton County—gave Voinovich an essential element in the folkloric syllabus of any recent Ohio governor: at least
one statewide loss before donning the gubernatorial toga.

Voinovich earned an undergraduate degree at Ohio University and,
in 1961, a law degree from Ohio State University. He served in the Ohio
House until 1971, resigning to become Cuyahoga County auditor, succeeding fellow Republican Ralph J. Perk, who had bested Voinovich in
the 1971 Cleveland mayoral primary. Later, Voinovich was elected a
Cuyahoga County commissioner. Then in 1978 he was elected lieutenant

governor on the fourth-term gubernatorial ticket of James A. Rhodes. In 1979, however, after less than a year as lieutenant governor, Voinovich left Columbus to become mayor of Cleveland by defeating incumbent Dennis Kucinich, who had presided over a controversial administration plagued by financial and political problems.

So after ten years as mayor of Cleveland and an unsuccessful campaign against Metzenbaum, Voinovich next set his sights on the governor's chair. First, the crucial Franklin County (Columbus) Republican organization endorsed Voinovich. Then, to avoid a divisive primary, party chiefs eased Cincinnati Republican Robert A. Taft II, who had also been seeking the governorship, into a winning challenge of Democratic secretary of state Sherrod C. Brown. That set the stage for Voinovich to undertake in 1990 what later was considered a close to faultless campaign against the Democratic gubernatorial nominee, Attorney General Anthony J. Celebrezze, Jr.

Voinovich's ten-year mayoral record (1979–89) was a central selling point in his victorious bid for the governorship. Persistent themes of the 1990 Voinovich campaign were his purported managerial skills and financial expertise. Voinovich fostered an independent image as mayor by winning support for a hike in the municipal income tax in 1981, by refusing to endorse (failed) efforts to repeal the mammoth state tax hikes that Democratic governor Richard F. Celeste had pried from the General Assembly in 1983, and by periodically breaking with the Reagan administration over urban issues.[2]

Some critics cited statistics that called into serious question whether the overall quality of life in Cleveland improved during Voinovich's administration. But maintenance of life-quality may have been a task beyond the talents of any mayor of any American city. Far more telling is the apparent intellectual consensus on Voinovich's time at City Hall: "[Voinovich's administration] was successful in restructuring Cleveland's finances, allowing the city to escape from default and remain solvent at a time when both the area's economy and federal funding of local programs were declining."[3]

After the dust settled in the Celebrezze-Voinovich contest, Voinovich's 1990 campaign manager, Curt Steiner, disclosed that Celebrezze—citing George Bush's purported tilt toward rich taxpayers in a congressional budget tiff—had crept to within 6 percentage points of Voinovich. But Celebrezze, during a televised debate, frittered that advantage away by saying he favored reconsideration of long-standing state policy that protects property owners from nonvoted inflation-fueled tax hikes. Voinovich's campaign organization, his consistent antiabortion stance (accompanied by a pledge that he would not actively seek new antiabortion laws from legislators), and the telegenic legacy of Voinovich's bricks-and-mortar record in Cleveland combined with Celebrezze's lackluster campaign to win the office for Voinovich.[4]

On the same day that Voinovich won the governorship, Ohio House Democrats actually increased the number of seats they had in the 1989–90 session, emerging election night with 61 seats, fueling Democratic boldness in 1991 and 1992 in reviewing Voinovich's programs. (By January 1993, however, halfway through Voinovich's term, and in part because of new legislative districts that a Republican-ruled Apportionment Board had drawn for the 1992 midterm election, the number of House Democrats had fallen to 53, a perilously narrow majority and the smallest Democrats had held since winning the House from the Republicans in November 1972.) In the 1990 election, the Senate's 19-to-14 Republican advantage rose to 21 to 12, although the party's comfortable majority was, as later events proved, far from a pushover for Voinovich.

The new governor's inaugural address was a blend of hope and concern, warning of serious state budget problems. But Voinovich said austerity could help Ohio make long-overdue policy choices, using a tag-line—"harder and smarter"—that became an endless (and, some critics said, mindless) theme of his subsequent speeches. "Gone are the days when public officials are measured by how much they spend on a problem. The new realities dictate that public officials are now judged on whether they can work harder and smarter, and do more with less."[5]

Like his predecessor, Democrat Richard F. Celeste, Voinovich's initial task was to accommodate state policy to larger economic and political realities. Perhaps learning a lesson from Celeste's experience, Voinovich took his time in appointing cabinet members. Political pros believed that some of Celeste's hasty appointments in 1983 later haunted his administration, fueling assorted managerial and financial scandals. Also like Celeste, Voinovich faced an Ohio that was rapidly changing economically. Ohio, once among the foremost manufacturing states, instead was becoming a supplier not primarily of goods but of services in a world that more than ever was a transnational marketplace. At times it ranked as high as third in population among the states, but it had lost ground—in wealth, in congressional seats—in the last quarter of the century to southerly and westerly sisters, some of them just howling wildernesses when Ohio became a state in 1803.[6]

In Voinovich's first State of the State address, on March 5, 1991, he urged the General Assembly to cut spending, saying that balancing the state budget—a constitutional requirement in Ohio—should be a top priority. He vowed to boost funding for children's programs and to protect current levels of state aid to education.[7] By "education," it turned out, the governor meant grades K–12, not state colleges and universities. Voinovich also called for enactment of two key programs: privatization of the state liquor monopoly's retail stores and mandatory deposits on beverage containers, a so-called "bottle bill." Legislators of both parties repeatedly balked at those goals, and by early 1993—though some ad hoc privatization had occurred in the liquor monopoly—neither broad privatization, opposed by House Democrats, nor a bottle bill, opposed by Senate Republicans and House members of both parties, was in the law books. And neither appeared to stand a chance of being enacted.

In that first State of the State speech, Voinovich, while not mentioning Celeste by name, alluded critically to the explosion of state spending from 1983 to 1991, a time when Ohio's population was stagnant. "When state government was spending and building and growing like there was no tomorrow, did the lives of the average Ohioan improve by similar proportions? I don't think so," Voinovich told legislators.[8] In the wake of the speech, Republican Senate president Stanley J. Aronoff of Cincinnati and Democratic House speaker Vernal G. Riffe, Jr., of Wheelersburg said Ohio's finances were not as gloomy as Voinovich had said. But even if fiscal differences in early 1991 among the Statehouse trio were only a semantic dispute, later events suggested that Voinovich was substantially correct. And in December 1992, Riffe and Aronoff implicitly conceded Voinovich's point. They and their caucuses agreed to enact a mammoth tax package requested by Voinovich to produce about $420 million a year in new state revenues. Object: To balance the state budget.

Setting the stage for that bipartisan turnabout was Voinovich's first state budget, proposed in March 1991, two months after his inauguration. He called for $26.8 billion in spending during the 1991–93 biennium. But instead of tax hikes, Voinovich proposed a series of "revenue enhancements" and siphoned $150 million from Ohio's $300-million rainy-day fund, a kind of state savings account for budget shortfalls.

The largest "revenue enhancement" Voinovich sought for the 1991–93 budget was abolition of a long-standing law that let retailers keep

1.5 percent of the sales taxes they collect for the state. Repeal would have produced $109.1 million for the state treasury over two years.[9] But the legislature refused to end the so-called "vendors' discount," and only as part of the December 1992 budget deal would Riffe and Aronoff agree to any change, to cutting the "discount" in half to 0.75 percent. The governor's first proposed budget also assumed the state would win a one-time, $47.8-million gain from privatizing retail liquor stores, a move legislators refused to make. And he called for changes in the calculations Ohio used to reimburse nursing homes for Medicaid patients. Legislators, in consort with Voinovich aides, did tackle the so-called Medicaid "formula," and by December 1992 budget data suggested the state had enjoyed some success in slowing down Medicaid spending growth. Because of the sheer size of the Medicaid budget, the largest single-line item in the state's books, a confirmed smaller-rise trend in Medicaid spending over time would have lasting positive impact.

Nevertheless, as Voinovich had warned legislators, Ohio's overall budgetary trends gave pause for thought. For example, in the Ohio fiscal year that began July 1, 1972—the first full year the state had imposed an income tax—total revenue from that source proved to be $373 million. In the Ohio fiscal year that ended June 30, 1991, total collections of the state income tax were $4.2 billion—a 1,000-percent increase in a period when Ohio's population was essentially flat and the Consumer Price Index had increased by less than 200 percent.[10]

Meanwhile, in a development with numerous political and social implications, the state's financial contribution to local public school districts was proportionally rising, even though enrollments fell. For example, in the 1978–79 school year, Ohio's public-school enrollment was about 2.1 million pupils. State "basic aid" to school districts was $452 per pupil. By the 1989–90 school year, there were 1.8 million pupils enrolled in Ohio's public schools—a 15-percent decline—but state per-pupil "basic aid" was $1,285, a 184 percent increase.[11] The statistics suggest that the rise in state aid to public schools was offset by declining contributions to school resources from federal sources and school district property owners.

Concurrently there was explosive growth in a less visible but highly significant sector of state school aid: the money Columbus returns to Ohio communities to make up for property-tax rollbacks—a 10-percent reduction in taxes on all real estate and an extra 2.5 percent cut in taxes on owner-occupied real estate. In the decade of fiscal years that ended

June 30, 1991, for example, state reimbursements for property-tax relief grew from $329 million in fiscal 1981 to $651 million in fiscal 1991, a 98-percent increase. Similarly, during the 1967–68 state budget biennium, for the two years that began July 1, 1967—a budget written by a General Assembly that included freshman representative George V. Voinovich, but one that lacked the state income tax—legislators authorized $2.05 billion in spending from the General Revenue Fund, Ohio's main budget account. Yet by the 1991–92 biennium, the first full biennium of Voinovich's governorship, total appropriations from the General Revenue Fund before subsequent adjustments, cuts, transfers, and corrections were $27.26 billion—a 1,230-percent increase over a twenty-four-year span when the Consumer Price Index had risen by 284 percent.[12]

A key feature of Voinovich's proposed 1991–93 budget was a radical reduction in the state-financed General Assistance Welfare Program for "able-bodied" adults who have no children. Although the Democratic House modified Voinovich's original proposal, both it and the Republican-led Senate agreed to the core of Voinovich's plan. The governor alone, however, was the politician damned for the cuts—not senators and representatives of both parties who had gone along with him.

Among legislators already long in office when Voinovich came to the House as a freshman in 1967 were Aronoff and Riffe. Cincinnati Republican Aronoff had served three terms in the House before he was elected to the Senate on the same day in 1966 that Voinovich had won his House seat. But senior even to Aronoff when Representative Voinovich arrived in Columbus in January 1967 was Riffe, the Scioto County Democrat who had first been elected to the House in November 1958. And when Voinovich returned to Columbus as governor in 1991, Aronoff was president of the Senate—thus leader of the governor's party in the General Assembly—and Riffe, speaker of the House, was leader of the official opposition. Riffe, Ohio's most powerful Democrat—a crucial fundraiser, a member of his party's national committee—was beginning his seventeenth year as speaker. As such, he was potentially a major obstacle to Voinovich's program.

The complex interrelationship of these three leaders set the tone for at least the first two years of Voinovich's four-year term. Adding to the complexity of those dealings were two notable factors. First, two more different personalities could not be imagined, at least in the context of Ohio politics, than Riffe, the product of old Protestant stock that reached back to the Appalachian South below the Ohio River, and Aronoff, a

Harvard-trained lawyer and a descendant of Russian Jews, a member in good standing of sophisticated circles in Cincinnati. Yet because of their thirty years of legislative dealings, in good times and bad, and despite their nominal party differences, Riffe and Aronoff had far more in common, politically and institutionally, than either had in common with their new governor. Second, taking office the same day as Voinovich was a new secretary of state, Robert A. Taft II, scion of one of Ohio's grandest Republican families. His arrival in Columbus meant that Republicans would have a majority on the Apportionment Board, the agency that would redraw Ohio's 33 state Senate districts and 99 Ohio House districts to Republican specifications. That reapportionment was a direct threat to Riffe, whose power rested in part on the Apportionment Board majority that Democrats had usually enjoyed since November 1970. Taft's defeat of Democratic secretary of state Sherrod C. Brown made the board 3 to 2 Republican.

Regardless of partisan goals, and in fact independent of them, Ohio's political landscape was transforming itself because of inexorable economic and demographic changes, spawning growth in Republican areas, and decline in Democratic areas but also presenting Voinovich with a legislature much different than the one he joined in 1967. For example, in the 1965–66 House session, a chamber of 137 members rather than the 99-member session Voinovich joined in 1967, only 7 state representatives, or 5.1 percent, were female. Only 2 of 137 state representatives in 1965 and 1966 were black. (One was future Cleveland mayor Carl Stokes).[13] But in a 1991–92 House of 99 members—the first session of Voinovich's governorship—there were 16 female state representatives, composing 16.2 percent of the House's roll, and 11 black state representatives, 11.1 percent of the House membership. (At the November 1992 election, voters sent 12 blacks and 23 women—13 Democrats, 10 Republicans—to the Ohio House.) And House Republicans later in 1992 chose Representative Jo Ann Davidson, of Reynoldsburg, a Columbus suburb, as leader of their caucus, the first woman ever elevated to such a House post in Ohio—potentially Ohio's first female House speaker, when and if the GOP captures the House.

Among the tensions of the Riffe-Aronoff-Voinovich triangle was the governor's evident frustration at the apparent independence of Aronoff's 21 Senate Republicans (20 after the November 1992 election). Those differences led on several occasions to private caucuses—respectful, if not altogether cordial—between the Republican governor and his nominal party allies in the upper house. Besides the "bottle bill," which was eventually junked, Voinovich's bid to raise so-called "sin taxes" on tobacco products and alcoholic beverages also hit brick walls. Ostensibly, the sin taxes faltered because of their regressive impact on blue-collar voters. In fact, and in political reality, legislators of both parties opposed the taxes because of potential negative impacts on retailers in the Cincinnati area, who already were being undercut by price competition from low-tax Kentucky, a tobacco and distilling state.

Because of the Senate's peculiar traditions, gubernatorial-senatorial relationships in Ohio require a governor to placate caucuses. Both Riffe and his House GOP counterparts periodically caucus with their party colleagues, but those rare House meetings typically are little more than glorified pep rallies or grievance sessions. In the Senate, however, both among Democrats and Republicans, "King Caucus" still reigns. Lengthy and secret Senate caucuses are a routine feature of the days in which the Senate is in formal session.

Another feature of gubernatorial-legislative dealings was mutual frustration, if not mutual incomprehension, fostered by Voinovich's long-distance volleys at legislators. For example, Voinovich startled both friends and foes in October 1991 by telling reporters at the Midwestern Governors' Conference, meeting in Sioux City, Iowa, that he supported term limits on Ohio General Assembly members. The governor, himself a legislator from 1967 to 1971, said legislative staffs had "grown and grown and grown," and he assailed "special interest influence" that swayed legislative deliberations. Aronoff, back in Ohio, was caught flat-footed by his party leader's comments. He knew Voinovich had long supported limiting the terms of all statewide executive officers but not state legislators. "That's something I hadn't heard," Aronoff said. A day later Riffe accused Voinovich of "using partisan politics at its ugliest" to bully the legislature into rubber-stamping executive decisions.[14] It was "the ultimate in hypocrisy," he said, for Voinovich to question the size of the legislature's staffing when costs of the governor's office had steadily increased over the years.

But Voinovich's Iowa remarks evidently reflected public opinion in Ohio. In November 1992 Ohioans overwhelmingly ratified a term-limits initiative that extended to other statewide executive officers—and state and federal senators and representatives—the same term limits that Voinovich and all Ohio governors had faced since November 1954: no more than eight consecutive years in a statewide executive or General

Assembly office (twelve years for U.S. senators). Legislative leaders, especially Riffe, intent on reelecting majorities the same month that voters ratified term limits, were generally mute about the term-limit proposals. When asked, however, Riffe did say that if terms were going to be limited, limits should apply to the terms of all Ohio officeholders—from township trustee on up.

Months after the referendum, speaking to a meeting of the Ohio Chamber of Commerce, Riffe finally emerged from cover, calling term limits "a mistake." The speaker said the limits would deter good candidates from seeking public office and, in Washington, would reduce Ohio's influence in a Congress where power is still mostly based on seniority.[15] Riffe suggested that the chamber (or similar statewide Ohio membership organizations) might eventually launch a repeal drive, though there was no evidence they would.

Additionally, Voinovich, who predictably—but unsuccessfully—had called for limits on the political contributions made by labor unions, also had publicly criticized what he implied were cozy ties between business lobbyists and legislators of both parties. Voinovich's accusation was not one expected from a Republican governor. And even when Governor Celeste, during his 1983–91 administration, assailed business interests, and that was rare enough, Celeste's darts were usually aimed at tobacco and liquor lobbyists, politically correct punching bags in Ohio.

By midsummer 1992, Voinovich publicly expressed his aggravation with the legislature's slow response to his requests. As before, he warned skeptical legislators that he would marshal public opinion against them, a threat made before and, as then, never carried out: "We are taking the case to the people. We came to change state government and, by God, we are going to change state government." The governor's repeated threats to rally public opinion, an unobserved vow, prompted one veteran Democrat, Senator Harry Meshel of Youngstown, just before his election as Democratic state chairman, to call Voinovich the "or-else" governor. Voinovich, Meshel said, started with "the 'bottle bill, or else,' then it was the 'sin taxes [on tobacco and alcoholic beverages] or else'; and then it was 'sell all the [state] liquor stores or else.' He's 'or-else'd' himself to death."[16]

One source of Voinovich's frustration was House speaker Riffe. Even as James A. Rhodes dominated Ohio's executive branch for a generation, Vern Riffe, who announced in early 1994 that he would retire when his House term ended on December 31, 1994, was and remained a colossus of Statehouse politics. Born in June 1925 and elected to the House in 1958, Riffe, the second-longest-serving member of the 1993–94 General Assembly, but the session's longest-serving House member, had been House speaker since January 1975, an Ohio record. Although hardly meant as flattery, consumer advocate Ralph Nader has called Riffe the most powerful floor leader in any American legislative body, including Congress. Lecturing in Riffe's district at Portsmouth's Shawnee State University, Nader said, "Take all the voters of Ohio who send representatives to the House—they have less power over what that House does than you do in this district." During a fight over workers' compensation legislation in 1987, an Ohio United Auto Workers leader denounced Riffe as "dictator of Ohio." And the Scioto County commissioners posted a road sign in the right-of-way of U.S. Route 23, at the county line, where motorists driving from Columbus to Portsmouth learned that they weren't just entering Scioto County; they were in "Vern Riffe Country."[17]

Riffe's mammoth political fund-raising reception, held annually on or near his June 26 birthday, has become a political folk-event. He originated the party in order to win and retain support as the number-one Ohio House Democrat: speaker. Similarly, every other autumn since the 1970s, Riffe has held a giant fund-raising dinner for members of the House's Democratic caucus, which, besides Riffe's House district, is the constitutional base of his political power. In recent years, annual receipts from the birthday party, which total close to $1 million, have been first banked in Riffe's House district campaign committee and then parceled out as needed to help Democrats running for the Ohio House (and, sometimes, for other offices). A *Plain Dealer* column set the stage for the 1991 gathering: "What amounts to the Statehouse's senior prom is tonight in northeast Columbus. [Riffe]—and a few thousand of his closest friends—will be celebrating the Speaker for Life's 66th birthday. . . . You'll see just as much of Ohio's political society in one night as if you'd stood for a year at Broad and High streets in Columbus—the crossroads of Ohio. Admission is $400 per person. . . . And no, this isn't a revel without a cause. The goal is re-election next year of a Democratic Ohio House."[18]

A visit to one of Riffe's birthday parties gives spectators an unscientific but peerless peek at the issueless, cross-party, coalitional, ad hoc politics that is at once the key feature and key determinant of Riffe's power.

Don Hanni, Democratic boss of Mahoning County. Janet Folger, of the Ohio Right to Life Society—as well as women (and men) of the 'pro-choice' persuasion. Lobbyists for the banks, great and small. George V. Voinovich, governor of Ohio, Paul Mifsud, Voinovich's viceroy. Theodore (Ted) Celeste, an Ohio State University trustee and brother of Ohio's most recent Democratic governor. Lobbyists for the unions. Lobbyists for the insurance companies. Lobbyists for the sick, the poor—and for children. Hilljacks and urbanites. Democrats, Republicans and independents. And where, prithee, did we see these grand and glorious Ohioans? The line formed in front of St. Peter's check-in desk on Judgment Day? No, but almost the same thing: the throng last week at Vern Riffe's mega-galactic, $400 per person 66th birthday party, the largest yet.[19]

A key question is the extent to which Riffe was the product or the creator of the system he has come to symbolize. Riffe held the House's gavel only by the sufferance of the other fifty-two Democrats in his caucus, at least since he—and they—unseated one-term Democratic speaker A. G. Lancione in 1974. Riffe took the heat when newspapers and the good-government reformers attacked the House for its actions and inactions. But, in return for the unspoken bargain that gave Riffe power, and rank-and-file Democrats political protection, House Democrats were expected to forget ideology, other than caucus loyalty, at the House chamber's door.

Still, as a matter of practical politics, Riffe had consistently taken into account—some might say co-opted—black or female Democrats in the House. For years, a key Riffe lieutenant was the late C. J. McLin, of Dayton, patriarch of Ohio's black politicians, and Riffe invariably had among members of his leadership circle several women from the House Democratic caucus, such as Cuyahoga County commissioner Mary O. Boyle, when she was a House member, and Representative Jane L. Campbell, Boyle's successor in the House. Still, the politics of Riffe's House was the politics of coalitional pragmatism, not ideology. Thus, for example, it was a Democratic House that ratified the Equal Rights Amendment and that made Dr. Martin Luther King's birthday a state holiday. But it was also a Democratic House that agreed to require women in Ohio to wait twenty-four hours before obtaining an abortion and that reinstated the death penalty, even though black defendants are believed to be disproportionately sentenced to death. (Ohio's last execution was in 1963; the prisoner was a white male.)

Riffe's advantages in winning and maintaining power were a combination of natural and historical factors. First, he had a prodigious memory—not just for names and faces, but also for the details of legislation. Second, although he slowed down somewhat on the orders of his physicians, Riffe's first dozen years as speaker were typified by long work days, which included weekends. After graduation from Scioto County's Glenwood High School in 1943, Riffe served in the Air Force's Mediterranean theater during the Second World War, rising to the rank of staff sergeant. Beginning in 1947, Riffe's father, Vernal G., Sr., began a twenty-three-year stretch as New Boston's mayor. He had briefly been in the New Boston police before becoming a grocer, and in 1940 he was appointed New Boston's municipal safety-service director. After the war Riffe Jr.—known as "Little Vern," "Junior," or "June," to distinguish him from his father—clerked at the family's grocery. From 1950 to 1958, he served as a New Boston fire fighter. Meanwhile, in 1954, Riffe opened the insurance agency he still owns.[20]

In 1958, Riffe was elected to the House as Scioto County's representative. As a House newcomer in the 1959–60 session, Riffe was silent, if watchful, one fellow freshman said. Lieutenant Governor Myrl Shoemaker, who entered the House with Riffe in January 1959, said, "Vern sat in the back of the [House Chamber] with his little bow tie on and didn't say a word for 10 years."[21] After years of quiet, behind-the-scenes politicking—being the "available man" for virtually any party task—Riffe became Lancione's deputy in the 1973–74 session, the first House session Democrats had controlled since 1959–60. Riffe's day-to-day management of the 1973–74 caucus set the stage for Lancione's less-than-fully-voluntary retirement from the speakership and Riffe's succession.

One prize that always eluded Riffe, assuming he ever really wanted it, was the governorship. As early as February 1975, only a month into his speakership, there was press speculation that a run for governor was Riffe's near-term goal. There was additional speculation in 1977 about a Riffe governorship in the run-up to the eventual (but failed) challenge that fellow Democrat Celeste aimed at Rhodes in 1978. And early in 1982, as Celeste was gearing up again for the governorship, Riffe and Cincinnati financier Marvin L. Warner, who was later imprisoned as one result of Ohio's 1985 savings and loan crisis, jointly announced that one or the other of them would seek the governorship that year.[22]

The election of Voinovich and Taft prompted House Republicans to declare a political war against Riffe and his Democratic caucus, which had been in power continuously since November 1972. Nevertheless, by mid-September 1992, six weeks before the November election, campaign committees controlled by Riffe had on hand fourteen times the money that the House Republican campaign committee reported. When the dust cleared in November 1992, Riffe emerged with 53 Democratic Ohio House seats, the narrowest majority of his speakership. (The previous low-water mark had been 56 seats, in the 1981–82 session after Ronald Reagan's 1980 landslide victory over Jimmy Carter.)

While far from the "boroughmongers" of Hanoverian England's par-liaments,[23] Aronoff and Riffe were uniquely positioned—because of se-niority and fund-raising skills—to determine not only the outcome of legislation but also the direction of their followers' careers. The House speaker and Senate president have significant patronage powers to place loyal ears and eyes throughout state government. The legislature's patronage power is usually seen only as a feature of the Ohio Senate's constitutional right to block, for any reason or for none, practically any gubernatorial appointee (except, notably, judges). But beyond ap-pointing standing House and Senate committees (directly by the House speaker, indirectly by the Senate president), which can bestow extra salaries on legislators, the two leaders control at least some appoint-ments to more than 120 special committees and state boards, councils, and commissions. Key examples include the legislature's own Joint Committee on Agency Rule Review, the Turnpike Commission, the Arts Council, the Board of Regents, the Power Siting Board, and scores more.

This power is one reason why the four legislative caucus campaign committees—Senate Republicans and Democrats, House Democrats and Republicans—reported spending a total of $4.8 million in 1990. Of that, a combined $3.5 million, was spent by caucus committees that are con-trolled by Riffe and Aronoff. Riffe's own Eighty-ninth (now Ninety-second) House District campaign committee raised $1.28 million in 1990, spent $2.6 million, and still had $962,000 left over.[24]

The story of the 1991–92 legislative session is largely a tale of a new governor and two wily, veteran legislative leaders trying to live with each other. After the traditional new-term honeymoon, Riffe—and, to a lesser degree, Aronoff—let it be known that Voinvich's proposals would have a much better chance of reaching the law books if the governor, like Rhodes and Celeste, would confide in them and seek their advice.

Contributing to the legislative-gubernatorial tension were strained relations between Aronoff, who as the legislature's top Republican was vital to enactment of Voinovich's program, and Republican state headquarters at the former Norwich Hotel, a block east of the Statehouse. The strain between Voinovich and Aronoff came because attacks by Republican regulars on Riffe threatened to sour the long-standing entente between Riffe and Aronoff. Riffe believed that, if Aronoff persuaded the governor, Voinovich could muzzle Republican state chairman Robert T. Bennett—a belief not all operatives of either party shared.

Meanwhile, as Meshel noted later, to Voinovich's intense frustration, legislators of both parties and chambers balked at Voinovich's demand for a law imposing deposits on beverage containers, Democrats spurned his appeal for privatization of the (unionized) state liquor monopoly, and, finally, both Democrats and Republican conservatives initially teamed up to block Voinovich's plea for higher state excise taxes on alcohol and tobacco—the demand of a governor who had won office in part by campaigning against new taxes.

Perhaps the low point of executive-legislative relations was during 1992, when, repeating an intermittent practice some earlier governors winked at, legislators quietly passed a special bill to allow the rerun of a local-option liquor election in Franklin County. At issue were precincts being developed into luxury housing by billionaire clothier Leslie H. Wexner, a major contributor to both parties: voters had turned down a liquor license for a plush new club on Wexner's property, and absent the special bill a rerun could not be held for several years. After the liquor bill was exposed simultaneously by the *Plain Dealer* and the *Columbus Dispatch,* Voinovich vetoed it, drawing quiet complaints of double-cross from Aronoff and Riffe, who said Voinovich aides had indicated no objections to the bill.

Another fissure between the governor and the legislative leaders came about fifteen months into Voinovich's term. Because of population losses recorded by the 1990 census, Riffe and Aronoff wrote a bipartisan, "agreed" bill, using a Senate-House conference, to reduce Ohio's congressional districts to 19, from the 21 the state had from 1982 through 1990. But House Republican conservatives, cheered on by Voinovich, blocked the compromise, despite Aronoff's coauthorship.

Moreover, the House Republicans acted in de facto coalition with the House's black Democrats, who had objections of their own. For example, black Democrats believed the congressional map plan could be reconfigured, most likely in the Columbus area, to create a district that gave African American voters greater influence there, even if a black-majority district was mathematically impossible. Defection of the House's 11 black Democrats meant Riffe had at most 50 votes for the re-districting bill—enough to pass it, but not enough to override the veto that Voinovich threatened.

A key target of Republican conservatives was Democratic former sec-retary of state Sherrod C. Brown, who was opposed by state GOP leader Bennett and Bennett's aides. Republicans feared that if the original "agreed" congressional remap were not changed, Brown could win a U.S. House seat in the outer Cleveland suburbs. Nevertheless, when all the huffing and puffing ended, and some changes in the map were made in northern Ohio and elsewhere, Brown won the redrawn Thirteenth U.S. House District in November 1992. (As if in counterpoint, Republi-can newcomer Martin Hoke retired veteran Democratic representative Mary Rose Oakar in her redrawn district.)

But the fate of Congress, as disliked by state legislators as it is by vot-ers, was not central to Riffe's and Aronoff's frustrations. The central issue was that Voinovich was believed to be unilaterally changing State-house etiquette by stoking opposition to a remap that both Riffe and Aronoff had supported.

Earlier, though the battle was confined to the courts, the two political parties had begun to spar over "reapportionment." The Ohio Constitu-tion requires reapportionment after every decennial federal census to conform the 99 House and 33 Senate districts to population shifts. And the task was to be undertaken by the Apportionment Board, a five-member body with a new Republican majority composed of Voinovich, Aronoff, and Taft. In that debate, Republican solidarity held.

The initial Republican reapportionment, unveiled in the autumn of 1991, was revised after a special panel of three federal judges, voting along party lines, demanded additional evidence to justify Republicans' creation of some black-majority House districts. The three-judge panel, again along party lines, rejected a revised version of the GOP plan, at-tempted to have its own legislative map drawn, and, for a time, threat-ened to reschedule state elections. Meanwhile, in a 4-to-3 party-line decision, the Republican-led Ohio Supreme Court upheld the remap. The U.S. Supreme Court blocked the federal three-judge panel's orders, letting the redrawn districts be used for the 1992 election. Finally, in mid-winter 1993, months after the general election, the U.S. Supreme Court unanimously upheld the remap of General Assembly districts and chided the three-judge panel, saying the panel's two Democratic judges had incorrectly interpreted federal voting-rights law.

For all the Democratic outcries about the Republican map, drawn by the Senate's chief Republican aide, James R. Tilling, the real problem for Democrats was Ohio's arguable Republican tilt—something the Democrats' 1971 and 1981 remaps had successfully bucked through thoroughly creative cartography. (Although Arkansas Democrat Bill Clinton carried Ohio in the 1992 presidential contest—besting George Bush by 90,000 votes, and taking 40.2 percent of the vote to Bush's 38.3 percent and H. Ross Perot's 21.0 percent—such a Democratic presidential victory was the exception in Ohio.) To show the skill of the Democrats' 1971 legislative remap, for example, Republicans observed that on the same day in 1972 that Republican Richard M. Nixon was swamping Democrat George S. McGovern in Ohio (and virtually everywhere else), Ohio Democrats—partly through a crafty remap—grabbed 13 Republican-held Ohio House seats, giving Democrats a 58-to-41 House majority, which they have held with varying margins every election year since.

Almost 140 years ago, Ohio was among the states that gave its electoral votes to the Republican party's first presidential nominee, John C. Frémont, in 1856. Ohio did not support its first Democratic presidential nominee until 1912 (Wilson, due to the William Howard Taft–Theodore Roosevelt split); the only other years that Democratic presidential nominees carried Ohio were in 1916 (Wilson's second term); 1932, 1936, 1940 (Franklin Roosevelt); 1948 (Truman); 1964 (Lyndon Johnson); 1976 (Carter, by only 11,116 votes, less than one vote per precinct); and 1992 (Clinton). Partisan leanings aside, population shifts made some parts of the 1991 Republican reapportionment virtually inevitable. As one constitutional father saw it, the General Assembly's primary task was to reconcile competing regional, not necessarily partisan, interests—the legislature as threshing floor, not assembly line. Said delegate Charles Reemelin, a German-born farmer from Hamilton County, and an author of Ohio's 1851 constitution, "The people of the Western Reserve are different from the people of the southern part of Ohio. They have their peculiar notions; but they cannot, under our government, get those opinions into the shape of law, without passing the scrutiny of the people south of the National Road. And it is this very spirit of our institutions, meeting each other in the common arena, for the determination of our legal enactments, which gives us, in my opinion, better laws."[25]

This suggests the 1991 apportionment of General Assembly seats may pose an additional issue. While today's differences between northern Ohioans and Ohioans "south of the National Road" may be as acute as they were 140 years ago, there are relatively fewer northerners now than in the 1960s. That may give southern Ohio, more conservative than the north, greater weight in the direction of state policy. For example, in the House elected in November 1966, Cuyahoga County (Cleveland) had 17 seats. Coupled with other House districts assigned to similar, Democratic-leaning metropolitan counties, urban northern Ohio had 30.2 districts in a 99-district House—almost 44 percent more seats than the 21 assigned to urban and suburban Republican-leaning southern Ohio (the Columbus, Cincinnati, and Dayton areas).

The 1991 reapportionment illustrates the relative shift of regional representation spurred by population declines in the industrial north and growth in the service-sector south. First used for the November 1992 election, the 1991 plan assigns 12.9 Ohio House districts to Cuyahoga County, a 24-percent decline from the 17 districts the county had when Voinovich arrived in January 1967. Those Cleveland area districts and districts assigned to neighboring northern Ohio metropolitan regions give the northern and urban areas 24.2 House districts for the General Assembly sessions from January 1993 through December 2002, a 20-percent decline in seats from the northern Ohio urban region's 1967–68 holdings. Notably, however, counties in the Columbus, Cincinnati, and Dayton areas will have 22.1 House seats during the same 1993–2002 period, conferring practical parity at the Statehouse between the Democrat-leaning north and GOP-leaning south.

But once-a-decade apportionment is a lagging indicator of demographic trends. Ohio's in-state population shift was compounded by job-growth in Columbus and Cincinnati, and the desire of new industries to dodge unionization by building rural, "greenfield" factories in central Ohio (and also, perhaps, to draw on southern Ohio's markedly cheaper electricity). The political and social consequences of these trends have not been fully assessed, said one policy review by scholars.

Given enough time, the outward expansion of urban areas ultimately would drain most cities. Over the past 40 years, Cleveland's population went from its peak of 914,000 to 500,000. This study shows that by the year 2000, the city's population could be near 400,000. By the year 2030 . . . Cleveland would be essentially emptied of its population, leaving mainly the poorest of the poor in the city. Youngstown would be emptied by 2030 as well, Akron would be diminished to half its current size. Change in a single year is small and not noticeable; the cumulative effect over several decades becomes very sizable. . . . The process of suburbanization in Ohio has reached the point where its dynamics, its impacts . . . and its future should be given serious attention.[26]

In his second State of the State address, on January 15, 1992, Governor Voinovich focused on balancing a budget that was believed likely to be $457 million short by June 30, 1992—the end of the fiscal year—and on the creation of new jobs. "The only person who has used the word 'jobs' more than Gov. Voinovich is [former] Gov. [James A.] Rhodes," Aronoff said later.[27]

Besides job promotion—realized, at least nominally, in an October 1992 package of economic development laws—the legislature's key task in the wake of Voinovich's speech was to find budget-balancing revenues without raising taxes. Riffe and Aronoff had vetoed higher tobacco and alcohol taxes and the abolition of the vendor's discount. "In my judgment, at this time the budget can be balanced without [tax hikes]," Riffe said. "We should exhaust every means we have to find revenues . . . without raising taxes."[28] The table had been set for chronic budget troubles long before, by the stop-and-start tax policies of Governor Celeste and legislators of both parties from 1983 to 1991. The result was that Celeste himself, before turning his office over to Voinovich, had to make various midterm cuts in the 1989–91 budget. Those preexisting budget problems, with six months of Celeste's 1989–91 budget left, were complicated by fears within both the House Democratic and Senate Republican caucuses about the then-unseen reapportionment of legislative districts. In combination, those factors made budget building during Voinovich's first year a perilous task. Indeed, budget cuts sounded like drumrolls across Capitol Square. First, in February 1991, less than a month in office, Voinovich cut spending $127 million. Further cuts came in December 1991 and, climactically, in July 1992.[29] In fact, for a variety of reasons, the 1991–93 budget was not enacted by legislators until mid-July, after the expiration on June 30 of the 1989–91 budget. Although the delay caused no meaningful disruption of state government, it was the first time the budget had been enacted late since the early 1980s.

On July 1, 1992, the first day of the new fiscal year, Voinovich cut planned state spending by $315.7 million, a reduction that was about 15 percent smaller than he had threatened. The cut amounted to an overall reduction of about 3 percent in the $10.93 billion in the new year's planned spending. Even so, actual state spending, year-to-year, was still expected to be about 3.9 percent greater than in the 1991–92 fiscal year. But that 3-percent overall reduction understated an important political reality. Some programs—spending on grades K–12 education, for example—were indeed spared any reductions in planned spending; but other programs suffered relatively (though not absolutely) big reductions. For example, more than half the $315.7-million July 1992 reduction was produced by withholding $170.2 million in state assistance that state-aided colleges and universities had expected to get during the year. Riffe had said there was no immediate need for the cuts because the budget could not, in fact, be out of balance on the very first day of the fiscal year. The total that counted was the one on the budget's final day, June 30, 1993.[30] And, as Voinovich honed the scalpel, Aronoff politely but publicly asked Voinovich to minimize cuts in state college and university subsidies.

But in effectively rejecting the advice of both Aronoff, his fellow Republican, and opposition leader Riffe, Voinovich departed from the more accommodationist politics of Celeste and Rhodes—something Voinovich himself acknowledged. "The new politics is lay it on the table, do the very best you can, tell the people the truth, and they'll understand," he said. One unnamed Voinovich ally put it more bluntly: "Don't you get it yet? It doesn't make any difference what Stan and Vern think. It's what the people think. And the people are on our side." While the governor's popularity, as indicated by public opinion surveys, remained relatively high, a Democratic critic—also unidentified—gave his party's side of the argument. "What have we got to show for a year-and-a-half of George Voinovich? The answer is zero. Tell me one thing he has done as governor of Ohio, other than try to raise taxes and cut government services to people?"[31]

Finally, however, after the November 1992 legislative elections, run by using GOP-drawn districts, the Voinovich–General Assembly standoff began to wane. First, speaking through state budget director R. Gregory Browning, Voinovich said he could hold further cuts in planned spending to $50 million if the Senate and House would agree to raise roughly $200 million in new taxes for the remaining six months of the 1992–93 fiscal year. He also indicated that if the state had more than $70 million in reserve on the last day of the fiscal year, any surplus greater than about $70 million would be deposited in Ohio's rainy-day fund, which by then had only 14 cents left in it. As well, the governor promised that any additional reductions in planned spending would not be imposed on either state aid to schools grades K–12 or to public colleges and universities. He publicized a series of cost-saving measures, not requiring legislation, that he had ordered, and finally—and perhaps most importantly—the governor began intense private talks with Riffe and Aronoff.

These private talks resulted in enactment in mid-December 1992 of a package that would raise $194.5 million for the six months through June 30, 1993, and an additional $858.7 million for the subsequent two-year, 1993–95 budget. As both a bait and a sweetener, the tax package, including a reduction to 0.75 percent in the embattled 1.5-percent sales tax vendor "discount," was folded into a two-year state construction bill to win the votes of wavering or fearful legislators. When the legislature, scripted by Riffe and Aronoff, produced the bill the governor requested, Voinovich lavishly praised people who had previously stymied him on other fronts. Thanking Riffe, Aronoff and other leaders by name, Voinovich said, "The passage of [the tax bill] was a team effort of public officials who worked together to save educational cuts of $164.6 million. . . . I know that it was a difficult vote for many [legislators] but I firmly believe the people . . . appreciate their willingness to make tough but necessary decisions."[32]

Early in February 1993, Voinovich and Browning unveiled Voinovich's proposed 1993–95 state budget. Voinovich aides said the $30.8 billion plan sought the "third-lowest biennial spending increase in 25 years." Requested spending would rise 5.6 percent in the year beginning June 30, 1993, and 6.6 percent in the second year, Voinovich said.[33] The governor called his proposal "a new paradigm" for Ohio budgeting that would "improve quality and lower costs" in the delivery of state services.

Indeed, Voinovich apparently had reined in state spending growth. For example, state spending on higher education in the 1991–93 budget was expected to rise 4.2 percent over Celeste's last, 1989–91, budget; on grades K–12, 4.4 percent; on welfare, 13.3 percent; and on prisons, 18.1 percent. In contrast, in the wake of the economy-wracked Rhodes years, Celeste's first budget—from mid-1983 through mid-1985—had hiked state spending 29.2 percent for state-aided colleges and universities; 26.1 percent for grades K–12; 19.4 percent for welfare; and 33.5 percent for prisons.[34] The spending hikes proposed by Celeste and approved by the General Assembly in 1983 were a natural consequence of needs neglected during the wretched state economy of the later Rhodes years. Nevertheless, even as Celeste's budget (and massive tax hikes) fueled expectations of ever-greater state spending, Voinovich's first two budgets—1991–93 and 1993–95—tried with some success to impose a new regime of targeted growth.

The December 1992 budget-balancing bill was a tour de force for Riffe. By orchestrating a lame-duck budget-balancing bill, in partnership with Aronoff, Speaker Riffe spared Democrats who would arrive as House freshmen in January 1993 a politically treacherous tax vote; cemented his cross-party alliance with Aronoff; got Voinovich to swallow traditional Democratic "soak the rich" dogma by increasing income taxes on wealthy Ohioans to offset blue-collar "sin taxes"; and rounded up votes from Republicans and lame-duck Democrats in the House, ensuring that 14 incumbent Democrats, who would also have seats in the 1993–95 session, could safely vote no and the tax bill would still pass. As a *Plain Dealer* column expressed it, "Last week showed that Riffe, despite GOP-drawn House districts, a siege of illness and, starting Jan. 4 [1993] the smallest Democratic majority of his speakership, could still parlay timing, luck and country-boy scheming [to pass the budget-balancer while protecting Democrats.] . . . If this is political failure, who needs success?"[35]

Voinovich's third State of the State speech, on January 26, 1993, was long on generalities but short on specifics, some legislators said. The governor repeated pledges to reform education, the federal-state Medicaid health-care plan, and the workers' compensation system. The latter pledge set the stage for a collision with Democrats, whose traditional alliance with organized labor required them to be highly suspicious that reforms proposed by a Republican governor would be tilted to favor premium-paying employers, not benefit-claiming employees. Said one report of the 1993 State of the State address, "Voinovich's speech gazed back at 1992 more than it peered into [1993]. Some lawmakers said they were left hungering for more. Others said Voinovich's broadly sketched speech set just the right tone."[36]

As if to sum up the first half of Voinovich's term, the Toledo *Blade* compiled a list of forty-two specific campaign promises Voinovich had made in 1990, ranging from limiting tuition increases at state colleges and universities (not accomplished) to creating a veterans' affairs office (delivered as promised). *Blade* reporters said they had determined that Voinovich had, halfway through his term, fulfilled nine of the forty-two campaign promises he made in 1990: "Nine for 42, or 21%. For a quarterback, those passing statistics lead to a seat on the bench. For a basketball player, those shooting statistics encourage more passing. For a goalie, that goal per shot ratio is a ticket to the minors. For a baseball player, that batting average is a pitcher's. But what does nine for 42 mean for a governor? You're the coach. You decide."[37]

With the new revenues provided by the December 1992 tax hike, programs—not funding—were central issues of the otherwise tepid Senate and House debates on the proposed 1993–95 budget. Among the budget's more pronounced programmatic shifts was to make a greater part of the state's environmental operations fee-based, financed by fees for assorted permits and services. The budget, enacted on time after a Senate-House conference proposed a compromise acceptable to both parties and chambers, provided for $30.8 billion in spending for the two years that began July 1, 1993. As much as anything, the 1993–95 budget was an agenda-setter for the 1994 elections.[38]

The biggest legislative-executive joust of Voinovich's third year was over his bid to "reform" Ohio's workers' compensation system, a state monopoly that has long been a concern of business interests, including newspaper publishers, and injured workers whose unpaid claims got lost by the system's Victorian-era business methods. After months of haggling, a compromise reform bill was finally enacted in July 1993, but it was opposed by organized labor, all Senate Democrats, and some but not all Democrats in the House. Riffe, to get a bill that would placate Voinovich while letting House Democrats from union-heavy districts safely vote no, in effect forced Voinovich to woo House Republican votes for a bill that did not go nearly so far as some GOP conservatives wanted. Whether the compensation reform bill would really lower costs to employers and improve services to workers remained to be seen. The bill did not, after all, formally make the compensation system's board any more accountable to Voinovich than it had been, something for which a substantive reform bill might seem to call. But there was one certainty about the measure: the reform bill would surely figure in Voinovich's 1994 reelection resume. And reelection, not necessarily reform, appeared to be a key goal of the summertime exercise.

But as the workers' compensation debate receded (at the Statehouse, if not in corporate boardrooms), a controversy about legislative ethics broke over Capitol Square like a September storm. At issue were speaking and appearances fees allegedly sought or accepted by a powerful House Democrat, Representative Paul H. Jones of Ravenna, chairman of the House Health and Retirement Committee, which oversees legislation dealing with Ohio's immense health-care industry. Compounding the controversy—some said spawning it as payback—was a concurrent and titanic Statehouse battle over a Jones bill, backed by Cleveland-based Blue Cross and Blue Shield Mutual, to force the merger of Ohio's three historic Blue Cross plans into one statewide company.

The House Legislative Ethics Committee, though it severely reprimanded Jones, cleared him of any illegality. Nevertheless, for Ohio's long-suffering reformers, there were sunbeams amid the Statehouse clouds. By January 1994 the uproar had resulted in a broad new legislative ethics law whose scope would have been unthinkable before the fingering of Jones. The ethics reform law "will require most public officials, including state lawmakers, to disclose all their sources of income and list the amounts in general ranges. In addition, state legislators will be forbidden to accept speaking fees, known as honoraria, and will be limited to $75 a year in free meals from each lobbyist. The legislation will also require lobbyists to file detailed reports on money spent on lawmakers, including free trips."[39]

On the statewide front, Voinovich, cloaking himself with the same "teflon" that coated recent Republican presidents, opened election year 1994 with a State of the State address that embraced a school-technology plan he had partially vetoed in July 1991—when Democrats had proposed it. Then, on January 14, in Ohio's most momentous political development in a generation, Democratic House speaker Riffe revealed that he would leave the House when his term expired. Despite claims that General Assembly incumbents were an endangered species, 89 of the 99 House members—44 of the 46 Republicans and 45 of the 53 Democrats—filed reelection petitions. But the retirement of Riffe, the "godfather of Ohio politics,"[40] called into question how many of Riffe's godchildren would survive the energetic offense that House Republicans planned for the fall 1994 election campaign.

House GOP strategists were counting on a surge from what they hoped would be an easy reelection victory by Governor Voinovich. The Democratic gubernatorial nomination fell to a dogged but underfunded state senator from Dover in Tuscarawas County, Robert Burch. He faced a decidedly uphill struggle, prompting Republican optimism that a House majority could be built on what they hoped would be a Voinovich landslide.

No matter how the gubernatorial election turns out, Ohio history will be made in the lieutenant governor's race. If Voinovich wins, the state will have its first woman in the number-two job because the governor named Nancy P. Hollister, a former Marietta mayor, as his 1994 running mate. Hollister, who was a two-term councilwoman before becoming mayor in 1984, joined the Voinovich administration in 1991 as director of the Governor's Office of Appalachia.[41]

And if Senator Burch should pull an upset, Ohio will get its first African American lieutenant governor in lawyer Peter Lawson Jones, a former Shaker Heights city councilman and vice mayor. In announcing the selection of Jones, Burch declared, "We are like another Democratic team that took on another 'invincible' George [a reference to President Bush's 1992 defeat]. Yes, we are Davids fighting Goliath, and proud of it."[42]

But pending the history that Ohio voters were expected to make in November, Voinovich made history on his own. Early in 1994 he named former Cincinnati mayor J. Kenneth Blackwell, a fellow Republican, as Ohio's first black statewide executive officer, to succeed state treasurer Mary Ellen Withrow, a Democrat appointed treasurer of the United States by President Clinton.

As Governor Voinovich readied his campaign arsenal to demonstrate that he's no George Bush, a host of other spirited statewide contests were shaping up for the fall, including the battle for the U.S. Senate seat being vacated by the retirement of Democrat Howard Metzenbaum. Only one thing was absolutely certain about November 8, 1994: Ohio voters would go to the polls and chart the next chapter in the state's political life.

❖

CHAPTER NINE

The News Media
& Ohio Politics

❖

SHARON CROOK WEST

❖ It was a hot summer afternoon and Governor James A. Rhodes was bored. So he sent for his favorite entertainment troupe—the Statehouse press corps. There was no news, but Rhodes made some up. Afterward, as reporters trooped back through the Statehouse rotunda, one of them started singing "Send in the Clowns." It became the theme song for the rest of the governor's term.

Reporters who covered Rhodes's second eight years as governor describe his tenure as a period of drift, when Rhodes kept himself out of sight except for selected occasions. He refused to publish a daily schedule and often spent four-day weekends playing golf in Florida. The press turned its attention elsewhere. Looking back, many reporters say they are embarrassed by Rhodes's lack of accountability.

When Richard F. Celeste became governor, reporters met him at the door demanding access and information. Celeste had campaigned on a theme of "no more business as usual," and reporters were determined to hold him to keeping those promises. An energized press corps scrutinized his every move, and the emphasis in reporting shifted from the legislature to the governor's office. Celeste admits that the intense coverage revealed "some issues that clearly needed our attention," but at the same time he charges that the competition for breaking stories often degenerated into "political gossip mongering."

George Voinovich's first years in office were marked by a new caution on the part of the media. One reporter after another describes Voinovich as an enigma, whose personality and political style often contradict one another. Even as he seeks reelection, reporters are still groping for a definitive picture of Voinovich as governor, and their tentative coverage of many issues illustrates their reluctance to draw the wrong conclusions. Paul Mifsud, Voinovich's chief of staff, recognizes the value of such a murky picture: he has said to other state officials that pure unpredictability is one of the administration's strongest weapons and that he intends to use it as long as he can get away with it.

Almost to a person, reporters in the Statehouse press corps use the terms politics and government interchangeably when describing their assignments in Columbus. And most admit that the political side of the story gets the first and best coverage because it has the "flash," "the glamour," "the sexy stuff," or, most honestly, "it's the most fun to do and read." But no one makes the argument that it is the most important; most reporters readily admit that more work should be done in covering the day-to-day workings of all three branches of state government—executive, legislative, and judicial. To be fair, the press corps is a small force in the face of a huge government bureaucracy: only sixteen news organizations, with thirty-five reporters, have full-time news staffs in Columbus. Most bureaus have tried to carve a niche for themselves, hoping to do one thing well.

The Cleveland *Plain Dealer*, the largest daily and Sunday paper in the state, also has the largest Statehouse bureau, with six full-time reporters. Tom Suddes and Mary Beth Lane, two of the six, say that the large bureau allows reporters to specialize but also creates enough "throw weight" so that everyone in the bureau gets tips and ready access. Suddes, whose beat is primarily the legislature, sees his job as threefold: telling people how their money is being spent, how their liberty is being expanded or reduced, and whether their interests are being served by the officials they send to Columbus. Part of his job, he says, is to give his readers a sense of perspective, connecting the present to the relevant past.[1]

The *Plain Dealer* has, in the past, led the state in breaking news stories and long-term investigative projects. With Mary Anne Sharkey as bureau chief and Gary Webb as the primary investigative reporter, the *Plain Dealer* broke stories all over state government. The *Plain Dealer* pursued stories beyond Capitol Square as well, turning its attention to The Ohio

State University hospitals, the firing of OSU's football coach, and the state's costs in the financial debacle that followed "Son of Heaven," a fantastic exhibit of Chinese artifacts in Columbus. After Sharkey moved to the daily's Cleveland office and Webb left the state, the bureau seemed quieter, although it continued to break big stories.

Now the *Plain Dealer* is being challenged by the newly aggressive *Akron Beacon Journal*. David Adams, with the *Beacon Journal,* says the *Plain Dealer* is still "the finger that pulls the trigger," but says the *Beacon Journal* has, over the past few years, become "a more . . . crusading newspaper."[2]

The first of the *Beacon Journal's* major "crusading" efforts was a series called "Pay to Play," which detailed the power of House speaker Vernal G. Riffe, Jr., to elicit political contributions from individuals and special interest groups affected by legislation. Those "players," the *Beacon Journal* alleged, know that they must contribute money to Riffe's cause or be frozen out of the legislative process. Adams is proud of the fact that the series got wide circulation, ruffled lots of powerful feathers, and prompted some of those mentioned to refuse all communication with the *Beacon Journal*. He swaggers a little when describing reaction to the series. "If we have to piss people off, then we do that. But our job is to look out for the taxpayers and the public," he says. "Some people now see getting a call from the *Beacon Journal* as coming to work and seeing Mike Wallace and his camera crew." Adams may be overstating the case a bit, but clearly the *Beacon Journal* has sent a message that the traditional "sacred cows" have been declared fair game for the time being by the Akron paper.

Mike Curtin, public affairs editor for the *Columbus Dispatch,* acknowledges that the *Beacon Journal's* work must be taken seriously but says that sometimes it goes too far. "They may have 10 yards of material and try to write a 15-20 yard story," he says. "At times they've tried to make a bigger splash than the facts called for." But Curtin doesn't discount the importance of the paper's newfound role in Columbus. The *Dispatch,* he acknowledges, is at times too conservative, too staid, too complacent. The paper is reluctant to paint stories in vivid black and white, often choosing shades of gray. "One thing you have in Ohio is a range of editorial positions that newspapers take. You can choose your poison in Ohio. . . . There is not a dominant urban center in Ohio and there is not a dominant newspaper in Ohio. That's a strength in terms of political coverage in the state."[3]

Curtin gives the *Dispatch* the highest marks for day-to-day coverage of state government; it has the staff, the proximity, and the responsibility as the "paper of record" in the capital city. It has also done some laudable special projects work in out-of-the-way areas of state government. Early in 1992 the paper broke a series of stories on the Ohio Department of Youth Services, the euphemistically named corrections authority for youth. The paper pointed out in graphic detail the horrendous conditions under which juvenile criminal offenders are held and the relative inattention by the legislature and administration to their treatment. Because juveniles do not have the legal rights of their adult criminal counterparts, adult offenders have far better physical facilities, educational programs, and treatment. The series prompted a flurry of bureaucratic attention. The reporter, Michael Berens, picks up on the story periodically to let readers know what real reform has resulted. Such detailed, regular follow-up is rare on a beat where stories are always breaking and looking back is a luxury.

A large measure of the success of a political reporter in Columbus is the attention his or her work receives. One of the most underexposed, and often undercredited, Statehouse bureaus in the capital is the *Dayton Daily News*, with bureau chief Tim Miller and reporter Sandy Theis. With the financial woes that have struck so many newspapers in recent years, the *Dayton Daily News* eliminated its circulation in Columbus, so stories by Theis and Miller were not appearing in the "clipping services" that circulate through every government office, news bureau, and lobbyist's office. The paper now is back in full circulation in Columbus, and both Miller and Theis are being recognized as major players. They concentrate on two things in their coverage: telling their readers very specifically how state government is affecting their lives and giving their readers a picture of state government that will not be available anywhere else. Theis and Miller pay close attention to financial and regulatory developments that affect the Miami Valley, and they watch for patterns that will make good reading.[4]

The backbone of political and government coverage in any statehouse is the wire services. Day in and day out, often while the rest of the press corps is out chasing a story that is a lot more fun, wire service reporters sit through the hearings and the legislative sessions and the press conferences. With only sixteen news organizations represented by their own reporters, the wire services are almost the only sources of information for Ohio's nearly one hundred daily newspapers, as well as radio and television stations that may touch briefly on state news.

The deans of the Statehouse press corps were until recently the heads of the two wire services, Bob Miller of Associated Press and Lee Leonard of United Press International. As UPI's financial fortunes deteriorated, Leonard fled to the *Columbus Dispatch*, where he continues to cover the Statehouse. Miller held forth from his crowded cubicle in the Statehouse Press Room until February 1994, when he retired after thirty years on the beat.

Both Miller and Leonard are praised by their younger counterparts for their complete, evenhanded coverage over the years. More than that, they are noted for their lack of cynicism about the cycles of officeholders and events they have watched. Their work has often provided historical perspective sorely lacking from most coverage.

Ironically, while younger and newer reporters often looked to Leonard and Miller as the "voices of reason" in Statehouse coverage, Leonard thinks the new breed of "head-hunting" reporters is doing a better job of keeping after state government. They are better prepared and take the job more seriously than reporters of his generation, Leonard says. They are more aggressive and the relationship between journalists and officials is more adversarial.[5] There is also, he notes, more competition for fewer jobs covering politics and government, and new reporters on the scene are sometimes better than their predecessors. He acknowledges, however, that the competition among reporters can lead to overkill and even to questionable reporting tactics. Leonard adds that prospective candidates for public office now factor press coverage into their decision. Many who know they will not survive close scrutiny simply do not run, he says. "You know you're doing pretty well when you start to scare these people from running for office."

Despite the relative youth of the Statehouse press corps, there are still reporters around who covered Rhodes and Celeste. Styles of coverage changed dramatically from one administration to the other, partly because reporters came and went, but partly as well because of changing expectations and standards by the media.

Leonard recalls James A. Rhodes's first eight years as governor as the "old school" of politics and reporting. "The rules of the game were different. You hung around your source, you drank with your source, you kibitzed with your source, and you would get stories that way," he says.

"Rhodes knew how to play that game. Then he had to adapt to the new breed in his second two terms. . . . But Rhodes succeeded in this. He could get the media to print the story he wanted. He knew reporters so well he could practically predict what they would say." Rhodes was a master at reducing most issues to "jobs and progress." He dismissed environmental concerns about Ohio's high-sulfur coal as a threat to the jobs of Ohio miners. (He was born in Coalton, after all). He battled the EPA and occasionally came up with a silly way to save Ohio's dirty coal industry. The fluidized bed, his multimillion-dollar boondoggle, was "demonstrated" to perplexed reporters and environmental skeptics one cold day as a way to mix high- and low-sulfur coals at power plants with no major pollution. It never worked. But no one ever reported that.

. When the steel and auto industries collapsed during the last two years of Rhodes's term, the state's economy went into a tailspin. Rhodes attended a summit meeting of Midwest governors in Detroit and hauled the press corps along on the state plane, leaving them at the airport while he attended a day-long closed meeting which accomplished exactly nothing. At the end of the day, Rhodes distributed the press release he had carried onto the plane that morning, herded the reporters back onto the plane, and went home.

But reporters were charmed by Rhodes's fractured rhetoric and lulled by his administration's seeming lack of activity, and let it go at that. They paid little attention to the siting of new state prisons in southern Ohio, far away from the homes of prisoners; the long-term implications of his environmental policies; his penchant for building technical colleges and branch campuses of state universities all over Ohio; or his use of bonds as a way to raise millions of dollars without increasing taxes.

All that changed with the arrival of a new governor. Richard Celeste came to state politics, first as a legislator and then as lieutenant governor, just as the country was feeling the effects of Watergate. Leonard recalls that when Celeste campaigned for lieutenant governor he was viewed by some voters and reporters as "a knight in shining armor" who would be untouched by the ugly realities of political life in a big state. Reporters had extremely high expectations of him, seeing him as a young idealist who would be the antidote to the old-school politics of Rhodes. Those expectations were further fueled by the near-perfect political campaign Celeste ran in 1982. The campaign looked even better in contrast to the inept effort of his Republican opponent, U.S. congressman Clarence Brown of Urbana. Brown's campaign operation double-scheduled events so that Brown routinely missed commitments, stranded reporters when promised transportation failed to show up, and could not get the long-time Washington politician to stop saying "out here in Ohio" during his speeches.

The defining moment in Celeste's eight years occurred almost immediately, when he persuaded the legislature to raise the state income taxes. In his final budget, Rhodes had stitched together a quilt of temporary tax and fee increases scheduled to expire six months after Celeste took office. Celeste, riding the wave of a huge victory, wanted to act decisively to balance the budget and guarantee funding for his programs. He tried to minimize the amount of the increase and maximize the need, and the media began accusing him of exaggeration. The Republicans quickly framed the issue as "Celeste's 90-percent tax increase," and the charge stuck, even when the tax was later reduced to essentially the same level as when Celeste took office.

Leonard says that the most important story of his thirty-year reporting career came on Celeste's watch: the collapse of the Home State Savings Bank. When Home State failed, it forced the closing of seventy other savings and loan banks all over the state. It was a huge story, as people faced the prospect of losing their life savings. The media had an immediate role to play: initial coverage of the crisis would determine to a large extent whether there would be a statewide panic. Once the first wave of closings was reported, the media had to decide who was at fault, how these institutions were regulated in Ohio, and how they could be restored. Reporters, Leonard says, rose to the occasion and the coverage was good, although it took a while to grasp the intricacies of savings and loan regulation. In the meantime, they treated the story as purely political—what would this crisis do to Celeste, fomented as it was by Marvin Warner, owner of the institutions and a major contributor to Celeste? Eventually, papers moved the story off the political beat and turned large portions of it over to their business writers. When all was said and done, Celeste got high marks for what proved to be the first of a nationwide chain of similar financial crises.

Most reporters still characterize the Celeste administration as riddled with ethical scandals, most often prompted by the governor's inability to make good appointments in critical departments. James Rogers, named head of the Department of Youth Services, was the first cabinet member in Ohio history to be indicted while in office. The *Columbus Dispatch*'s Mike Curtin thinks that those early bad personnel decisions set a tone in the coverage that overshadowed good people and major accomplishments. Things happened so fast, and the media were watching so intensely, that the governor's relationship with the press corps quickly reached a point of no return, he says.[6] When Curtin lists adjectives associated with relationships between the press and the governors, it reads: Rhodes—laughable, critical, frustrated, groping; Celeste—adversarial, condemning, tough; Voinovich—evolving, ambivalent, curious, wait-and-see, tentative.

At the end of his first term, Voinovich continued to perplex reporters. He was endorsed in 1990 by every major paper in Ohio, and reporters were anxious to see what he could do. Increasingly, they seem to have concluded that he is a good man personally but not necessarily a good governor. Curtin notes that reporters do not want to be made fools of. They do not want to "buy into George Voinovich the good man," he says, "and fail to see some of the not-so-good manifestations of his governance."

Sandy Theis of the *Dayton Daily News* says that Voinovich has been very good so far at avoiding blame.[7] For example, the Ohio State Fair, traditionally a big party that the governor throws for Ohioans, was a public relations disaster in August 1992. Voinovich supporter Billy Inmon was named fair manager and promptly turned the fairgrounds upside down, changing the way admissions and rides were paid for, trying to ban a gay-rights group from distributing literature, and negotiating an exclusive contract with Pepsi which forced out Wendy's and other major vendors who serve Coca-Cola. Voinovich deserted his friend, saying it was up to the fair board to keep or fire Inmon.

It is Voinovich's personality, not his record, that still seems most fascinating to the press corps. Reporters are particularly taken with his tendency to anger without provocation, and they try different approaches to elicit an explosion. David Adams at the *Beacon Journal* says Voinovich "will just blow up. He'll start pounding his desk and his face will turn red. . . . You never know what will trigger it." Setting off these episodes is almost a sport, Adams says. "Some topics that seem to work are lobbyists and whenever someone insists that he's wrong. Tell him that he's wrong and he goes crazy." Mary Beth Lane of the *Plain Dealer* says that while Celeste was unflappable in the face of even the most provocative question Voinovich "goes ballistic."[8]

Nobody follows political coverage more avidly or critically than the politicians themselves. Officeholders and party officials alike devour newspapers and monitor newscasts. When it comes to the Ohio news media, the state chairs of both the Democratic and Republican parties have at least one thing in common: both offer lukewarm reviews of the work of Ohio's political reporters. Robert Bennett, chair of the Ohio Republicans since 1988, says he has seen political coverage deteriorate over the past couple of decades. "Years ago, you had a few reporters who had a genuine love of politics," Bennett says. "Now, most reporters approach politics as pretty adversarial. But politics is the people's business and it needs to be covered."[9] He thinks that questions about the fairness of political coverage will continue. A candidate's personal life, for example, has become too central. Instead, he says, the media should return to covering the issues that most affect the public. The media need to look at important public policy questions like infrastructure and national issues like defense spending increases or cuts and force candidates to do likewise. "We need a watchdog press," he says.

Bennett acknowledges that such a change will not occur without a change in the way candidates run their campaigns, particularly in terms of negative campaigning, but says that will not end soon because "it's what works and what moves numbers." Instead, he would like to see campaign finance reform coupled with some sort of "ethics review body" that could pass judgment on the fairness of ads, for example. The media cannot do it alone, he admits.

Gene Branstool, chair of the Ohio Democratic party from 1991 until 1993, also does not expect the press to singlehandedly reform the electoral process, but he does think it is reasonable to expect the media, particularly print reporters, to be more analytical and less sensational. Reporters have an "obligation to call attention to the numerous hypocrisies that creep out . . . to point out people who say one thing and do another . . . who pander."[10] He would also like to see more attention paid to what does *not* succeed "to tell why a lost cause failed." In the 1970s, when Branstool was a state representative, bills dealing with hazardous and toxic waste disappeared as quickly as they were introduced. "The fact is that the [Ohio] Manufacturers Association had them locked up. Why wasn't that a story?" Understanding the process is as important as understanding the results, he says. He thinks the media could help to reduce public cynicism about government by occasionally writing a positive story. "Most of government that is delivered works," he says. "The school buses run on time, prisoners are held safely in prisons, water runs and toilets flush—that's government working. And why not write about a group of legislators sitting down on a bipartisan basis, working on a problem, getting the votes to solve it and having some oversight? That's government working too."

Branstool and Bennett are not alone in believing that the media tend to emphasize the negative elements of politics. Robert H. Bohle wrote about it in his article "Negativism as News Selection Predictor," in which journalists were given a series of story leads from which to choose. Although they had indicated earlier that positive and negative stories were equally important, they tended to select the negative stories, dealing with crime, corruption, and disasters as being more newsworthy. Bohle speculates that this is because negative stories are easier to report.[11]

Although the small circle of politicians and reporters who inhabit the Statehouse and its environs live and die by the newest development in state government and politics, that interest dwindles rapidly away from the Statehouse grounds. Most people spend little time contemplating the state of state government. This is not a new phenomenon. In a spring 1979 article in the journal *State Government*, W. T. Gomley, Jr., writes that mass media pay less attention to state government than to any other level of government. Overall, he says, state politics is characterized by relatively low levels of public awareness, knowledge, and participation. Statehouse bureaus are inadequately staffed for in-depth reporting and instead show a preference for "comprehensible conflicts between two easily identifiable sides." That view is reinforced in a 1982 article in which Malcolm E. Jewell writes that state government and politics have for too long received too low a priority and too few resources in research.[12] Jewell argues for increased single-state studies and comparative studies in the area.

Richard Celeste agrees that there is too little attention paid to state government. Still smarting over his treatment by the press corps during his eight years as governor, he gives the quality of coverage low marks.[13] "Over the last 20 years, as there has been more and more responsibility delegated to state government, there has been less coverage," he says. "And generally the trend in the quality of coverage has declined. . . . People know less about state government today, though it's more important to them, than they knew when Frank Lausche was governor."

While Mike Curtin sees the number of roughly equal-sized papers as a boon to coverage statewide, Celeste sees it as part of the reason coverage has not been strong. "Because there's no one dominant market— there's not a Chicago, a New York, a Philadelphia, an Atlanta—it's hard to maintain a high quality press corps," he says. "You step way up when you go to a dominant market. The good reporters tend to move on." The other impediment to good coverage in Ohio, Celeste says, is the increasing number of one newspaper cities. Multiple papers in the same city vie with one another for stories and fairness. One paper attacks, the other defends. A one paper town "creates a phony objectivity, where a single writer tries to cover both sides. . . . In that case, balance is mostly in the minds of the writers."

As long as the press sees government as politics, the story will not be told, Celeste predicts. "The classic example was the way the press took the notion of 'no more business as usual' and applied it to politics, but not to the way state business was conducted." During his administration he recalls that Ohio used all of the federal highway money to which it was entitled, moving projects forward very quickly. (There was much commentary about "orange barrels" throughout the Celeste years.) "That was 'no more business as usual,' but it wasn't a story," Celeste charges. "There were many examples where we undertook initiatives to make things different, but they were too complicated for the press to understand, or it wasn't a political faceoff, so it wasn't controversial enough for the press to cover."

Celeste is astounded that Ohioans have not been upset by the cuts Voinovich has made in higher education, and he blames the press for not making clear the relationship between higher education and the economy of the state. He is also concerned about the increasing power of television news, despite the fact that most is "clip and read." It minimizes, once again, the quality and quantity of information citizens receive. "There has always been a notion of playing to the gallery, and now the gallery is television."

What Celeste does not see is the "media as watchdog" role that many reporters ascribe to themselves and to which Branstool and Bennett believe they should aspire. The real watchdog, Celeste says, is the competitiveness of politics itself. "No one has a lock on an office," he says, "and that's where you get your real accountability."

Like Celeste, Republican political consultant Curt Steiner has serious concerns about the role of the media in covering politics in Ohio. Steiner began his career—still acclaimed by the Statehouse press corps—as press secretary to Thomas VanMeter when he served in the Senate, finally becoming press secretary to Voinovich before leaving in mid-1992 to head the failed U.S. Senate campaign of Lieutenant Governor Michael

DeWine and establish his own political consulting business. He says there is a "serious contradiction" in Ohio when it comes to political coverage.[14] People now get most information from television, he says, but there is virtually no real reporting by the electronic media about politics and government. As a result, Steiner says, print media and the wire services actually set the agenda for radio and television newscasts, giving newspapers a disproportionate amount of influence. Ohio, with only two electronic media organizations covering the Statehouse full time, falls behind other states. "Most major states have some level of electronic government news, at least when the legislature is in session." As a result, there is no consistency in the coverage the audience sees and hears. "In the last two weeks of a major campaign, the lights will come on and there will be some coverage," he says. "So most information comes from either televised political ads or print. We're lucky that overall the Statehouse press corps have been overall a pretty responsible group of people. But the system as it is now puts a tremendous amount of power in the hands of the *Columbus Dispatch* and the Cleveland *Plain Dealer.*" The powerful endorsements around the state are from those two papers and the *Dayton Daily News,* Steiner says, while the *Akron Beacon Journal* probably carries the most weight locally of any paper in the state and runs more state-issue editorials than any other paper.

Steiner has two other observations about the media in Ohio: polling has become very important, and true campaign finance reform has not. "A tradition of polling has evolved in Ohio papers that has a tremendous influence on the money flow in a campaign," he claims. In 1986 the *Beacon Journal* conducted a poll early in the Republican primary election season that showed former governor Rhodes with 70 percent of the vote and state senators Paul Gillmor and Paul Pfeifer sharing the remaining 30 percent. The poll did not allow for "undecided," Steiner noted, and was the only poll taken during the campaign. Rhodes used the poll results to dry up money to both Gillmor and Pfeifer and became the Republican gubernatorial nominee, with disastrous results for the party. Since then, virtually every major paper in the state has begun some sort of poll, Steiner says. Is that too much polling? "We're probably better off having more than less; it keeps any one poll from having too much influence."

While Steiner is generally complimentary of the Statehouse press corps, he does note "a real proclivity" on its part "to make too many issues political. It's fun, but it's not very good for creating informed readers in Ohio." Although conventional wisdom says that most people get

their information from television and radio, the number of full-time reporters from the electronic media has dwindled to three: two for Ohio
Public Radio/Public TV and one from WHIO-TV, a commercial station
in Dayton. No Columbus television station has a reporter regularly assigned to the Statehouse or to politics in general. Jim Otte, Columbus
bureau chief for WHIO-TV, says that regular Statehouse coverage is
one of the ways his station sets itself apart from the local competition.[15]
With the demise of an afternoon paper in Dayton, Otte says he can
often beat out the *Dayton Daily News* by twelve hours with a story on
the six o'clock news.

"State government is terrible television," Otte says. "Every producer's
dream is a story that tells itself totally in pictures. There's not one story in
state government that lends itself to pictures. A standard response to a
political story idea is 'that might be interesting, but it's not good television.' We have to bend over backwards to think of a different way to handle the story." An example he cites is when legislators were considering
a bill to make the stalking of a person a crime. Since the story could not
be done in the hearing room, he and his cameraman went out to talk to a
woman who had been stalked, putting the local scene into the story.

Otte finds it ironic that stations complain about having no time in
their news schedules for political and state government stories at a time
when newscasts are proliferating. Newscasts used to be aired at 6:00 and
11:00 P.M. Now they are scheduled for 6:00 A.M., 6:30 A.M., noon, 5:30
P.M., 6:00 P.M., 7:00 P.M., and 11:00 P.M. And, he charges, they are either
filled with fluff or use canned stories.

Deborah Countiss, news anchor for WSYX-TV in Columbus, began
her television reporting career at the Ohio Statehouse in the early 1980s
in the position now occupied by Otte. She agrees that local television
news does not often cover politics mostly because it is so difficult to
make visually interesting.[16] She notes, however, that state politics is increasingly complex and difficult to handle effectively in short news stories. Countiss disagrees with Otte's argument that the increase in the
number of television newscasts should allow increased political coverage. The flaw in that position, she says, is that there are few new reporters and photographers to fill the time on the new programs.

While a long story for Otte is ninety seconds, Bill Cohen, bureau chief
of the Ohio Public Radio/Public Television Statehouse News Bureau,
has as long as three and a half minutes to tell his lead story of the day.
That means he can put the story in perspective and, over time, help his

audience come to grips with the enormity of state government.[17] Of concern to both Otte and Cohen is the proliferation of video news releases by politicians and companies. With so much emphasis on health issues, stations are scrambling for features. A drug company, for example, may send a video-taped report featuring the "malady and cure of the week," Otte says, which may well be aired with no acknowledgment that it was not produced by the station itself. Political campaign managers, Cohen says, often offer tape of a candidate speaking. While it is against Ohio Public Radio and Television policy to use such tape, it does get used in small markets without the resources to send a reporter. "The line between news and public relations is being blurred, largely by the newsmakers, and they try to get around reporters," Cohen said. "I don't fault the newsmakers. It's the responsibility of the newspeople to say 'no, we're not going to use this. We're either going to do it ourselves or we won't do it.' But it gets manipulative. When there's a void in reporting, the public relations people will move in to fill it."

Although Ohio has a diverse population, Ohio's political reporters are white, and most of them are male. In the early 1980s, an influx of women to the Statehouse press corps created great confusion for legislators and other male officials, who assumed that all women in the Statehouse were clerks and aides. More than one female reporter was called "honey" or sent out for coffee during a committee meeting. After several "by the book" efforts at introductory interviews, the women decided to meet political leaders where they lived—in bars and restaurants. A series of off-the-record sessions proved so successful that male reporters demanded to be included. Only Rhodes resisted the efforts of the women to name the time and place and pick up the tab. He insisted on lunch at the Athletic Club, an all-male Columbus club where women traditionally were not allowed above the first floor. The governor was late. Just as the ten women sitting around the table were concluding that they had been stood-up, Rhodes's voice, in a stage whisper, was heard asking his press secretary, "Jack, what the hell do these women want?"

As several bureaus in the Statehouse have been closed or reduced, the number of women reporters has dwindled as well. Until recently there was no African American reporter in the Ohio Statehouse press corps.

Reporters and politicians have come and gone over the years, but the system has remained largely unchanged. While that was fine with officeholders, lobbyists, and the media, Ohioans were clearly tired of the status quo. Their overwhelming approval in November 1992 of term limitations for Ohio's congressional delegates, state legislators, and state-wide officeholders has the potential to turn the Statehouse upside down over the next few years as the effect of the new provisions becomes known. It will be the turn of the century before the first elected officials are forced to retire after eight years in office (if no court decision throws out the restrictions before then), but Ohio politicians and political reporters alike will spend the rest of the 1990s speculating about what it all means. In the meantime, however, Ohio government will continue to grow in both size and influence.

Conversely, the resources devoted to informing Ohioans about their state government seem likely to dwindle. Statehouse reporters who view themselves first as political reporters will continue to focus on the political implications of everything from the state's $31 billion budget to the repercussions of the inmate riot at Lucasville's Southern Ohio Correctional Facility in the spring of 1993.

And the details of state government are unlikely to receive the attention they deserve. Ohioans will know about the personal animosities among the justices of the Ohio Supreme Court but will know little, if anything, about the impact of the court's decisions. Agencies like the Ohio Environmental Protection Agency and the Department of Insurance, the Ohio Department of Education, or the Public Utilities Commission of Ohio will operate in relative obscurity unless there is a political scandal or something happens to capture the attention of someone in the press corps. Politics, which should be the process by which voters decide how their government will be operated, has unfortunately become the product as well.

❖

CHAPTER TEN

Ohio in Washington:
The Congressional Delegation

❖

TOM DIEMER

❖ Resting on the grassy northwest slope of Capitol Hill, the Taft Memorial is not on the main line of Washington, D.C., tourist attractions. This handsome bell tower is one of the capital's best-kept secrets.

But the legacy of Robert Alphonso Taft lingers. It is never far from the mind of George J. Mitchell, the Senate majority leader. "Outside of my office building, I can look and see the memorial to Robert Taft, Mr. Republican of his time," Mitchell, a Maine Democrat, once said. "His entire career was directed at the objective of restraining the power of the executive and enhancing the power of the legislature." "Mr. Republican," Taft was called, a critic of Franklin Delano Roosevelt and Harry Truman and a formidable rival to Dwight D. Eisenhower at the 1952 Republican National Convention. This Ohioan was a pillar of classical conservative Republicanism. The four-story Taft Memorial is inscribed with his philosophy of government: "Let us abide by the fundamental principles laid down by the Constitution. Let us see that the State is the servant of its people and that the people are not servants of the State."

Since Taft's death in 1953, halfway through his third Senate term, Ohio's influence and fortunes in the nation's capital have gone gradually downhill. Senior Ohio congressmen like Ralph Regula or Tony Hall stroll through the press gallery in the U.S. House unnoticed by reporters awaiting bigger game. (The dean of the Ohio delegation at the outset of the 1990s, Clarence Miller of Lancaster, was even named chairman of the ficticious "Caucus of the Obscure" by a whimsical Capitol Hill publication.[1])

Ohio references abound in the Capitol: a magnificent W. H. Powell oil painting of the Battle of Lake Erie adorns a wall outside the House chamber; a Toledo Mud Hens baseball pennant hung for a decade or more in the bill room; and William Allen, a long-forgotten mid–nineteenth century senator from Chillicothe, stands amid other more famous statesmen in Statuary Hall. Across the Rotunda from the House, the most important "Ohio connection" for journalists is the Ohio Clock, a fixture since 1816. The handsome mahogany antique near the entrance to the Senate chamber serves as a "stake out" area for word from closed door meetings. (Once a good place to stash whiskey, it kept ticking after a 1983 terrorist bomb blast shattered the glass front.) No one is certain of the origin of the name, but legend has it that the seventeen stars on the carved shield face of the lower case represent Ohio as the seventeenth state admitted to the Union. Another clue is found in an 1897 picture of a group of politicians standing in front of the clock. Foremost among them is Marcus Hanna, the Cleveland political boss, then a freshman senator apparently posing with a landmark identified with his home state.[2]

Now fast-forward a half-century or so.

Taft, a committed individual-rights conservative who nearly captured the presidential nomination in 1952, was a consummate statesman. He became a symbol of Republican resistance to the expanding power of the federal government under Roosevelt. As Taft faded from the scene, so did classic conservatism with its libertarian, isolationist bent.

Taft was groomed for politics. The son of President William Howard Taft, a Cincinnati native, he graduated from Yale University while his father sat in the White House and completed Harvard Law School three years later as the war was about to erupt in Europe. He was elected to the U.S. Senate during a year of resurgence for the Republican party, which had fallen to fewer than 100 seats in the House at the height of Roosevelt's power. In 1938 Republicans across the land capitalized on another slump in the economy. They also fed on resentment of Roosevelt's unpopular attempt to pack the Supreme Court. With Taft as one of their leaders, the Republicans rebuilt their strength in Congress, capturing both houses in 1946.

The same year Taft won his Senate seat, attorney John Bricker of Columbus was elected governor of Ohio and quickly gained national prominence as a tight-fisted, anti–New Deal conservative. In 1944 he ran as Republican Thomas Dewey's vice presidential nominee and then joined Taft in the Senate in 1946. Bricker took the Senate seat that had been held by Harold H. Burton, the former Republican mayor of Cleveland. Burton resigned in September of 1945 to accept an appointment from President Truman to the U.S. Supreme Court, where he served until 1958. But it was Bricker and Taft, along with Democratic governor Frank J. Lausche of Cleveland, who dominated Ohio politics in the postwar era, giving the state a conservative stamp.

"Honest John" Bricker was a political middleweight compared to the erudite Taft, a complex lawmaker, a man of the Right, passionate about limited government but progressive on aid to education and housing issues. "[Taft] was saying we have got to face facts that we cannot legislate prosperity, we cannot legislate equality, or legislate opportunity," said retired Mount Union College political scientist Byron H. Walker, a student of Taft's career. "[Taft believed] free Americans should freely work out their own destiny."[3]

Pearl Harbor ended debate about U.S. entry into World War II. Taft, hurt by a lackluster campaign and his criticism of Roosevelt's handling of the war, narrowly survived defeat in 1944 at the hands of Democrat lawyer William G. "Big Bill" Pickrel of Dayton with 50.3 percent of the vote. Even so, he led the ticket in Ohio, attracting more votes than any other candidate. Dewey and running mate Bricker bested Roosevelt with 50.2 percent in Ohio, an 11,530-vote margin.

In the Senate, Taft was despised by labor leaders. He viewed the increasing strength of the Congress of Industrial Organization (CIO) as creeping socialism. Following his reelection, he cosponsored the Taft-Hartley Labor Management Act, which banned closed shops and forced union officers to renounce any ties to the Communist party. Anathema to the labor unions, the bill was vetoed by President Truman on June 20, 1947, but both the House and Senate overrode the president. The Senate barely achieved the required two-thirds majority in its 68-to-25 veto override.

In 1948, Taft challenged Dewey for the Republican nomination at the Republican National Convention in Philadelphia, but he was unable to form a coalition that was the equal of what came to be known as the party's eastern establishment. Taft finished second to Dewey on each of the first two ballots and then withdrew, giving the New York governor a unanimous third-ballot victory.

By 1950, admiration of Taft's integrity was deeply rooted in Ohio, where his unwillingness to compromise on matters of principle mattered more than the changing political currents. In the country at large, the ideal of supremacy of individual liberties and noninterventionist foreign policy was losing its grip on Republicans. Taft won a third term, easily defeating a weak opponent, state auditor Joseph T. "Jumping Joe" Ferguson, and returned to Washington as Senate majority leader.

With his drab lawyer's suit, glasses, and balding pate, Taft was not a colorful or charismatic politician. Fortunately for him, television was not yet deciding political campaigns. "He was an extremely shy man and he really relaxed with his family," said his grandson, Ohio secretary of state Robert A. Taft II. "He was intensely focused on whatever it was he was thinking about."[4] This was so much the case that he would occasionally fail to greet acquaintances on the street, rushing by them deep in thought.

Once, reacting to a meat shortage, he blithely advised consumers to "eat less." Another often-told story has Taft leaving a fashionable Washington restaurant with a doorman beckoning to an attendant for "Senator Taft's car." "Well," replied Taft with amusement, "it is a good car but it does not come when it is called." That was his idea of a joke.

His taciturn, scholarly bearing was a poor match for the "I Like Ike" mania at the 1952 Republican National Convention. Eisenhower was said to have agreed to run only to stop Taft and prevent a resurgence of isolationism. Taft, who was cool to the Marshall Plan for rebuilding Europe, supported the "police action" in Korea. "It was surprising that he went along with the armed intervention in Korea," Professor Walker said. "He joined in with the China Lobby, and he was critical of not supporting Chiang Kai-shek. He was concerned about the Communist takeover in China."[5]

Taft made his last national stand in Chicago in 1952. He finished a strong second to Eisenhower on the first ballot at the convention. Then when Minnesota abandoned favorite son Harold Stassen and threw nineteen votes to Ike, the war hero and favorite of moderates and liberals in the party went over the top without a second roll call of the states.

A year later, Taft was dead of cancer. He was buried in an Episcopalian cemetery in Cincinnati after a service in the Rotunda of the

U.S. Capitol. The memorial in Washington was dedicated in 1958 to the "honesty, indomitable courage and high principles of free government symbolized by his life."

In a special election in 1954, Republican representative George Bender of Cleveland won Taft's seat by 3,000 votes over Cleveland mayor Thomas A. Burke, who was appointed to the seat by Governor Lausche in October 1953, three months after Taft's death. On the House side, two young Democratic lawyers, Charles A. Vanik of Cleveland, and Thomas "Lud" Ashley of Toledo, upset incumbents in 1954 and persevered during the next twenty-six years as mainstays of northern urban liberalism in the Congress.

But liberal Democrats like Vanik and Ashley were a small minority in postwar Ohio. Republicans dominated the congressional delegation in the late 1950s and early 1960s, just as they held sway in the Senate, where Bricker won a second term in 1952 against Toledo mayor Michael V. DiSalle. Most of the time, the Ohio Republicans were out of step with Democratic majorities in both bodies on Capitol Hill, diminishing Ohio's influence on the national political scene. "You have states that are off-synch," said John Morgan, a Republican political consultant in Washington. "I think how it explains itself is that Ohio led the fight against the New Deal. It is kind of the backbone of the Republican party."[6]

The 15-7-1 Republican edge in the Ohio delegation after the 1950 election was part of the next-to-last Republican majority in the U.S. House for more than four decades. Democrats have controlled the House since 1955, but Republican congressmen had the majority in Ohio until the mid-1980s. "The Ohio congressional delegation has never quite had the clout that the political power of the state would warrant," said Randall Ripley, professor of political science at Ohio State University. "Some of it is just bad luck."[7]

Vanik, Ashley, and Democratic populists like Michael J. Kirwan of Youngstown and Michael A. Feighan of Cleveland were exceptions to the conservative rule in Ohio; more influential members of the delegation were Republicans William M. McCulloch of Piqua, Clarence J. Brown, Sr., of Urbana, and Frank T. Bow of Canton.

Dominance in the House rested with one man: Mr. Speaker, Sam Rayburn of Texas. "Policy was made at the top and filtered down," Ashley said. "The Democratic caucus was practically non-existent. The only memory I had of the caucus was to ratify the Speaker. Then the caucus faded and was called upon no more." Rayburn, while partisan to the core, liked working with Eisenhower, especially on foreign policy. The concept of divided government as a deterrent to governance, a hallmark of the 1980s, was not recognized as a major obstacle. "Those were years of bipartisan government," said Vanik. "Sam Rayburn would kill us if we trespassed: 'He is our president,' you know, 'we don't want any partisan hotshot.' " Dissent was swiftly punished. "You were dealt with," Ashley said, smiling as if recalling a boyhood whipping, "and I'll tell you, *you were* dealt with."[8]

Near the close of the decade, Kirwan, who was close to Rayburn (as was Clarence Brown, Sr., on the other side of the aisle), approached Ashley about becoming a deputy whip, a rung up on the leadership ladder. Ashley, thrilled, assumed the deal was done and notified his hometown newspaper, the *Blade,* which ran a favorable editorial. Then Kirwan brought him bad news. Someone else had been promised the slot and he would have to wait. "I said, 'what on earth am I going to say?' And he said, 'Tell 'em it don't make any difference anyway. Sam Rayburn runs the place.' " And when asked by a *New York Times* reporter about the foul-up, Ashley brashly declared, "We have one-man rule in the House." Rayburn, told of this comment, deadpanned to the reporter, "Ashley who?" "From that point on," Ashley said, "Nothing good happened to me and he [Rayburn] was very open about it."

The Toledoan tried. Allowing for a decent interval, he asked Rayburn for a seat on the prestigious Joint Economic Committee. "He looked at me squarely with those blue eyes of his and he said, 'you are not going to be on the Joint Economic Committee as long as I am the Speaker of the House.' And he said, 'you of course understand the reason for that.' And I said, 'Mr. Sam, indeed I do,' and I turned around and walked out and I thought, 'Well goddamnit, there is at least a guy who doesn't equivocate, who doesn't pretend.' That's when I realized how the place was run."[9]

No one man could control the freelancers in the Senate. In 1956 Lausche, miffed that his appointee, Thomas Burke, had lost the special election, ran against George Bender and won easily. Lausche, however, was closer in spirit to Bricker than to the smallish Ohio Democratic delegation in the House. He was so independent-minded that Eisenhower briefly considered replacing Nixon with Lausche as a vice presidential candidate in 1956 despite his party affiliation.[10]

Bricker was his own man too. He challenged the authority of his party's president, the popular Eisenhower, who once said, "if it's true that when you die the things that bothered you most are engraved on your skull, I am sure I'll have there the mud and dirt of France . . . and the name of Senator Bricker." The so-called Bricker Amendment, introduced in 1953, was a direct assault on presidential power. It was designed to limit the power of the president to make executive agreements with foreign governments. Eisenhower, of course, resented the intrusion and wondered once if Bricker's supporters "had lost all their brains."[11] For his part, Taft had battled relentlessly against executive branch power, but, as Senator Mitchell pointed out, "that was in an era [the 1940s] in which presidents were Democrats." The Bricker Amendment embarrassed a *Republican* president before being beaten by a single vote in 1954, leaving Eisenhower, who was slow to react, looking indecisive on a fundamental separation-of-powers issue.

In Ohio, the conservatives went too far in 1958, backing a state right-to-work ballot initiative that would have severely curtailed the power of labor unions to organize workers. It energized the labor movement, which defeated it, and also swept out many Republican sympathizers, including Bricker, taken down by Stephen M. Young of Cleveland.

Young's campaign was run by a political activist from Cleveland, a former state lawmaker and parking-lot owner named Howard M. Metzenbaum. "A 69-year-old man came and asked me to run his campaign for the Senate," Metzenbaum said. "His name was Steve Young. We were not real close, but I thought John Bricker was the antithesis of everything I believed in. We raised $45,000 and won one of the greatest upsets in Ohio political history."[12] Young was cantankerous, outspoken, crafty, not particularly effective, and not at all beloved, but he was in line with the leftward drift of his party.

By contrast, Wayne Lavere Hays was a far cry from the popular cultural interpretation of the 1960s Democrat. As Hubert H. Humphrey put it at a Democratic dinner in eastern Ohio, circa 1974, "Every Congress needs one Wayne Hays but only one!" Hays was a bread-and-butter politician from Belmont County who got his share of Great Society largesse for his eastern Ohio district, which was impoverished, largely rural, and dotted with coal mines. But he was downright reactionary when it came to the so-called small-*d* Democrats, those seeking reform within the party and the Congress. Neal R. Peirce wrote of Hays: "Of all the power brokers (and abusers) few if any rivaled Wayne Hays, representative of a poor southeastern Ohio district for 30 years, who rose to twin pinnacles of power: chairman of the House Administration Committee and the Democratic Congressional Campaign Committee. Hays wheeled, dealed, placed other congressmen in his political debt, bullied opponents, fought election reform, and as the press finally revealed in 1976, placed a mistress (Elizabeth Ray) on his committee payroll."[13]

Hays was also known as one of the most traveled members of Congress in his role as a NATO parliamentarian—despite his reputation as a constituent-based congressman. At one point a Hays amendment stopped publication (and media scrutiny) of House members' travel records; but under protest, publication resumed a year later. Hays was clever. Quietly expanding the authority of the House Administration Committee, an obscure housekeeping body with little legislative authority; he became a tyrant with power over his colleagues office allowances, perquisites, and fringe benefits. He dished out rewards and punishment, as well as vitriol from the House floor, where, under congressional immunity, he abused political opponents with acidic floor speeches. He was free with a stinging quip or crude insult. President Ford, he once said, was the only guy "who could back himself into a corner in the Oval Office." Vanik said with a laugh when reminded of Hays's antics, "Congress was a stage. Members would go down there and we would act out our parts. Actors read the lines of others. We read our *own* goddamn few lines. It was fascinating theater."[14]

But Vanik and Hays were bit players in their own state throughout the 1960s, as Republicans maintained an overwhelming majority in the Ohio delegation. In the House, Sam Rayburn's successor, John McCormack of Massachusetts, controlled the agenda, although he delegated more authority than did Rayburn. "The only people that benefited were people from Massachusetts, because they weren't worth jackshit with Rayburn," said Ashley. "With Kennedy and McCormack, strength shifted from Texas to Massachusetts. From an electoral vote standpoint Ohio is not as important to the Democrats. It [the delegation] is split, the state is split. The leadership looks to [the states that can deliver]. Ohio was of only modest consequence."[15] With Republicans holding the state by an 18-to-6 margin in 1962, Ohio could not compete for federal projects against bigger Democratic delegations in states like California, New York, Pennsylvania, Texas, and Massachusetts. Slowly, the economy was shifting, too. A bicoastal bias emerged on Capitol Hill.

Mike Kirwan, mentor to younger Democrats like Ashley, wielded power as chairman of the Appropriations subcommittee on public works, a source of pork-barrel largesse. He chaired the Democratic Congressional Campaign Committee, which gave him a say over who would get critically needed campaign funds. He was, however, turned down on one scheme—a grandiose plan to build a canal connecting the Ohio River with Lake Erie. It was dismissed as "Mike's Ditch."

At the other end of Pennsylvania Avenue, Lyndon Johnson was in the White House as Kennedy's vice president. The former Senate leader was not shy about calling in his chits. "We used to get telephone calls from Lyndon at 6:30 A.M.," Vanik said of Johnson's days as president during the latter half of the decade. " 'Listen, partner,' he'd say, 'I have to have you on this farm bill.' 'Well, Mr. President, this is very serious,' I'd say, and he would say, 'Look what you have gotten for Cleveland,' and he would have a whole litany." By his account, Vanik was among the few Democrats with the gumption to say no to Johnson when he was running for president. In succeeding years, he would change his mind about Johnson, but in 1960 Vanik was still uncomfortable with the Texan's racial views. "In June, Lyndon called me and he wanted me to host a meeting for him in Cleveland. I had this mixed district, had a lot of people, a lot of blacks, and he wanted me to arrange a meeting. He just wanted exposure in a northern state. And I said, 'Lyndon, I just can't do it.' I just felt it would be a problem. If I had done that, he would have helped me. He never forgot."[16]

John F. Kennedy defeated Johnson for the Democratic nomination in 1960, but he failed to carry Ohio in November despite vigorous support from Governor DiSalle, who ran his campaign in the state. Later, Kennedy supposedly told aides he wanted that "Italian guy from Ohio" as his secretary of Health, Education and Welfare. Cleveland mayor Anthony J. Celebrezze got the cabinet post in 1962.

Was there a misunderstanding? Some Ohio politicos joke that Kennedy really wanted Governor DiSalle, not Celebrezze. Robert F. Kennedy debunked the tale in a 1964 interview when he revealed that the Celebrezze appointment was a precise political calculation. "He had a good reputation out in Cleveland. The fact that he was Italian was a major factor to be considered. It was an election year [1962]. . . . We did have a saying that, 'Celebrezze makes it easy.' He was very helpful in the congressional elections around the country because he got the Italians."[17]

Lausche did not need the liberal Celebrezze's help. He won a second Senate term in 1962, drubbing Republican John Marshall Briley with 62 percent of the vote. Briley, a Toledo lawyer, ran a negative campaign, saying the sixty-two-year-old Lausche was "a little old and tottery and can't remember what happened just four and a half weeks ago."[18] Lausche died twenty-nine years later at the age of ninety-four.

What a year 1962 was. A third-generation Taft, Robert Taft, Jr., was elected to the House, but that was no surprise—he had the pedigree. The Democrats has a future star just coming into focus: John Glenn of tiny New Concord, who that year became the first American to orbit the earth.

Two years later, fresh out of the Marine Corps and against the advice of his friend, Robert F. Kennedy, Glenn decided to challenge Steve Young in the 1964 Democratic primary. But lingering effects from a freak fall on a shower stall door caused Glenn to withdraw, ending the adventure prematurely. Lyndon Johnson swept the state, carrying Young along to a second-term victory over Congressman Taft by less than 17,000 votes. Democrats made gains in the House, too, cutting the Republican edge in the delegation to 14 to 10. Among the freshmen was a blunt-spoken redhead named John J. Gilligan, a victor over Republican Carl W. Rich of Cincinnati.

With the Goldwater "counterrevolution" under way, Republicans surged back to a 19-to-5 advantage in 1966, as nationally the party picked up 47 seats and cut substantially into the Democratic majority. After the 1966 election, President Johnson conceded that "the other party strengthened its position," but he brushed off the Republican surge as a midcourse correction by voters after two years of inordinately large Democratic majorities. Johnson could not know that soon a revitalized Republican party, spurred by newly discovered strength in the once-Solid South, would capture the White House for twenty of the next twenty-four years beginning in 1968. After all, Johnson's party still held the House by a 248-to-187 margin. Johnson attributed Democratic losses in states like Ohio, Michigan, and California to the drawing power of Republican governors James Rhodes, George Romney, and Ronald Reagan. "In Ohio, Gov. Rhodes had a great majority and has been a very effective leader of the Republican party, a very popular one and very cooperative with our administration and with me personally," Johnson told reporters gathered at his Texas ranch that November. "We lost five seats there because he ran hundreds of thousands [of votes] ahead of his opponent."[19]

Republican national party chairman, Ray Bliss of Akron, saw a bigger picture: the makings of a political realignment and a new Republican majority with a coalition built "from the bottom up," taking votes of city-dwellers, blacks, union families, and the young away from the Democrats. "It looks as if we have a very live elephant," Bliss said of a party that seemed moribund after the 1964 election. A *New York Times* editorial on November 13, 1966, said that the "Republican party for the first time in its history is well on its way to becoming a party with a nationwide base." And *Times* columnist James Reston said that Democrats "can no longer count on the allegiance of a massive, unified labor vote . . . the race issue, the rise of taxes, the cost of the war are breaking up the old Roosevelt coalition of the south, urban and poor and intellectuals. What one group wants the other rejects."[20]

In Ohio, Republicans had more than held their own with the FDR Democrats throughout the postwar era. By 1966, veterans like Frank Bow, Jack Betts, Bill McCulloch, and Frances Bolton were ranking minority members of important committees. And it was no accident. Clarence Brown, a senior member of the House Republican Committee on Committees and a chum of Rayburn's, had maneuvered over the years to get the Ohioans in key posts. "What he was trying to do was structure Ohio's power in Congress," said his son, Clarence "Bud" Brown, Jr. "It was an era that was Ohio's high point. This was a moveable feast."[21] Clarence Brown died in 1965 after forty-seven years in politics (he was elected lieutenant governor in 1918 at age twenty-three) and was succeeded by his son, Bud, a moderate who quickly earned respect for his mastery of energy issues.

Moderation was in style for Ohio Republicans by the mid-1960s. William M. McCulloch of Piqua, ranking member on the Judiciary Committee, was the leading voice for a progressive Republican position in the House on race relations during the great civil rights battles of the mid-1960s. The courageous McCulloch, a cosponsor of the landmark 1964 Civil Rights Act, represented a district bordering Indiana that had only a small minority population. Brown, also from western Ohio, was an ally. McCulloch felt so strongly about the "inherent equality of man" that he later took on President Nixon, saying, "He doesn't see eye to eye with me and I don't see eye to eye with him on constitutional rights in the field of skin color."[22] To Republicans, he was "Mr. Civil Rights." Before Nixon came along, McCulloch was one of President Johnson's closest political friends in the opposition party. The news media called him LBJ's "right arm" in the House. Johnson named him in 1968 to the National Advisory Commission on Civil Disorders, which investigated the race riots in Los Angeles, Detroit, Newark, Cleveland, and other cities. Yet McCulloch was conservative on other issues, signing on as a cosponsor of several anticrime and wiretap bills.

Young newcomers Charles Whalen of Dayton and J. William Stanton of Painesville identified with the small liberal wing of the Republican party. Robert Taft, Jr., was back in Congress in 1966, knocking out Gilligan, but he was a soft-spoken moderate-conservative not destined for leadership. The *New York Times* overestimated young Taft's potential. "Whereas his father, the late Sen. Robert Taft, who was referred to as Mr. Republican, conducted formal campaigns relying on written speeches, the son was big on visits to plant gates, bowling alleys and even bars," the newspaper reported. "Mr. Taft is nearly certain to be heard from again."[23] Taft proved less conservative than his father, but also less ambitious. And he was no ally of the emerging Reaganites.

John M. Ashbrook of Johnstown, elected in 1960, and Donald E. "Buz" Lukens, who arrived in 1966, represented the New Right: fiercely anti-Communist, hawkish, resistant to civil rights legislation, and moralistic.

In 1968, the Ohio political landscape changed. Jack Gilligan, an opponent of the Vietnam War, stunned the state with an upset victory in the Senate primary over Lausche, who had worn out his welcome and seemed sadly out of touch. Lausche was hated by unions and disaffected from African American voters even in his hometown of Cleveland, which had elected Carl Stokes as the first black mayor of a major American city in 1967. Despite the warning signs, Lausche did not take Gilligan seriously and ran a ho-hum campaign until the final days. After years of frustration, Lausche's enemies had taken him out at age seventy-eight. "For 25 years, labor leaders fought me," he said. "In 1968, they beat me. They flooded Ohio with money from the unions throughout the country. I wasn't conscious of what was going on. I was late recognizing it and the turn against me occurred in the very last part of the campaign. By then, it was too late." William B. Saxbe, the Republican Senate nominee that year, said, "Lausche would go to a session and get up and make some wild statement and leave and go play golf. That is why he lost."[24] Saxbe, the former Ohio attorney general, was a tobacco-chewing gentleman-farmer from Mechanicsburg. Just over 51 percent of the voters chose his folksy ways over the urbane Gilligan in the general election for the Senate in November.

Before the May 7 primary, a federal court approved a new congressional map for the U.S. House, mandated by the Supreme Court's 1964 "one man, one vote" decisions, which halted huge population disparities among legislative districts. The remap, stalled due to a series of lawsuits and conflicting plans, was finally drawn up based on a Supreme

Court opinion in a case brought by attorney Louis Stokes on behalf of the Cleveland NAACP. Districts were allowed population variances of no more than 2.4 percent, or about 9,000 people. Even though Republicans in the legislature controlled the redistricting process, this proved to be a death knell for the "cornstalk brigade." Low-population rural districts, usually held by Republicans, had to be expanded to pick up voters from urban and suburban areas.

Fiendishly clever remapping by a Republican-controlled state legislature after the 1970 census and strong candidate recruitment by party chairmen like Ray Bliss in Akron, Robert E. Hughes in Cleveland, and Earl T. Barnes in Cincinnati saved a disproportionate number of GOP seats. Bliss, with quiet backing from Eisenhower, served as the Republican party's national chairman after the Goldwater debacle. As Neal Peirce makes clear, he was no Lee Atwater, the take-no-prisoners architect of George Bush's 1988 White House triumph:

> The chief architect of postwar Republican organizational strength in Ohio was Ray C. Bliss, a man whose modest demeanor (that of a small town banker, or the Akron insurance broker that he was) belied unusual intensity when it came to political matters. Scrupulously careful organization, year-round fundraising, never leaving a detail unattended—those were the secrets of the Bliss formula. The one thing Bliss never, never did as a party chairman was to talk in public about issues. He was essentially a technician to whom issues were a propaganda tool, not an end. His ideological neutrality assured him longevity on the job in Columbus and made him the natural choice [for national chairman].[25]

In the 1968 election, Congressman Vanik, whose redrawn east-side district was now 60 percent black, wisely decided to run against Frances Bolton for a seat that included parts of suburban Cuyahoga County. "One of her issues was that I was a carpetbagger because I did not [live in the district]," Vanik said of the campaign. "Mrs. Bolton overstayed her time."[26] After succeeding her late husband, Chester C. Bolton, Frances Bolton had been in Washington for twenty-eight years. She lost to Vanik by almost 18,000 votes, capturing only 45 percent of her district. (Her loss left Ohio without female representation until Cleveland west sider Mary Rose Oakar won the Democratic nomination in a crowded 1976 primary.) Vanik's move opened the door for Louis Stokes, known then

mainly as the brother of Cleveland mayor Carl Stokes. He bested thirteen other candidates in a primary and then defeated Charles P. Lucas,
a black Republican. Ironically, Stokes had represented Lucas in the gerrymandering suit that was decided in 1968, in effect creating a district for
him. He remained through the mid-1990s as Ohio's first and only African
American congressman.

The "one man, one vote" rulings had a profound impact in the new
decade as political power moved finally toward Ohio's Democratic-
controlled urban areas. Twenty-year veteran William H. Ayres, a moderate Republican, lost in 1970 to Democrat John Seiberling of Akron,
scion of the Goodyear Tire family and an opponent of the Vietnam
War. Cleveland City Council president James V. Stanton, a practiced
Kennedy-style Democrat, succeeded Michael Feighan. Kirwan died in
1970; McCulloch, Bow, and Betts retired in 1972.

The old guard was bowing out. But John Glenn, on the sidelines since
1964, was waiting for another opportunity as the decade opened. Behind
the hero's sheen and Boy Scout modesty, Glenn was ambitious and
determined to succeed in politics. He joined RC Cola as an executive
and made a fortune investing in Holiday Inns in Ohio and Florida near
Disney World. But he was eyeing the Senate in 1970 when Senator
Young, by then eighty-one, the oldest man in the Senate, decided to step
down. A former Ohio colleague commented, "John got a taste of it and
that is why he wanted to go immediately to the U.S. Senate—no House
of Representatives, no administration post. He would properly take his
position in the Hall of Fame. . . . He is always thinking about his place in
history. You look at his single-minded determination, which he has
plenty of. When he announced against Steve Young [in 1964], it was
there, and he was going to go for it. Until he slipped in the shower, it
was a forgone conclusion he was going to the United States Senate."[27]

Glenn was nagged by questions about his slow recovery from the
bathroom mishap six years earlier, making a household accident part of
Ohio political folklore: somehow the hero who roared through a nearly
flawless three orbits in space in Friendship 7 failed to negotiate a shower
door. "I was trying to slide the [medicine cabinet] mirror shut, and
slipped, and the throw-rug went out and my head hit the little metal rail
at the top of the tub where the shower door slides. The mirror [falling]
hit my head and broke."[28]

Howard Metzenbaum of Cleveland, himself a millionaire, had also
been waiting for Young to step aside. He leaped into the primary against

Glenn with a well-financed, professionally run campaign. He was little known outside Cuyahoga County, but he was a savvy campaigner, outmatching the inexperienced Glenn. Using television advertising more extensively than any previous Senate candidate had in Ohio, Metzenbaum made inroads in heavily Democratic areas in the industrial north of Ohio. He attracted strong support from trade unions.

Metzenbaum won the hard-fought 1970 primary by 13,443 votes. In addition to his sophisticated television advertising campaign, he capitalized on the success of New York's "Amazin' Mets" in the 1969 World Series, rallying his followers as "Metz fans." The overconfident Glenn was embarrassed and bitter. Representative Robert Taft, Jr., defeated Governor James Rhodes in a nasty Republican primary held the day after the shootings of four students by National Guard troops at Kent State University.

Now running against Taft, Metzenbaum asked the crusty Young about getting a mailing list or other help in fund raising for the fall campaign. Ever the eccentric, Young would not help. "He looked at me and said, 'I don't know anybody.' He never gave me a name."[29] Metzenbaum was staggered by a smear in the general election campaign when a Columbus radio reporter accused him of having connections with Communist front groups, such as the National Lawyers Guild, in the 1930s and 1940s. Metzenbaum later conceded he had naively gotten too close to some leftist organizations. He was "red-baited" throughout his career. So Taft, fitting into the state's moderate politics like a comfortable shoe, edged the Democrat by 2 percentage points—74,000 votes out of more than 3 million cast in the election.

As a political footnote, Congressman Ashbrook, deciding that Nixon was not conservative enough, challenged the incumbent president in 1972 in the New Hampshire primary but was badly beaten and dropped out. (Ashbrook was principled and sincere, but not credible. Nixon's few problems with the far-right wing of his party were soon overshadowed by Watergate.) And Senator Saxbe, though he once said he feared Nixon had lost his senses after an escalation of bombing in southeast Asia, was chosen as U.S. attorney general in 1974, replacing Elliot Richardson, who resigned in protest during Watergate.

Back in Ohio, Governor Gilligan, pressured by organized labor, appointed Metzenbaum to the Saxbe vacancy. Infuriated, Glenn immediately challenged the Clevelander in the 1974 primary. The acrimonious campaign exceeded the Democrats' worst fears. Metzenbaum, playing on the antiwar sentiment of the times, repeatedly referred to his rival, a retired Marine officer, as "Colonel Glenn." But on one occasion, he overdid it, intimating that Glenn had never held a job in private life. At the City Club debate in Cleveland on May 3, 1974, Glenn brought up the subject on his own. "Go with me and tell a Gold Star mother her son didn't hold a job," he told Metzenbaum, who had never served in the armed forces. "Go to Arlington National Cemetery, watch those flags, stand there and tell me those people didn't have a job." This time, Glenn hired professionals to run his campaign, accepting his fate as a political being. "In the primary against Metzenbaum, he had tremendous courage," said his press secretary, Steve Avakian, "the courage to surround himself with people he basically did not like."[30]

Glenn won the primary and rolled over Cleveland mayor Ralph Perk in the general election. To his credit, Metzenbaum worked at a furious pace in Washington, even as a lame duck, establishing himself as an aggressive, consumer-oriented senator with a quick grasp of the Senate's protocols.

He battled back in 1976, defeating Congressman James Stanton and two minor candidates in the Democratic primary with 53.6 percent of the vote and then upsetting Senator Taft by 3 percentage points in the general election. Metzenbaum was bewildered by the appeal of Jimmy Carter, a moderate former governor from Georgia, but he campaigned with Carter and his running mate, Walter F. "Fritz" Mondale, and produced bumper stickers that looked like delicatessen advertisements: "Fritz, Grits and Metz."

Taft was only forty-nine, but he had suffered a heart attack the year before and was hurt by questions about his health. "It was post-Watergate, of course. No question about that," he said when asked about the race sixteen years later. "There was no reason why I should not have run ahead of Jerry Ford, but I did not." Taft did not take a strong position on Nixon in 1974 because he thought he might be called upon to vote if impeachment proceedings reached the Senate. In his one term in the Senate, Taft was respected for his integrity and quiet effectiveness, but he did not leave big footprints on Capitol Hill, as had his father. He died in December 1993 at age seventy-six. A friend of Taft's, Bud Brown, himself a second-generation congressman, told of once being accused by a shallow Reagan administration aide of not being a "true conservative." "You were not for Reagan, you are not a conservative," the angry Reaganite told him. "I said, 'my family comes from a long line of people that supported Senator Taft.' " He meant the senior Taft, of course, but his accuser misunderstood. "She said, 'He is a liberal. That is why he was defeated by Metzenbaum.' That was the depth of her history about the Republican party and the liberal-conservative split in the Republican party."[31]

Glenn refused to endorse Metzenbaum during the 1976 campaign against Taft. After Metzenbaum's election, the two men barely spoke. Their working relationship was so poor that at one point Carter's attorney general, Griffin Bell, called them to the Justice Department and insisted they agree on appointees to the federal judiciary. Their stand-off had caused a backlog of vacancies for the federal bench in Ohio. Newspapers called it the "civil war" of Ohio politics. "The staffs were at each others throats. We were all charged up to be competitive. It was almost like machismo," a former staffer told the *Plain Dealer*. "To my mind, it transcended the bounds of healthy competition."[32]

Republicans still controlled the House delegation, but the Democrats were developing a liberal nucleus that would support Carter's programs later in the decade and resist Reagan in the 1980s. Tom Luken of Cincinnati, Donald J. Pease of Oberlin, and Mary Rose Oakar, all elected in 1976, formed lasting alliances with more senior members and soon landed assignments on powerful committees.

By mid-decade, Congressmen Seiberling, whose gentle, dignified manner and common sense, belied the stereotype of "far-out" liberalism, had emerged as one of Ohio's most effective legislators, though he was never a national figure. In 1974, Seiberling, amid criticism from many who thought the notion incredulous, persuaded Congress to set aside a "greenbelt" around the Cuyahoga River between Akron and Cleveland—a national park surrounded by megalopolis. Aided by Vanik and a progressive young Republican from the Canton area, Ralph S. Regula, he won approval for the Cuyahoga Valley National Recreation Area, Ohio's only national park. As he gained seniority, Seiberling became chairman of the public lands subcommittee of the Interior Committee and played a leading role in preserving 100 million acres of wilderness in Alaska. He was the bane of development-minded western state Republicans.

He was a problem for the White House, too. Seiberling coauthored the landmark War Powers Resolution, which was adopted over President Nixon's veto. He was a champion of nuclear disarmament, historic preservation and the environment. Once outlining his legislative philosophy for a reporter, he said, "What we are trying to do is maintain a liveable world, free of nuclear disaster, a world that we have not polluted to the point where we can't breathe, and where we preserve some natural beauty so that we can have the solace and the experience of being out in God's world." After Seiberling announced his retirement in 1986, the *Plain Dealer Magazine* wrote, "His voice is scratchy now and his walk slowed, but Seiberling still looks almost boyish at times, with his hands stuffed in his pockets and his head cocked up a little, as if he is trying to hear something just out of earshot. On good days, he still rides a bicycle from his town house near Capitol Hill to his House office."[33]

In 1974 Seiberling sat on the Judiciary Committee and voted with the majority to impeach Richard Nixon. His counterpart was Delbert Latta of Bowling Green, one of the president's diehard loyalists. Latta, a flinty Main-Street conservative, was one of eleven Republicans on the committee who voted against impeachment. When a GOP effort to narrow the articles of impeachment failed, Latta defiantly said, "We're bowing because we don't have the votes. We are not abandoning our position."[34] The Ohio delegation had enjoyed friendly, cooperative relations through much of the 1960s as outnumbered, compliant Democrats worked with Republicans to seek favors from the House leadership. But relations became strained between Latta and his allies and the liberal activists on the Democrat side after the Watergate scandal. A humorless sort, Latta became chairman of the Ohio delegation in the mid-1970s and was a senior member of the Rules Committee. He rarely held bipartisan delegation meetings, but he did maintain respectful, working relationships with Democratic leader Thomas P. "Tip" O'Neill and Congressman Stokes.

Wayne Hays was every bit as hard-edged as Latta. He took over as chairman of the House Administration Committee following the 1970 election and quickly made a grab for power. A year later, Gerald Ford, the House minority leader, warned that the power ceded to Hays's committee "will never be returned to the House as a whole until and unless there is a scandal."[35] He was right. Hardly a crusader for good government, Hays and his committee fashioned the 1974 campaign finance reform act. During the infighting, Hays added loopholes to the law.

Making enemies on Capitol Hill with his abrasive style and vindictive tactics, Hays "brought home pork" to the folks in his eastern Ohio Eighteenth Congressional District. He went home often to Red Gate Farm in Belmont County, where he raised angus cattle and Tennessee Walking Horses. "He took care of his district and worked well with a good constituency-oriented office and I think that is what gets you elected," said his successor, Douglas Applegate of Steubenville. "His problem was he had an ego that was as fat as the globe. I think he expected a lot of people to cater to his whims. But I have to give the devil his due, he did take care of his people." "He could be real tough," said Charlie Vanik, who knew Hays from their days together in the Ohio Senate in the late 1940s. "He was sort of a bully. He would pick on weak people and pounce all over them." Yet sometimes he went after more deserving targets. "He really shook up the foreign service," said Vanik. "They were living lush. He had them all stirred up."[36]

But Hays's undoing was a blonde party-girl, Elizabeth Ray, a receptionist for the House Administration Committee, with whom Hays had an affair. After he got a quickie divorce from his wife, Martha Judkins, in the Dominican Republic, Hays began courting another woman, Patricia Peak, and dumped Ray.

When Hays decided to have his wedding reception in House Administration offices, the staff was invited—except for Liz Ray. When she protested, making a general nuisance out of herself, Hays called Capitol Hill police to remove her, forcibly, squirming and screaming. "He should have let her come. Everybody knew about Elizabeth, but he told her if she came he was going to have her put out and he put her out, or he had the police come and put her out," Vanik recalled. "It was not wise. She was a sensitive person and it offended and hurt her very much."[37]

On a train trip to New York, Ray once had a chance encounter with a *Washington Post* reporter and mentioned, unabashed, that she "slept with congressmen."[38] Now, remembering that contact at the *Post*, Ray went to a phone booth and called the reporter with her story about Hays.

"In another era, Ray, angry at Hays' snub and anxious about what he could do to her, might have sent an anonymous letter to his new wife, phoned some of his fellow politicians, or slashed her wrists and left a tragic incriminating note," Suzanne Garment writes in *Scandal: The Culture of Mistrust in American Politics*. "But Ray went directly to the press to take her revenge. A child of the *Playboy* culture, she did not in the least mind being revealed as Hays' mistress. Moreover, when she stepped into that phone booth, she was confident that her story would be welcomed even by such a prestigious news organization as the *Washington Post*." In the subsequent story Ray said she was kept on the payroll to serve as Hays's mistress. "I can't type. I can't file. I can't even answer the phone," she declared.[39]

Hays's enemies fell on him. He was stripped of his committee chairmanship and the coveted post of chairman of the Democratic Congressional Campaign Committee. He managed to win the June 1976 primary in Ohio, but later in the summer he suddenly resigned. Jim Hart, onetime aide to Hays, argues against the conventional wisdom that Hays was one of the most powerful members of the House. Hays wanted to be "the ultimate politician" in the context of exerting control, he said. That kind of arrogance led to his downfall in the treatment of Liz Ray. "I don't believe, by my definition, that he was a powerful congressman, not in terms of influencing the direction of the country," said Hart. "It was institutional power." (A final note on Liz Ray, according to Hart, who knew her: "She *could* type.")[40]

Vanik, a determined individualist who wore a black suit and bow tie every day in defiance of Washington's "power" dress codes, passed legislation that would have implications for the fall of the Soviet empire. The Jackson-Vanik amendment of 1974 used a carrot-and-stick approach to force the Soviet Union to allow more Jewish emigration. The measure linked most-favored-nation trade status to the human rights record of a trading partner. "It considers immigration a human rights issue," said Vanik, himself of Czech descent. "It was a law that tried to restore some power to the Congress. [Until then] the silk hats at the State Department would decide what the trade rules were; Congress had nothing to do with it."[41] (When Mikhail Gorbachev introduced *glasnost* in 1985 and opened Soviet borders, former congressman Vanik urged that Jackson-Vanik restrictions be waived. They soon were.) Had he stayed in Congress into the new decade, Vanik might have become a household name, since he was in line to take over as chairman of the Ways and Means Committee. That would have given him the kind of power Hart was referring to—the ability to shape national policy.

Ohio's best hope for national leadership in the latter half of the 1970s was John Glenn. But Glenn chose not to capitalize on his astronaut fame, and his inexperience as a politician showed. Over the protests of political advisers, he stubbornly insisted on writing his own keynote speech for the 1976 Democratic National Convention in New York (and wound up following charismatic Barbara Jordan to the podium) and bombed.

"He's got that fighter-pilot mentality," said Steve Kovacik, his onetime political guru. "I'll fly this ship [is his attitude], just get me a good ground crew." Glenn steered away from national appearances. Avakian and Kovacik led a faction that thought he had as good a chance of being the Democratic presidential nominee as a peanut farmer from Georgia, but Glenn squelched an incipient write-in campaign in New Hampshire. "I still believe that was John's best chance to become president—nothing has deterred me from thinking that," Kovacik said. "There comes an opportunity and you have to make your move. I thought that was John's chance. I think he would have knocked Jimmy Carter back to Georgia."[42]

Senator Glenn's ill-timed and uneven political career was in some ways mirrored by the Ohio House delegation, which often seemed outside the loop of Washington's Beltway. Enormously popular and seemingly "teflon-coated" back home, Glenn was a second-tier senator in Washington during his first two terms. When Democrats reclaimed control of the Senate in 1986 after a six-year interlude, he became chairman of the obscure Governmental Affairs Committee, which is occupied with the minutiae of government. Busy, busy Metzenbaum was named chairman of two subcommittees and served with Glenn on the select intelligence panel.

Ohio Democrats lost only one seat to the Reagan 1980 sweep as twenty-six-year veteran Lud Ashley was knocked out by Republican Ed Weber of Toledo. (Ashley surfaced later as an influential banking lobbyist and George Bush's best Democratic friend, chums since their college days at Yale.) Glenn easily won reelection in 1980, disposing of a likeable state representative from Rocky River named James E. Betts.[43] A Republican warhorse, one-time FBI agent Sam Devine of Columbus lost to Democratic lawyer Robert Shamansky. (Hurt by redistricting and political miscalculations, Shamansky was the only House Democratic incumbent in the country ousted in 1982, losing to conservative populist John Kasich.) Dennis E. Eckart, representing Cleveland's east suburbs, also began a productive career in the House in 1980, taking Vanik's seat when he retired, not wishing to "overstay." Edward F. Feighan, nephew of Michael Feighan, arrived two years later, defeating antibusing activist Ronald Mottl of Parma in a primary. The publicity-hungry Mottl took fiscal conservatism to an extreme, often sleeping overnight in his Capitol Hill office rather than renting an apartment.

Glenn's Senate seat was secure; so was Metzenbaum's. A classic contest with John Ashbrook ended prematurely in 1982 when Ashbrook collapsed and died at his Johnstown headquarters in the midst of a campaign against Metzenbaum. (He is memorialized at the John M. Ashbrook Center for Public Affairs at Ashland University.) Republican state senator Paul Pfeifer, a Bucyrus lawyer, took up the fight but was run over by the Metzenbaum machine. Governor James A. Rhodes seriously considered challenging Metzenbaum that year but was advised against it. (When GOP state chairman Earl Barnes asked him why he would want to go to Capitol Hill after a career of beating up Washington politicians, he answered simply: "Burning Tree, Earl, Burning Tree." Rhodes, an avid golfer, was referring to the toney all-male golf club in Maryland.)

Rhodes and Metzenbaum stirred strong emotions among Ohio voters. A hero to organized labor, consumer activists, and the party's left wing, Metzenbaum was feared by business interests and loathed by conservatives. Glenn, however, remained somewhat the detached hero. He was held in affection by average Joes, tolerated by Republicans, considered a reliable vote for the Democratic party. "Where Metzenbaum is a porcupine, getting prickly with people, John is neither a porcupine, nor a political doer," said a Cleveland politician.[44] Unlike the aura surrounding Taft, there were relatively few "Glenn Democrats" in Ohio and only a slim constituency in the country at large, as he discovered during a disastrous 1984 bid for the Democratic presidential nomination. Glenn's amateurish campaign and middle-of-the-road compass were no match for former vice president Walter Mondale's veteran crew. In hindsight, Glenn would have had a better chance in 1976 against Carter or in 1988 against Michael S. Dukakis. And adding to his pain, both of those nominees bypassed him as a vice presidential running mate. Instead, he was left with a huge debt and a critical finding from the Federal Election Commission that $2 million in loans he took from four Ohio banks should not have been extended because of the absence of collateral.

He was a lousy fundraiser; he hated to ask. By his reelection in 1992, the unpaid debts from the 1984 presidential campaign owed to creditors had reached more than $3.2 million. One year he raised only $250 toward retiring it. Finally, in 1993, the Federal Election Commission made an exception for Glenn and authorized him to use his own money to pay off the debt. Until getting the waiver, Glenn had been legally barred from giving more than $50,000 to his own campaign.

His opponent in 1986, banjo-strumming representative Thomas N. Kindness of Hamilton, tried to make the old campaign debt an issue, calling Glenn a deadbeat because he defaulted to the banks and had not paid vendors. The voters paid no mind to the bland Kindness and reelected Glenn with 62 percent of the vote.

The next year Glenn and four other senators met privately with savings and loan regulators on behalf of embattled financier Charles H. Keating, Jr., who had given a $200,000 contribution to Glenn. Keating, an old acquaintance of Glenn, was the brother of former Cincinnati representative William Keating, who served from 1970 to 1974. His money was funneled to a dormant political action committee, which used some of it to partially subsidize operations of Glenn's debt retirement and Senate campaign committees.

The "Keating Five" scandal became public the following year. Glenn and the other four senators were accused of using their influence in 1987 to help Keating ward off regulators. Glenn was eventually cleared of wrongdoing in his intervention on behalf of Keating (Glenn called him "Charlie"), but the Senate Ethics Committee said he used poor judgment in going to Keating's aid. Glenn, defiant, insisted he was only helping an embattled constituent and would do the same for any Ohioan. Phoenix developer Keating, who went to prison in 1992, had not lived in Ohio for ten years.

As a man who had looked down on his world from 162 miles in space, Glenn had vision. But his political instincts often failed him. "More than anyone I have ever known he realized how one person can influence another person's life," said former press aide Avakian, a Columbus-based political consultant.[45] Two years into his first term, Glenn was prescient about voters attitudes and their lack of confidence in government. "I think in theory at least part of the problem is that the people have lost control of their future," he told a 1976 symposium on directions for our third century. "The government is writing regulations in the *Federal Register* that say you can do this, and you cannot do that, and it affects your future. The average person is mad at the government." In Washington, he is known as a champion of nuclear nonproliferation, an advocate for the homeless, a thoughtful planner of the scaling-down of the military after the cold war, and author of the benefits package for Persian Gulf war veterans. But he is a cautious politician, reluctant to lead on controversial issues. He and Metzenbaum initially opposed use of force against Iraq, and Glenn was noncommittal about President Bill Clinton's plan to lift the ban against gays in the armed forces. His forte was the arcane; his playground the General Accounting Office. The *Washington Post* called him "Mr. Checklist."

Unlike Glenn, Metzenbaum rarely shied away from controversy. Until the mid-1980s, he was better known for his ability to block legislation—often through filibusters—than for advancing important works. He was a master at uncovering boondoggles hidden in thousand-page bills, stopping them in their tracks. When the new Democratic majority gave him two subcommittee chairs in 1986, he proved he could legislate constructively also, winning enactment for a plant closing notification law, pension reform, and stronger antitrust enforcement. He coauthored the Civil Rights Act of 1991 and was one of Israel's best friends in Washington. He is a death penalty foe, yet once suggested Mu'ammar Qaddafi should be assassinated.

Metzenbaum and Glenn reconciled and worked well together during the Reagan and Bush years. Like Senator Edward M. Kennedy, Metzenbaum was a lightning rod for the Right—targeted without success by the National Rifle Association and other conservative activist groups. He relished those attacks, even baiting the NRA, an organization feared by many of his colleagues. But Metzenbaum was embarrassed by the revelation that he had accepted $250,000 as a "finder's fee" for making a telephone call that helped strike a deal for the sale of the elegant Hay-Adams Hotel. And he hurt himself with an awkward performance during the nationally televised confirmation hearings of Supreme Court justice Clarence Thomas, who was accused of sexual harassment by Anita Hill. The old white tiger was never a made-for-television act. He called it his low point in politics.

While Senators Metzenbaum and Glenn had their share of notoriety, most of the House members from Ohio toiled in anonymity and measured their progress in inches rather than miles. House Democrats achieved a breakthrough in 1984 when they captured an 11-to-10 majority in the Ohio delegation, gaining at least a symbolic advantage for the first time in the postwar era. The shift of political power in Ohio from the farmbelt to the cities and suburbs was complete.

Representative Louis Stokes of Cleveland, who headed the delegation when Democrats claimed their majority, was one of the most prominent black politicians in the country. He was chairman of the Ethics Committee and a senior member of the mighty Appropriations Committee, a position that proved of great benefit to his east-side district, which included the inner-city Hough and Glenville neighborhoods. Stokes starred on television in the Iran-Contra investigation as one of Oliver North's most aggressive inquisitors. He also led a special House inquiry in 1977 into the assassinations of John F. Kennedy and Martin Luther King, Jr. He was also a valued troubleshooter for three House speakers: Tip O'Neill,

Jim Wright, and Tom Foley. When he was named with Mary Rose Oakar and Edward Feighan in the House Bank fiasco, he stepped aside as Ethics Committee chairman while the panel conducted an investigation, which eventually cleared him.

Dayton's Tony Hall, whose father was the colorful mayor of Dayton and whose older brother, Sam, a soldier of fortune who was captured and later released by the Sandinistas in Nicaragua, was a member of the Rules Committee and Ohio's only House committee chairman through much of the decade. The former college athlete at Denison University and Ohio State and Peace Corps volunteer chaired the Select Committee on Hunger until 1993. Hall, an independent-minded liberal, took on issues such as international human rights and poverty, and as a committed Christian he consistently voted antiabortion.

Congressman Delbert Latta, who deeply admired Reagan, was a symbol for the stubborn, prairie conservatism that characterized the Ohio Republican delegation during the two previous decades. Near the end of Reagan's second administration, he proposed a constitutional amendment to allow the president to serve a third term—it went nowhere. Ironically, the Twenty-second Amendment was the brainchild of Republicans reacting to Roosevelt's dominance. Latta's high point came in 1982 when he and Senator Phil Gramm of Texas (then a Democrat), helped Reagan form an "ideological majority" relying on what Latta called "Jeffersonian Democrats." The Gramm-Latta budget resolution of 1982 was a blueprint for Reaganomics. Latta, ranking Republican on the Budget Committee, helped reduce domestic spending and income tax rates. The ideological majority vanished during Reagan's second term. Latta retired in 1988 with $123,000 in leftover campaign funds, which he donated to candidates and Ohio institutions.

Immediately to Latta's east on the congressional map was Lorain County representative Don Pease, Ohio's answer to "Mr. Smith Goes to Washington." Pease, a Fulbright Scholar elected in the Bicentennial year, was an architect of the Tax Reform Act of 1986 and the budget deal of 1990. The serious, low-key lawmaker grounded in college-town journalism at Oberlin, was one of Ohio's most effective representatives. Conservatively dressed and cursed with a thin reedy voice, he was a respected member of the Ways and Means Committee and an unlikely confidante of its tough-talking chairman, Dan Rostenkowski of Illinois. Like the Mr. Smith of the movies, Pease was an idealist, ill at ease with glad-handing, back-scratching, or boozy backroom deal-making. Unlike the fictional Mr. Smith, however, he was a full-blooded politician, disciplined, patient, and not given to tirades on the House floor.

The 1990 "Pease Plan," as it came to be known, shrank deductions for taxpayers whose adjusted gross incomes were more than $100,000. In addition to his work on tax law, Pease was cosponsor of the 1988 trade reform act and tried in vain to reform unemployment compensation. Because he came to Congress before 1980, Pease could have kept his leftover campaign funds, which exceeded $245,000, after announcing his retirement in October 1991 "at the height of my influence." He instead returned what he could to contributors he had tracked down and gave the rest to the nonprofit Community Foundation of Greater Lorain. "I value my reputation as a straight arrow," he said.[46]

Pease was convinced that television, more than money, was the corrupting influence of the 1980s, since in statewide races, most campaign dollars went into television commercials. "Campaigns are expensive because television is expensive," Pease said. "Television is such a powerful medium that negative TV ads will determine the outcome of almost any election, if the ads go unchallenged." Pease believed that the growth of cable television and the trivialization of the news by television distracted voters from serious analyses of candidates and left them "essentially blank slates." "The media consultants come along with their negative TV ads and fill in the slates."[47]

Ohio had another strong off-camera voice on the Ways and Means Committee, Willis Gradison of Cincinnati. Like Pease, he was a serious fellow and a stalwart of the Wednesday Group, a collection of Republican moderates cofounded by Pease's predecessor, Charles A. Mosher of Oberlin. Gradison, a millionaire, was an institutional reformer interested in streamlining needlessly complicated procedures of the House. "I recognize the Founding Fathers deliberately sought to make it difficult to pass legislation," he said after a Democratic-inspired sleight-of-hand on a budget bill, "but did they intend to provide this degree of frivolity?" And when mischievous Democrats linked an ethics package to a legislative pay raise in 1989, he registered his disgust. "This is the first pay increase I have voted for in my 15 years in Congress," he said. "In doing so, it is my hope, which may be naive, that my constituents will recognize that my goal is more effective government and not feathering my own nest."[48]

Ohio had its wild men, too. Representative Tom Luken, a garrulous pro-labor populist who came to Capitol Hill as an opponent of the

Vietnam War in 1974 but grew more conservative, particularly on environmental matters, was a bullying prosecutor in committee and just as tough on his own staff. When David N. Colbert left as counsel to Luken's transportation and hazardous waste subcommittee, he wrote to Representative John Dingell, chairman of the full committee, about his old boss: "The manner in which Chairman Luken treats the professional staff of the subcommittee is nothing less than scandalous. In the time I have served the subcommittee as counsel, I have been subjected to my share of the chairman's personal tirades and temper tantrums. I have witnessed behavior I would not condone in a two-year-old."[49]

Luken, of German-Irish heritage, was an ordinary looking middle-aged man from a distance, but a scowling, intimidating presence up close. Stocky, with a large head, he got right in the face of his target, haranguing in rapid fire like an aging drill sergeant, leaving little space for rebuttal. In the book *Hill Rat,* John L. Jackley recounts a confrontation with Luken, known to his staff as "the Duke." Jackley, a new legislative assistant at the time, was briefing on an innocuous bill designating "Our Merchant Marine Hymn" as the official song of the United States Merchant Marine. Luken accused Jackley of trying to sandbag him on the trivial measure. Jackley describes the horrific scene: "Silence. More silence. Then almost mildly: 'How's it go?' I furrowed my brow, looked at him, and without thinking, stepped off the edge: 'Uh, it's going fine, sir, how about you?' 'No goddamnit, how's it go, go, go!' he exploded. 'How's it go? How does it go? Which word don't you understand? Which one? How does it fucking go? Go! Dumdee dum dum dum! Go! Go!' almost choking out and screaming the final syllable. 'Dum deedum go go dum dum dee dum de fucking go!' "[50] Jackley did not know how it went.

Tom Luken retired in 1990 and was succeeded by his son, Charles Luken, the affable former mayor of Cincinnati who bore little resemblance to his incendiary father. In fact, Charlie Luken was so turned off by the hardball game on Capitol Hill that he quit after one-term to return to Cincinnati, where he went into television news.

Neither Cincinnati Luken, however, should be confused with the inimitable Donald E. "Buz" Lukens of Middletown, who returned to Congress in 1986 after a sixteen-year absence, taking Kindness's seat. Most of Lukens's time away had been spent in the Ohio Senate and in an unsuccessful attempt to build a winemaking business in southwestern Ohio. Weakened by a bout with throat cancer, he was no longer *l'enfant terrible* of the conservative movement, as he had been in the mid-to-late 1960s. But in 1989, Lukens, who was divorced and in his late fifties, was accused of having sex with a Columbus teenager. The girl's mother had videotaped a meeting with Lukens in a fast-food restaurant where the congressman appeared to offer to help find a job for the girl's mother. It was aired on Columbus television. He was subsequently convicted of contributing to the delinquency of a minor, a misdemeanor, but fought to hold his seat in Congress. After losing a primary to John Boehner of West Chester in 1990, Lukens was forced to resign in the midst of an ethics investigation. He had been accused of fondling a young female elevator operator in the Capitol.

Throughout the Reagan decade, the liberals of the urban north actively opposed the president. Representatives Dennis Eckart, Ed Feighan, Marcy Kaptur, Mary Rose Oakar, and James Traficant were not the Jeffersonian Democrats that Latta admired. They were fast with sound bites and anxious to move up in the Democratic leadership.

Eckart, who kept a condominium in Mentor, had the confidence of "Big John" Dingell of Michigan, the imperious chairman of the Energy and Commerce Committee. Eckart was a doer. He sponsored the 1986 Superfund bill, which promised to strengthen clean-ups of hazardous-waste dumps, and he tried mightily to balance Ohio's industrial and high-sulfur coal interests against his environmental conscience in the 1990 Clean Air Act. Feighan and Kaptur were not as flashy, crafty, or driven as Eckart, but they were respected. Feighan worked hard on legislation combating the international drug trade and authored the Brady Bill, the handgun waiting-period plan named after former White House press secretary James Brady. Oakar rose to vice chair of the Democratic caucus after cultivating a close relationship with Speaker O'Neill. Favored by women's groups, she was persistent in her efforts to gain more funding for breast cancer research and to expand benefits for mammogram testing. She was a friend to senior citizens and public employees and brought millions of dollars' worth of federal development grants to Cleveland. In 1987, however, it was reported that Oakar kept an aide on her House payroll for almost two years after the woman moved to New York. An ethics committee report concluded that she broke the law by paying the staffer in New York. No action was taken since Oakar had repaid the $45,386 to the treasury.

In 1992, Oakar and Feighan were listed as two of the worst abusers of the privileges of the House bank. The two Ohioans were among twenty-two singled out because they had frequently overdrawn accounts for large sums. Stokes and Chalmers Wylie of Columbus, among 280 who also had overdrafts, each had more than five hundred, though usually for small amounts. And while the "rubbergate" scandal had more to do with arrogance than illegality, it played into voter revulsion at the perks and inefficiency of Congress. The scandal, combined with redistricting, caused a record turnover in the 1992 election. "They [Democrats] ran the House bank and oversaw the post office [another mess]," grumbled Lukens's successor, John Boehner. "They've run the place lock, stock and barrel and look what they've produced."[51]

The purging could not have come at a worst time for Ohio. The maturing Ohio delegation was advancing to upper management in the House, discarding the label of chronic underachiever. But disaster struck in 1992. The state lost two seats after the census, continuing a thirty-year trend of stagnant population growth. Eckart, Feighan, Pease, Charles Luken, and Wylie, the ranking Republican on the Banking Committee, all retired.

Clarence Miller, one of four Ohioans on the Appropriations Committee, was beaten in a Republican primary by Bob McEwen of Hillsboro when they were thrown together in a southeastern Ohio district remapped to McEwen's advantage. But McEwen, another veteran with an overdrawn House bank account, was beaten in November by Democrat Ted Strickland, who had lost three earlier bids for Congress. McEwen, a strong stump campaigner, was bloodied by the primary fight against fellow Republican Miller, who remained bitter and did not endorse him in the general election. Strickland pilloried McEwen with radio commercials denouncing his check-writing habits and taxpayer-funded junketeering.

Oakar, running in a less-Democratic district that November, was upset by Republican businessman Martin Hoke, a political neophyte. The mud flew from both sides, as Hoke, focusing on Oakar's ethical lapses, ousted the incumbent of sixteen years.

Gradison easily won reelection, but in January 1993 he resigned to become president of the Health Insurance Association of America and emerged as a leading voice against President Clinton's health-care reform plan. "What's going on in Cincinnati these days?" a puzzled *Plain Dealer* columnist wrote of the rash of retirements. "Sibling rivalry aside, something about our sister city to the southwest appears to be scaring off their congressmen."[52]

At the outset of the 1990s, the delegation was ready to rival the clout of California, Texas, New York, Illinois, and Pennsylvania. Pease, through quiet lobbying, had helped bring the Democratic and Republican sides together monthly—unheard of in Latta's day. He and Gradison were men to be reckoned with on Ways and Means. Kaptur, Stokes, Miller, and Regula all had seats on the Appropriations Committee. And Stokes, Feighan, and Eckart were poised for subcommittee chairmanships. But then it fell apart.

After the 1992 election, the delegation retrenched. Six freshman were sworn in—almost one-third of the delegation—including former municipal judge Deborah Pryce of Columbus, the first Republican woman to serve since Frances Bolton. Ohio was shut out of the Ways and Means Committee for the first time in decades, and the state lost influence on the Energy and Commerce Committee, which held sway over issues important to Great Lakes states. Pryce moved to the front of the Republican freshman class in 1993; she was the "big tent" kind of pro-choice Republican that many analysts thought the party needed.

Stokes became chairman of an Appropriations subcommittee, joining the envied "College of Cardinals" that controlled spending bills. He was the dean of the delegation, a confidante of Jesse Jackson, and an inside player respected by the majority leadership. In the era of Clinton's "new kind" of Democratic party, he remained an unrepentant Great Society liberal.

Kaptur, Hall, and Akron representative Tom Sawyer settled into middle-management roles. Sawyer, who hesitated and lost an opportunity to succeed Pease on the Ways and Means Committee, made a name as a leading critic of the sloppy 1990 census. He studied hard, but was excessively cautious and given to uninspired speeches that in Akron were ridiculed as "Sawyerese." Tom Sawyer was never mistaken for his freewheeling namesake.

Kaptur, a Baby Boomer (but no yuppie), stayed arms length from the Clinton crowd. The pro-labor, single woman led opposition to the North American Free Trade Agreement, fearing it would take more industrial jobs away from Toledo. A handwringer when she first arrived on Capitol Hill, she grew smarter and tougher while many of her contemporaries—notably Eckart and Feighan—bailed out. She gained the confidence of House leaders and emerged as a force in the Ohio delegation. Enraged after losing the North American

Free Trade Agreement (NAFTA) vote, she said she would not welcome President Clinton to her northwest Ohio district.

Hall was also well thought of, but the shy Daytonian was not on a leadership track. Seniority still counted, and the Ohio Democrats were not staying around long enough. In a dramatic move, when his House Select Committee on Hunger was abolished by a budget cut, Hall fasted for twenty-two days to draw attention to hunger issues.

Traficant, a sight in bellbottoms and cowboy boots, was drawn to television cameras like a dog to a steakbone. The former Mahoning County sheriff, a nonlawyer who once represented himself successfully against a federal bribery charge, delighted in roughhouse tactics and bellicose speeches. He was a protectionist and brutal Japan-basher. And few of his colleagues took him seriously. He did have some success with his "Buy American" amendments, designed to force the government to purchase only domestic goods, and he championed the cause of accused Nazi death-camp guard John Demjanjuk, the Cleveland-area autoworker. Traficant had a chip on his shoulder, which suited his hard-scrabble constituents in Youngstown, but he was not very effective inside the Beltway. When Congress was in session, he lived on a boat docked in the Washington Channel.

Just downstate from Traficant, Douglas Applegate, the successor to Wayne Hays, took over in 1993 as chairman of the Public Works subcommittee on water resources and the environment. During the Reagan-Bush era, Applegate was given to blustery one-minute speeches on the House floor attacking Republican trade policies. But he was often out of step with his own party, siding with conservatives on abortion and other social issues. "Dapper Doug," known for expensive high-collared shirts and well-tailored suits, was well positioned on the Veterans Affairs Committee and proved to be one of the best friends of military veterans on Capitol Hill. He decided to step down in 1994, giving Republicans their best chance to win the seat since Wayne Hays captured it in 1948, defeating the incumbent Earl R. Lewis, a Republican.

Across the aisle, Regula was among the most respected Republicans in the House. The steady-as-she-goes moderate kept a telephone in the barn of his Stark County farm so he could talk politics. He was the ranking member of the Appropriations subcommittee on the interior, where he helped expand the Cuyahoga Valley National Recreation Area, protected coal interests, and fended off efforts to change the name of Mount McKinley in Alaska. He was close to President Bush, but not a rubber

(*Top*) Governor John J. Gilligan debated an empty chair at the Cleveland City Club on November 2, 1974, when his challenger, former governor Rhodes, did not show up for a joint election-eve appearance. Gilligan, a Cincinnati Democrat who had pushed through a controversial income tax early in his 1971–75 term, was narrowly defeated by Rhodes, who charged Gilligan with "taxing everything that walks, crawls, or flies."

Accompanied by John Nardella, president of Local 2 of the United Rubber Workers Union, Governor Gilligan (*center*) greets voters on an Akron street in early November 1974, a few days before his reelection defeat, which he later described as a "wrenching, harrowing shock." Gilligan contended that he had been victimized by Rhodes's "super saturation lie" campaign.

(*Top*) During his winning fall campaign for a third term in 1974, former governor Rhodes addressed this airport rally in Jackson County, where he was born in 1909 in the village of Coalton. His second eight years in office are generally rated as less successful than his first two terms.

Democrat Vernal G. Riffe, Jr. (*left*), the speaker of the Ohio House, and Republican Stanley Aronoff, president of the Ohio Senate, share a light moment during a 1989 luncheon at the Press Club in Columbus. Riffe, who became speaker in January 1975, wielded great power in state government during his record-breaking tenure, maintaining generally good relations with Republicans like Aronoff.

Governor Richard F. Celeste, the Cleveland Democrat who dominated Ohio politics during his two terms from 1983 to 1991, is shown during his second inaugural in late January 1987. Assessments of his tenure vary widely from "tremendous potential not realized" to "an innovative governor, perhaps the first 'global' governor at the end of the twentieth century."

Governor George V. Voinovich and his wife, Janet, wave to the crowd during his inaugural parade in January 1991. The former Republican mayor of Cleveland promised Ohioans that he and others in state government would work "harder and smarter and do more with less." He was considered a solid favorite to win reelection in November 1994.

stamp for his administration. He was denied presidential box theater tickets at the Kennedy Center when he refused to go along with the infamous 1990 budget deal that broke Bush's "read my lips" tax promise. Regula's reasonable bill to give Washington residents voting rights by making most of the District of Columbia part of Maryland did not advance because of opposition from advocates of D.C. statehood.

In central Ohio, John Kasich became ranking member of the House Budget Committee and offered one of the first challenges to President Clinton's economic plan by drafting an alternative budget making deeper spending cuts than those sought by the president. The subsequent Penny-Kasich spending cuts of 1993 came within a few votes of passing the House, as President Clinton lobbied hard to avert a major embarrassment. Kasich was known on the Armed Services Committee as a Republican who was tough on Pentagon waste. He was a career politician who broke in fresh out of Ohio State as a mop-topped intern for Buz Lukens in the Ohio Senate.

Paul Gillmor, the former Ohio Senate president, was also on the way up and secure politically in the lakeshore Fifth District between Toledo and Cleveland. Gillmor came to Congress late in life but worked hard and won a seat on the Energy and Commerce Committee at the outset of the 103d Congress. He was a legislator's legislator who fit the mold of a Taft conservative more closely than anyone in the delegation. His wife, Karen, served in the Ohio Senate.

Representative Michael G. Oxley of Findlay, gave Ohio a second Republican voice on Energy and Commerce, the committee that wrote the Clean Air and Superfund laws and reregulated cable television. Oxley was a major player, defending Ohio utility interests in the 1990 acid rain debate. The one-time FBI agent was one of the Bush administration's most reliable Hill votes. Oxley, capable and very conservative, seemed content to tend to his rural, solidly Republican Fourth District in northwest Ohio. He got unwanted media attention with his frequent travel and golf outings at the expense of lobbyists.

David L. Hobson of Springfield was another late bloomer, like Gillmor, who came to Congress by way of the state Senate after amassing considerable wealth as a lawyer, financier, and oil man. Hobson was an easy-going moderate who wrote a strong AIDS detection and treatment bill in Columbus. He was pro–civil rights and worked well with Democrats, positioning himself to help Ohio on the Public Works and Transportation Committee, a big dispenser of "pork."

To the west of Hobson's Seventh District, John Boehner aligned with the partisan, combative wing of the Republican party in the House. Boehner and six other freshman elected in 1990, called the "Gang of Seven," tried to embarrass majority Democrats with strident calls for institutional reform. He seemed fearless and quite secure politically in the rural and suburban Eighth District, which bordered on Indiana.

The surprise winner of a crowded GOP primary in 1992, Martin Hoke, bested Oakar in the Democratic-leaning district in the fall by running an outsider's campaign. The Cleveland lawyer was green politically, but ambitious. He made his money in the cellular telephone business before embarking on a career in government, and unlike other self-styled outsiders he was legitimate.

To the east of Cleveland, in a redrawn suburban district, a liberal state senator, Eric Fingerhut, was elected to Congress at age thirty-three. His strong pro-union Democratic credentials helped him with thousands of autoworkers and steelworkers, but he campaigned hard to gain the confidence of voters in bedroom communities after whipping former Cleveland mayor Dennis Kucinich and several others in a hard-fought primary. Fingerhut tempered his liberalism with a pro–economic growth agenda calling for reasonable limits on government regulation.

In another remapped district including most of Lorain, Medina, and Portage counties, Sherrod Brown was elected, reviving a career started at age twenty-two in the Ohio House. In 1990 he lost a bid for a third term as Ohio secretary of state to Robert Taft II. The Mansfield native was a foe of NAFTA and a health-care reformer who often took positions popular with organized labor. He lobbied hard for a seat on the Energy and Commerce Committee.

Two other Democrats were elected to first terms downstate. David Mann, a beacon of Cincinnati's small liberal community, took Charles Luken's seat after a close primary victory over state senator William Bowen. Mann, a graduate of Harvard Law School and an eighteen-year veteran of Cincinnati's city council, came to Washington as a middle-aged, yet wide-eyed, freshman. He had maverick tendencies; one of his first major votes was against President Clinton's 1993 tax package. Mann knew his GOP-leaning district was far from safe from a Republican takeover. And in the Appalachian foothills to the east of Cincinnati, the earnest Ted Strickland, a college professor and AIDS counselor at the troubled state penitentiary in Lucasville, prevailed in a marginally Republican district. Strickland, an ally of Ohio House speaker Vernal G.

Riffe, Jr., made reform of the public education system his top priority on the House Education and Labor Committee.

In the Senate, Metzenbaum and Glenn were well into their seventies. As the "junior senator," Metzenbaum won reelection in 1988 with 57 percent of the vote over outmatched Cleveland mayor George V. Voinovich. Metzenbaum had helped Stephen Young defeat Robert Taft, Jr., twenty-four years earlier in a contest that cost $175,000; against Voinovich, he spent more than $8 million, and the Republican almost matched it. When he announced in June 1993 that he would not seek another term, partisans on both sides of the aisle praised his tenacity and acknowledged that he saved taxpayers millions of dollars by killing special interest boondoggles. "He is a Democrat's Democrat," said his friend, Senator Tom Harkin of Iowa. Glenn, in a tough reelection battle against Ohio's lieutenant governor Mike DeWine, raised money furiously while taking his lumps in the media for the unpaid 1984 debt. He was not sanguine. Glenn could have been speaking for many of his colleagues, when he conceded, "I have had my nicks, there is not any doubt about that."[53] He survived, gaining a measure of vindication as he rolled over DeWine by almost 9 percentage points to become the first senator from Ohio popularly elected to four consecutive terms.

In 1994 Metzenbaum, at age seventy-seven, was in his last year in the Senate. His son-in-law, Joel Hyatt, campaigned for the seat even before the old warrior announced his retirement. Recognizable to Ohioans for his television commercials on behalf of his legal services business, Hyatt raised $1.4 million and visited nearly every county in a bid to prove he was more than a pseudo-pretender to the Metzenbaum seat. Hyatt withstood a strong Democratic primary challenge from Mary O. Boyle, a Cuyahoga County commissioner and former state legislator. On the Republican side, Lieutenant Governor Mike DeWine, back for another try at the Senate, easily defeated an intriguing newcomer, Bernadine Healy of Cleveland. Ousted as director of the National Institutes of Health by the Clinton administration, Healy, a formidable personality, was proabortion rights but stressed mainstream conservative themes in her campaign. Eugene Watts, a state senator and history professor at The Ohio State University, ran a feisty, if underfunded, campaign, but finished a poor third in the fight for the GOP nomination. Republicans had not elected a senator in Ohio since 1970.

Aggressive would-be reformers like Hyatt and DeWine ran for the Senate convinced that they could make a difference in Washington and maybe even reform the institution, which was held in scorn by much of the public in the late 1980s and early 1990s. The old timers were not so sure. Repeated attempts to tighten up the campaign finance law failed, partisan feuds got personal, and media scrutiny of a lawmaker's every deed—or so it seemed—was at an all-time high. Ross Perot, the millionaire-turned-populist, bashed Congress relentlessly for its closeness to special interests at the expense of ordinary citizens. Saxbe said the news media made certain no heroes were left standing. "It is a hell of a job up there anymore. I don't know why anyone wants to run."[54]

Vanik said one reason he never ran for Senate was because he "could not afford the mortgage." "The money-raising chased me out of the Congress," said a man who needed only $1,500 to unseat incumbent Democrat Robert Crosser in his first race in 1954. "You are really not free . . . every contribution is a mortgage on your integrity. . . . The Congress has become a citadel of political futures. You buy your futures with contributions for desired political actions."[55]

Camaraderie was strained by the fierce partisanship of divided government under a Republican administration and a Democratic-run Congress. The Democrats took heart from the election of President Bill Clinton, who narrowly carried Ohio in 1992. For most of the previous decade on Capitol Hill, it just hadn't been much fun. How times had changed. Twenty-five years earlier, William McCulloch declared: "I have never taken the position that one ought to oppose everything the majority proposes."[56]

During the go-go 1980s, most lawmakers returned to their districts almost every weekend, leaving Washington's social whirl behind in an effort to "stay in touch" with finicky constituents at dusty county fairs and Kiwanis Club meetings. Balancing congressional and personal responsibilities was too much for sensitive Baby Boom lawmakers who lacked the drive of the old bulls. Congressman Feighan, in 1989, recalled a troubling conversation with his nine-year-old daughter, Lauren. "She said, 'you're leaving in the morning?' And I said, 'Yeah,' and she looked at me and said—she wasn't trying to be manipulative—'are you going to do this the rest of your life?' I said 'no.' "[57]

Bud Brown said America's mall culture had traumatized his former colleagues, resulting in a collective personality change on Capitol Hill. "You have this terrific amount of democratization of the Congress and the 'little r' republican concept of a Congress that elects people who 'represent an area.' That is the change: now you have this homogenization of representatives, and the country. There is a mall in every one of these towns and the members and their constituents are literally on top of each other all the time. . . . In the old days, these guys were together all the time. They stayed here on weekends and went home when Congress was out of session for several months a year."[58]

That was the personal side. But the state's power was threatened by economic and demographic factors. Ohio, the seventh largest state after the 1990 census, had lost 250,000 manufacturing jobs during the previous two decades; another 70,000 evaporated during the 1991–92 recession as the state faced an extended period of flat growth. After the 1990 census, Ohio claimed only 21 electoral votes, compared to Florida's 25, New York's 33, and California's 54. In 1936, the state had 26 electoral votes to California's 22.[59]

For most of the postwar era, Ohio politicians in Washington were behind the curve—similar to Glenn, they zigged when they should have zagged. Under the watchful eye of the sixth-largest delegation on Capitol Hill, Lake Erie nearly died, industry fled to lower-cost sunbelt locations, and defense contracts were lost to coastal states. The delegation was polarized and divided by the same diversity Ohio politicians love to brag about. Congressmen from Cleveland really had more in common with Pittsburgh lawmakers than with those in Cincinnati. In contrast, Texans were fairly successful in blending the interests of agriculture, oil, and the other industries in their state.

During the decades after World War II, Republican majorities in Ohio were elected by rural and small-town conservatives and big money Republican industrialists (like the Timken family in Canton) in a coalition formed by William McKinley. The Democrats were splintered, confined to a half-dozen big cities and a handful of coal-mining counties. Two of Ohio's largest population centers, Franklin and Hamilton counties, tilted Republican. "In that period, the Republican Party really was a state party and the Democratic Party was essentially a collection of fiefdoms," said John Kessel, a political scientist at Ohio State University. "Mahoning County did not like Cuyahoga County and neither of them spoke to Toledo."[60]

Ohio "is the only 'megastate' with Republican House delegations most of the last 40 years, and the only one not to have voted for a Republican senator for the last 20," according to political analyst Michael

Barone. "It has oscillated fairly regularly between Democratic and Republican governors. In effect, politics in Ohio has become two very different contests—the heavy industry, CIO-dominated north-and-east, and the rest of the state."[61]

While Ohio Republicans outnumbered the state's Democrats most of the time, they had to deal with national Democratic majorities in the House. When Democrats took command in Ohio in 1984, they were stymied by a Republican White House under the Reagan and Bush administrations. "You are laboring against a period from 1865 to 1925 when practically every candidate for president was from Ohio," Bud Brown said in a small overstatement. "We are in the center of the country—where the population center of the country was moving. We were a developing industrial state, and a developing agricultural state to begin with. I hate to say it, it isn't just decline politically, it is decline in some other elements of leadership which I wish I could put my finger on."[62]

Call it timing, blame it on the sunbelt or television. As the turn of the century approached, the glory days were gone, the talent pool shrinking. The last of eight presidents from Ohio was Warren Gamiel Harding, remembered more for scandal than for leading the nation. The last two to try—the late congressman Ashbrook in 1972 and John Glenn in 1984—failed ignominiously. On Capitol Hill, Ohio has not claimed a chair of a House standing committee since the late Wayne Hays went home to his wife at Red Gate Farm in 1976.

❖

CHAPTER ELEVEN

Legislative Politics in Ohio

❖

SAMUEL C. PATTERSON

❖ There is a puzzling contradiction about the role of the legislatures in the politics of the American states. On the one hand, these legislatures are centerpieces in the decentralized system of political representation that marks American democracy. Our constitutional system, etched in the convictions and expectations of the American people, accords the representative assembly a primacy in voicing public demands on government and formulating domestic policies. To govern our states without vibrant, effective, powerful legislative institutions would, to almost all Americans, seem unthinkable. There is a constancy in Americans' abstract faith in the efficacy of legislative representation.

On the other hand, Americans' support for the real, work-a-day legislatures that convene in their state capitols is equivocal. Sometimes, public opinion is highly supportive of the state legislatures. But that citizens' orientations toward the legislatures can plummet to very negative depths is exemplified by the "legislature bashing" so common in the 1990s.[1] Americans may harbor more favorable appraisals of their own legislator than they do of the legislative collectivity. But public affection for the representative may dwindle, too, when legislators come to be conjured as self-serving "incumbents" who have perpetuated themselves in office at public expense. When such affection slides, efforts to restrict the sovereign voters and their freely elected representatives through term limitations or constraints on legislative decision making can increase accordingly.

Ironically, state legislatures have become much more effective, professional, representative assemblies over the last three decades. The reapportionment decisions of legislatures and courts beginning with the 1962 U.S. Supreme Court case of *Baker v. Carr* engendered legislatures much more representative of the people of the states. "A new generation of members," says legislative scholar Alan Rosenthal, "went to work to reshape legislative institutions."[2] There followed an era of legislative reform. Leadership in the state legislatures came to be more effective; committee systems were streamlined; more adequate staff support was provided to members, leaders, legislative party caucuses, and committees. Modern media and transportation technology came to permit much better communication between representatives and the represented, affording legislators extraordinary knowledge of the needs and preferences of their constituents. Yet, the legislatures are under siege and legislators are under fire from a public that little appreciates, and often condemns, the reformed institution.

In fact, today it is fair to assert that "state legislatures are in better shape now than they were twenty-five years ago" and that "whatever the public assessment of legislative performance, legislatures are meeting their responsibilities, they are active participants in the policy process, and they are producing informed debate and legislation."[3] At the same time, an assessment of the legislative condition made more than a quarter of a century ago still holds:

> The state legislature is one of the anomalies of the American political system. It has very few public supporters. Its own members sometimes turn out to be its most inflexible critics. The communications media are most likely to report its affairs when the matters at hand are bizarre or when legislators are intransigent, whether with one another or with the governor. The public reputation of the legislature with the public is seldom as good as its actual warrant to public respect. Its contributions to significant public policy are seen more often as legislative response to the initiatives of others than as legislative accomplishments. Its partisanship is perhaps as likely to be attributed to the perversity of party members as it is to the fact that legislative parties struggle over issues that count. Its independence is about as likely to be interpreted as abstinacy as it is to legislative option. Its powers seldom appear commensurate

with its responsibilities. The American state legislature is an institution waning in everything except resilience.[4]

The Ohio legislature of the 1990s epitomizes this anomaly in civic perspectives about politics and representation.

The oldest of the state legislatures is the Virginia House of Burgesses, which first met in 1619 and had established itself as an autonomous, independent, powerful representative assembly by the mid–eighteenth century.[5] The start of the legislature in Ohio awaited congressional enactment of the Northwest Ordinance in 1787. After an interim period of government by the territorial governor and three judges appointed by the president of the United States, the first General Assembly met in Cincinnati in 1799. This body was made up of a House of Representatives of twenty-two elected members and a five-member Council appointed by the U.S. Congress from a list of ten nominees submitted by the territorial House of Representatives. Convening the first Ohio legislature was no easy task in those pioneer days. It is recorded that

> the representatives from Marietta, after leaving Belpre found only the monotony of the woods until they reached the Scioto Salt Works, near the present town of Jackson; from there to Chillicothe there was no human habitation, and after leaving that place they passed no settlement on their way to Cincinnati until they crossed the Little Miami River. On this winter journey through a wilderness those travelers carried provisions and blankets, camped at night, swam their horses across streams and penetrated the forest, guided only by blazed trees or compass. The only roads were bridle paths or Indian trails. It was under these conditions and by this type of men that were laid solid and deep the foundations of popular government for the people of Ohio.[6]

Legislators today hardly face such an arduous struggle to get to the capital for legislative sessions! This first Ohio legislature passed thirty-nine bills into law, among other things establishing a system of taxation, regulating the practices of lawyers, creating land policies, initiating law enforcement offices, and creating an incipient criminal code.

Ohio became a state in 1803, following a protracted squabble between the legislature and the governor, Arthur St. Clair.[7] The state constitution reestablished the bicameral General Assembly, consisting of a House of Representatives and a Senate. The new legislature was migratory. First, it met in Chillicothe until 1808, then for two years in Zanesville, then back to Chillicothe, and again to Zanesville. At last, in 1812 the legislature established the permanent state capital at Columbus, where the legislature first met in 1816 following the construction of a new capitol building. The cornerstone of the present capitol, with its spacious chambers for the Senate and House of Representatives, was laid in 1839, but because of political squabbling the Statehouse was not occupied until 1857 and not completed until 1861.

The constitution of 1851 established the basic structure for the Ohio legislature for the years thereafter. The legislature functioned as a largely part-time, amateur body for more than a century. Change began in the late 1950s, when the term of office for state senators was increased from two to four years, with half of the body elected every two years. Later in the 1950s both houses streamlined their committee systems.

Then, in the mid-1960s, "the reapportionment revolution struck Ohio."[8] The ensuing struggle brought about major changes in legislative representation in the state. The size of the House was reduced from 130–40 to 99 members, and the Senate to 33 members. House districts were made equal in census population, and Senate districts were composed of three contiguous House districts. All multiple-member districts were abolished. Then, the reapportioned legislature began annual sessions, improved the staffing of committees and party leaders, strengthened the central staff of the legislature (the Legislative Service Commission), increased the pay of legislators, and took steps to improve the office space and facilities available to members. By the 1980s the Ohio legislature had developed as a professional legislature with members paid a salary more in keeping with full-time employment; a professional staff; a modernized committee system; businesslike offices, facilities, and equipment; and stable membership turnover. In the professionalization of its legislature, Ohio joins seven other states—California, Illinois, Massachusetts, Michigan, New York, Pennsylvania, and Wisconsin— considered to have comparable state legislative institutions.

Members of the Ohio legislature must be qualified voters who have resided in their districts for at least a year. The single-member district boundary lines are redrawn after every decennial census by a five-member apportionment board composed of the governor, the state auditor, the secretary of state, and representatives of House and Senate

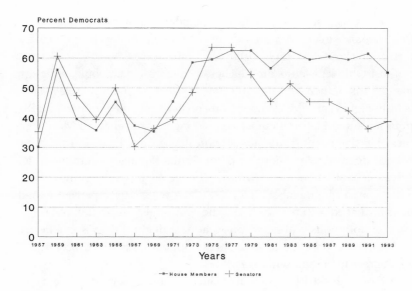

FIGURE 11.1
Political Party Composition of the Ohio Legislature, 1957–93

party leaders. In 1992, the apportionment board adjusted the district boundaries based on the 1990 federal census. House districts average about 110,000 people; Senate districts are three times larger. Like their counterparts in most other states, Ohio legislators are partisans—either Republicans or Democrats. Party fortunes have waxed and waned over the past thirty-five years (see fig. 11.1). With the 1972 election, the Democratic party captured majority status in the House of Representatives, maintaining a majority averaging 15 to 20 seats in the 99-member body. In the Senate, they held a majority for a time in the 1970s, but the Republicans have enjoyed the Senate majorityship throughout the 1980s and into the 1990s, except for the one-seat Democratic majority in the 115th General Assembly (1983–84).[9] The 1992 election witnessed the commanding House Democratic majority fall to 53 to 46, with the Republicans, losing one seat that November, holding a 19-to-14 majority in the 33-member Senate.

Political scientists have studied the members of the Ohio legislature first-hand over a number of years, conducting personal interviews with members. This was first done systematically in 1957 and then most recently in 1988, so it is possible to describe the membership in some detail.[10] The 1988 interviews provide an especially complete portfolio of information about the Ohio legislative membership.

Most Ohio legislators are business or professional people, although many think of themselves as full-time legislators. The typical legislator is forty-eight years old; Democrats are on average a bit younger than Republicans, and House members are younger than senators. Moreover, these legislators constitute a well-educated group. Three-fourths have college degrees, with more than four-fifths having postgraduate degrees. Most of the members without college degrees have some college education; of the members interviewed in 1988, only 6 percent ended their formal education with high school. A larger proportion of Democrats in both houses attained postgraduate degrees than Republicans, and a larger proportion of senators in both parties attained postgraduate degrees than representatives.

Although most legislators are men, 15 women served in the 117th General Assembly (1987–88)—13 in the House and 2 in the Senate (the membership elected in 1992 included more women—23 representatives and 6 senators). The delegation of Democratic women in the House is proportionally twice as great as Republican women, but Republican women in the Senate outnumber Democratic women 3 to 1. By the same token, most legislators are caucasian. However, a well-established black caucus, Black Elected Democrats of Ohio (BEDO), included 11 representatives and 2 senators. There was a time when black Republicans were elected to the Ohio legislatures, but today all the African American legislators are Democrats.

The composition of the legislature as it was assessed in 1988 was far different than in 1957. There were five women in the Ohio legislature of thirty years ago and only one black. Today's Ohio legislators are much better educated than their forebearers of the 1950s. At the same time, Ohioans today are serving in the General Assembly at about the same ages as three decades ago, the average age of the membership not having changed substantially.

Above all, legislators are politicians—people who, for one reason or another, are deeply interested in politics and government. When Ohio legislators were asked how they became interested in going into politics, many of them said they had been fascinated by politics as long as they could remember (about 38 percent of both representatives and senators). Others became activated through personal experience, a sense of civic duty, or working in a campaign. Some acquired political urges as a result of political activity in school or through the academic study of politics. Only a handful said they had not been involved in politics at all before they became legislators.

Some decide to run for public office on their own—"self-starters," entrepreneurs in politics who are strongly motivated to seek political roles and have the resources to enter politics without sponsorship or intervention by others. Other people are actively recruited for politics by party leaders or activists, often in the local constituencies. About half of the legislators interviewed in 1988 indicated that they ran on their own volition, as self-starters. Senators were more likely to be self-starters; 66 percent of them said they decided to run on their own, compared to 43 percent of House members. The 1988 legislators reported that they were encouraged to run by various actors, among whom incumbent legislators and party officials were by far the most prominent. Political associates and family members play an important role in stimulating Ohioans to run for the legislature, even for a good many of those who consider themselves self-starters. The towering role of active party recruitment of legislators is very significant in Ohio, a fact of political life that looms even larger when all candidates for the legislature, not just those who won primary and general election victories, are taken into account.[11]

A "new breed" of politicians serves in the Ohio legislature today. Most of the members interviewed in 1957 were part-time politicians, "citizen legislators," whose principal occupations lay elsewhere and for whom legislative service was an avocation. Nowadays, for most members being a state legislator is a vocation. Two-thirds of those interviewed in 1988 indicated they were full-time legislators. At the same time, two-thirds of the House members and three-fourths of the senators reported pursuing a second occupation as well. More than half the senators (52 percent) were lawyers, compared to less than a third (29 percent) of representatives. Preponderantly, House members are in business as their second occupation (46 percent in 1988)—as businessmen, insurance or real estate agents, accountants, or stock brokers. In contrast, fewer than a third of senators (31 percent) are in business. Other legislators are educators or are in "helping" professions or are farmers or workers or labor union officials.

The Ohio legislators of thirty years ago were amateurs in another way as well: sizeable proportions of them had little experience in public office, and most had not held political party offices or been active in party work. Today's legislators are more professionalized when they enter the legislature. The 1988 interviews showed that only 27 percent of representatives and 17 percent of senators had not served in party or elective offices prior to their election to the legislature.

A sizeable proportion of Ohio legislators have run for reelection in recent years, but term limits imposed by the voters in 1992 will affect future turnover. Moreover, most legislators aspire to run for other political offices if the opportunity arises. In 1988, a third of the representatives and two-fifths of senators indicated they were definitely interested in running for other offices, and an additional fourth in both houses indicated a tentative interest. Fully a third of House members expressed a hope to run for the Ohio Senate; a fourth showed interest in a congressional candidacy; and a fifth aspired to run for a statewide office. Slightly more than half the state senators aspired to statewide office, including a few who expressed interest in running for the U.S. Senate. And, 38 percent of senators indicated an interest in running for the U.S. House of Representatives.

A legislator's job can be divided into two broad responsibilities: representing the constituency that elected him or her and engaging in the activities required to make public policies. Representing and governing are not mutually exclusive activities, but they are different. Interestingly, Ohio legislators themselves reflect this distinction when they talk about their work.

Legislators interviewed in 1988 were asked what legislators should do in order to be most effective. A majority—56 percent of representatives and 62 percent of senators—referred to representational activities, working directly with constituents and representing groups.[12] Other legislators stress governing or lawmaking activities. Forty-four percent of House members characterized the legislator's job in lawmaking terms. For them the most salient features of being a legislator are introducing legislation, working on major state issues, and engaging in committee work. Like these representatives, 38 percent of senators expressed the view that their jobs involved legislative work, although senators stressed familiarity with issues and expertise when they talked about the legislator's job while House members emphasized bill introduction and committee work.

In the 1988 interviews, legislators were asked, "On the one hand, it is sometimes said that the job of legislators is to carry out the wishes of their constituents even if they disagree. On the other hand, sometimes legislators expect to use their own best judgment on policy issues even if their constituents disagree. Which of these views comes closest to your own conception of the legislator's job?"

This question put in rather bald form the classic division in the role of representatives as posited in the eighteenth century by Edmund Burke. In a famous speech to his constituents, Burke said he thought his job as their representative was to serve as a *trustee,* weighing arguments about issues in parliament and making judgments about the best interest of his constituents. He did not think, he said, that he should be merely their "delegate," mandated to reflect their particularistic wishes against his own studied judgment. Burke's distinction between the delegate and the trustee roles remains useful today. The label "politico" has been adopted to denote legislators who describe their role as a mixture of delegate and trustee orientations.[13]

Attentive as Ohio legislators are to the needs and opinions of their constituents, in the 1988 interviews most (47 percent) took the trustee orientation when asked about their conception of the representative role. Forty percent were classified as politicos because they indicated both delegate and trustee orientations were important to them. Finally, 13 percent accepted the delegate orientation, believing that representatives should be at the beck and call of their constituents. This general distribution of representative role orientations differs from the pattern shown by Ohio legislators who were interviewed thirty years previously.[14] Fewer contemporary legislators articulate their job as either delegates or trustees (as fully 71 percent of the 1957 legislators had done), and a larger proportion view their function in more sophisticated fashion, as a mixture of constituency representation and expert judgment.

Legislators interviewed in 1988 were asked whether they considered themselves to be very conservative, conservative, moderate, liberal, or very liberal on issues of public policy. Not surprisingly, Republican legislators classified themselves as more conservative than Democratic legislators (see fig. 11.2). At the same time, only a minority of Democrats among Ohio legislators—just 25 percent—indicated they were liberal; most Democratic legislators considered themselves moderates. In contrast, most Republican legislators—about 69 percent—said they were conservative.

Ideologically speaking, Ohio legislators resemble their partisans in the general public. In July 1988, a sample of Ohioans interviewed by the

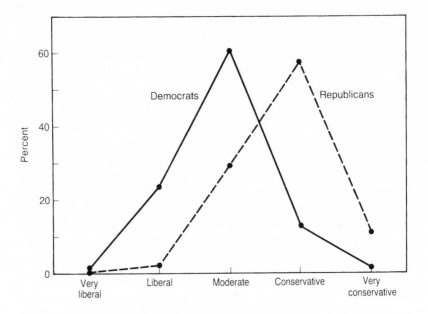

FIGURE 11.2
Ideological Orientations of Ohio Legislators, 1988

survey unit of the Ohio State University Polimetrics Laboratory was asked to designate themselves strong conservative, weak conservative, leaning conservative, neither conservative nor liberal, leaning liberal, weak liberal, or strong liberal. These are not precisely the same liberal-conservative categories offered to legislators, but rough comparison is possible. Like Republican legislators, Republican Ohioans think of themselves as quite conservative. Similarly, Ohio Democrats tend to be liberals, just as their representatives in the legislature. And, just as a significant proportion of Democratic legislators in 1988 were conservatives (14 percent), so there existed a sizeable percentage (23 percent) of conservatives among Ohio Democrats generally. Accordingly, both in the general public and in the legislature the Republican party is quite homogeneous ideologically. In contrast, Ohio Democrats, both citizens and legislators, are ideologically divided, with each indicating a significant conservative minority.

A highly significant feature of the internal environment of the Ohio legislature is its party organization. There are only two parties organized in each house: the House Democrats and Republicans and the Senate Democrats and Republicans. These four legislative parties are distinctive in their leadership patterns, structures, and practices. Each is composed of a leadership team and the rank-and-file members organized as a caucus.

In the 119th General Assembly (1992–93), where the Democrats were the House majority party and the Republicans were the Senate majority party, the leadership teams looked like this:

House Democrats	*Senate Republicans*
Speaker of the House	President of the Senate
Speaker pro tempore	President pro tempore
Majority floor leader	Assistant president pro tempore
Assistant majority floor leader	Majority whip
Majority whip	
Assistant majority whip	

House Republicans	*Senate Democrats*
Minority leader	Minority leader
Assistant minority leader	Assistant minority leader
Minority whip	Minority whip
Assistant minority whip	Assistant minority whip

The leaders of the majority parties, speaker of the House and president of the Senate, have dual responsibilities. They are the presiding officers of their respective houses, duty-bound to manage legislative business fairly and effectively, protect the decorum of legislative proceedings, and preserve the integrity of the legislative process. But they are also the political leaders of their parties.

In Ohio, as in many state legislatures, the formal powers of speaker and Senate president are considerably greater than their counterparts in the U.S. Congress. They chair the rules committees of their houses and have an important influence on the substance of the rules of procedure. They appoint members to committees and designate committee chairs. The speaker and president may use their powers as presiding officers to control debate, regulate who can speak in debate, apply the rules of procedure to influence policy outcomes, participate actively in debate on legislation, and vote on all questions put to their houses. The "pro tems," the speaker and president pro tempore, are second in command, although other members may preside, as well, when the speaker and the president are not in the chair. The House majority leaders and the whips are part of the leadership team, and their responsibilities may vary depending upon the expectations and requirements of the leadership over the course of the legislative process.

The speaker of the House is the dominant leadership figure in the Ohio legislature.[15] As presiding officer of the House and leader of the majority Democratic party from 1975–94, Vernal G. Riffe, Jr., was able to function as a central legislative leader. He skillfully deployed his official powers and prerogatives as presiding officer of the House, drawing upon his long-time experience in the legislature and his passion for leadership. Riffe was elected to the House in 1958 and ultimately became its longest-serving member. He was first elected speaker in 1975 and served longer than any speaker in Ohio history. Friends and detractors alike acknowledge the pervasiveness of his leadership of the House and influence in state politics generally.

Riffe's success as a party and House leader depended on three important considerations: his personality and interpersonal style; his competence in managing and directing the work of the House; and his political leadership. He grew up in a highly political family and turned to a career in politics as a natural family inheritance. As a new member of the legislature in the 1950s, he absorbed political life and was fascinated by the workings of state government; soon, he knew a great deal about both political realities and governmental processes. He found that serving as speaker of the House suited his ambitions, interests, and temperament very well. "I love being speaker," he often said. Moreover, Riffe loved working with his members, doing favors for them, helping them get reelected, and assisting them in fulfilling their own ambitions and objectives as legislators. As a political leader he was supportive, and his success depended on his reliability and trust. Riffe's friendliness and his southern Ohio, small-town, "down home" demeanor endeared him to his supporters and disarmed many of his opponents. He was not stridently partisan, a quality underscored by the fact that two prominent Ohio Republicans, former long-time governor James A. Rhodes and former House Republican leader Corwin Nixon, are among his closest personal friends.

Equally important, Riffe found ways to remain accessible to his members and to the cast of important players in politics in the capital. He did this not through formal party caucuses, but through an interesting pattern of informal access. An important locale for regular access to the leader was a downtown Columbus restaurant and bar, the Galleria. One close observer of Ohio legislative politics describes Riffe's typical mealtime activity:

[For lunch] he selects a restaurant where everyone will know where he is. For the past decade this has been the *Galleria Restaurant* located directly across from the State House on Third Street.

While at the restaurant the leader is flanked by several of his lieutenants and later is joined by the leader from the other house. Throughout his stay, lobbyists and members from both chambers and from both parties join him, say a few words, and leave. He is here deliberately at a place where anyone can get access to him on an informal basis. Mostly supplicants are giving the leader information, the commodity on which the legislature thrives. Some are pleading their cases; pleading for time with him; pleading for support in getting a bill referred, brought out of committee, changed, or stalled; pleading for help with a constituent problem; pleading for assistance with a state agency or with the governor; pleading for any of the kinds of things that the leader can deliver. It is the leader's time to be in touch with a lot of folks he might not have time or be willing to see except in this informal way. . . .

After dinner, the leader returns to the *Galleria* for two more hours of "face time" with those who want to chat with him in a more informal setting.[16]

The support Riffe received from House members is no mystery; his skills in personal relations created tight bonds of mutual respect, admiration, obligation, and loyalty.

But effective political leadership requires more than being a good fellow willing to talk to anyone. Leadership requires the management of affairs, and Riffe certainly proved to be a skillful legislative manager. A tireless worker, he immersed himself in the "nuts and bolts" of the legislative process, and his fellow legislators came to accept and appreciate his businesslike, efficient conduct of floor action on bills. Moreover, he succeeded in assembling and effectively directing an able, well-trained staff.

Finally, Vern Riffe proved skillful as a negotiator, in politically nurturing his party majority and in exercising sanctions to preserve member loyalty. His reputation as a skilled negotiator is punctuated by celebrated stories and folklore. There is the famous case of bringing the black caucus (BEDO) into the fold of loyal Democrats. Early in his speakership, in the mid-1970s, BEDO leaders threatened to sabotage the Democratic budget bill unless the speaker added more welfare funding and made demands regarding the administration of Central State University, the state's historically black college in Wilberforce. Riffe resolved the problem through successful negotiations with the BEDO leader, Representative C. J. McLin, and thereafter enjoyed firm support from black Democrats.[17] His strong ties of friendship to Republican governor Jim Rhodes and to his closest friend in the House and long-time roommate, Corwin Nixon, the former minority leader, and his effective working relationship with Republican Senate president Aronoff epitomize Riffe's capacities as a political compromiser and bargainer. Interestingly, during the 1980s, when there was a Democrat in the Governor's Mansion, Richard F. Celeste, the speaker's working relationship with the governor was such that he was dubbed "the prime minister," indicating his leading role in securing adoption of the governor's legislative program.

Riffe was effective at supporting the reelection of House Democrats. He began using his birthday as a vehicle for fund-raising in the 1970s at the suggestion of former U.S. House speaker Thomas P. "Tip" O'Neill, Jr. Once under full steam, the speaker's "Birthday Party" alone was raising annually six- to seven-figure amounts for the House Democratic war chest. Additional funding for campaigns came from the House Democratic Campaign Committee, also organized by Riffe. These party funds, although representing only a minority of the aggregate campaign expenditures in Ohio House districts, are influential mainly because they can be targeted and concentrated so as to maximize their effect.[18] Riffe's fund-raising and fund-dispensing role, along with other personal efforts to get Democrats elected or reelected to the House, provided an important source of party loyalty.

Riffe also developed as a leader who could impose discipline upon his party. Stories of his disciplinary strategies are legion, mostly having to do with disciplining individual Democrats who held committee chairmanships and, thereby, enjoyed several thousand dollars in additional salary. There are several accounts of such action over the years, but the experience of Representative Mike Stinziano of Columbus is instructive:

"House Insurance Committee Chairman Mike Stinziano . . . was booted off the House Finance Committee in 1981 and 1982 because he voted against a Riffe-backed temporary tax increase. Stinziano said he didn't know the bill bore Riffe's imprimatur. . . . 'The lesson I learned is that if you don't talk with the speaker and vote the other way, you're going to pay the price,' Stinziano said."[19] Riffe disciplining Stinziano and other committee chairs without much rancor or prejudice, restoring disciplined members to leadership posts when they seemed to have learned their lesson.

Riffe's leadership of the House majority party was not without criticism. Some complained that he was a "benevolent dictator." Periodically, sustained attacks have been leveled at him in the press, exemplified by the widely circulated series of stories in the *Akron Beacon Journal* in 1988 under the headline "Pay to Play." The newspaper's stories asserted that Riffe took campaign contributions from lobbyists explicitly in return for considering their bills favorably. The speaker vehemently denied this. Consumer advocate Ralph Nader once said that Riffe "had developed a system where the legislators in the House are more afraid of him than they are the voters." And Riffe's trial balloons exploring a possible candidacy for governor never received very warm responses. But as a legislative politician, advocates and critics alike agree that Riffe was remarkably successful.

The minority-party leaderships of the two houses are similarly organized. They function as political managers for their legislative party—raising campaign funding for their partisans, recruiting candidates, and otherwise endeavoring to enhance the political position of their party in the legislature. Minority leaders also play a role in the assignment of minority-party members to committees and the designation of the committees' minority leaders, or ranking minority members. The speaker and Senate president customarily consult the minority leaders in making committee appointments. The work of the minority leaders is complex because on the one hand they seek to transform their party into a majority, while on the other hand they may often need to work cooperatively with the majority-party leadership in bipartisan efforts or in negotiating compromises that allow the minority to have some influence over public policy.

Minority-party leaders often come under criticism and challenge. Serving in the minority is frustrating to members who enjoy exercising power or want to have some impact upon public policy. Minority legislators may use the ability of the leader to strengthen the party's position, or even the leader's capacity to transform the minority into a majority, as criteria for success. The two Ohio minority parties have experienced internal conflict in these terms. For example, in 1988 the Senate Democrats suffered a loss of seats. Dissatisfaction with the leadership of Youngstown senator Harry Meshel surfaced at the first party caucus following the November election. Meshel had served as leader since 1981 and was president of the Senate when the Democrats momentarily captured a majority in the 1982 election. His leadership was challenged by Senator Robert J. Boggs of Jefferson, but Boggs was able to get the support of only five other Democratic senators from the fourteen-member caucus. Following the attempt to replace him, Meshel sought to punish Boggs and his supporters by denying them their preferred committee assignments. Boggs lost his places on the education and finance committees and was, along with two supporters, relegated to the state and local government committee. Meshel made it clear that he might have punished his caucus opponents more roundly—-indicating that he might have reduced their legislative pay by denying them designation as ranking committee members, "if I really wanted to hurt somebody." But Boggs and his supporters won in the long run: he was elected Democratic leader when his caucus met after the 1990 election, which had resulted in a loss of Democratic seats.[20]

The House Republican minority has endured conflict over its leadership as well. Representative Corwin M. Nixon, minority leader from 1979 until his retirement in 1993, was often under fire for his cooperation with the Democratic majority, typically from conservative and freshmen members who prefer a more partisan advocate as leader. Nixon generally took the view that the minority Republicans had more to gain by cooperating with the Democratic leadership than by engaging in partisan opposition. Specifically, Nixon's well-known close, personal friendship with Speaker Riffe drew criticism from some Republican representatives. Challenges to his leadership were common but unsuccessful (some believe the speaker himself had done enough arm-twisting among Republicans to prevent Nixon's defeat). The most recent effort to displace Nixon as leader occurred in March 1992, when some members of the Republican caucus complained that he was soliciting minority members' votes for a congressional redistricting bill at the request of Speaker Riffe. But Nixon deflected the "coup" attempt by announcing that he would not seek reelection.

Political-party leadership carries substantial weight in the Ohio legislature, but party caucuses have a variable role to play. On the Senate
side, party caucuses are the routine site for discussing and hashing out
party stands, for the exchange of information between leaders and back-
benchers, for educating senators and staff members, and for party campaign and organizational planning. In contrast, party caucuses are
infrequent for the House parties, although more often convened by the
House Republicans than by the majority party.

The level of partisanship of legislative parties can be assessed in various ways. One way is to analyze legislators' attitudes toward their party,
party leadership, and intraparty agreement. Another appraisal of legislative partisanship can develop from analyzing roll-call voting to gauge
levels of partisan voting and intraparty voting cohesiveness. In a highly
partisan legislative body, members might express strong partisan attitudes, favoring party voting, partisan leadership, loyalty, and partisan
choice in elections. The extent of partisan state legislative politics varies
quite widely across the fifty states. In Ohio, partisanship is ambiguous.

Legislators interviewed in 1988 were asked a number of questions regarding their feelings about party. Two of these questions had been
asked of Ohio legislators in previous rounds of interviews, in 1957 and
again in 1969. One item concerns members' feelings of party loyalty: do
they think that, on party matters, a member should support his or her
party in the face of potential loss of support in their districts. The other
question concerns legislators' baseline senses of the importance of partisanship: members were asked whether or not they thought legislators
should be elected in a nonpartisan election without party labels (just as
elected judges in Ohio are chosen). The results are shown in table 11.1.

On the party loyalty item, 37 percent of the 1988 members agreed that
members should vote with their party on party issues, but 55 percent disagreed. Moreover, supportive attitudes toward party loyalty seem to
have declined: in 1957, 63 percent expressed loyal partisan attitudes; in
1969, 53 percent harbored such views. On the question of electing legislators without party labels, the change is more subtle. While large majorities of members have always opppposed removing party labels from
the ballot in legislative elections, the extent of disagreement seems to
have waned over the years (65 percent "strongly disagreed" in 1957,
compared to 59 percent in 1969 and only 46 percent in 1988). In 1988, on
the party loyalty indicator, Democratic legislators were measureably
more partisan than Republicans, but this party difference was almost

TABLE 11.1

Ohio Legislators' Attitudes toward Party in 1957, 1969, and 1988

Item, Year, and Number in Survey	Strongly Agree	Agree	No Opinion	Disagree	Strongly Disagree	Total*
"If a bill is important for his or her party's record, a member should vote with the party even if it costs some support in the district."						
1957 (156 surveyed)	26%	37%	2%	17%	19%	101%
1969 (51 surveyed)	8	45	12	22	14	101
1988 (127 surveyed)	4	33	8	42	13	100
"The best interests of the people would be better served if legislators were elected without party labels."						
1957 (162 surveyed)	4%	4%	1%	27%	65%	101%
1969 (51 surveyed)	0	8	2	31	59	100
1988 (127 surveyed)	3	9	3	39	46	100

*Totals equal more than 100 percent because of rounding.

Source: The 1957 and 1969 data come from Thomas A. Flinn, "The Ohio General Assembly: A Developmental Analysis," in James A. Robinson, ed., *State Legislative Innovation* (New York: Praeger, 1973), 268; the 1988 results are from the survey of legislators conducted by the Ohio Legislative Research Project, Ohio State University.

entirely attributable to the much stronger expression of partisanship among Senate Democrats (46 percent of whom agreed that members should vote with their party) and the much weaker expressed partisanship of Senate Republicans (only 28 percent of whom agreed). Such differences did not materialize on the question of electing members without party labels.

Additionally, in the 1988 interviews legislators were invited to express their attitudes about the leadership of their party. Democratic and Republican legislators differed quite sharply in their assessments of the role of party leadership. Democrats substantially agreed, and Republicans disagreed, that "party leadership makes a concerted effort to hold the party together on roll calls." Here we observe back-bench member responses to the differential leaderships of the two legislative parties, especially in the House of Representatives. In contrast, Democrats and Republicans alike express attachment to the legislative rather than the gubernatorial leadership. Ohio legislators exhibit this reticence to embrace gubernatorial leadership even when legislators are part of the majority party and the governor is one of them. As Thomas Flinn once said, "it seems that legislators do not necessarily see themselves as troopers for gubernatorial armies ... "[21] Ohio legislators are inclined to feel a fairly strong sense of autonomy from the governor of any political party and to circle their wagons ferociously when there are confrontations between the governor, on one side, and the speaker or Senate president on the other.

Apart from taking stock of legislative partisanship through the expression of partisan attitudes, levels of party conflict can be assessed by observing the legislators' decision-making behavior. With or without frequent party caucuses, the Ohio legislative parties are relatively cohesive in their voting on policy issues. Studies of party voting in the Ohio legislature of the late 1950s and 1960s indicated moderately partisan houses and senates. Seventy percent of controversial Senate votes and nearly half of the contested votes in the House were found to be "party votes," in which at least half the Democrats voted against at least half the Republicans.[22] On these party votes, the legislative parties were quite cohesive.

Yet, even when party competitiveness in legislative voting was relatively pronounced, legislators were not particularly inclined to show consensus about the extent of party conflict, and there did not seem to be a correlation between members' partisan attitudes and their partisan voting behavior. A penetrating analysis of the 1957 Ohio legislature revealed the ambivalence and ambiguity of partisanship among legislative politicians: "though Ohio has a reasonably competitive party system on the state legislative level, and though in fact party divisions are significant in legislative voting, there is a good deal of perceptual confusion in regard to the importance of party conflict." Comparable data for 1969 showed the same ambivalence between partisan behavior and perception of party conflict more than a decade later.[23]

Throughout the 1970s and 1980s, there was evidence of a persistent partisan structure in voting. For instance, for the early 1970s about half of all contested legislative roll calls were found to be party votes. It could be said that "state legislators . . . base their decision on the peculiar arrangement of attitudes, pressures, and cues," and "where regular alignments exist they tend to be closely related to party." Yet the legislature's partisan behavior often appears detached from consistent policy differences, may seem issueless, and frequently underscores personal calculations of advantages and disadvantages rather than reflecting policy or ideological considerations.[24]

The political strength of a legislative assembly is dependent upon the durability, power, and viability of its committee systems. Representative bodies may provide arenas or forums for great debates and eloquent expressions of the popular will, but the real capacity of the people's representatives to govern depends on the development of a division of labor and policy expertise. Committees provide a division of labor and constitute the environments in which representatives can acquire information and expert knowledge. That is why Woodrow Wilson once said that "it is not far from the truth to say that Congress in session is Congress on public exhibition, whilst Congress in its committee-rooms is Congress at work."[25]

The committee systems are provided for in the houses' rules. In the 119th General Assembly, for example, the House established 27 standing committees and the Senate operated with 14 standing committees. The average representative served on 3.7 committees, and the average senator served on 2.4 committees. The committee structures of the two houses are not entirely parallel. The committees on commerce and labor, finance, reference, rules, and ways and means are essentially parallel. Otherwise, in general Senate committee jurisdictions are split among two or more House committees. Subcommittees are a pervasive part of the congressional committee structures, but in the Ohio legislature only the finance committees of the two houses and the House education committee employ subcommittees.

Committees serve a variety of purposes in the House and Senate. Fundamentally, they do provide a division of labor, although the work loads of the various committees of each house are not the same. The budgeting and taxing committees (finance and ways and means), the education committees, the human services committees, and the committees concerned with crimes carry the heaviest burden of work in a typical legislative session. In the minds of legislators, committee chairs and long-time committee members tend to be considered experts in the area of committee concerns. Committees sift and winnow legislative proposals, and, in the end, the House and Senate rules committees, chaired by the speaker and the president of the Senate, respectively, select and schedule committee-reported bills for floor action.

At the same time, the committee systems perform functions beyond those related to making laws. The chairmanships of committees and subcommittees, and the ranking minority-member status accorded to the leading minority member of each committee, provide jobs and status for legislators that justify moderate salary increments for them. The pay structure of the Ohio legislature is greatly influenced by the existence of these committee chairs and ranking-member designations. In this way, the committees provide a structure for rewarding ability, loyalty to the leadership, and service.

In the course of their work, the legislative committees hold hearings—usually two hearing for each bill, one for its proponents and one for its opponents. These hearings are two pronged in their value to the legislative process. On the one hand, they provide valuable information to the committee and the legislature about the substance of public policy proposals, about the probable effects of policy alternatives, and about the political landscape of public and private interests concerned with the particular policy arena. On the other hand, committee deliberation provides a safety valve for venting the frustration, antagonism, disappointment, hostility, or deprivation that citizens, groups, and interests may feel about the imperfections of modern life. Since the legislature cannot resolve all of the problems and anxieties of human experience, this cathartic function of committee hearings—-giving people a voice—-can be vitally important.

As mentioned above, representatives and senators are appointed to committees and committee leaders are designated by the speaker of the House and the president of the Senate. These majority-party leaders generally respect the requests of the minority leaders in determining the selection of posts for minority-party members. Seniority is not a very significant factor in the appointment of Ohio legislators to committees, but members understand that the most important factor in getting good committee assignments, and certainly winning a chairmanship, is their personal relationship to the leader.[26] Appointments to the appropriations committees are the most highly prized (in the 1988 interviews, 54 percent of the legislators chose the finance committees as "most desireable"), with the rules committees a rather distant second, and the revenue committees last. The more-senior legislators tend to receive assignments to the most prestigious committees.

Committee processes are crucial in the Ohio legislature, but the fate of bills varies greatly in the hands of different committees. The most important committees (for example, the appropriations, tax-writing, judiciary, education, and insurance committees) bear the largest work loads in bills. These committees are relatively less likely to approve bills referred to them and send them to the floor. A very high proportion of bills referred to committees are altered to some extent in the committee process (75 percent, according to a study of the 112th General Assembly, 1977–78). Again, the most important committees are most prone to revise and amend bills or offer substitutes. Moreover, committee-reported bills are frequently amended during consideration by the plenary session of the house, and the "batting average" of committees during floor consideration is a measure of committee standing and prestige. Floor amendments of bills is pervasive, although much amending activity is routine, involving editing and correcting. Legislators do know that the most important committees do a better job of perfecting legislation and present bills less likely to require floor amendments.[27]

The Ohio legislative committee system is comparable in structure and function to the committee system of Congress. But legislative committees in Ohio are much more directly under the control of the house party leaders, explicitly the speaker and the Senate president, than their congressional counterparts. Seniority, fundamental to committees of Congress, plays a relatively minor role in the Ohio legislative committees. The Ohio committees have modest staffs, coordinated by a central staff agency, the Legislative Service Commission (or, for the finance committees, by the Legislative Budget Office). Membership turnover is greater for the Ohio committees than for congressional committees. All standing committees of Congress have subcommittees, but subcommittees are used sparingly by Ohio legislative committees. Interest groups and their lobbyists probably are not as closely tied to Ohio legislative committees as to congressional subcommittees. Conference committees, invoked when the houses of a bicameral legislature pass bills in different forms in order to iron out the differences, are extensively used in the congressional setting but less commonly employed by the Ohio houses. Taken together, it is fair to say that the similarities and differences between congressional and Ohio legislative committees indicate that Ohio's committees are less important to the state legislative process than the committees of Congress are to the congressional process.

The legislative process in Ohio is, in many respects, typical of state legislatures, but it contains distinctive features. In the last two decades its most distinctive feature was Speaker Vern Riffe, the redoubtable retiring Democratic leader of the House. His reputation for strong leadership made him something of a legend in his own time. A large bronze plaque bearing Riffe's name carved in large letters adorned the front of the desk on the speaker's dias during his tenure. Across the street from the capitol stands the Vern Riffe Center for Government and the Arts; in front of the building a large sign carries Riffe's name in softly glowing lights. The thirty-two-story office tower, among other purposes, provides modern offices to members of the House of Representatives and their staffs.

President Stanley Aronoff does not dominate the Senate the way Vern Riffe dominated the House, but Aronoff provides effective leadership to the Senate Republican majority. Both legislative party leaders compete with the governor for power and influence in state government. Divided control of the legislature creates a strategic environment in which the two leaders can joust and play one house against the other. Over the years of divided control, Democratic governors have provided leverage for the speaker and Republican governors for the Senate president. A good case of recent intercameral jousting involved the 1992 campaign finance reform bill. The Democratic House bill contained limits on individual contributions to candidates; Senate Republicans insisted on limiting the use of labor union dues in campaign finance; and, Republican governor George V. Voinovich threatened to veto any campaign finance bill that did not include the anti-labor provision. The Senate bill excluded the limits on individual contributions, and in June 1992 the Senate tabled Democratic amendments to include such limits. The Senate omission provided a bargaining chip in dealing with the House: the Senate would add the individual contribution limits if the House would accept the limits on labor-union contributions.

For a legislature in an urban, industrial state, the Ohio House and Senate operate with relatively lean staffs. Moreover, although lobbying by interest groups is very much in evidence in the capital, the firm majority-party leadership in both houses constrains and channels interest-group influence.[28] Lobbyists cannot achieve their legislative purposes without the agreement of the speaker and the Senate president. These leaders channel the attempts of interest groups to influence elections through their control of legislative party campaign funding. The instrumental nature of the House and Senate leaders' styles and objectives dampens ideological cleavage between the parties, stimulates a social climate in the legislature in which there is considerable interparty fraternization, and attenuates partisan conflict. These features give the Ohio legislature a distinctive climate.

To these observations about the Ohio legislature's distinctive characteristics should be added the marked differences between the organizational life of the two component houses. The House is a policymaking environment pivoting around the speaker. The Senate is a more collegial body, where the party caucuses are important parts of the landscape. These distinctions can be elucidated by considering the members' perceptions and observations about where important legislative decisions are made. In interviews conducted in 1988, members were asked about the locus of significant decision making. House members think decisions are made mostly in the speaker's office (or in other leadership offices). Ten percent mention the Galleria and other watering holes. A third of the representatives cite committees and subcommittees as important decision-making loci. Only 8 percent of House members mention party caucuses as important locations where decisions are made. The governor and lobbyists appear as only minor actors, not center stage for most purposes.

The Senate contrasts dramatically to the House in members' perceptions of the locus of big decision making. Nearly 10 percent of the senators think the major decisions are made in the speaker's office, and 15 percent believe the Senate president's office is the decision-making center. Senate committees and subcommittees do not rival their House counterparts as perceived loci for decision making, but fully a fourth of senators attribute important decisional activity to the party caucuses. Moreover, senators are more willing than representatives to accord decision-making influence to the governor. Decisional locations are, for senators, more dispersed than for House members.

The institutional life of the Ohio legislature has been shaped by the political culture of the state and by the state's particular human ecology. The legislature takes on the contours of the political organization, conflicts, and electoral successes and failures that mark the political realities of its time. Of course, the existing legislature is not inevitable; nor was it brought about by immutable forces; nor is it without need for perfecting through reform. But the Ohio legislature in the 1990s does reflect the political topography and public mores of Ohio remarkably well.

❖

CHAPTER TWELVE

The Ohio Executive Branch

❖

JOHN J. GARGAN

❖ The election of William Jefferson Clinton as the forty-second president of the United States was widely interpreted as a manifestation of generational and policy change in American politics. The election also reflected a continuity—the persistent importance of state government and politics as the starting point for a presidential career. Over the course of the twentieth century alone, former governors have occupied the White House more than half the time.[1]

The significance of the governorship in national politics is based in the visibility potential inherent in the office and the opportunities it provides an occupant to formulate a record of achievement. Since the United States is still a federal system, individual states continue to be autonomous policy laboratories.[2] Many significant public programs have been formulated and tested in state governments before being adopted and implemented at the national level. Governors promoting such programs have enhanced their reputations as policy innovators with their colleagues in the National Governors' Association and with the attentive public through the mass media.

Despite Clinton's success, the political lives of governors have become more complicated. The problems governors confront have become more complex because of long-term structural changes in America's economic, demographic, and cultural life as well as short-term fluctuations in consumer spending and tax yields. Though support from the federal government for some programs has declined since the early 1980s, new federal regulations and court decisions promulgated in the same period have expanded state government responsibilities. Revenue shortages and near-uncontrollable spending in vital functions have made fiscal policy the test of a governor's ability to govern.

In light of the complex decision and policy environments governors must consider, Thad Beyle has predicted that they are likely to find themselves fulfilling one or more of three identifiable legacies—the "no-saying" bearer of bad news, the entrepreneurial advocate of new approaches to public services, or the proponent of patchwork (and largely irrelevant) approaches to problem solving.[3]

In his influential work *Goodbye to Good-Time Charlie*, Larry Sabato tells the story of the constitutional, institutional, and political transformation of the governorship in recent decades.[4] State constitutions have been rewritten to cut the number of state agencies, support staff available to the governor has grown, and better educated candidates have run for office. The era of the back-slapping "good-time Charlie" has been replaced by the politically astute and administratively competent chief executive officer. The Ohio experience fits well into Professor Sabato's central theme.

To understand politics in the Buckeye State, and particularly the operations of the executive branch, it is essential to recognize the centrality of the governor's role. Article 3, section 5, of the Ohio Constitution states: "The supreme executive power of this state shall be vested in the governor." Formal powers, of course, are supplemented by personal leadership skills. Thus, the record of any Ohio governor will hinge on the interplay of personality, formal powers, and the circumstances of a specific term of office. As to the latter, governing is far less problem laden in a period of economic growth than in one of economic decline, as several post–World War II Ohio governors have found out.

Election as governor is not a random exercise. Indeed, in his analysis of the 194 individuals who became governor in the fifty states between 1970 and 1989, Beyle has identified several distinct career paths to the governorship, allowing for regional and party differences.[5] An elemental fact is that the governorship goes to the politically active; only 12 of the 194 governors came to power without having held a prior office. While a number of political experiences—including Congress, local elective office, and nonelective administrative positions—were evident, the most common were in the state legislature, state elective office, and law enforcement.

Sixteen gubernatorial elections were conducted in Ohio from 1944 to 1990. Twelve of the thirty-two candidacies involved Frank J. Lausche and James A. Rhodes, each of whom ran for governor six times. Thirteen candidates, eight Republicans and five Democrats, account for the remaining twenty candidacies.

Like their counterparts in most other states, candidates for governor in Ohio are not political novices. Nominations are gained by those seasoned in state politics, frequently those long seasoned. Candidates often began their political careers in the state legislature. Seven candidates (three of nine Republicans and four of six Democrats) were members of the Ohio House or Senate. In some cases legislative experience was extensive; two of the three Republicans (O'Neill and Cloud) were speakers of the House. State legislative service has been a background characteristic of gubernatorial candidates rather than the last office held before winning the state's top office; only one candidate during the 1944–90 period—Democratic state senator Frazier Reams, Jr., in 1966—moved directly from the legislature to the gubernatorial nomination.

Election to one of the lesser statewide offices (auditor, treasurer, secretary of state, attorney general) has been somewhat more the case for Republican (six of nine) than for Democratic (two of six) candidates. The offices held were attorney general (Herbert, O'Neill, Celebrezze), state auditor (Rhodes, Cloud), lieutenant governor (Celeste, Voinovich), and state treasurer (Ebright). Anthony Celebrezze, Democratic candidate for governor in 1990, moved through a series of state offices; from the state Senate he was elected secretary of state and then attorney general, from which he gained the nomination for governor.

Experience in state government and politics is not a prerequisite for nomination. For some, holding an elected or appointed local office has been an early step in a political career, like service in the state legislature. On occasion, candidates have gained their party nomination directly from a local or (though rarely) from a national office. The mayoralty of a major city has been the principal office from which several candidates have moved to the nomination for governor—James Stewart (Cincinnati) and Frank Lausche (Cleveland) in 1944; Michael DiSalle (Toledo) in 1956; and George Voinovich (Cleveland), who had served as lieutenant governor prior to his election as mayor, in 1990.

Because gubernatorial politics in Ohio is so intensively state based, national government credentials have not been particularly important.

Three of the fifteen candidates served in appointed federal government positions prior to seeking the governorship—Charles Taft, Michael DiSalle, and Richard Celeste. Defeated after a single term in the U.S. House of Representatives, John Gilligan won the 1968 Democratic primary for the U.S. Senate against incumbent Frank Lausche, but lost the election before becoming the Democratic candidate for governor in 1970. Not evident in Ohio is a minor pattern found in other states, that of members of Congress returning to their states to run for governor.[6] Only one incumbent member of Congress, Republican Clarence Brown in 1982, won the nomination for governor in the post–World War II era.

Any meaningful transformation of a governorship or executive branch is contingent upon basic changes in state politics—electoral, policy, legislative, and judicial. In fundamental ways, patterns of Ohio politics in the 1990s are as John Fenton described them in the 1950s—partisan, pragmatic, issueless, and patronage oriented. All is not unchanged. For example, groups interested in ideological questions, environmental concerns, minority rights, and class-based issues have been vocal and have sought to place their concerns on the political agenda. Nonetheless, the general patterns Fenton outlined remain.[7]

Executive leadership requires a governor to define policy direction and to set strategic goals. To empower governors to meet the requirements, "a principal focus of . . . reform initiatives" to reorganize state government has been "to make the chief executive the center of energy, direction, and administrative management."[8] Thus, reorganization proposals and comparative studies of state government have devoted considerable attention to strengthening the formal powers of governors—tenure potential, appointment authority, budget control. Somewhat less attention has been devoted to tracing the relation of those powers to the governor's several roles—chief policy strategist, chief administrator, chief legislator, and chief political leader.

From a historical perspective, the formal powers of the Ohio governor have notably increased. Under terms of the 1802 constitution, power was "entrusted . . . almost absolutely to the legislature." Reacting to their experiences with the territorial governor, the convention delegates responsible for the 1802 constitution weakened the office. The governor was to be elected every two years, was to have no veto power, and would need legislative approval of all appointments. At the 1851 constitutional convention, provision was made for the direct election of officials in the executive branch, although the "legislature remained the most powerful branch" of state government.[9] Through constitutional amendments adopted over the twentieth century, the powers of the governor have been periodically expanded.

On measures of formal institutional power, Ohio chief executives are classified as "strong governors." This is apparent in Ohio's score on a composite index of six measures developed by the National Governors' Association.[10] Three measures—tenure potential, appointments, budget authority—relate to "the governor's power within the executive branch." The other three—the legislature's role in the budget, veto power, political strength in legislature—relate to "the governor's power vis-a-vis the legislature." Ohio's scores on the individual measures are as follows:

Tenure potential: Ohio is one of the "Strong" (4 on a 5-point scale) states in which the governor has a four-year term but is limited to two consecutive terms. "Very Strong" (5 points) states are those in which the governor has a four-year term and no limit on the terms served.

Appointment power: Ohio is classified as "Strong" with a score of 4.5 on a 7-point scale. On the scale, 4 is "cabinet appointment without governor's approval"; 5 is "appointment with board, council, or legislative approval"; and 7 is "Governor's appointment with no other approval needed."

Budget-making power: Ohio is among forty-four states designated "Very Strong" (5 on a 5-point scale); "very strong" governors have "full responsibility" for preparation of the state budget.

Legislative budget-changing authority: Ohio is one of forty-three "Very Weak" states (1 on a 5-point scale); in such states the legislature has "unlimited power . . . to change the executive budget."

Veto power: Ohio is one of thirty-eight states considered "Very Strong" (5 on a 5-point scale); the governor has the item veto and the votes of three-fifths of the legislators elected are necessary to override the veto.

Gubernatorial party control: Ohio is one of thirteen states classified as "Moderate" (3 on a 5-point scale). In "moderate" states there is "split party control in the legislature or non-partisan legislature." "Very Strong" (5 points) states are those in which the governor's party "controls both houses substantially"; "Very Weak" (1 point) indicates the "Governor's party in substantial minority in both houses."

The formal institutional powers of Ohio governors are not uniformly strong. The governor scores above the fifty-state average on three (appointment power, budget-making power, and veto power) of the six measures and below average on the other three (tenure potential, legislative budget changing power, and political strength in the legislature). Overall, Ohio has a score of 23 of a possible 32 points on the National Governors' Association composite index, slightly higher than the fifty-state average of 22. By way of comparison, Maryland had the highest composite index score of 29, and Rhode Island had the lowest score of 15.

Formal powers are neither necessary nor sufficient for executive leadership or governing effectiveness. Still, the mix of formal powers available has political implications for Ohio governors. On some matters the implications are very specific. Richard Sheridan notes that in Ohio the line-item veto "is an important budgeting tool, and one used even when all three branches of government are controlled by the same political party."[11] On other matters the implications are somewhat more indirect. For example, a constitutional amendment adopted in 1954 to take effect in 1959 extended the governor's term from two to four years and limited a governor to two consecutive terms. Prior to 1959, governors could serve two-year terms for as long they could be reelected. With the change, a governor's power begins to wane at the outset of a second term; opponents can have their way by simply waiting.

The scope of a governor's responsibilities and the enormity of state operations are such that gubernatorial success depends on the qualities of appointed and career governmental and political surrogates. The most important of these are appointed department heads who oversee operations in executive branch agencies. Institutional arrangements designed to assist the governor include the governor's immediate staff, budget and policy development support, agencies responsible for management details, and political appointees in departments and on boards and commissions.[12] The arrangements and instrumentalities vary from the personal and political to the technical and bureaucratic and from the hourly to the gubernatorial term and beyond.

State law provides for twenty-three cabinet departments headed by gubernatorial appointees who must receive the consent of the Ohio Senate. The relevance of cabinet rank and status must always be considered in context, as departments vary substantially in number of employees and budget size. A number of noncabinet agencies, including the Department of Education and the Board of Regents, are more substantial than cabinet agencies, and Ohio governors frequently bring some of the noncabinet agency heads into cabinet deliberations.

The cabinet departments of the Ohio executive branch are:

Administrative Services
Alcohol and Drug Addiction Services
Aging
Agriculture
Office of Budget and Management
Commerce
Development
Employment Services
Environmental Protection Agency
Health
Public Safety
Taxation
Transportation

Industrial Relations
Insurance
Liquor Control
Mental Health
Mental Retardation and
    Developmental Disabilities
Natural Resources
Public Utilities Commission
Rehabilitation and
    Correction
Human Services
Youth Services

Among the first, and most crucial, decisions a governor makes on taking office are appointments to administrative positions, particularly directors of these departments. A second decision is the extent to which political appointments of the governor will affect the departmental structure. Balance has to be achieved between the political competency of appointees and the substantive competency of the bureaucracy. The directors and their assistants are the governor's link to the career service and are expected to be more sensitive to the needs and aspirations of the governor, other things being equal.

From a governor's perspective, there is always a risk that political appointees, along with the departmental bureaucracy, will become captives of constituencies.[13] In addition to supporting the governor's policy agenda, directors and their assistants are expected to be advocates of the interests of their departments to the governor's office and representatives of departmental constituencies at all stages of the policy process. Representation of constituencies becomes distinctly important when departmental interests differ, as, for example, with the Departments of Insurance and Health on health insurance or with the Departments of Taxation and Development on legislative proposals for tax abatement.

In selecting directors and assistant directors, governors must face the realities of the state's political recruitment pool. For any gubernatorial appointment, several bases for selection compete: long-term loyalty to the governor, a reputation for political skill and influence in the state, substantive policy knowledge and management experience, and advocacy of the interests of specific groups and constituencies. Ideally, gubernatorial choices to head departments and agencies will combine all bases.

A former department director in the Celeste administration outlined the more typical case and the selection process. Certain positions were reserved for representatives of key Democratic constituencies, such as African Americans. For other positions, professional reputations rather than relations with the governor were determining, "part of the cabinet was chosen as a result of their credentials rising to the top" so that "some people being chosen for positions didn't meet Dick Celeste until the final interview." A third grouping involved "others like me who had political backgrounds, our credentials were judged differently."[14]

Whatever the basis for the initial appointment, forecasting the performance of a political appointee is demanding. Appointees who demonstrate administrative talent may become "management troubleshooters." Governor Celeste's Department of Health director, Dr. David L. Jackson, took a short-term assignment to manage a problem-laden Department of Mental Retardation and Developmental Disabilities and was acknowledged as one of the "key troubleshooters [who] pulled some of Celeste's fat from various fires." During his first two years in office, Governor Voinovich moved a long-time "trusted lieutenant," C. James Conrad, into three cabinet posts to handle difficult assignments.[15] Individuals like these are close to ideal appointments, demonstrating loyalty, political sophistication, professional knowledge, and management skill. They contribute substantially to a governor's success and to an effective executive branch.

Other political appointees detract from a governor's reputation and subvert the effective operation of the executive branch. However worthy the efforts of Richard Celeste and his supporters to recruit the best professionals available and to increase the representation of minorities and women in higher level positions, the efforts involved political costs. Throughout the Celeste years, problems with major administrative positions were widely reported in the press and contributed to negative public perception of the administration's record. The director of the Department of Public Welfare was forced to resign in 1984 after publicized disagreements with subordinates and internal departmental conflicts. In

1985 the director of the Department of Mental Retardation and Developmental Disabilities left office after a newspaper reported "mismanagement and patient abuse at state facilities and at group homes for the mentally retarded." Another director, James E. Rogers of the Department of Youth Services, not only left office but subsequently went to federal prison "for extorting bribes from contractors."[16] Other members of the administration were accused of bad political judgment and ethical lapses, which interfered with Governor Celeste's efforts to report on and highlight a number of very innovative policies.

Difficulties in recruiting competent political appointees cross party lines and governing styles. Governor Voinovich, a moderate Republican with considerable management experience as a mayor, early in his administration faced politically embarrassing personnel problems, not unlike those of his predecessor. One involved a state fair director hired by the Expositions Commission, members of which are appointed by the governor. The state fair is a high visibility, usually noncontroversial annual event at which governors frequently receive favorable publicity. The director of the 1992 fair, Billy Inmon, was criticized in the media when he "hired friends from Kentucky, started charging for rides, skirted the state's prevailing-wage laws, proposed banning a gay-rights group from renting a booth at the fairgrounds and signed a $2.6 million contract making Pepsi-Cola the fair's exclusive soft drink."[17] Only after direct intervention by the governor and the Expositions Commission was it possible to remove Inmon.

Other of Governor Voinovich's personnel problems were more serious, involving agencies responsible for major programs. After weeks of news coverage and release of a report critical of problems in his department, Terry A. Wallace, director of the Department of Human Services, resigned in October 1992. According to one newspaper account of the resignation, "Inspector General David Sturtz found politically connected hiring on a widespread basis in Wallace's administration. Generous pay raises were given to top management and jobs were created for Wallace's friends when certain welfare and assistance-to-the-homeless programs were going through enormous cuts. Among controversial hirings was a former stripper who could barely type. Voinovich appointed Wallace as director 18 months ago and vowed to stand by him as a growing number of critics wanted Wallace ousted."[18]

The governor receives day-to-day assistance from a staff attached to the Office of the Governor. Headed by a chief of staff, it is made up of individuals who provide support essential to any executive—director of communications, director of administration, director of policy and legislative initiatives, director of constituent affairs, legal counsel, legislative liaison.

Also on the staff are several executive assistants who report to the chief of staff and who serve as the governor's liaison to various "cluster groups." Among the cluster groups established by the Voinovich administration are criminal justice and public safety, business and industry-government, health and human services, environmental and natural resources, and education. Each group is made up of several state departments, agencies, and commissions, usually in the same substantive policy area. The health and human services cluster, for example, is composed of the Departments of Aging, Health, Human Services, Insurance, Mental Health, and Mental Retardation and Developmental Disabilities. In the environmental and natural resources cluster are the Regional Governors' Association, Department of Agriculture, Environmental Protection Agency, Environmental Board of Review, Department of Natural Resources, Emergency Management, and the Public Utilities Commission.

Duties and responsibilities of the immediate staff will change from one administration to another and, as in the Celeste administration, from the first term to the second, according to one former staff member. In general, the executive assistants oversee developments in their cluster. Assistants serve as the governor's contact or point person in promoting the governor's program and dealing with the details of policy implementation, following up on requests for information or clarification from the governor, handling potentially embarrassing departmental or agency problems before they emerge—or as they arise—in the media or the legislature.

While executive assistants and the politically appointed department heads are presumably promoting the same goal—the governor's policy and political agenda—tensions do develop. As in other states, assistants are frequently recruited from the governor's political campaign staff. One department head in the Celeste administration recalled that even though assistants were young and inexperienced, "the staff had influence and power" when "many cabinet members had no power or influence." Not surprisingly, resentments develop.

A former executive assistant in the Celeste administration cited tensions within the governor's staff, aside from those between the staff and cabinet. On any given major issue, he pointed out, there were three possible perspectives: that of members of the communications staff, who were mainly concerned with promoting the governor's image; that of members of the policy staff, who were concerned with effective policy processes; and that of the members of the legal staff, who were concerned with the legalities of any gubernatorial actions. Each perspective may well be valid; which prevails on an issue contributes to a governor's overall record.

The governor's overall record is also shaped by personal and staff relations with the state legislature. These relations change from administration to administration. A Democratic legislator who chaired a major committee during both the Celeste and Voinovich administrations indicated that while Governor Celeste and his staff initiated policy discussions things had changed under Governor Voinovich: "I'll call and ask if they want to comment on a major piece of legislation. They'll say 'We'll get back to you.' Later I'll contact them again and they'll say, 'No, we don't have a position.' "

The initiatives and decisions of the executive assistants are always subject to review and may be overridden by the chief of staff and others. At least for a time, Governor Celeste used a "superstaff" to complement the work of the governor's office. Celeste supporters in the Office of Budget and Management (OBM) and the Department of Administrative Services (DAS) served as "gatekeepers," with authority to give a final procedural sign-off, beyond formal legal requirements, on matters of hiring, salary increases, and contracts. According to one familiar with the procedures, OBM and DAS were responsible for making sure of "crossing the t's and dotting the i's and of overseeing the agencies and what they did."

Sitting at the center of the state government communication network is the chief of staff. One lobbyist familiar with recent gubernatorial administrations claims that Governor Voinovich's chief of staff, Paul C. Mifsud, has been quite powerful. Typically, policy initiatives are produced on matters in which the chief of staff is interested. When he is not particularly interested in the issue, notes the lobbyist, the problem is delegated to a staff subordinate with the possibility that no action will be taken.

The influence of the immediate staff and the executive assistants, in particular, will depend on the personality and operating style of the governor, the relationship between the chief of staff and the governor, and the professional reputation and political independence of a department or agency head. When the governor has a "hands on" operating style and a close relationship with the chief of staff, and the department head has a national reputation as a policy professional or a strong political base in the state, the influence of the executive assistant is minimized. As conditions change—a highly technical issue becomes controversial, a department head fails to gain administrative control, an important campaign contributor requests a policy change—the influence of the executive assistant grows.

Of the tools available to assist governors, the single most important is the biennial budget. In the past two decades, state government budgets have grown in importance as instruments of policy guidance, priority setting, and productivity measurement. Budgets can be used by a governor to control individual agencies, manage the state government, and plan the state's future. Greater emphasis has been given in Ohio to the control and management aspects than to the planning, according to the leading scholar of Ohio public finance, Richard Sheridan. Sheridan wrote in 1990 that "The Rhodes and Celeste administrations have been far more concerned about the budget as a control mechanism and have exercised strong central controls to achieve this end."[19]

The largest part of any state budget is based on legal and political commitments to continuing programs. The governor can, however, influence developments at the budgetary margins. When tax revenues are plentiful, the governor can allocate surpluses to new initiatives or to expansions in selected programs. Faced with revenue shortages, the governor uses reductions in the budget to redefine program priorities.

Budget formation is handled by the Office of Budget and Management, a cabinet agency headed by a gubernatorial appointee and staffed by career civil service employees. A division of labor characterizes OBM: the revenue section estimates state revenues in line with changing economic conditions; the budget section, operating within a framework developed in the governor's office, collects agency requests for operating and capital budgets, prepares the budget for submission to the legislature, and watches over budget implementation; and the controlling board section staffs the controlling board, a legislative-executive body that modifies legislative appropriations and considers and approves agency spending requests during the fiscal year.[20]

Students of comparative state politics who seek to strengthen the governor's office have stressed the key role of budgeting in management.

They have advocated as well greater use of planning by the governor's office to improve decision making and to coordinate decisions that have a significant impact on the state's future.

Certain types of planning have been adopted to cope with changing administrative environments. The demands of managing the complex affairs of a modern state government require a high level of operations and logistical planning sophistication. State departments of administration or general services, like Ohio's Department of Administrative Services, do long-term planning on matters as disparate as personnel, purchasing, printing, facilities, telecommunications, and vehicle fleet management.[21]

Nationally, efforts to improve broadly based state planning have been mixed. By the 1980s, after decades of searching for a purpose and political acceptance, state planners had achieved acceptance and some status. The planning function has been integrated with budgeting in a few states, located in a separate department or a division of a functional agency in others, and, most typically, administered from the governor's office. State planning activities have come to focus on economic development, land use, and policy formulation.[22]

In Ohio the quality and nature of state planning has depended on the occupant of the governor's office. Governor John Gilligan sought to integrate budgeting and planning when he established the Office of Budget and Management. Located in OBM was the responsibility for administering federally mandated land-use and capital-facilities planning requirements. According to one observer, "This might have served as a way of bringing statewide planning to Ohio, but it did not have a chance to mature since Rhodes abolished the office as one of his first acts when he returned to office after Gilligan's four-year term ended. He transferred the two federal functions to his own office and they then became purely clerical functions performed in compliance with federal law." State planning efforts also have been targeted to the delivery of state services. To improve the coordination of services in geographic areas, the Gilligan administration recommended "a small number of large districts for use by state agencies in their planning and service delivery and a large number of planning regions."[23] The Voinovich administration established new districts for the administration of Department of Development programs, reflecting a policy decision to increase local influence over state economic development.

While crucially important in support of any governor's work, planning for administrative operations and service delivery is less relevant in the 1990s than policy planning. That chief executives need to adopt strategic and creative approaches toward their organizational and external environments is a point regularly made at meetings of governors.[24]

The most impressive innovations in Ohio's state planning were those adopted in the early years of the Celeste administration. Initially, a Governor's Cabinet Cluster on Strategic Planning was co-chaired by Alfred Dietzel, director of the Department of Development. Assisted by process facilitators, ranking officials from several departments met in policy cabinet clusters, defined as "working groups formed to address interdepartmental issues." Cluster-formulated strategic plans were generated for economic development, human services, and natural and physical environments. For each of the strategies or initiatives, a plan specified an "implementation time frame," a "funding level and mechanism," "linkages" of public and private organizations, and the organization or organizations with "lead responsibility."[25]

Altered conditions in the 1990s changed planning emphases. Faced with severe fiscal constraints, Governor Voinovich relied on strategic-planning task forces to study problems. An Operations Improvement Task Force in 1991 generated an analysis by "over 250 private sector people" who contributed "over 150,000 hours of volunteer time."[26] The task force report called for a revamping of the entire executive branch into a generic type that administrative reformers have labeled the Secretary-Coordinator. All existing units of state government would be grouped under five secretary-coordinators—Health and Human Services, Environmental Resources and Transportation, Finance, Business and Labor, and Public Safety—who would report directly to the governor.

To improve the existing system, both general recommendations ("Develop and communicate a departmental mission statement and establish unit goals and objectives") and specific recommendations ("Develop minimum standards for vendors") were made by the task force for each agency studied. Even more sweeping proposals for change in state government were contained in a report prepared by a task force appointed by the Ohio Board of Regents at Governor Voinovich's request "to examine higher education's operations and to suggest ways in which public higher education in Ohio could become more effective and efficient."[27]

In addition to the governor and lieutenant governor (who since 1978 have been paired on the ballot), Ohio voters elect a secretary of state, auditor of state, treasurer of state, and attorney general. These offices are included under the rubric of "the executive branch," and the duties and responsibilities of each are detailed in state constitutional and statutory provisions. The term of office is four years and, until the voters approved a constitutional amendment in 1992, there were no limits on the number of terms an incumbent could serve. To be elected to one of the executive offices is to assume responsibility for bureaucracies of fairly limited size and scope. General-fund budgets in 1991 for the four offices ranged from just under $7 million (secretary of state) to just over $57 million (treasurer), and the number of full-time permanent employees varied from 148 (secretary of state) to 997 (attorney general).[28] The four offices accounted for 3.8 percent of total state government employment in 1992.

The primary duties of the four elected officials are the oversight, housekeeping, and system maintenance policies and activities. While significant, these activities do not profoundly affect the quality of life in the state. This is not to deny their relevance to a well-ordered society. In such a society, elections are fairly conducted, local finances are honestly audited, state funds are safely invested, and legal opinions are professionally crafted. Yet most of the time such activities are neither highly visible nor particularly controversial.

The limited size and scope of these domains should not be overstated. In meeting their formal responsibilities the elected officials are generally concerned with problems and issues that are very specialized and that raise complex technical questions. They exercise considerable discretion in the day-to-day operations of their offices. Typical cases might include the following:

- The secretary of state casts the deciding vote in the case of tie votes in the deliberations of county boards of elections.
- The auditor issues findings on the fiscal conditions in local governments.
- The treasurer makes decisions as to which banks and investments will receive state funds.
- The attorney general hires local attorneys to represent the state in local legal cases in which the state has an interest.

The discretion available to the elected officials in each of the cases allows them both to carry out duties and serve political interests. Whatever their impact on the public at large, the four officials affect such specialized constituencies as local political party leaders, lawyers, bankers, and investment brokers. In appointing local attorneys to represent the state in legal proceedings, the attorney general is also distributing patronage to lawyers throughout the state. Patronage recipients become a source of campaign and fund-raising support. Similar kinds of arrangements—the use of the powers of office to carry out the law and to provide financial and prestige benefits to supporters—hold for the other offices as well.

The structure of executive offices has additional political consequences. After every national census, boundaries of Ohio state legislative districts are redrawn by a five-member Apportionment Board. The secretary of state and the auditor are members along with the governor and one member of each party from both houses of the legislature. Since the board's decisions fashion power alignments in the legislature for the ensuing decade, the stakes are very high for a political party to win at least two of the three executive offices. Extraordinary effort and expenditures will be put forth in the first statewide election of each decade to retain or gain one or both offices. This was the case in 1990 when a Republican defeated an incumbent Democratic secretary of state and shifted partisan control of the Apportionment Board.

The offices perform other functions. Election to any one of the offices allows an aspiring politician to gain stature, experience in state government, and a reputation of accomplishment on difficult issues. In 1975 Richard F. Celeste was the Democratic incumbent in the all-but-powerless office of lieutenant governor in the gubernatorial administration of Republican James A. Rhodes. That year Celeste campaigned aggressively against four ballot measures vigorously supported by Rhodes, who had a track record for gaining repeated voter approval of bond issues in the 1960s. Defeat of the four issues was interpreted by the mass media as "a substantial political defeat for the governor and a political plus for Lt. Gov. Richard F. Celeste, chief foe of the package."[29] With several independently elected statewide officers, the political party out of power in the governor's office or the legislature can establish a bastion from which to campaign to regain power. Political pundits regularly cite the lieutenant governor, attorney general, secretary of state, auditor, and treasurer as logical candidates for the more prestigious posts of governor and U.S. senator.

Immediately after Governor Celeste was elected in 1986 to the second of his constitutionally limited two consecutive terms, Thomas Ferguson, elected to the third of his then–constitutionally unlimited number of terms as state auditor, announced, "Right now my inclination is to run for governor." Four years later, the Democratic candidate for governor was not state auditor Ferguson, who had generated a spate of unfavorable publicity in the meantime (sexual harassment charges by a former employee had clouded the political future of Auditor Ferguson), but one of his 1986 party running mates, Ohio's attorney general Anthony Celebrezze. Following the 1990 election, two of the three successful Democratic candidates—newly elected attorney general Lee Fisher and state treasurer Mary Ellen Withrow, reelected for her third term—were designated by the media as potential candidates for governor in 1994.[30] The lone Republican elected, Secretary of State Bob Taft, had seriously considered running for governor in 1990 before party leaders prevailed upon him to avoid a potentially divisive primary against Voinovich.

A sizeable number of boards and commissions comprise a segment of the executive branch. Since there is no single office at which the formation of boards and commissions is recorded, and because enabling legislation often permits state agencies to create boards and commissions at their own discretion, the precise number is not easily determined. One publication of the secretary of state reports information on 201 boards and commissions. A 1992 report of the Operations Improvement Task Force puts the number at 452. The number of listings, either the higher or lower, is an indicator of political salience. Boards and commissions are generally established by a provision of the Ohio Revised Code or by executive order for any of a number of reasons. Interest-group leaders recognize that autonomous board or commission status can carry with it a separate funding line in the state budget and protection for their policy concerns from switches in partisan control of the governor's office or legislature. On the longer term administrative implications, Sheridan points out, "The legislature has been especially attentive to such requests and has isolated a good part of the executive branch from the direct control of the Governor by creating boards to head up the agencies that administer the programs, and by making the board members subject to special rules governing their dismissal."[31] Boards and commissions are frequently given responsibility for state regulatory policies. Many boards oversee and regulate, or simply advise, occupations and professions. Some sense of this role can be gained from a partial listing of occupation-related state boards: State Board of Cosmetology, Board of Chiropractic Examiners, Auctioneers Advisory Commission, the Dental

Board, Board of Bar Examiners, Hearing Aid Dealers and Fitters Licensing Board, Motor Vehicle Salvage Dealers Licensing Board, State Board of Optometry, State Board of Psychology, State Board of Registration for Professional Engineers and Surveyors, Ohio Board of Speech Pathology and Audiology, Veterinary Medical Board, State Medical Board of Ohio.

The growth and influence of the professions present a dilemma of sorts to state officials. The potential for monopolistic control of their fields by professionals raises serious questions of protection of the public interest. Alternatively, the coercive powers of state government routinely affect the lives of professions and professionals. Political activity by a professional association and its members is often directed to gaining or maintaining legal protection of the profession's occupational status and distinctive subculture, including attempts to gain control of regulatory boards. The quality of services received by the public may well be upgraded by a board's oversight of an occupation or profession. That practitioners are setting standards and mandating admission criteria undoubtedly increases the likelihood that those coming into the professions will have mastered the state-of-the-art and core knowledge of the field.

Other boards and commissions make policy and set strategic direction for major functions. Two of the most important relate to education. Members of the State Board of Education, the policymaking body for the Department of Education and for primary and secondary education, are elected on a nonpartisan basis. Membership on the nine-member Board of Regents, which sets policy for higher education, is by gubernatorial appointment for a nine-year term, one year longer than the maximum time in office allowed an appointing governor. Education consumes a significant portion of every biennial budget. The Department of Education and the Board of Regents received 26.5 percent and 13.6 percent respectively of the 1991–93 general fund budget. Because practically every family in the state has had contact with the educational system, education policy is relevant to a significant percentage of the population. Governors are regularly held responsible for developments in education and, on occasion, campaign on promises of being an "education governor." However, because of the board arrangement, a governor lacks direct control—legal and political—over those making basic decisions.

Efforts have been made to alter the system. In the 1982 gubernatorial campaign, Celeste proposed creation of a single education agency to administer programs from kindergarten through university graduate study. Implementation of the proposal required changes in the Ohio Constitution and approval of enabling legislation by the General Assembly. Neither occurred during Governor Celeste's eight years in office. And despite statements on behalf of educational reform, Governor Voinovich achieved only modest change during the initial years of his administration. As noted above, a detailed study was completed and policy recommendations put forth to consolidate higher education units and missions. For primary and secondary education, legislation was adopted, with Voinovich's active support, to reduce the size of the elected State Board of Education from twenty-one to eleven. The rest of the system remained in place.

Education is only one of the state government functions directed by boards and commissions. Fundamental decisions regarding elements of the state's transportation network are made by the Turnpike Commission. Other boards such as the State Teachers Retirement Board and the Police and Firemen's Disability and Pension Fund manage the investment of funds to assure the continued viability of public employee pension systems. The fact that hundreds of autonomous or quasi-independent boards and commissions operate in Ohio, as in many other states, is inherently neither good nor bad. Large numbers of citizens participating, either ex officio or by appointment, on the boards and commissions promises that a variety of views and perspectives will be given consideration in policy and administrative deliberations. Along with the benefits, there are potential negative consequences of the large number of boards and commissions. The success of any policy change will frequently be contingent on the coordination of actions by these numerous state entities. Those wishing to sabotage have many avenues of attack. The greater the number of autonomous agencies, the greater the number of opportunities for delay.

Judgments about the leadership and bureaucracies of state agencies depend to a considerable degree on the vantage point of the analyst. Membership in the governor's cabinet is no assurance of political influence; a board majority of an obscure commission may control policy developments. There are, however, two empirical measures of the relative importance of activities carried out in the executive branch, state government employment and state government expenditures. The first is considered in table 12.1, which ranks eight state agencies by the number of full-time permanent employees and the agency's share of total state government employment.

TABLE 12.1

Full-Time Permanent Ohio State Government Employees, 1992

Agency	Full-Time Permanent Employees (percentage of state total)	
Department of Rehabilitation and Correction	8,975	(15.5%)
Department of Transportation	7,834	(13.5)
Department of Mental Health	5,308	(9.2)
Department of Mental Retardation and Developmental Disabilities	4,090	(7.1)
Department of Public Safety	3,198	(5.5)
Bureau of Workers' Compensation	2,857	(4.9)
Bureau of Employment Services	2,545	(4.4)
Department of Natural Resources	2,103	(3.6)

There were 57,857 full-time permanent employees working for Ohio state government in September 1992. Excluded from this total are employees of the state's university system and primary- and secondary-school teachers. That relatively few executive branch agencies account for most of the employees can be seen in table 12.1. The eight agencies listed employ 63.7 percent of all nonuniversity state workers. Many of these are custodial workers, those who control people who have broken the law (Department of Rehabilitation and Corrections), or those who care for those who need help in coping in contemporary society (Department of Mental Health and Department of Mental Retardation and Developmental Disabilities). Maintaining the state's basic transportation system accounts for a second major set of workers (Department of Transportation and Department of Public Safety). Problems of employment—injury, disability, or lack of a job—require 9.3 percent of the state work force (Bureau of Workers' Compensation and Bureau of Employment Services).

Ohio public employment can be considered in a functional sense. To facilitate interstate comparisons, the U.S. Bureau of the Census reports public employment data by function, including higher education.[32]

TABLE 12.2

Ohio State Government Employment by Function, 1991

Function	Percentage of State Total
Higher education	46.5%
Hospitals	13.9
Corrections	7.7
Highways	6.3
Social insurance administration	4.4
Financial administration	4.1
Natural resources	3.0
Health	2.8
Other	11.3

Each function's percentage share of total state government employment, calculated from 1991 census data, is reported in table 12.2. Nearly 75 percent of Ohio state government employment is in higher education, hospitals, corrections, and highways, a pattern comparable in state government throughout the country. Relative to other states, Ohio is not a major employer, ranking forty-fifth in the number of state employees per capita.

Another perspective on the executive branch can be gained from budget data. Budget allocations are not the sole indicator of policy or functional relevance or quality, but they do measure claims on scarce state resources. Expenditures proposed in the general fund budget at least partially answer the question: When officials have some discretionary control, for what purposes are state funds spent?

The 1991 budgets of the eight agencies listed in table 12.3 amounted to 92.8 percent of the general revenue fund total. The single largest allocation of nearly five billion dollars, just under four of every ten general revenue fund dollars, was for policies administered by the Department of Human Services. Ranking second and third were the two state education agencies. The other five departments had allocations ranging from slightly under half a billion dollars (Department of Rehabilitation and Correction) to slightly more than one hundred million dollars (Department of Youth Services).

TABLE 12.3

State General Fund Budgets by Agency, 1991

Agency	Total Revenue (in thousands)	Percent of General Revenue Fund Total
Department of Human Services	$4,968,478	39.7%
Department of Education	3,311,599	26.5
Board of Regents	1,705,372	13.6
Department of Rehabilitation and Correction	479,130	3.8
Department of Mental Health	401,392	3.2
Department of Taxation	347,589	2.8
Department of Mental Retardation and Developmental Disabilities	282,915	2.3
Department of Youth Services	107,811	0.9

Much of what is currently done in the executive branch and how it is done reflect changes in state government in the past quarter century, partly in response to changes in the federal system. The changes most frequently cited are associated with reductions in federal grant support and increases in the number of federal regulations. Others involve the diminution of gubernatorial control as state agencies become more dependent on federal funds. For example, in 1991 several state agencies—including the Bureau of Employment Services, Department of Health, Department of Alcohol and Drug Addiction Services, Department of Aging—received over half their funding from the federal government. In the case of the Ohio Bureau of Employment Services, federal funds for unemployment insurance, employment services, and job training are such a significant percentage of the bureau's budget (96.2 percent) that bureau personnel may be more concerned, much of the time, with developments in the U.S. Congress than with those in the Ohio General Assembly.

Policymakers in Ohio and other states have confronted a double bind over the past few decades: a heightened demand for public-sector services and a scarcity of resources.[33] The heightened demand is rooted in sweeping societal change. Unemployment levels and employment opportunities have been shaped by national and international economic forces over which state governments have virtually no control. Social attitudes regarding family formation, divorce, teenage pregnancy, and substance abuse have brought into being a public-sector-dependent population with concentrations in central cities.

The very economic changes that have increased public needs have weakened the fiscal bases of state government. Successful governors are therefore those who most adroitly carry off the roles of economic developer, within-state entrepreneur promoter, and out-of-state traveler in search of foreign investment capital. Governors Rhodes, Celeste, and Voinovich devoted considerable time and energy to these roles, and Ohio state government has been recognized as innovative in economic development policy.[34]

This double bind confronting Ohio government is not of recent origin. A changing economic base has been the single most important aspect of public and private life in Ohio during the 1970s, 1980s, and 1990s. Like the Great Lakes region as a whole, the state's economic well-being has been impaired by a severe contraction in manufacturing industries. Since the 1950s, Ohio's share of national manufacturing and other non-agricultural employment has declined. The loss of well-paying jobs has drastically transformed many communities and increased the need for state-financed social services. And these economic changes have significantly altered Ohio's fiscal patterns. Decreasing manufacturing has shrunk the income, real property, tangible personal property, and corporate franchise tax bases available to the state and local governments.

The fiscal bind has been compounded by decreased assistance from the federal government and the rate of increase in spending for selected state programs. According to the Advisory Commission on Intergovernmental Relations, federal aid accounted for 26.3 percent of the Ohio state government general revenue in 1980 and 22.6 percent in 1990. The decrease in federal support is more stark when inflation and population factors are considered. One analyst estimates that from 1980 to 1990, controlling for inflation and excluding welfare grants, per capita federal aid to Ohio state government fell 15.8 percent, aid to Ohio local governments fell 51.5 percent.[35]

Pressures for increased spending have been most evident in programs targeted to the poor and the medically indigent, by way of the Medicaid program in the Department of Human Services, and for imprisoning criminals, by way of the Department of Rehabilitation and Correction. Between 1981 and 1991, the state's share of Medicaid spending increased 218 percent. Spending by the Department of Rehabilitation and Correction grew through the decade by 361 percent, and, for roughly the same period, departmental employment increased from 3,831 to some 8,800. In those ten years, general revenue spending for primary and secondary education increased 88 percent, and for higher education 126 percent.[36] Given these fiscal pressures, governors, legislators, and interest groups seeking to respond to political demands for new programs in the 1990s will find few uncommitted resources.

State revenues and expenditures are manifestations of Ohio's political culture. For over half of the post–World War II years, the governor's office has been held by fiscal conservatives, Democrat Frank J. Lausche (1945–47, 1949–57) and Republican James A. Rhodes (1963–71, 1975–83). Recurrent campaign and governing themes of Governor Rhodes were "no new taxes" and the positive benefits of low taxes and a limited number of state employees.[37] On occasion during the Lausche-Rhodes era others came to power and advocated new state taxation and spending. Governor Michael V. DiSalle (1959–63) sought adjustments in several state tax rates. Governor John J. Gilligan (1971–75) achieved adoption of a graduated state income tax and inclusion of an income base in the state corporation franchise tax. Both DiSalle and Gilligan were defeated after single terms by Rhodes, who, in campaigning against Gilligan, attacked the incumbent for taxing "everything in Ohio that walks, crawls or flies."

The politics of taxation shaped state politics in the 1980s. Faced with major revenue shortfalls on taking office, Governor Celeste increased income and public utility taxes with unanimous Democratic support and Republican opposition in both houses of the legislature. Higher tax rates and a growing economy allowed the governor to support new spending and, in time, even reduce taxes. But for the remainder of Celeste's tenure and into the 1990s, Republican candidates ran for office on a record of opposing tax increases.

The recurring patterns were evident early in the Voinovich administration. Revenue shortages and spending pressures received much of the attention of state officials throughout 1991 and 1992. Despite reductions in spending for higher education and for certain welfare programs, projections of revenue-spending shortfalls continued. Calls by the governor for higher minor taxes were initially resisted by Democratic legislative leaders. In a "lame duck" legislative session following the 1992 elections, a compromise was reached and adjustments were made in the tax structure to raise an additional one billion dollars over two and a half years.

Fiscal conditions are a key element of the environment facing the executive branch of Ohio state government—but only one element. Those charged with preparing the executive branch to enter a new century need to give careful thought to other elements. Most fundamentally, stability and change in the state's political culture—citizen attitudes about the ends of government and acceptable political practices—will determine state government quality. Also vital will be the willingness of political elites to build institutional capacity in the executive branch and throughout the state. This will entail support for the use of state-of-the-art strategic planning, budgeting, and management practices.

In the final analysis, executive branch effectiveness will be determined by the intellectual breadth, political skill, and moral courage successful candidates, particularly gubernatorial candidates, bring to office. For Ohio to progress, those who would be governor in the twenty-first century need to ponder what can be accomplished when political vision and high capacity are joined.

❖

CHAPTER THIRTEEN

The Ohio Judiciary

❖

LAWRENCE BAUM & MARK KEMPER

❖ The Ohio judiciary fades in and out of public attention.[1] Judges and courts attract public interest when something noteworthy occurs: a hard-fought contest for judicial office, a controversial decision, a scandal. Once that episode has passed, the judicial branch returns to its accustomed obscurity.

Ohio's courts merit more attention because they make important policy choices. The Ohio Supreme Court establishes legal rules on matters ranging from freedom of speech to compensation for personal injuries. Trial courts affect the lives of a great many individuals every year through decisions in criminal and civil cases. And all those decisions, aggregated over time and across the state, have considerable effect on how Ohio law works.

This chapter examines various aspects of the state's judiciary. We begin by looking briefly at the judicial system as a whole, then turn to the selection of judges, and, finally, conclude with an examination of the Ohio Supreme Court as an institution and policy-maker.

At the trial level, most of Ohio's judicial business is conducted by two types of courts. The common pleas courts are general jurisdiction courts that hear civil and criminal cases with relatively large stakes, along with the special categories of domestic relations, juvenile, and probate cases, and appeals from some administrative decisions. Municipal and county courts are limited jurisdiction courts, which typically hear cases with smaller stakes. Every large city and many smaller ones have municipal courts. In most Ohio counties, the jurisdiction of one or more municipal courts covers the whole county; in most other counties there is a county court whose jurisdiction covers the whole county; and in several counties the area is divided between municipal and county courts.

Limited jurisdiction courts handle far more cases than do courts of common pleas, though this is primarily because of their jurisdiction over most traffic violations. Excluding traffic cases, in 1990 common pleas courts decided about 600,000 cases, municipal courts 800,000 cases, and county courts 70,000.[2]

Specialization in the trial courts goes further. Common pleas courts have divisions for probate, juvenile, and domestic relations; depending on county size, these divisions may be staffed by their own judges. The great majority of counties have judges who specialize in probate cases or, less often, probate and juvenile cases. Probate judges have power over matters of great importance: estates, guardianships, and adoptions. They also dispense a good deal of patronage through the appointments of appraisers, administrators, and guardians. One lawyer has said that "nobody wants to be probate judge. Everybody just wants to be the probate judge's best friend."[3] Within the municipal courts, there are specialized housing divisions in Cleveland and Toledo and an environmental division in Franklin County (Columbus); each has its own judge. Like many other specialized courts, these divisions were created largely to advance certain policy goals: improvement of housing, better enforcement of environmental laws.[4]

Ohio also has two trial courts with narrow jurisdiction. The Court of Claims was created in 1974 to adjudicate monetary claims against the state. Mayor's courts, which exist in some localities, are basically specialists in traffic and parking cases. In 1972 the U.S. Supreme Court ruled that an Ohio mayor whose village received a substantial share of its revenue from fines levied in mayor's court was not an impartial judge in cases involving possible fines;[5] despite that decision, there have been complaints that some mayors whose governments rely heavily on fines continue to preside over local courts. The continued existence of mayor's courts owes something to the political power of small-town mayors and to the money-making potential of these courts for local governments.[6]

At the appellate level, the courts of appeals hear appeals from decisions of trial courts and some administrative agencies.[7] Because their jurisdiction is mandatory, they must address every appeal, although they need not—and do not—give the same full consideration to each. Thus, much of their business consists of cases with only narrow significance. But the sheer number of decisions by the courts of appeals—nearly 11,000 in 1990, as compared with fewer than 700 in the Ohio Supreme Court—helps to make them important.[8]

The Supreme Court hears appeals from decisions of the courts of appeals. Depending on the type of case, that jurisdiction may be mandatory or discretionary. If a case is brought under the court's discretionary jurisdiction, the court can decide the case on the merits or reject it and thus leave the lower court decision standing. The court also hears appeals directly from rulings of some administrative agencies. The Supreme Court is the only court that adjudicates matters related to the practice of law, including discipline of lawyers. The court also has general power of "superintendence" over Ohio courts. The chief justice can assign judges temporarily to other courts, and the court establishes rules of practice and procedure. The use of these powers sometimes has aroused controversy. C. William O'Neill, chief justice from 1970 to 1978, used his powers aggressively to attack backlogs of cases in trial courts. Seeking to enforce time limits that the Supreme Court had established for disposition of cases, O'Neill employed publicity to embarrass judges who fell behind and rewarded judges who had met the limits with "Superior Judicial Service" awards. According to a study, the time limits and their enforcement "succeeded in reducing delay, but only at the cost of making many judges feel they had become case expediters rather than arbiters of justice."[9]

Except on the mayor's courts, Ohio's judges must be licensed attorneys with a certain amount of experience in practice or as a judge—six years on most courts. No judge may take office or begin a new term after reaching the age of seventy. Except for those courts and the Court of Claims, judges are elected to six-year terms. (Judges sit temporarily on the Court of Claims through assignment by the chief justice.) They are nominated in partisan primary elections but run in the general election under a nonpartisan ballot. This unusual "semi-partisan" system apparently resulted from complex historical circumstances rather than a deliberate effort to balance partisan and nonpartisan elements in the selection system.[10] Where multiple judges serve in the same geographical area, they have been selected through at-large elections across that whole area; a 1991 decision by the U.S. Supreme Court, applying the Voting Rights Act to judicial elections, will result in the election of judges by districts within some large counties.[11] If a vacancy appears during a judge's term, the governor unilaterally appoints a replacement; an election for that seat is held within two years even if the term has not yet expired.

The most widespread alternative to election of state judges is the Missouri Plan, sometimes called "merit selection." Ohio voters have had two opportunities to adopt the Missouri Plan for their appellate courts, in 1938 and in 1987. (Missouri did not adopt this system until 1940, so approval in 1938 would have made it the "Ohio Plan.") They disapproved Missouri Plan proposals by 2-to-1 margins both times, and there was a striking similarity in the lineup of groups for and against the two proposals.[12] The defeat of the 1987 proposal illuminates the politics involved in choosing among systems for selecting judges.[13] Under this version of the Missouri Plan, nominations for appellate court vacancies would be made by commissions composed equally of lawyers selected by appellate judges and lay members chosen by the governor and approved by the state Senate. The governor would choose from three nominees for each vacancy. Each judge would go before the voters two to four years after appointment and then every six years for a "yes" or "no" vote, needing 55-percent approval to remain in office. Counties would be allowed to adopt the same system for their trial courts.

The public campaign for this proposal was led by the Ohio Bar Association and the state League of Women Voters, groups that had made several earlier attempts to get a Missouri Plan proposal on the ballot. Like their counterparts in other states, they identified the Missouri Plan with good government and a reduced role for "politics" in the selection of judges. Less public was the role of Ohio's business community, led by insurance companies, which contributed the majority of funds used in support of the Missouri Plan proposal. Organized labor was the main financial contributor to the campaign against the proposal and the leading public opponent. Both sides believed that adoption of the Missouri Plan might make the courts more conservative on economic issues such as liability for personal injuries.

Organized labor framed the proposal as one that would take from the public the "right to vote" on judges. This framing seemed to be highly effective. Proponents of the Missouri Plan could not provide voters with an equally compelling reason to support their proposal. Their overwhelming defeat suggests that Ohio will retain judicial elections well into the future.

Below the Supreme Court level, most campaigns for Ohio judgeships are small in scale and receive limited coverage in the public media. In large part, these characteristics simply reflect the greater perceived importance of contests for other offices, contests that garner a larger share of campaign effort (including funding) and attention from news organizations. The canons of judicial ethics add a further limitation, constraining candidates from discussion of policy issues.

Despite these canons, questions of judicial policy sometimes find their way into lower court campaigns. Most common are explicit or implicit messages by trial judges that they favor "tough" treatment of criminal defendants. But the appeals that candidates make in person or through media advertising are more likely to focus on other matters: competence, as indicated by such information as bar association endorsements and judicial experience; links to voters, such as long-time residence in the area and endorsements by associations that represent ethnic groups; and attractive personal traits, such as family and service to good causes.

Lower-court contests can have a significant partisan element. Leaders of Ohio's political parties view judgeships as important prizes, similar to other offices that they would like their party members to hold.[14] As a result, the parties often play an active role in judicial elections, making pre-primary endorsements of candidates and contributing money and personnel to general election campaigns. More visible to voters, a party's candidates in a particular county may run as a "team," and campaign materials may refer to the candidates' party affiliations. Perhaps most important are the lists of candidates that parties often distribute to their registered voters.

Still, voters typically are exposed to little information about the candidates. Moreover, most voters give a low priority to judicial contests. As a result, they generally know little about the candidates when they reach the polling place. The ballot itself is not very helpful, listing only the candidates' names. Voters sometimes can make inferences from those names, inferences that may include party affiliations, incumbency status, ethnicity, and gender. Some voters use lists of party candidates, and others undoubtedly employ newspaper and interest-group endorsements. But a good many voters are likely to encounter difficulty in making meaningful choices among the candidates.

In the absence of survey research, it is difficult to determine how Ohio voters make their choices in lower-court elections. But studies of outcomes in contests for seats on the courts of appeals and courts of common pleas, supplemented by additional data, allow some tentative generalizations about lower-court elections.[15]

First, lower-court elections frequently are uncontested. Between 1982 and 1990, 60 percent of the general elections for the courts of appeals were contested; in 1990, the rate of contests for common pleas was 44 percent.

Second, incumbents generally fare well. To begin with, incumbency discourages competition. In the 1962–80 period, common pleas judges who had won previous contests for that office were unopposed 73 percent of the time, appointees facing their first contests 44 percent; races with no incumbent had only a single candidate 33 percent of the time. Even when they face opposition, incumbents have a high success rate. Between 1962 and 1980, incumbent common pleas judges defeated opponents in the general election 84 percent of the time, and a slight majority of those victories were by at least a 2-to-1 margin. This success rate is striking when we consider that vulnerable incumbents are more likely to attract opponents. Taking into account both contested and uncontested races, the overall general election success rate for incumbents who had won previous elections was 95 percent; for appointees facing their first elections it was 86 percent.

The advantages of incumbency for a lower-court judge probably differ somewhat from those of incumbents in more visible offices. Name recognition plays a particularly important role in contests that provide relatively little information to voters. (Of course, nonincumbents who are well known can gain a similar advantage; the same is true of people who gain "false" recognition because they share names with sitting judges or other political figures.) On the other hand, incumbent judges have only limited opportunities to build support through their conduct in office.

Third, the pattern of party strength in an appellate district or county has considerable impact. Like incumbency, a strong party advantage discourages competition. The strongest advantage lies in the most heavily Republican counties, where there frequently is no Democratic candidate for a common pleas judgeship even if the seat is open. The relative strength of the two parties also affects outcomes of contested races, particularly when neither candidate has the advantage of incumbency. In the 1962–80 period, Democrats won 59 percent of the contests for open common pleas seats in the most Democratic counties but only 31 percent in other counties (in which Republicans generally have the electoral advantage).[16] The impact of party strength on election outcomes indicates that many voters—what proportion is impossible to determine—use judicial candidates' party affiliations as a basis for their choices. To do so, of course, voters must ascertain those affiliations. Candidates' past political activity, campaign publicity, and lists of party candidates all identify party affiliations for some voters; in some instances, voters use candidates' names as cues to their affiliations.

Finally, common pleas elections operate somewhat differently in populous urban counties and sparsely populated rural counties. There is less competition for judgeships in the smaller counties, largely because there are fewer potential aspirants. Incumbents are especially likely to win by default. In the forty-five smallest Ohio counties, 85 percent of the judges who had won previous elections were unopposed in the 1962–80 period.

When seats are contested, those contests produce more voter participation in smaller counties. In 1990, of the people who turned out at the polls in Ohio's three largest counties, typically between 70 and 85 percent cast votes in specific common pleas races. In relatively small counties, the proportion was over 90 percent most of the time. In the 1962–80 period there was an interesting pattern of outcomes across counties of different sizes. Even though incumbents were considerably more likely to face opposition in larger counties, about the same proportion of incumbents lost their seats in groupings of counties ranging from largest to smallest. In other words, those incumbents who did have opponents were defeated at a much higher rate in smaller counties.

The differences between larger and smaller counties, taken together, suggest that voters in smaller counties tend to know more about the judicial candidates. Counties with smaller populations have fewer judges to observe, so citizens have a better opportunity to assess their performance. Perhaps more important, a higher proportion of people will have personal knowledge of judicial candidates, and word-of-mouth may spread that knowledge widely by election day. Thus, trial-court elections in counties such as Cuyahoga and Hamilton can differ fundamentally from those in counties such as Vinton and Noble.

The Ohio Supreme Court is not only the state's highest court but also its only statewide court. These characteristics increase competition and the visibility of campaigns for seats on the Supreme Court, especially for chief justice. And the character of Supreme Court elections has varied over time. Supreme Court elections of the 1980s featured more campaign activity and media coverage than in the preceding era, and the relatively high visibility of these contests increased voter participation and seemed to affect the ways that voters made their decisions.

Even before the 1980s, the level of competition for the Supreme Court was relatively high. Of the fifty-five general elections to the court between 1942 and 1978, only five were uncontested.[17] This level of competition reflects lawyers' ambition for seats on the highest court and the parties' desire for maximum representation on that court. Because of the reasonably close balance between the parties in Ohio as a whole, runaway victories were exceptions to the rule. Even so, the general visibility of Supreme Court contests seemed to be fairly limited. During the 1974–80 period, the highest level of spending by a Supreme Court candidate was $72,000, and the mean was less than one-third of that total.[18] Similarly, the media paid relatively little attention to most Supreme Court contests.

As in common pleas elections, voting patterns in the electorate followed partisan lines: Supreme Court candidates generally fared better in counties where their party's gubernatorial candidates did better. In large part, this relationship seemed to reflect voters' use of candidates' names as cues to their party affiliations. The county-level correlation between voting for the Supreme Court and for governor generally increased when one candidate had a party-identified name, even more when both had such names. And in one memorable contest in 1970, a Democrat with a name that sounded "Republican" ran against a Republican with a "Democratic" name; in that contest the Democratic candidate did substantially better in counties where his party's gubernatorial candidate did *worse*.[19]

More generally, name recognition helped candidates. Such recognition might derive from the holding of high public offices, and a familiar political name also seemed to help. The perceived advantage of such a name is illustrated by the proliferation of Supreme Court candidates named Brown, a popular name in Ohio politics; between 1964 and 1980, Browns were listed on the general election ballot thirteen times, including two Brown-versus-Brown races.[20]

Incumbency is one potential source of name recognition, but sitting Supreme Court justices fared only moderately well between 1960 and 1980; only seventeen of twenty-four previously elected incumbents were successful. This result reflected the limited visibility of Supreme Court justices and the advantages of Republican candidates in nonpartisan contests (Republican incumbents did considerably better than Democrats). Indeed, Republican candidates dominated Supreme Court elections in general. Between 1950 and 1974, Republican candidates won more than two-thirds of all elections to the court.

Beginning in the early 1980s, the character of Supreme Court contests changed. The scope of campaigns grew, with levels of spending and media coverage substantially higher. Meaningful issues, including judicial policy, became more prominent. These changes reflected several related developments.[21] The establishment of a Democratic majority on the court in 1978 led to a liberal doctrinal trend on economic issues, arousing opposition from business groups and increasing the stakes in Supreme Court elections. The conduct of Democratic chief justice Frank Celebrezze became a focus of controversy; critics charged that Celebrezze had committed ethical violations in connection with his short-lived gubernatorial candidacy in 1981, that he was the cause of poor working relations on the court, and that he acted in a vindictive fashion toward the state bar.[22] Both economic issues and allegations about Celebrezze's conduct lent themselves to campaign appeals; the former created a powerful incentive for monetary contributions from interest groups, and the latter provided excellent fodder for stories and editorials in the state's mass media.

The level of publicity and campaign activity was at its highest in the mid-1980s. In 1984, considerable attention was given to the unsuccessful reelection campaign of James Celebrezze, brother of the chief justice, against Republican Craig Wright (James Celebrezze was treated largely as a surrogate for his brother). Interest in Supreme Court contests peaked in 1986, with Frank Celebrezze running for reelection and the parties battling for a court majority. Celebrezze and his opponent, Thomas Moyer, spent a total of $2.8 million on the campaign, eclipsing earlier spending levels. The media also gave unprecedented attention to the contest for chief justice, with major newspapers uniformly supporting the Republican candidates in all three contests. The economic issues that motivated many contributors played only a limited role in the campaigns and media coverage; rather, the Republicans and Ohio's newspapers emphasized the alleged misdeeds of the chief justice and the need to "clean up" the court. Moyer defeated Celebrezze by more than 200,000 votes, winning 53.8 percent of the total votes. That win, along with a party split of the two associate justice contests, gave the Republicans a 4-to-3 majority on the court. In 1988 the Democrats won both races for associate justice, while in 1990 the Republicans won both races. In 1992 Moyer was reelected as chief justice, and the parties split the two associate races. Each of these elections maintained the 4-to-3 Republican advantage.

The impact on the voters of this growth in visibility was evident as early as 1982, when James Celebrezze defeated Republican appointee Blanche Krupansky in a heated battle. Voter participation in that contest, as a proportion of people who turned out at the polls, was the highest (82 percent) of any associate justice contest in the period beginning in 1942. That record was broken two years later when James Celebrezze was defeated for reelection. In 1986, participation in the two associate justice contests by this measure was just over 80 percent; in the chief justice contest, participation was 89 percent—far higher than in any other Supreme Court contest in the past half century. Participation declined after 1986, but it remained relatively high.[23]

Surveys of the voters that were conducted between 1984 and 1988 provide some sense of how voters choose Supreme Court candidates.[24] These surveys have verified that voters respond to candidates' party affiliations and that partisan voting is strongest when information on those affiliations is most widespread. In 1986, for instance, the correlation between voters' party identifications and their votes was highest in the chief justice contest, where the candidates' affiliations were well publicized; weaker in one contest for associate justice, where the Democratic candidate had a Democratic-identified name (Sweeney); and weakest in the other associate justice contest where neither candidate had a party-identified name.[25]

Name recognition in itself is an advantage. When voters were asked the reasons for their choices, significant numbers indicated that their recognition of one candidate swayed them in favor of that candidate.[26] In some instances, particularly the Sweeneys who ran in 1986 and 1988, it was probably the name itself more than the individual that produced these responses. Francis Sweeney, who had lost a Supreme Court contest in 1986, won in 1992; by doing so, he joined A. William Sweeney on the court.

Interest groups also can have a meaningful impact on voters' choices. Ohio's labor unions strongly supported the Democratic candidates in 1986 and 1988, and they seemed to communicate their message with some effectiveness. When party identification and other relevant factors are held constant, union membership increased the likelihood of voting for the Democratic candidates considerably in some contests.[27]

In contrast, policy issues seem to have little direct impact on voters' choices even when those issues receive publicity. The Democratic candidates in 1984 and 1986 gave considerable emphasis to personal injury issues, arguing that the Democratic court was favoring the interests of the common person. Yet relatively few voters indicated that their 1986 choices were based on those issues.[28] These responses may underestimate the impact of issues on voters' choices, but they suggest the difficulty of communicating policy issues effectively in even the best publicized judicial contests.

Finally, voting in 1984 and 1986 indicates that nonpolicy issues can have a major impact. As noted earlier, Republican candidates and most of the mass media in those years emphasized the alleged failings of Chief Justice Celebrezze—and, by extension, the Democratic majority on the Supreme Court. In two contests, those involving the chief justice in 1986 and his brother in 1984, many voters referred to negative impressions of the Democratic candidates as reasons for choosing Republican candidates. To that extent, the Republican message about judicial conduct was communicated to voters more effectively than the Democratic message about judicial issues.[29]

The survey responses underline the difference between elections to the Supreme Court, even the well-publicized elections of the 1980s, and those to high offices such as governor and U.S. senator. The nonpartisan ballot limits voters' knowledge of candidates' party affiliations, and the smaller scale of campaigns limits what voters can learn more generally about the candidates. The nonpartisan ballot aside, differences between elections to the Supreme Court and to nonjudicial contests below the highest level, such as state treasurer, are not as dramatic.

The governor's power to fill judicial vacancies between elections has real significance because such vacancies are not rare. Between 1961 and 1978, 40 percent of the new common pleas judges were appointees; between 1960 and 1980, 16 percent of the judges who joined the appellate courts did so through appointments.[30] Appointments are made largely on a partisan basis, with the procedures reportedly used by Governor George Voinovich for trial-court vacancies being fairly typical.[31] When a vacancy occurs, according to a 1992 description, a gubernatorial assistant contacts the chair of the Republican party for the county involved.

The county party is asked to submit two to three names, along with supporting information, to the governor; before making its recommendations, the party organization is to consult informally with the local bar association on the qualifications of potential appointees. In the governor's office more information is gathered, and the governor then makes an appointment. At the Supreme Court level, appointed judges have been vulnerable to defeat in their first election; since 1960, a slight majority of Supreme Court appointees have lost.[32] Common pleas appointees have done better, winning 86 percent of the time against opposition or by default in 1962–80. Thus the appointment power is particularly useful to the governor below the Supreme Court level.

Courts at every level of the Ohio system have considerable effect on the state and its people. But it is the Ohio Supreme Court whose impact is most sweeping. It is also the court whose work is most closely entwined with other political institutions. And in recent years the court and its decisions have been especially visible and controversial.

In their backgrounds, Ohio Supreme Court justices are fairly similar to their counterparts in other states.[33] Of the justices serving in the 1980s and early 1990s, the great majority had engaged in the private practice of law, several having spent twenty years or more in private practice.[34] The great majority also had served on lower courts, either at the trial level or on a court of appeals and a few on both. Another common characteristic was government service. Several justices had held high-level government positions: state attorney general (Paul Brown), state legislator (Frank Celebrezze, Robert Holmes, Paul Pfeifer), gubernatorial assistant (Thomas Moyer, Ralph Locher), big-city mayor (Locher). But none of the recent justices matches the record of Chief Justice C. William O'Neill, who had been both speaker of the state House and governor before heading the judicial branch. The holding of high nonjudicial positions by several justices is the most visible manifestation of another trait that most justices share, past involvement in politics. The justice who comes essentially from outside politics to gain a seat on the Supreme Court, as Herbert Brown did in 1986, is a clear exception to the rule.

The cases that come to the Supreme Court include original cases involving appeals from administrative decisions and questions concerning governance of the state bar, along with an array of mandatory and discretionary appeals from the courts of appeals. (Each year the court also hears several cases that have been certified to it by a court of appeals because of a conflict between that court's decision and the position of another court of appeals on the same legal issue.) Most of the cases brought to the Supreme Court are under its discretionary jurisdiction. Because the court is so selective in accepting discretionary cases—it turned down about 90 percent of these cases in 1990[35]—only about a quarter of the cases that it actually decides on the merits are discretionary. But many of the mandatory cases are decided without full consideration and full written opinions; among the full-opinion cases—those that constitute the court's central agenda—discretionary cases constitute a much higher proportion of the agenda. Thus a large share of the court's work is imposed on it, but another large share is subject to the justices' own assessments of what merits their consideration.

Substantively, the Supreme Court's agenda is diverse in two respects: it decides significant numbers of cases involving statutory law, constitutional law, and the common law (this category includes fields such as contracts and property, in which state law developed primarily through court decisions independent of statutes), and it addresses a great many kinds of legal and policy issues.[36] But the court generally devotes a large portion of its agenda to a small number of issues. In 1990 and 1991, for instance, more than half its decisions fell into four areas: regulation of the legal profession, workers' compensation, taxation, and criminal law and procedure.[37] This specialization reflects the court's jurisdiction; a good many workers' compensation and tax cases come to it on a mandatory basis, and the court's exclusive responsibility for regulation of the legal profession also brings it a considerable number of cases.[38] Of the cases under its discretionary jurisdiction decided in 1990–91, 16.5 percent concerned criminal matters, 15.2 percent employment and labor relations, 12.7 percent torts, and 6.3 percent insurance, with other cases spread across a wide array of issues.

One potentially important factor in the policy choices of a state supreme court is its partisan composition. Not surprisingly, Republican judges across the country generally support more conservative policies than do their Democratic counterparts.[39] Yet not all judges follow the dominant tendencies in their parties, and other forces may complicate the relationship between a court's party membership and its policies.

For most of Ohio's pre-1978 history, the Supreme Court had a Republican majority, with a predictable effect: "The Ohio high court was dominated from the close of the Civil War to 1978 by conservative, 'old stock' Republicans who fashioned the law to conform to the values and interests they shared with small town and rural Ohioans, with business and industry."[40] Yet we should be careful not to overstate the court's adherence to conservative positions. One of the major continuing battles in state law has been between the interests of plaintiffs (primarily individuals) and defendants (in practice, primarily large institutions) in personal injury law. In the nineteenth century, the law promulgated by state supreme courts tended to favor defendant interests; in this century, particularly after World War II, the law shifted to expand the rights of injured parties to obtain compensation.[41] During its period of Republican dominance in the decades prior to 1979, the Ohio Supreme Court ranked above average in the speed and extent with which it adopted new doctrines favorable to plaintiffs.[42] While this standing undoubtedly reflected the availability of relevant cases as well as the justices' inclinations, it could not have developed if the Supreme Court had been uniformly conservative.

In the period from 1979 through 1986, in contrast with most of its earlier history, the Supreme Court had both a Democratic majority and a Democratic chief justice, Frank Celebrezze. During this period the court became considerably more liberal on economic issues, most notably in personal injury law, a liberalism that was reflected in a number of major doctrinal shifts.[43] The change in the court's stance was one proclaimed by Celebrezze himself,[44] and it received considerable attention even outside the legal community. One controversial set of decisions allowed injured employees to sue their employers for damages in addition to workers' compensation, decisions that earned Celebrezze a mention from *Forbes* magazine as one of "the hanging judges of business."[45] In 1986, business groups secured legislation that largely overturned this line of decisions.

The court's liberalism, however, did not extend to civil liberties. During the early 1980s, state supreme courts increasingly were using state constitutions to extend the scope of individual liberties beyond those established under the U.S. Constitution by an increasingly conservative U.S. Supreme Court.[46] The Ohio Supreme Court maintained a fairly conservative stance on civil liberties issues—particularly in criminal law, the area in which state supreme courts as a whole were most active in expanding rights. James Leonard found that for the court's decisions across all fields, the proportion of liberal decisions was at about the same level in 1985 as the average for the years 1970, 1975, and 1980; in criminal cases the court's record was actually at its most conservative, by far, in 1985.[47] (Such comparisons should be made with caution, however, because of the content of the cases heard by the court changes over time.)

Since the Republicans maintained a 4-to-3 court majority from 1987 through 1992, the court might have been expected to move strongly in a conservative direction during that period. The actual record is more ambiguous. There is no longer a clear movement favoring plaintiffs in personal injury cases, but by no means has the court been uniformly conservative on economic issues. In addition, the post-1986 court has not been distinctly less friendly to civil liberties than its predecessor.

The absence of a more dramatic shift reflects complexities in the relationship between party affiliation and the policy positions of individual justices. While the court's Democratic justices generally establish more liberal voting records than their Republican colleagues, there are exceptions to that rule.[48] In 1990 and 1991, three Democrats were distinctly more liberal in their votes than three Republicans—but the fourth Republican, Andrew "Andy" Douglas, had a voting record closer to those of his Democratic colleagues than to the other Republicans. Further, the positions of justices relative to each other are not uniform across areas of policy. The justices' records in three types of economic cases (torts, insurance, and employment) showed a difference between the three Democrats and Douglas and the other three Republicans. But the ordering of justices in criminal cases was quite different, and there was not a clear relationship between party affiliation and voting behavior in that field.

Another way to gauge the justices' voting behavior is through the proportions of nonunanimous decisions in which pairs of justices voted alike. Except for Douglas, justices were more likely to side with their party colleagues than with other justices. But there was not a sharp division into two camps; no pair of justices agreed in as many as three-quarters of the nonunanimous decisions or as few as one-quarter of these cases. With the absence of such a division, it is not surprising that a shift from a Democratic majority to a narrow Republican majority failed to produce a revolutionary change in court policy. The new court lacked the cohesive conservative majority that would be necessary for a fundamental shift in policy.[49]

Judges enjoy greater insulation from political influences and pressures than do legislators, but their insulation is far from total. That certainly is true of Ohio Supreme Court justices. Most were active in politics before reaching the bench. Their links with the state's politics are strengthened by the role of the political parties in helping them to win and retain their seats and by their relationships with interest groups that care about

Supreme Court decisions. It is noteworthy that Ohio legislators tend to describe the court and its justices in partisan and "political" terms.[50]

Partisan influence on judges is most easily detected in the occasional cases that directly affect political parties.[51] Certainly this is true of the Ohio Supreme Court. In cases that have a direct impact on the parties, the court frequently splits perfectly along partisan lines. This was true, for instance, of a critical 1973 decision that allowed popular Republican former governor James Rhodes to run for a third term and of two 1980 cases involving election issues.[52] In 1991, a 4-to-3 party-line vote allowed a former employee of Democratic auditor Thomas Ferguson to bring a potentially damaging lawsuit against Ferguson.[53] In 1992 another party-line vote produced a ruling in favor of a Republican plan for state legislative districts, thereby justifying the efforts of the Republicans to get the issue into state court and of the Democrats to get it to federal court.[54]

Yet the court does not always respond to partisan cases in partisan terms, as one important case illustrates. Democrat Lee Fisher defeated Republican Paul Pfeifer by a very small margin in the 1990 contest for attorney general, and Pfeifer brought a lawsuit alleging that Fisher had benefited from illegal practices in one county. Despite the high stakes in the lawsuit, the court (with three justices from each party participating) voted unanimously to uphold Fisher's election.[55] And in some other party-related cases, most justices have followed their party, but one or two have deviated. This was what happened in the 1990 cases involving the tax liability of the Republican candidate for state treasurer and the criminal conviction of a former Democratic party official growing out of her fundraising activities.[56]

Parties, of course, are not the only political organizations that may influence Supreme Court decisions; interest groups also play a role.[57] In 1990–91, 212 *amicus curiae* briefs were submitted to the Ohio Supreme Court, with 279 groups and individuals associated with those briefs. (These briefs came in 131 separate cases, suggesting that a significant minority of Supreme Court decisions are regarded as important by people other than the litigants.) The groups submitting briefs included professional associations, businesses and business groups, labor unions, and public interest groups. Amicus briefs were scattered across a wide range of cases, with criminal and employment relations cases garnering the highest proportion (15 percent each). Of the briefs that could be classified ideologically, a small majority (54 percent) took a liberal position.

Interest groups also participate in Supreme Court elections. The most active groups are on both sides of personal-injury law and other economic issues. Insurance companies and other business groups, as well as medical groups, seek the election of justices who would favor conservative policies in these fields; labor unions work for the election of justices with liberal positions on economic issues. Both sides proselytize their own members and make monetary contributions to candidates. In Ohio's most expensive Supreme Court campaign, the contest for chief justice in 1986, labor unions contributed at least $350,000 to Frank Celebrezze, while the insurance industry alone gave at least $185,000 to Thomas Moyer.[58] Although the level of interest-group contributions in other campaigns has been considerably lower, such contributions have provided a substantial amount of funding for candidates.[59]

Public concern about the effects of campaign contributions on the Supreme Court's decisions has been most widespread when justices took visible actions in cases that benefited campaign contributors, particularly in 1987 and 1991 decisions about whether to rehear cases. In each instance the justices were criticized in the press and action was then taken within the court to repair the damage.[60] Members of the court also have been criticized for other actions that raised questions about their impartiality, such as continuing relationships with party organizations, expressions of loyalty to interest groups, and participation in cases involving associates and acquaintances. Such concerns have not been limited to Ohio, and they have grown nationally as increased campaign funding raises the potential for direct conflicts of interest.[61]

Every state supreme court features some dissent, but the frequency of dissent varies considerably. In years for which state dissent rates have been calculated, the Ohio rate has always been above average. In 1980–81, for instance, 36.8 percent of the published Ohio decisions included dissenting votes, the sixth highest rate in the country and exactly double the mean for all fifty states.[62]

A high dissent rate does not necessarily reflect conflict among the justices. The greater a court's freedom to accept or reject cases, the higher the proportion of its cases that contain potentially divisive issues. Courts whose members have strongly divergent views about legal issues are likely to have high dissent rates even if personal relations are harmonious. And some courts are more favorable to open expression of disagreement than others.

Yet the Ohio Supreme Court has a reputation as a contentious body, a reputation based on public disclosures of serious personal differences since the early 1980s. Chief Justice Frank Celebrezze became involved in open conflict with some of the court's Republican members.[63] Celebrezze criticized Republican appointee Blance Krupansky in strong language in two 1982 opinions.[64] Conflict surfaced again after the election in 1984 of two new Republican justices, Craig Wright and Andy Douglas. "On just one day," a reporter noted, "two jurists exchanged accusations of case-fixing, payoffs, lying, electronic surveillance and political orchestration. And then things really got nasty."[65]

One striking episode was the aftermath of a 1985 decision in which the court reinstated a suspended attorney to the practice of law. One of three dissenters, Celebrezze wrote an opinion in which he asked, "What is the silent and sinister cause for this unprecedented action?"[66] Wright and Douglas then asked for a legislative hearing on Celebrezze's charge, but the chief justice did not appear for the hearing. When Celebrezze held a press conference about the matter, Douglas tried to get in, but a staff member blocked him and there reportedly "was some bumping."[67] Afterward, the *Dayton Daily News* illustrated an editorial on the court's conflicts with pictures from professional wrestling matches.[68] These conflicts were one issue used against Celebrezze in Thomas Moyer's successful campaign in 1986. After that election many observers assumed that the source of internal battling had been eliminated. As one commentator wrote, "Gone are the days of shoving matches, heated public exchanges and nasty jabs in court."[69] Indeed, the court remained relatively quiet for several years.

But conflicts within the court again became visible in the early 1990s. Much of the reported friction on the court involved suspicions and charges by some justices that colleagues had leaked information to the media, including information about alleged improper conduct by justices. In 1991 Douglas and Craig Wright engaged in a physical scuffle, reportedly resulting from Wright's belief that Douglas was the source of unfavorable information about Wright's activities that the *Akron Beacon Journal* had published.[70] News stories in 1992 indicated that Douglas and Moyer each had taken actions intended to reduce the other's chances for reelection.[71] While Douglas was involved in much of the conflict that was visible outside the court, discord seemed to extend more widely.[72]

The most serious reported conflicts on the court have involved justices on opposite sides of partisan or ideological divides. The disputes between Frank Celebrezze and Republican justices were part of a larger battle over partisan control of the court. While Wright, Moyer, and Douglas are all Republicans, Douglas is a liberal maverick who said in 1992 that Moyer and another Republican colleague "get very upset with me because I don't vote the Republican line."[73]

Conditions in supreme courts are often conducive to conflict; justices work together intensively over long periods of time, and inevitably they disagree about matters of policy. It is hardly surprising that some justices should come to dislike some colleagues or even attack them directly. More often than not, such conflict is kept quiet; the pre-Celebrezze Ohio Supreme Court was not entirely harmonious, but the departures from harmony did not become public.[74] And the Ohio court is not the only one in which messy disputes have become public. In the 1980s and 1990s internal battles have surfaced in such states as California, Nevada, Missouri, Montana, and Pennsylvania.[75] This does not mean, of course, that such conflicts are unimportant or that they do not affect a court's work. Conversely, a degree of conflict may be one price of an active role in policy making.[76]

This chapter has pointed to the multifaceted role of the Ohio judiciary—especially the Supreme Court—in state politics. While Ohio's courts are insulated from their political environment in some ways, their insulation is far less than total: the courts have strong links with the larger world of Ohio politics. These links take many forms, but they are largely the result of activities by Ohio's political parties and interest groups. Primarily because of efforts by parties and groups, partisanship and controversial policy issues often influence both the style and the outcomes of judicial elections in the state. Interest groups frequently seek to influence the policy choices made by Ohio courts through litigation and amicus briefs, along with other methods. Finally, internal conflicts in the Ohio Supreme Court reflect partisan and ideological divisions that run throughout Ohio politics.

For those who would prefer that courts stand outside the world of "politics," much of this chapter's description of Ohio's courts must seem unsettling. But courts in Ohio are not unique in their relationship with the larger political process. For instance, partisan considerations play a large part in the selection of judges in a great many states, and such considerations affect decisions on issues such as legislative redistricting in both state and federal courts. Elsewhere, as in Ohio, the importance of what courts do inevitably makes them targets of "political" influence.

This does not mean that the links between courts and the larger political system look the same everywhere. The form and strength of those links are the product of both a state's political culture and its institutional arrangements. This reality should be a source of both hope and modesty for those who want to change the relationship between Ohio's courts and their political environment: institutional change can have an impact, but that impact will be constrained by the continuing effects of Ohio's political culture.

One important example concerns the selection of judges. Ohio's system of judicial elections with partisan primaries facilitates links between Supreme Court justices and political parties and interest groups. Thus, replacement of that system with the Missouri Plan might well weaken some of these links. For instance, facing less difficulty in retaining their offices, Supreme Court justices might be less concerned with amassing campaign funds or pleasing important interest groups. But in a state where partisanship pervades government and politics, it is highly unlikely that partisan considerations would disappear from the selection and behavior of Supreme Court justices.[77] Indeed, by limiting the role of the electorate in selecting judges, the Missouri Plan might make the selection process even more susceptible to control by political elites—who are probably more partisan in their orientation than the electorate as a whole. This does not mean that it is futile to consider changes in such institutional arrangements as the system for selection of judges, but it cautions against expecting such changes to transform Ohio's courts in fundamental ways.

Whatever their relationship with the political process, Ohio's courts can be expected to continue to play a vital role in shaping the state's public life. In this respect, the courts of Ohio strongly resemble the state's other governmental institutions: all are engaged in the important and complex enterprise of making public policy.

❖

CHAPTER FOURTEEN

Interest Groups in Ohio Politics

❖

CHARLES FUNDERBURK & ROBERT W. ADAMS

❖ Lobbying is as American as apple pie. It is the most effective way for citizens to communicate their interests to government. As critical as they are to representative government, elections are more a judgment of past performance and a referendum on the times than an expression of policy preferences.

In practice, of course, lobbying works best for citizens organized into permanent interest groups able to monitor and influence government every day. And the large number of organized groups lobbying government in this country and in Ohio might suggest that most citizens have their views well represented. It is an article of near-religious faith among many students of American politics that interest groups comprise the main means of expression for the diverse interests of American citizens. The most succinct commentary on this belief is E. E. Schaatschneider's remark that "the interest group choir sings with a distinctly upper class accent."[1]

It is clear that groups most successful in promoting their political agendas have disproportionate control of critical political resources—money, organizational skills, useful connections, access to information, proximity to decision makers—compared to ordinary citizens. In some cases, the size and unity of a group's membership may offset the greater financial power, for example, of a state manufacturers' association. Employee unions and associations are examples of such groups. However, only a small minority of Americans belong to unions, leaving most workers with no direct representation in the lobbying system. Despite the appearance of every category of citizens having one or more associations speak for them, it is mainly on behalf of the most advantaged members of society that lobbyists ply their trade.

This chapter's survey of interest groups and lobbying in Ohio reveals the following trends:[2]

A great proliferation of interest groups since the 1960s. Interviews with members of the General Assembly confirm that there are now more interest groups, a greater variety of types of groups, and a significantly increased level of activity by them. This is a national trend, not just one affecting Ohio. As federal policy mandates to states increase and financial support from Washington goes down, states have had to assume more responsibility for solving their own problems—a change especially affecting major urban states like Ohio. As state government in Ohio has seen its policy agenda lengthen, interest-group activity in the capital had increased accordingly.

A centralization of group activities in Columbus. Citizen contacts with state legislators and other grass-roots efforts to influence decision making on bills are effective in some situations. However, our interviews leave no doubt that the most effective way to influence legislation in Ohio is by regular face-to-face contact with key General Assembly leaders—only possible through the services of experienced, well-compensated professional lobbyists working the capitol corridors every day. The extraordinary power centralized in the legislative leadership of the Ohio General Assembly virtually requires interest groups to hire full-time advocates with reliable connections to the leadership.

The rise of single-issue groups. In this context the legislators most frequently cited pro-life and pro-choice groups on the abortion issue, along with environmental activists, the American Association of Retired People, consumer groups, and advocates of term limitations for elected officials. A common complaint by the legislators was that some single-issue activists were zealots who did not appreciate the necessity in politics for compromise.

The increase in the number, activity, and visibility of public-interest groups. Interestingly, Ohio legislators reported only modest levels of activity by public interest groups (such as Common Cause), and they did not consider these groups to be particularly effective.

The growth of activity and impact by institutions, including corporations, universities, and state and local governments. The importance of public schools and universities in Ohio legislative politics cannot be underestimated. The Ohio Education Association (OEA), with more than 80,000 members, is probably the most powerful union in the state. Legislators regard the OEA as a significant force in Columbus. Our interviews show that the traditional business and corporate interest groups, including the manufacturers, bankers, insurance companies, and utilities, remain very influential in Ohio politics. Of increasing importance are hospitals and other health-care providers.

Across the street from the Statehouse in Columbus is a gleaming chrome-and-glass tower that bears the name of the outgoing speaker of the Ohio House of Representatives, Vernal G. Riffe, Jr. That Riffe was successful in getting this structure constructed to provide new offices for the members of the legislature and that the tower bears his name is a testament to his power, as is the decision a few years ago to establish a state university in his district. The window in Riffe's office on the fourteenth floor of his monument overlooked the Statehouse; major traffic arteries converge at the base of the building that bears his name, seeming to bring people and power to him. It is an impressive image, and an appropriate one. Indeed, one legislator described Riffe as "the Governor without the title," adding, "It's what Vern wants, that's what matters."

The Ohio General Assembly has a tradition of strong leadership. Riffe, who decided to retire in 1994, is the latest in a long line of powerful Ohio House speakers. Not only are the formal powers of his office impressive, but equally important were the skill and assertiveness with which Riffe used his formal powers and the informal ways he expanded his influence after becoming speaker in 1975. He added to his power by raising hundreds of thousands of dollars in each election for Democratic candidates for the legislature. Those who were elected soon found that the speaker demanded team-play and readily disciplined uncooperative members.[3]

The president of the Ohio Senate, currently Stanley Aronoff, a Republican from Cincinnati, also enjoys an impressive list of formal powers as well as a unified party. The speaker and the president are without question the most important and powerful members of the General Assembly. This is of considerable significance for interest groups and their lobbyists. When power is centralized in the party leadership, the task of interest groups is to find a direct route to the leadership. In Ohio, this task is simplified by the availability of high-priced professional consultants with close connections to the legislative leadership. Groups that can afford to purchase this service are in a good position to promote their interests. This centralization of power in the legislative leadership is the single most important and distinctive aspect of interest-group lobbying in Ohio.

Although legislative leadership is important, legislators also work in a localized environment that requires them to be entrepreneurs as they work on behalf of their constituents—and for their own reelections. Into this fluid negotiating system comes the lobbyist in command of significant political resources important to legislators. And, with over two thousand organizations and agents registered to lobby the Ohio General Assembly and the executive branch of state government, there is no lack of possible assistance.

Key among the needed forms of help is reliable policy information that is usefully packaged and persuasive. Most members do not enter the legislature as policy experts, and, even if they do develop expertise on some issues, their capacity for documenting legislative need, cost, and utility is always limited. Since lobbyists belong to networks of other lobbyists and legislators, they can be good sources of political as well as policy information. They can offer intelligence about what other interest groups or legislators might do on pending legislation and what may be necessary to overcome opposition at critical junctures along the road to a floor vote. In this manner, they become strategists and advisers on the complex business of steering measures through the legislative maze.

Lobbyists have access to another critical resource in these days of spiraling election campaign costs: direct control or a major say in the distribution of large sums of campaign money. Lobbyists who also manage political action committees—for example, the lobbyist for the Ohio Hospital Association—have a "cash lever" in their hands. However, even if a political action committee (PAC) is run separately, the organization's lobbyist will have input into campaign contribution decisions of the PAC. If no PAC has been set up, at the very least, the lobbyist can recommend to affluent organizational members which legislators deserve their support. In what is rightly called a "pay-to-play" legislative process, the ability to distribute campaign funds is the political ante for a seat at the legislative gaming table.

Despite the fears of many, especially in the media, that "the special interests" have too much say in what government does, most legislators do not see themselves as targets for marauding bands of lobbyists—victims of evil forces beyond their power to resist. A large body of research has shown the relationship between legislators and lobbyists to be more symbiotic than adversarial. Quite simply, they need each other.[4] In state legislatures, especially, where staff support, good information, and assistance is at a premium, the typical member is more likely to see lobbyists as partners, valued advisers, and political allies with common goals. And, even though some may be seen more as basically unfriendly to their concerns, legislators generally see lobbyists as the most available and authoritative sources of expertise on the issues they face. As the agenda of issues and problems grows, so does the influence of lobbyists.

Since 1890, when Massachusetts passed the first state law regulating lobbying, every state has sought to regulate it. Disclosure has been the main approach to regulation, since more restrictive laws invite First Amendment court challenges. Today all states mandate that individuals paid to influence legislation register and identify the organizations or persons who contract for their services. In forty-five states lobbyists must register and file periodic reports describing their activity. In forty states, expenditures on behalf of the legislative interests of clients also must be reported.[5]

In Ohio, individuals employed to lobby the legislature and the organizations that hire them must register with the Joint Legislative Ethics Committee, a bipartisan committee of twelve members representing both chambers of the General Assembly. The committee employs a director and a small staff, including at least one attorney, to administer the lobbying statute and issue periodic reports identifying the organizations and individuals lobbying the legislature. Since 1991 individuals lobbying state executive agencies also must register and report their activities to the committee. Expenditures by lobbyists to influence specific bills through direct communication with members and executive officials regarding contracts and other financial matters also much be reported. Failures to register or other infractions of the statute are reported by the director to the attorney general's office for review—provided they are detected, which is not always the case. In Dayton, for example, the failure by lobbyists for the Greater Dayton Area Chamber of Commerce to register was revealed during the Montgomery County sheriff's 1993–94 criminal investigation of alleged financial irregularities and other abuses in the chamber's operations. However, there are more important problems with the law than weak enforcement.

A glaring problem arises from lobbying done by lawyers for clients having political stakes in what state government does. Attorneys have always enjoyed a highly visible and influential role in state government, usually as members of the legislature. However, their advocacy skills and experience representing clients before state agencies, commissions, and boards plus their detailed knowledge of state law also equip attorneys very well to lobby. In fact, in recent years, attorneys increasingly have offered their services as paid advocates for the legislative and administrative interests of a broad range of clients. Yet, in most cases they are exempt from state regulation of such activity, because in Ohio, and in most states, governance of the legal profession, including professional conduct, is the prerogative of the state supreme court.

In 1988, Governor Richard F. Celeste issued an executive order requiring all lobbyists who appeared before executive agencies in his administration to register; at that time state regulations covered only legislative lobbying efforts. However, he exempted lawyers from the order because of the jurisdiction of the Ohio Supreme Court over the state bar membership. At the same time, the governor wrote to Chief Justice Thomas Moyer to express his disapproval of the double standard in the executive order, urging the court to change the code of professional responsibility to include paid lobbying efforts by members of the state bar. Justice Moyer responded that he felt it would be inappropriate for the court to do this but that he would be willing to cooperate with the administration in drafting legislation regulating the conduct of lawyers as lobbyists.[6] Thus, at best, regulation of lobbying provides minimum control of the increasingly significant "shadow government" in the state capital.

Restrictions, however, have tightened in recent years, largely due to the watchdog efforts of two of the state's most influential newspapers, the *Akron Beacon Journal* and the *Dayton Daily News*. Their media spotlights revealed several examples of why a growing number of elected officials view their careers in state government as basic training for much more lucrative future opportunities in the lobbying business. Their reports pushed the General Assembly in 1991 and again in 1994 to adopt a series of strengthening amendments to the state lobbying regulations—the first important changes since the 1970s.

In 1986, articles first appeared in the *Daily News* documenting how certain former state legislators and political party leaders had parlayed their connections and legislative know-how into second careers as high-profile, high-fee Columbus lobbyists. A former Celeste administration insider and state legislator, Dennis Wojtanowski, came in for special attention. His rise to power exemplified the growing importance of what *Daily News* reporters Tim Miller and Joel Rutchick dubbed "the government across the street."

Major targets of criticism in the media series included the Celeste administration, which had developed a reputation for ethical conduct lapses among people close to the governor. Dennis Wojtanowski was featured because he personified the growing power and sophistication of the "new lobby." His firm, Success Group, Inc., was portrayed as a prototype for the new breed of independent lobbyists—the so-called "hired guns"—that simultaneously represent several clients. The contract lobbyists have elevated lobbying to a high-tech level of expertise not seen before in Columbus. An icon for the new-style lobbyist was a *Daily News* photograph of Wojtanowski, cellular phone to his mouth, walking from his Broad Street office across from the Statehouse to a meeting, plugged in always to the influence system. (Earning retainers ranging from $2,500 to over $10,000 per month, per client, Success Group is well named.)

During an interview for the series, Wojtanowski spoke matter of factly about his achievements, noting that he goes far beyond the old-fashioned schmoozing and glad-handing methods of his predecessors. One of his main tools is a comprehensive, constantly updated computerized information system providing instant access to the legislative records, political views, personal backgrounds, interests, and idiosyncracies of every General Assembly member and key executive agency people. He and others like him have raised the business of marketing influence in Columbus to a very effective level. Wojtanowski typifies what many observers of state government fear most about the growing power of lobbyists.

Paul Tipps, a former Montgomery County and state Democratic party chair and a Vern Riffe confidante, exceeds even the high-powered success of Dennis Wojtanowski. Tipps's lobbying partnership, with Neil Clark, former aide to Ohio Senate Republican leader Aronoff, represents what many Statehouse observers assert is the Cadillac of the lobbying business in Columbus. With easy access to both parties—a major asset in an era of divided party leadership in state government—Tipps and Clark and their firm, Public Policy Consultants, Inc., seem well positioned for a long run in Columbus.

Many other examples of exploitation of public position and trust, as perceived by the media, were spotlighted by the press. "Exhibit A" was Dayton's former Ohio House member, Edward J. Orlett. He was a major target of the *Dayton Daily News* throughout 1986–88 for lobbying activities that occurred at the same time he held the elected job of clerk of Dayton municipal courts. His public job paid him $58,000 a year while he operated his own consulting business in Columbus, Edward J. Orlett Associates. As a long-time, close political ally of outgoing speaker Riffe and a former member of the State Controlling Board, Orlett had instant access to two of the four major power centers in Columbus—and through Riffe to a third, the governor's office. Upon Orlett's request for a ruling, the Ohio Ethics Commission determined that there was no law against Orlett holding elected office while working as a Statehouse lobbyist. However, the commission tempered its decision by warning that the potential for a conflict of interest was there, not to mention the question of whether he could properly perform his official duties as municipal court clerk in Dayton while pursuing his expanding lobbying business in Columbus.[7]

Orlett's critics were not reassured when he responded to criticism by hiring a former Dayton police officer to run the clerk's office while he was in Columbus and by claiming he was only using vacation days to work as a lobbyist, which he alone could approve for himself. The Orlett case made especially good ammunition for those seeking revision of the state's lobbying regulations. However, as already noted, any law is a very limited instrument of control in the rapidly expanding influence industry in Columbus.

In Ohio, since 1975, lobbyists have had to comply with registration, activity, and expenditure reporting requirements administered by an arm of the General Assembly. Operating until 1993 from cramped quarters in the basement of the Statehouse, file cabinets bursting with reporting forms, the Joint Committee on Agency Rule Review (JCARR) administered the regulations and maintained the required filings of lobbyists and the organizations, associations, and individuals who hire them. The 1991 amendments to the Ohio law made significant changes in the scope and effectiveness of the regulations.

The vehicle of change, House Bill 174, became effective on April 10, 1991. Most of the revisions were in direct response to media criticisms and to the growing sentiment among a small band of General Assembly members that, if nothing else, the appearance of impropriety and undue lobbying influence had to be addressed.[8] Of the weaknesses the bill corrected, the most important was "agency lobbying." Before 1991, lobbying the executive branch—elected department heads and appointed administrators and board and commission members and staff—was exempt from any regulation. And in connection with this omission of coverage, perhaps the most glaring deficiency was that attempts to influence actions of the powerful State Controlling Board, considered to be part of the executive branch, also were exempt from any reporting or registration requirements.

American legislative bodies tend to pass laws and authorize expenditures for programs cast in very broad terms. Vague descriptions of problems, ambiguous goals, and imprecise standards of performance all lead to increased administrative discretion to determine what should be done, how, and by whom. This is an open invitation for interest groups to press their own interpretations of programs and to determine whose private interests are to be enhanced. When there is no accountability for agency lobbyists, it is difficult to assess the objectivity and integrity of the administrative process. Even when the legitimate part interest groups play in government is granted, the lack of any reporting or registration requirement raises suspicions about a policy process in which so many key decisions are hidden from public view.

The state purchases millions of dollars worth of goods and services every year—from high-tech data processing equipment to automated accounting systems for collection of delinquent taxes, to imaging systems for production of drivers' licenses, to buildings, highways, vehicles, office supplies, food, and contracts for printing. Some procurement occurs through competitive bidding where specifications and standards limit administrative discretion, and the decision-making process is more or less public. However, a large volume of state business is negotiated between administrators and vendors with unbid contracts awarded to providers who, in the judgment of an administrator, best meet agency requirements.

All unbid contracts are reviewed—hurriedly, at best—by the State Controlling Board in biweekly meetings where lobbying pressures can be fierce. The seven-person board (six of whom are legislators appointed by the House speaker and Senate president) is supposed to be a checkpoint, ensuring that public monies are properly spent. However, given the size of the task and the insufficient time for careful review, timely intervention by a well-connected lobbyist often may be critical in board actions. In practice, the lobbying-through of an unbid contract would begin with the executive agency purchasing the goods or services for which the contract provides. Last-minute telephone calls to board members or consultations in the hallway during a break, so visible to observers, are simply follow-up to an influence effort begun much earlier.

Since the amendments were enacted in 1991, executive branch and Controlling Board lobbying must be reported. Probably the most important part of the change was to extend the definition of lobbying efforts directed at the award of state contracts through the Controlling Board. This may make the process somewhat more visible and accountable; however, the substantive "bottom line," the capacity for great influence in the administration of law in Ohio, remains as great as ever, despite the expanded identification of players in the influence game in Columbus.

Prior to the 1991 revisions in lobbying regulations, it was often impossible to learn who a lobbyist was really working for. Organizations and individuals routinely represented by legal counsel would often ask their lawyers to hire a lobbyist to advocate their cause in Columbus. Under the old law, lobbyists needed to register and identify the immediate source of compensation—the person or organization that had formally contracted for their services. Many times lobbyists themselves did not know for whom they were really working. Now the "party of real interest," the ultimate employer of a lobbyist, must be indentified in addition to the immediate source of employment.[9]

Even after the 1991 revisions were enacted, the definition of lobbying remains narrow. Lobbying in Ohio is defined only as seeking to influence the content or passage of a specific bill through direct communication with legislators; attempting to affect the contract award or other expenditure decisions of major executive branch officials; or trying to sway Controlling Board actions—excepting public meetings of the board or committees of the General Assembly.

Before 1991, lobbying state administrative officials was unregulated by law. Only through the executive order of former governor Celeste requiring lobbyists working the corridors of his administration to register had executive branch lobbying ever been officially acknowledged. Administrative officials included in the law's coverage are all elected state executives and bureau-level managers or staff personnel in policy-making roles. In addition, the law also covers all departments, boards, and commissions of state government accountable to elected executives. Attempts to influence the decisions of regulatory boards and agencies is also considered to be lobbying. However, while attempts to influence administrative actions on contracts and other specific financial matters must be reported, there are important types of executive activity that escape coverage.

For example, policy advocacy—trying to influence the legislative proposals, including budgets, of executives—is not considered lobbying in Ohio. To most students of the lobbying process, policy advocacy is the very essence of the practice. Another key executive activity exempt from the lobbying regulations is assigning contracts for competitive bid on the ground that administrative discretion is limited, although not precluded, by bidding procedures for contract awards. Other administrative purchasing decisions also are exempt from the law provided a vendor did not use a lobbyist to affect the outcome and did not contribute more than $1,000 to the executive's election campaign fund within two years of the transaction.

However, there is a significant omission in the current campaign contribution restrictions placed on vendors of services and goods to state administrators. They do not apply to members of the state Controlling Board, which has approval power over millions of dollars in contract awards. Briefly, in the summer of 1986, thanks to the efforts of the House Ethics Committee chair, Democrat Jolyn Boster from Gallipolis, who got the appropriate language inserted into the law, the campaign contribution limits did cover members of this very powerful keeper of the state purse strings. However, when the General Assembly reconvened in November, the loud protests of powerful legislators on the board, complaining that the new limits would cripple their efforts to maintain the accustomed flow of political money, fell on the sympathetic ears of Speaker Riffe and the Republican Senate leader Paul Gillmor. In short order, the legislature responded, as always, to its powerful leaders, and Controlling Board members were exempted from the campaign contribution limits on vendors dealing with elected executive officials.[10]

Money spent by lobbyists on legislators (excluding campaign contributions covered in a separate statute) must be reported since May 1994 to the Office of the Legislative Inspector General, which now performs the implementation duties formerly entrusted to the Joint Committee on Agency Rule Review (JCARR). Also, two separate ethics committees in the House and Senate were replaced in the 1994 revisions by the bipartisan Joint Legislative Ethics Committee. These changes, unlike in 1991, were prompted by the press notoriety gained from a legislator's flagrant efforts to wring maximum advantage from his position as chair of the powerful House Committee on Health and Retirement.

In several newspaper accounts in the fall of 1993 and early 1994, including articles in the *Dayton Daily News*, Democratic representative Paul Jones from Ravenna was reported regularly demanding $500 honoraria as a condition for his attendance at meetings with lobbyists and interest-group members—sometimes under the most hurried circumstances. He even "charged" his fellow Democrat, Representative Rhine McLin of Dayton, $500 for meeting at her request with a group of constituents.[11] This kind of raw cupidity was even too much for Statehouse veterans who certainly had benefited from the honorarium slush funds maintained by groups wanting to ingratiate themselves with legislative leaders. Undoubtedly, the fact that an election season was approaching finally spurred the Democratic leadership in the House to take steps to further tighten the restrictions on the use of lobby money in Columbus.

Thus prodded, in February 1994 the General Assembly passed its second major ethics bill in less than three years—although not without a continuing drumfire of media criticism over various foot-dragging tactics by the leadership—no doubt brought on by the awful prospect of going "cold turkey" on the honorarium habit.

While the end of all honoraria was the most dramatic change approved, there were other notable restrictions enacted. For example, all lobbyist-paid travel and lodging expenses, in and out of Ohio, now must be reported, ending the $500 threshold previously in effect. The maximum expenditure for "wining and dining" legislators and executive officials was considerably tightened from $150 per individual to $50, and a nonreporting ceiling of $25 was placed on gifts from lobbyists (or their spouses). As usual, however, major loopholes remain. Lobbyist-financed parties, receptions, and similar events where all members of the General Assembly or either chamber separately or a full committee membership are invited are exempt from the reporting provisions as specific events. However, total lobbying expenditures in a calendar year must be reported. The requirement to report all business transactions (for profit) between covered public officials and lobbyists was continued as before. Also escaping scrutiny are lobbyist expenditures entertaining officials in attendance at national conferences and conventions of associations to which the General Assembly or other state bodies pay membership dues. And, similar expenditures for the participation of legislators in seminars, panels, and speaking engagements also do not need to be reported.

The most important single condition of successful lobbying is, and always has been, access. Developing good relationships in which key players know and trust each other, where easy, open working relationships exist, takes time and cultivation. Informal, small social occasions offer the ideal receptive environment for the lobbyist to simply "keep people informed" about the general concerns of the organization represented and to build receptivity for future "covered" lobbying overtures. This kind of "old boy/old girl" networking is perfectly normal and not necessarily a threat to the integrity or quality of government. But, at the very least, it is another example of the way so much of the real governing in Columbus occurs away from public view.

On a somewhat more visible level, organizations lobbying the General Assembly routinely invite members of the critical committees from the Senate and House to background seminars and weekend excursions—as much social as working in nature—to grease the wheels of the legislative process. As noted previously, none of this activity is considered lobbying and thus reportable as a lobbying expenditure. Here again the problem is not so much "corruption" as it is accountability. The practice deprives the public of the full knowledge needed to assess whether or not the game of "pay-to-play" has exceeded the murky boundaries of propriety.

Any discussion of money and lobbying should also take into account the role of campaign contributions in Ohio elections. To put it mildly, there is an abundance of the "mother's milk of politics" being poured into state election campaigns. A great deal of it flows directly or indirectly from the interests represented in Columbus. Campaign finance laws in Ohio do not limit how much may be collected and spent. There is a $25 limit on unreported cash contributions and a $100 ceiling on reported cash contributions. Candidates, of course, may personally finance as much of their own campaigns as they wish as established in 1976 by the U.S. Supreme Court in *Buckley v. Valeo*. The other important facts of Ohio campaign finance are these: There is no limit on the amount of money an individual may contribute to a political campaign or party; neither is there a restriction on how much a corporate political action committee or a labor union may contribute. And no law limits what a candidate or issues campaign committee or political party may spend in an election. But corporations may not spend corporate funds on campaigns. Essentially, Ohio law seeks only to record what is raised and spent on state and local political campaigns and to identify the individuals and groups involved. These rather free-and-easy campaign spending regulations invite very large infusions of political money into Ohio elections. However, what is most politically significant about campaign spending in Ohio is the degree of centralized control of very large sums of campaign money.

At or near the top of any list of campaign war chests are almost certain to be those controlled by occupants of the positions of House speaker and Senate president. These legislative leaders exert decisive control in their respective legislative domains. As noted elsewhere, outgoing speaker Vern Riffe set the institutional standard for leadership effectiveness during his record tenure. Long-time observers in Columbus say that there are four centers of power in state government; the governor's office, the Controlling Board, the office of Senate president, and the House speakership. By most assessments, "Mr. Speaker" ranks first—certainly no worse than second, even when an opposition-party governor sits in the Statehouse. It is obvious that interest groups in Ohio also know where power is located in Columbus. Over the years their generous support of the Riffe election committee was practical acknowledgment that if you wanted something from state government you asked Vern.

To take a recent example of the speaker's fund-raising prowess, the July 14, 1992, campaign finance report filed by the Riffe Election Committee recorded over forty pages of interest-group/lobbyist contributions for the reporting period just concluded. On that day, the committee report showed a balance on hand of $2.4 million—$539,000 of which had been collected at one fund-raiser on June 24, 1992.[12] These figures would seem disproportionate for the reelection campaign of a multiterm member of the Ohio House of Representatives from a one-party, rural, southern Ohio district unless it is understood that the Riffe campaign fund was perhaps the most powerful lever of all in his leadership of the majority party in the House. Other Democrats in need of campaign help often looked to the speaker and, at the opportune moment, he to them for critical votes.

The campaign fund controlled by Ohio Senate president Stanley Aronoff is nearly as impressive—less so only because the Senate is one-third the size, and senators must seek election only half as often as members of the House. Senator Aronoff was the formidable upper-house partner in the leadership duo that ran the General Assembly for so many years. Much like his former House counterpart, "Stan" is someone with whom majority Republicans in the Senate enjoy a highly beneficial mutual-support relationship—one based on the controlled flow of campaign cash from the Aronoff election committee.

The listing of registered lobbyists and organizations that employ either legislative or executive agents issued by the Office of the Legislative Inspector General is the official "Who's Who" of the influence industry in Columbus. The July 1992 edition (published by JCARR) lists the names of 2,209 individuals hired to promote and defend the interests of nearly 2,000 organizations in Ohio. The range of groups represented is very broad.[13] For example, nearly every state government agency, board, and commission, including the governor's office, employs at least one person whose main duty is to lobby the General Assembly. Increasingly, political subdivisions in Ohio also employ agents; county governments, municipalities, and school districts recognize that they benefit from (and may be hurt badly by the lack of) expert representation. Associations of local government elected officials—county commissioners, school board members, township trustees, sheriffs, engineers—are more and more in the influence business as well. Civil service and other public sector employee groups and unions are also well represented in this category.

The vast majority of organizations represented, however, are private. Individual corporations and associations of business—retail, manufacturing, banking, insurance—and health-care providers and professional practitioners of every description by far dominate the rolls of people and groups registered to lobby the General Assembly and the executive branch of state government. Industrial and trade unions, while comprising a very small number of separate organizations, represent large, even if declining, memberships.

In order to gain a view from the "inside" of the influence industry in Columbus, we interviewed ten registered lobbyists representing institutional and independent agents during the summer of 1992. They were chosen on the basis of our personal acquaintance with some of them and referrals by these individuals to others whom they felt were active and experienced enough to offer useful information about lobbying practices in state government. All but one of the interviews were conducted by telephone, lasting anywhere from twenty minutes to an hour each. Anonymity was a condition required by each respondent for the interviews.

Initially each lobbyist was asked to assign a "power rating" to each category of interest group represented in Columbus. The power ratings were based on each lobbyist's perception of a composite visibility and effectiveness status for each of twenty-five types of lobbying groups registered with the Joint Committee on Agency Rule Review as of July 28, 1992. A power-rating scale from 1 to 5 was used where 1 was the lowest perceived level of visibility and effectiveness and 5 a perception of maximum activity and influence. Individual ratings were averaged to produce the ranked power values presented in table 14.1.

The power ratings reflect an overall assessment of the influence of each group over time. Respondents often offered caveats for their assessments. For example, when groups form coalitions, the influence of interests generally perceived as weak may be significantly enhanced on an issue of joint concern. Also, intensity of concern may compensate for the lack of other lobbying resources. For example, the power of single-issue and ideological groups generally was discounted by respondents. However, on occasions that such groups can "kick up such a god-awful stink," as one lobbyist put it, they may get their way—the price legislators and other groups pay to move on to "more important things." Abortion and gun-control interests, for example, advocate positions on which compromise is unlikely. Thus, the fervency with which they pursue their goals may become a significant lever of influence.

Other circumstantial factors may alter the status of a group. For example, the 1989 death of John Hall, long-time Ohio Education Association lobbyist, has had a disastrous impact on the effectiveness of the OEA in the view of lobbyists interviewed. Hall was described as a "legend in Columbus" who made the teachers' union one of the top lobbying groups in state government. Also, special contacts—friends in high places—at critical times such as the biennial budget scramble or at the point of Controlling Board consideration may make giants out of groups normally lightly regarded. Respondents cited Ohio arts organizations as an example. The Ohio Endowment for the Arts and allied arts interests have two very powerful, long-time friends in Senate president Aronoff and the chair of the House Finance and Appropriations Committee, Representative Patrick Sweeney, a Cleveland Democrat. When the chips

TABLE 14.1

Power Ranking of Twenty-five Types of Lobbying Interests
in Ohio State Government

Rank	Type of Lobbying Interest	Mean Rating
1	Insurance	4.5
2	Retail business	4.3
3	Health-care providers	4.2
4	Legal professionals	4.1
5	Industrial/Trade unions	4.0
6	Public utilities	3.9
	Banking and finance	3.9
7	Manufacturing	3.8
8	Contractors for goods/services	3.7
9	Real estate and land development	3.6
10	Alcohol and tobacco	3.4
	Teachers' unions	3.4
11	Agribusiness	3.3
	Retirees' associations	3.3
	Transportation	3.3
12	Public service unions (noneducator)	3.0
	County and municipal governments	3.0
13	Communications media	2.8
	Public universities	2.8
	Single-issue and ideological groups	2.8
14	Administrators elementary/secondary schools	2.7
15	Community two-year colleges	2.6
16	Arts organizations	2.5
17	Public interest/environmental	2.3
18	Public human-service providers	2.1

are down, these two Statehouse veterans could not be better positioned
to "put their mouths where the money is."

Another example of the power of special contacts is the critical
relationship between the governor's office and organized labor. For a

Democratic governor, statewide union organization and campaign finance contributions are a large part of a winning campaign. Thus, Democratic administrations are very accessible to union lobbyists. But when Republicans capture the governorship, precisely because of the very close relationship between labor and the Democrats, they virtually exclude unions from access to the executive branch. Thus, the entree enjoyed by labor lobbyists is highly variable, depending on which party controls the executive.

A more favorable political environment also may alter the status of particular groups. The "children's lobby" was seen by respondents as definitely on the rise because of growing popular awareness of a range of child-welfare issues. New knowledge of an alarming incidence of child abuse, violation of child-support obligations, infants born drug addicted or with AIDS, and a host of other disturbing child welfare issues (with guaranteed political appeal) greatly enhance the clout of lobbyists working in this area.

Another favorable political advantage the children's lobby enjoys in Columbus is the highly visible presence of the Children's Defense Fund—the most powerful national lobbying organization on children's issues. The CDF has only seven offices outside of Washington, D.C., three of them in Ohio. The well-known Hillary Rodham Clinton connection with the CDF did not prevent Republican governor George Voinovich from addressing its 1994 national convention in Cincinnati. The recent rise of the children's lobby demonstrates the dynamic nature of the interest-group system in Columbus.

There is a mixed picture of change and stability in the influence industry in Columbus, say practicing lobbyists. The major players tend to remain the same over time, and the "way things get done" changes little. However, all agreed that there has been an explosion in the volume of activity since the mid-1970s. This poses problems for newcomers or the minor players. The greater demand for access to legislators, especially, means long waiting periods in outer offices (downtime) and hurried contacts. The "old boy/girl" network" in the capital favors the veteran lobbyists even more as the competition for access grows. They are the ones who can get by an office gatekeeper, "stick their heads in the door" to exchange a few quick remarks with an official, and move on to the next contact point while the lesser-known or minor player watches in envy. One lobbyist said that her organization produced videocassette tapes packaging their message in a concise, attractive, familiar form that a legislator could review in private whenever a spare fifteen minutes became available. The videos are professionally produced and periodically updated. Certainly, she agreed, this is no substitute for an hour meeting with Vern Riffe or the chair of an important committee, but these days, she said, you have to be creative sometimes.

Other than the volume of lobbying, the second major exception to general continuity has been the emergence of the so-called "hired guns." Independent lobbyists like Paul Tipps, Neil Clark, Tom Fries, and Dennis Wojtanowski, among others, who offer their knowledge, skills, and contacts for sale to all "shoppers" in the influence marketplace represent the most important change in how lobbying is done. The traditional "institutional lobbyist," someone hired by a corporation, a professional association, employee group, or a chamber of commerce to advocate their cause, is no longer the only model for sale. Large, wealthy trade associations like the Ohio Manufacturers' Association and the Ohio Hospital Association, probably will continue to prefer (and be able to afford) having one person's undiluted efforts and undivided loyalty working for them. However, independent lobbying firms, like shopping malls and department stores, can offer "full-service lobbying" and personnel who specialize in particular areas of government activity. Specialized services, ranging from media and public relations to data banks of legislative votes to guide distribution of PAC monies, and grass-roots mobilization expertise are all available in one lobbying firm. One-stop shopping has come to the lobbying marketplace. Smaller, poorer organizations, unable to provide themselves with their own exclusive representation, more and more look to the contract lobbying firms to advocate for them.

Finally, despite the tendency toward continuity, evolutionary changes do occur in the pecking order of influence interests in Columbus. The most important examples of decline among the "big hitters" are:

> Education: The Ohio Education Association has lost some of its former influence due to the loss of its long-time champion, John Hall. Moreover, as public education has encountered criticism and pressures for change build nationally as well as in the state, the effect has been less influence in Columbus.

> Manufacturing: As the national and state economy move toward a postindustrial stage, the traditional "smoke-stack" industries decline in political influence.

> Railroads: This industry is a shadow of what it once was.

Consumer and Environmental Groups: Structural change and uncertainty about the future make elected officials wary of going along with the goals of these groups, and, even more important, lobbyists we interviewed noted the long-standing antipathy Vern Riffe felt toward groups like the Sierra Club and Ohio Citizen Action.

Farmers: The agriculture industry is still important; but as the economic priorities of the state change, farming interests continue to lose influence in Columbus.

Alcohol and Tobacco Interests: While they can still "dig in their heels" and be formidable when "sin tax" proposals emerge, because of an increasingly hostile environment, these groups are on the political defensive.

In our interviews we asked lobbyists to assess the effectiveness of the traditional methods employed to affect what government does. Most of the methods we asked them to rate are mainly applicable to the legislative branch. As with the ratings of major interests, we used a five-point scale in which each method was assigned a number from 1 to 5 where 1 means the least effective and 5 the most effective lobbying method. The mean rating score for each method and a ranking of the methods are presented in table 14.2.

Building mutual trust and friendly personal relationships with legislators was the unanimously preferred method for the ten lobbyists we interviewed. To them, credibility is the most valuable asset they have in working with legislators. This aspect of the relationship goes beyond keeping one's word and giving accurate information; it also means protecting legislators from any embarrassment or serious political risk that might flow from a relationship with a lobbyist. If a lobbyist compromises that trust or puts a legislator in political jeopardy, "you are dead in Columbus." An example of this occurred in 1991 when a lobbyist for the Association of Community Colleges in Ohio was found to be making illegal campaign contributions of public funds to legislators from monies provided by several community-college administrators. Because of their past associations with him, many legislators with community colleges in their districts (which includes a large number of legislators) feared for their reputations simply because they had trusted and worked with him for many years.

In second place is providing useful information and ideas. Ohio is no exception to the national trend of greater and more complex responsi-

Senator Robert A. Taft of Cincinnati, majority leader of the U.S. Senate when this photo was taken, listens in a 1953 Labor Committee hearing while John L. Lewis, head of the United Mine Workers, blasts the Taft-Hartley Act as "a thorn and a spear in the side of American labor." The legislation is part of the legacy of Ohio's most prominent senator of the early post–World War II era, who was known as "Mr. Republican."

Senator Robert A. Taft, Jr., surprised former governor James A. Rhodes when he showed up at the last minute at an August 1972 dinner Rhodes was giving for reporters and Republican party donors. Two years earlier, on his way to securing his first and only term in the Senate, Taft had defeated Rhodes for the Republican nomination.

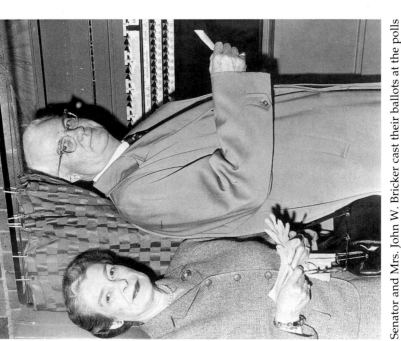

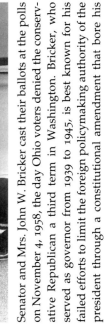

Senator and Mrs. John W. Bricker cast their ballots at the polls on November 4, 1958, the day Ohio voters denied the conservative Republican a third term in Washington. Bricker, who served as governor from 1939 to 1945, is best known for his failed efforts to limit the foreign policymaking authority of the president through a constitutional amendment that bore his

(*Top*) For a full decade, Colonel John Glenn, U.S. Marine Corps, the first American to orbit the earth, doggedly pursued his goal of representing his home state in the U.S. Senate before winning a seat in 1974. A moderate democrat from Cambridge, the former astronaut is shown with his family in this 1962 photo.

Vice President Gerald Ford reenacts the swearing in of Senator Howard Metzenbaum, the liberal Cleveland Democrat who had been named to an unexpired term in January 1974. Later that year John Glenn denied him the Democratic nomination for a full term, but Metzenbaum persevered and won Ohio's other Senate seat in 1976.

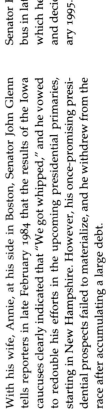

Senator Howard Metzenbaum is shown here in Columbus in late October during his 1982 reelection campaign, which he won handily. He was reelected again in 1988 and decided to retire when his third term ended in January 1995.

With his wife, Annie, at his side in Boston, Senator John Glenn tells reporters in late February 1984 that the results of the Iowa caucuses clearly indicated that "We got whipped," and he vowed to redouble his efforts in the upcoming presidential primaries, starting in New Hampshire. However, his once-promising presidential prospects failed to materialize, and he withdrew from the race after accumulating a large debt.

TABLE 14.2

Effectiveness of Lobbying Methods—Lobbyists' View

Rank	Method	Mean Rating
1	Building trust and friendly relations	5.0
2	Providing information and ideas	4.3
3	Campaign contributions	4.2
4	Wining and dining	3.4
5	Working through agencies to affect legislation	3.1
6	Testifying at hearings	3.0
7	PR with media	2.8
8	Grass-roots pressures	2.3
9	Targeting unfriendly legislators for defeat	1.3

bility for state legislatures, with shrinking resources to meet the new problems. More than ever, members must depend on the facts, figures, and problem-solving ideas from organizations that represent the interests and needs of specific constituencies. Although the state budget is an enigma wrapped in statistics for most legislators, knowledge of the budget process is critical to legislators looking for ways (and means) to further the interests of their districts. They do not enjoy the benefits of large staff allowances as members of Congress do. And, unlike members of Congress, most legislators are less-than-full-time public officials.

Campaign contributions came in a close third, not surprisingly, given the escalating cost of modern election campaigns. The amount of money going into state election campaigns gives credibility to the oft-heard remark around the Statehouse that "you must pay to play." And, certainly, the volume of money flowing from PACs and lobbying groups into the campaign coffers of Speaker Riffe, which he used to reward those who cooperated with him, cannot be dismissed as unrelated to the success lobbyists enjoy in Columbus.

Lobbyists readily concede the validity of the "pay-to-play" paradigm in the influence industry. But, as one lobbyist said, "It is expected that you will help your friends. You can cry all you want about the awful cost of campaigns and what it looks like from the outside. The bottom line is that it takes lots of bucks to win elections and most members [of the General Assembly] are not rich." Another lobbyist said that it really is not the amount that you contribute so much as it is that you show your appreciation: "They [legislators] know and even Vern Riffe knows that not every association can write a check for ten or twenty thousand. They're more interested that you show up at the fund-raiser and do what you can to help a friend. Until they find a different way to pay for campaigns or put a lid on spending, this is the way it's going to be." Indeed, "wining and dining" goes with cultivating trust and personal ties with legislators, lobbyists said. "It is expected—it's just something you do. By itself it doesn't mean much but it's a way of getting them out of the office so that you have a better chance to talk—about a bill or a budget line. It's just a way to get to know them a little better and build rapport."

For a while, one lobbyist recalled, some legislators were taking flagrant advantage of lobbyists in the "free-lunch game." He recounted how often a certain senator would run up a hefty tab at the Galleria, a popular watering hole for legislators and lobbyists across Third Street from the Statehouse, and leave it for Mr. ———— to pay the next time Mr. ———— came in! Finally, other lobbyists whom the senator was also "stiffing" went to the manager of the restaurant, instructing him to accept no more bills for the lobbyists from the senator unless the person paying was actually with the legislator.

While lobbyists generally agreed on the desirability of persuading an agency, or especially, the governor, to include in the budget or other requests to the General Assembly what the lobbying group wanted, it is no guarantee that at the end of the long process what went in at the beginning will still be there. Constant vigilance is necessary at every step of the way, which takes time and effort. In most cases, it was generally agreed, they would rather work through a few strategically placed legislative leaders, committee chairs, and the party leadership—who could intervene at the appropriate time. In the General Assembly, they said, power flows from the top and the support of a few leaders like Stan Aronoff, Pat Sweeney (chairman of House Finance and Appropriations), Ted Gray (chairman of Senate Finance Committee), or, of course, Speaker Riffe is tantamount to success.

Lobbyists do not think testifying before committees is very important to the outcome of legislation. In most cases, hearings are rituals where witnesses say expected things and legislators ask predictable questions. Lobbyists themselves seldom testify, since, as "hired guns" for the organization, what they say will be discounted. The best witnesses are members of the organizations; and sometimes a particularly compelling, sincere witness whose life would be directly touched by the legislation can make a difference, especially on matters that touch emotions, draw public attention, and are closely contested.

Seeking good public relations through the media was virtually written off by the respondents. Press releases from an organization are usually ignored; attempts to get "covered" in ways that are positive and still perceived as legitimate news is very difficult, especially in the major media outlets. In some cases media with limited news-gathering capacity (for example, small-town weekly newspapers) may print the "good" stories supplied to them by the lobbyists; however, it has very little effect because of their limited circulation.

Lobbyists agreed that grass-roots campaigns—mass letter-writing efforts, mobilization of a constituency through demonstrations, or other large-scale expressions of support for organizational goals—may be appropriate for groups with large membership lists, especially if they lack "inside clout." However, it is very difficult to establish credibility for these techniques. Legislators tend to discount them as "put-up jobs" organized for a media show. Newsletters to memberships containing information about legislators' voting records are useful and help draw the attention of members to issues affecting them. While it is a way of reminding members who their friends in government are, it is more useful as a long-term strategy than as a means of affecting particular votes on bills or budgets.

The least important of the traditional methods that organizations may use, according to lobbyists interviewed for this study, was to target consistently unfriendly legislators for election defeat. It would be almost impossible to do this without media and the intended victim discovering what was happening, and thus feeding the already-negative public perception of "the special interests." Targeting legislators for defeat could very well backfire by arousing sympathy for the intended victim, casting him in the role of the underdog fighting "the interests."

Legislators deal with interest groups and lobbyists on a regular and routine basis and are a key source of information about interest-group activities. In order to get the legislative perspective, we conducted open-ended interviews with seventeen members of the General Assembly during the summer of 1992. Since interest-group activities, techniques of influence, campaign contributions, and legislative leadership were being discussed during this election year, all legislators were promised anonymity. Several were adamant in insisting that their responses remain unattributed.

The legislators interviewed—four senators and thirteen House members—served in the General Assembly for an average of thirteen and a half years. Three were women, and three were African American; ten were Democrats, and seven were Republicans. Seven of them chaired at least one standing committee, and seven were ranking minority members on one of their committees. Five were vice chairs, and three held party leadership positions. All major House committees, including Ways and Means, Finance and Appropriations, Rules, Judiciary, and Insurance were represented by at least three members. Other committees represented included Commerce and Labor (3), Public Utilities (2), Small Business and Economic Development (2), Public Safety and Highways (3), Legislative Reference (2), Health and Retirement, and an assortment of others, including the Controlling Board.

When asked for their impression of "how visible and actively involved with the General Assembly" various interest groups are, the legislators ranked interest-group activity accordingly (a score of 1.0 is high). The responses, summarized in table 14.3, produced relatively few surprises. The low ranking of civil rights groups is mitigated considerably by the fact that there is a "built-in" lobby, or caucus, in the form of the Black Elected Democrats of Ohio (BEDO), which exercises considerable influence in the legislature by means of bloc voting.[14]

When asked to identify groups that "are much less active and important today than in the past," four of the legislators mentioned labor unions, three citing the AFL-CIO specifically. When asked which interest groups "are much more active and important today than in the past," the legislators nominated those listed in table 14.4.

These responses confirm findings described earlier—namely, that a new kind of player of some significance has entered the lobbying game in Columbus. Private consultants, or freelance contract lobbyists, have become increasingly active and important in promoting the interests of organized groups in Ohio politics. One veteran member of the House described the increasing lobbying activity of private consultants as "the most significant trend in the last ten years."

When asked which are "the most influential interest groups in Ohio politics today," the legislators answered as depicted in table 14.5. The legislators' rankings of the most influential interest groups in Ohio show

TABLE 14.3

Interest-Group Activity in the Ohio General Assembly

Rank	Interest Group	Raw Score
1	Insurance	1.41
2	Teacher and public employee unions	1.47
3	Public utilities	1.53
4	Manufacturing associations	1.59
5	Hospitals and medical interests	1.76
6	Banking, finance	1.88
7	Trade and business associations	1.94
	Higher education	1.94
	Elementary and secondary education	1.94
8	Single-issue groups	2.00
	Industrial and craft unions	2.00
9	Farming and agribusiness	2.12
10	Environmental protection	2.29
11	Local and state government	2.53
12	Construction	2.76
13	Retired persons	3.18
14	Religious and social service associations	3.24
15	Public interest	3.29
16	Civil rights	3.53

that traditionally powerful interests in Ohio, including the bankers, insurance companies, and manufacturers, are still regarded as influential. Labor unions are perhaps less influential since the industrial base of the state has shrunk. (The notable exception is the Ohio Education Association, which is a public sector union.) One legislator stated that the AFL-CIO "used to be big, but that's not true any longer." Another added that "their [the AFL-CIO] endorsement used to carry a lot of clout, but not so much any more." Yet another commented, "During the battles over collective bargaining for public employees they tried to throw their weight around. They were not successful, so it made them look weak."

The most interesting result in the legislators' rankings is the fact that twelve of them listed private consulting groups as among the most

TABLE 14.4

Interest Groups More Active Today Than in the Past

Rank	Interest Group	Number of Nominations
1	Contract lobbyists, consultants	6
2	Health care, medical	5
3	Single-issue groups	4
	Environment	4
4	All groups are more active	3
5	Utilities	2
	Higher education	2
	Professional associations	2
	Insurance	2
	Consumer groups	2
6	Government employees	1
	American Association of Retired Persons	1

TABLE 14.5

Seven Most Influential Interest Groups in Ohio

Rank	Interest Group	Number of Nominations
1	Consultants, contract lobbyists	12
	(Public Policy Consultants, Inc.)	7
	(Government Solutions)	4
	(Success Group, Inc.)	4
2	Ohio Education Association (OEA)	7
3	Insurance	6
	Health care, medical	6
4	Bankers	5
	Ohio Manufacturers' Association	5
5	Utilities	3
6	Unions	2
7	Higher education, BEDO, bar association, mining, local government, highway lobby	1

influential lobbying groups in Ohio. Three consulting firms were singled out by the legislators: Public Policy Consultants, Inc. (PPC), Government Solutions, and Success Group, Inc. The background of these consultants provides insights into their effectiveness. As mentioned earlier, Public Policy Consultants is the creation of Paul Tipps and Neil Clark. Tipps, one of the best connected political consultants in the state, is the former chairman of the Ohio Democratic Party, as well as the Montgomery County Democratic Party. He has years of experience, knows practically every Democratic official in Ohio, including Vern Riffe. Tipps's associate, Neil Clark, is well connected to the Republican leadership in the Senate, having worked with Senator Aronoff, the president of the Ohio Senate. In a legislature where power is concentrated in the party leadership, PPC has all the bases covered. Their strong connections to the legislative leadership puts PPC in a class by itself when it comes to delivering the goods in the Ohio legislature. Government Solutions offers the services of Tom Fries and Daryl Deaver. Fries is a former Democratic Dayton-area legislator who is well liked and regarded as trustworthy by legislators. Success Group, also mentioned earlier, is the consulting firm of Dennis Wojtanowski, another former member of the General Assembly.

How effective are the consultants in influencing the legislative process for their clients? One legislator, a thirty-year veteran of the political wars in Columbus, said, "These contract lobbyists can stop any bill." Another stated that "They can go right around the committees and the membership, directly to the leadership." He added, "I don't like it. I resent it." Several legislators were troubled by the "cozy relationship" between the consultants and the leadership. "It's government for sale to the highest bidder," one member complained. "You play ball, or you lose your chairmanship," said another.

Other members were less critical of the growing influence of the consultants. One legislator explained the situation this way: "They've all worked in the legislature, they know everybody. They're hired by the big interests because they're better at it. They're smarter and they work harder at it. They have better connections. They go back a long way with the leadership. They know all the players."

For those interest groups and citizens unable to afford six-figure consulting fees, there are still the traditional tried-and-true lobbying techniques. Asked to evaluate their effectiveness, the legislators rated them as listed in table 14.6 (a score of 4 is high).

TABLE 14.6

Effectiveness of Lobbying Techniques—Legislators' View

Rank	Technique	Raw Score
1	Employing a professional consultant	3.88
2	Personal persuasion/one-on-one	3.75
3	Provide information/assistance drafting bill	3.38
4	Campaign contributions/help	3.13
5	Appearances at committee hearings	2.50
6	Receptions, social events	2.31
7	Go directly to executive officials	2.13
8	Letter-writing campaigns	2.06
9	Use media to publicize issues	1.69
10	Targeting legislators for defeat	1.13

These results generally conform to expectations, based on decades of past research, and closely parallel the opinions of our sample of professional lobbyists. The high effectiveness rating of private consultants again underscores their growing importance in the governmental process, as well as their value to the interest groups that can afford to hire them. In states such as Ohio, where considerable power is centralized in the hands of legislative leadership, this is especially the case.

In conclusion, our research shows that interests that have historically been influential in Ohio politics—especially banking, insurance, and manufacturing—remain so today. Private sector labor unions have less political influence due to changing economic circumstances, but public-sector unions (especially the OEA) and health care interests are increasingly influential in Ohio politics. A significant development in lobbying in Ohio is the increasing importance of private consulting firms in the legislative process. The effectiveness of private consultants in Ohio politics is attributable partly to the fact that party leaders in the Ohio General Assembly have a great deal of power, and several top consultants enjoy close access to these leaders.

❖

CHAPTER FIFTEEN

Ohio Elections &

Political Parties in the 1990s

❖

DAVID E. STURROCK, MICHAEL MARGOLIS,
JOHN C. GREEN, & DICK KIMMINS

❖ Despite the changes that have marked its electoral politics in recent decades, Ohio remains a good index of larger national partisan trends.[1] The 1992 elections, for example, showed that Ohio is still viewed as a key state (if not the crucial prize) in presidential politics. Also, recent elections indicate that the state is a showcase for many of the ways in which Americans have recently exhibited both their testy discontent with—and grudging acceptance of—the political status quo. On the other hand, many of the patterns that have traditionally defined Buckeye State politics retain their vitality as Ohio moves toward the bicentennial of its statehood in 2003.

Long-established patterns of two-party competition reasserted themselves in 1990. If the 1970s and 1980s were difficult years for Ohio Republicans in statewide elections (six consecutive defeats in U.S. Senate races, two hairsbreadth wins balanced by two landslide losses in gubernatorial contests, and only three wins in twenty-two elections for the four lesser constitutional offices), then 1990 marked the end of their years in the wilderness.

Former Cleveland mayor George Voinovich regained the governorship for the Republicans with a 55.7 percent to 44.3 percent victory over a fellow Clevelander, Attorney General Anthony Celebrezze. His victory was built on a sweep of traditionally Republican western and central Ohio (where he ran far ahead of his showing in a losing 1988 U.S. Senate race); the capture of such key swing counties as Clark (Springfield), Montgomery (Dayton), and Stark (Canton); and home-turf strength in northeast Ohio. (Indeed, Voinovich was the first Republican to carry Cuyahoga County in a gubernatorial race since 1966). The county-by-county contours of Voinovich's support can be seen in figure 15.1. Voinovich's win also kept alive a remarkable law of Ohio politics: neither party has controlled the Ohio governorship for longer than eight years running since 1906. No other state has even approached this regularity of gubernatorial rotation in the twentieth century.

The renewal of Ohio's traditional partisan balance was also apparent in races for the other constitutional offices. Republican control of redistricting was assured when Hamilton County commissioner Robert Taft unseated incumbent secretary of state Sherrod Brown by a 52-to-48 margin. The party's ticket also ran strongly in contests for state auditor (47 percent against a long-time incumbent) and attorney general (a 1,200-vote loss). Only Mary Ellen Withrow, the state treasurer, comfortably rode out the Republican tide with a 60-to-40 re-election romp.

Patterns of Republican revival and anti-incumbency were also present in Supreme Court elections. Two Republican associate justices first elected in 1984 were reelected, but Craig Wright prevailed by only a 46-to-44 margin in a three-way race. On balance, 1990 was the party's best showing in statewide races since 1966, when James A. Rhodes's reelection landslide helped ensure a Republican sweep of all statewide races.

In voting for the General Assembly, Ohio voters affirmed their taste for divided party control. In the Senate, the Republicans gained two seats to widen their margin to 21 to 12, while House Democrats defied the Voinovich landslide with a net gain of two seats, for a new majority of 61 to 38. Evidence of anti-incumbent sentiment was modest; only five sitting members were defeated. Meanwhile, the state's U.S. House races presented a picture of deceptive stability. The Democrats preserved their 11-to-10 majority, as all incumbents were returned with at least 57 percent of the vote, and none of the three open seats changed partisan hands. However, the state reflected the national pattern of narrowed re-election margins for House incumbents, as 12 of the 16 who faced major party opposition in both 1988 and 1990 saw their victory margins reduced, five of them by ten points or more.

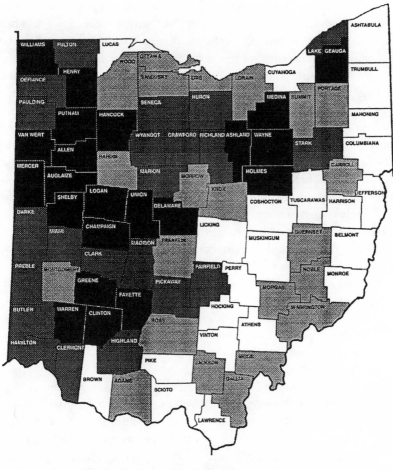

■ Highest Quartile (64.3–69.9%)
■ Second Highest Quartile (58.1–64.2%)
□ Third Highest Quartile (53.2–57.9%)
□ Lowest Quartile (38.4–53.0%)

FIGURE 15.1
Republican Strength in the 1990 Ohio Gubernatorial Election,
by Quartile

In Ohio, as elsewhere, 1992 was widely viewed as a year of deep voter unhappiness with the political order. Not surprisingly, voter turnout rose 12.4 percent over 1988 levels, an increase that exactly matched the national trend, and turnover occurred in a number of offices.

Ohio was important to Bill Clinton's victory over George Bush, as the state gave its electoral votes to a Democrat for only the fourth time in twelve elections since World War II (and rejected the incumbent for only the second time in eight such opportunities). The state was recognized early on as a critical battleground, if not *the* key state, by both campaigns. The frequency of visits by candidates, spouses, and surrogates prompted Senate candidate Mike DeWine to observe that "they're running this like a gubernatorial campaign." For Clinton this meant working the state both early (two bus tours before Labor Day) and late (an airport rally in Cleveland was part of his seven-state barnstorming marathon on election eve). This solicitude was justified, as the last wave of polls indicated a narrowing of the lead Clinton had enjoyed all fall.[2]

Clinton built his Ohio victory with strong support from union members, blacks, and urbanites and with smaller but crucial margins among younger voters and women. The county-level profile of his support correlated almost perfectly with Michael Dukakis's strength four years earlier, with the traditionally Democratic industrial counties of east and northeast Ohio leading the way.[3]

The final outcome in Ohio—40.2 percent for Clinton, 38.4 for George Bush, and 21.0 for Ross Perot—proved closer than the national division, as Clinton ran nearly three points behind his national showing. Indeed, the outcome was so uncertain that the three major networks did not declare Ohio a Clinton state until nearly 11:00 P.M. This artifact of the election night timetable provided dramatic, if purely symbolic, confirmation of Ohio's critical role in the campaign, as those 21 electoral votes gave Clinton the 270 he needed to claim the White House. (Curiously, Ohio had also clinched Clinton's victory at the Democratic convention in July.)

This pivotal role is nothing new: no Republican has ever been elected president without carrying Ohio; Republicans were able to cement their 1984 and 1988 victories with early and specialized attention to Ohio; and Ohio's support for Bill Clinton mirrored the crucial role it played in helping elect Harry Truman in 1948 and Jimmy Carter in 1976. Indeed, Ohio has been as reliable a predictor of the national outcome as any state, failing to support the winner only twice (the state voted for Thomas Dewey in 1944 and Richard Nixon in 1960) in the twenty-four presidential elections since 1900.

In Ohio, as elsewhere, the most visible measure of voter fractiousness in 1992 was Ross Perot's independent presidential campaign. Although he never campaigned in the state and had only a limited organization, he nonetheless ran 2.1 points ahead of his national percentage, and very probably cost George Bush Ohio's 21 electoral votes.[4]

Notwithstanding Perot's role as a lightning rod for voter disenchantment, Ohioans' clearest mandate for housecleaning in Ohio was their overwhelming endorsement of the term-limit movement. Three such proposals, which had been placed on the ballot by the initiative process, imposed limits of eight consecutive years on congressmen, state legislators, and lesser executive officers (Ohio's governors have been subject to this restriction since 1958) and twelve years for U.S. senators. Each measure received between 66 percent and 69 percent voter approval.

Evidence of a voters' revolt was also apparent, if less dramatic, in other statewide races. Although U.S. senator John Glenn's 51.0 percent to 42.3 percent margin over Republican lieutenant governor Mike DeWine was decisive, this was Glenn's closest call in four elections. Meanwhile, Supreme Court chief justice Thomas Moyer was reelected by only 2.8 percentage points, while the parties swapped the two associate justice positions that were open because of retirements. These results preserved the GOP's 4-to-3 majority.

Ohio's U.S. House delegation was the scene of the state's biggest political shake-up in 1992. Two changes were guaranteed as soon as the ink was dry on the 1990 U.S. Census; Ohio's minimal population growth during the 1980s (50,000, or only 0.5 percent) reduced the state's allocation from 21 seats to 19. The prospects for wholesale turnover were further boosted when five incumbents—three of them under forty-six years of age—retired. However, anti-incumbent fever claimed only two victims in November, both of whom labored under similar multiple burdens. Democrat Mary Rose Oakar (Cleveland) and Republican Bob McEwen (Hillsboro) had to explain numerous check overdrafts at the House bank, survive bitter primary battles (McEwen barely edged out a long-time House colleague, while Oakar won renomination only because of divided opposition), and contend with considerably reshaped districts. Not surprisingly, both lost to political newcomers on November 3. All of this electoral turmoil left the delegation's partisan balance where it had started, with a one-seat Democratic edge.

Were Ohioans fed up with gridlock? Not entirely; for all the orneriness they showed in other races, they were willing to extend the bipartisan control of the General Assembly they had first established in 1984. The Republicans cut deeply into the Democrats' twenty-year domination of the House, reducing the latter's majority to 53 to 46. However, most of their seven-seat gain seemed to be the result of friendlier district boundaries; only 6 of 84 House incumbents were defeated, and 3 of them were forced by redistricting to square off against fellow legislators. In the Senate, only 1 of 15 incumbents fell, enabling the Democrats to gain a seat, which still left them on the short end of a 20-to-13 division. All of this points to the fact that even in 1992, Ohioans, like voters elsewhere, were of two minds on the subject of incumbency.

Recent history gives Ohio politicians reason to expect that the state's political gyroscope will continue to impose its wobbly equilibrium on both parties. Buoyed by Governor Voinovich's apparently favorable public approval ratings, Republicans had cause to hope for a strong year in 1994. However, they should be sobered (and Democrats encouraged) by historical lessons: in neither 1986 nor 1990 did gubernatorial landslides produce legislative gains, and a win in 1994 would mean the GOP would have to buck the eight-year rule in 1998.

Another law of Ohio politics—though its reach is less absolute—will be tested in 1994, when U.S. senator Howard Metzenbaum retires. GOP Senate nominee Mike DeWine is hoping that Ohio's "once to meet, twice to win" rule remains in force: every Ohio governor and U.S. senator elected since 1958 has previously lost at least one statewide race. This pattern reflects the difficulties of campaigning in a state with many media markets and a political culture that features voter patience and rewards candidate persistence. More than in some states, Ohio voters are willing to give candidates a second hearing, even when their debut was unimpressive (as with Voinovich's rocky 1988 Senate bid) and to encourage repeat visits. Of course, the ultimate example of this tolerance is Jim Rhodes, who ran eleven times for three statewide offices in thirty-six years. Although he had lost three times—twice in primaries—he did not exhaust his welcome with the voters until 1986, when they roundly rejected his bid for a fifth gubernatorial term.

Geography should also help sustain Ohio's competitive party balance for the foreseeable future. In 1991, only ten county governments were controlled completely by one party, most of them in smaller counties,[5] and each party maintained a strong presence in the strongholds of the other. The Republicans' decisive majorities in the Ohio Senate have been bolstered by major inroads into mostly Democratic northeast Ohio, where the party now holds 5 of 12 seats, including a remarkable 3 of 5 in Cuyahoga County. Meanwhile, city council majorities in Cincinnati and Columbus give the Democrats highly visible power bases within the usually Republican counties of Hamilton and Franklin. Local success behind enemy lines can also lead to great rewards at the state level, as the gubernatorial victories of Cincinnati Democrat John Gilligan and Cleveland Republican George Voinovich attest.

Considerable electoral change does seem likely in the year 2000, when legislative incumbents will be subject to the term limits adopted in 1992. The partisan fallout from this is difficult to handicap, as each party's knack for controlling "its" chamber in the Statehouse has relied heavily on the continued reelection of incumbents. However, the efforts of both parties to cultivate strong "farm teams" at both the state and local levels suggest that neither will be unprepared when term limits take effect. In 1992, for example, only 8 of 116 General Assembly races were uncontested. If this and other recent results are any guide, it would seem that Ohio Republicans have gone a long way toward closing the "candidate gap" that plagues their brethren in many other states.[6]

Clearly then, Ohio election results cannot be understood apart from considerations of party. But how do the state's parties operate? What roles are played by state and county party organizations in Ohio politics? These questions can only be answered when one understands the impact of Ohio election laws on party politics. While the rules and regulations that apply to the Democratic and Republican parties may seem onerous, these laws help to preserve their duopoly of partisan political power in Ohio.

State election law defines a political party as any group of voters who (1) polled at least 5 percent for its candidate for governor or slate of presidential electors in the last preceding regular state election or who (2), subsequent to any election in which it polled less than 5 percent, filed a petition with the Ohio secretary of state signed by a number of registered voters which equals at least 1 percent of the total vote cast for governor or presidential electors at the most recent election. The law also classifies political parties as major, intermediate, or minor. Major political parties are those whose gubernatorial or presidential elector nominees received at least 20 percent of the total vote in the last regular statewide election, while intermediate parties must reach at least 10 (but less than 20) percent in one of those contests. Minor parties need to garner at least 5 (but less than 10) percent in either race. Parties qualifying via petition are designated as minor until their first gubernatorial or presidential election. If a minor party fails to meet the 5-percent threshold, it loses official recognition and must begin the petition process all over again.[7]

Ohio law also prescribes the general organizational structure and procedures to which officially recognized parties must conform. The party's foundation lies with those voters who participate in its primary elections in even-numbered years. Ohio is technically a "closed primary" state, which means that in primary elections Ohioans must declare a party affiliation and can vote only in that party's primary. However, affiliation requires only a statement that the voter desires to affiliate with and support the principles of a particular party. These affiliations can be easily changed at the polling place on primary election day.

Primary voters select their party's county central committee, which consists either of one member from each precinct, or one from each city ward and county township. (The outgoing central committee is empowered to choose which of these formulas will be used.) State law requires that the newly elected committee hold an organizational meeting between six and fifteen days after election results have been certified. Prior public notice of the meeting must be issued, and the notice must stipulate which officers are to be elected at that meeting. It also mandates the selection of a county executive committee, to which the central committee may delegate as much of its power as it sees fit. Among these is the power to establish city, township, or district committees. In practice, the executive committee then assumes most real authority for party matters. The central committee meets only periodically during its term of office, which can be either two or four years.[8]

Primary voters also elect one man and one woman per congressional district to the state central committee for four-year terms. This body's organizational meeting must be held under the same requirements as those for county committees, and like those groups it delegates most of its power to a smaller executive committee. The state convention, which is held in even-numbered years, drafts a party platform and nominates presidential electors. Most of its delegates are chosen by the county executive committees, and the remainder are included by virtue of the offices they hold. These include county central committee and executive committee chairmen; state central and executive committee members; nominees for statewide, legislative, and congressional offices; and state and federal incumbents not up for election.[9] The convention's time and location are established by the state central committee.

Should one again emerge,[10] an intermediate political party would elect a state central committee in the same manner and at the same time as the major-party state committees. However, intermediate parties would not be required to hold a biennial state convention nor elect county central committees. Minor parties would need only file a plan of organization with the secretary of state at least ninety days prior to the primary election.

In addition to those organizations stipulated by law, numerous party auxiliaries exist. The most important are the Senate and House caucus committees. Although they are likely to work closely with the official party committees, these bodies raise their own funds and use them to help elect legislative candidates. The state and county parties may also be closely associated with women's federations or youth, college, or high school organizations or other groups that are not legally recognized as formal party entities. These groups have the same status in law as interest groups and political action committees, even though they are more closely tied to a particular party.

Although the regulations that apply to major parties seem more burdensome than those that govern intermediate and minor parties, the majors also enjoy compensating privileges. Most notably, each county executive committee is entitled to nominate (subject to the secretary of state's approval) two paid members to its county's board of elections. In turn, these boards hire a permanent staff to register voters, maintain registration records, establish and staff polling places, prepare and distribute ballots, count votes, certify results, and perform any other tasks associated with the administration of elections within their county.

In a like manner, the law also grants the two major parties formal representation on the Ohio Elections Commission. Four of its five members are appointed by the secretary of state (and confirmed by the Senate) from lists submitted by the state party chairmen.[11] In turn, these four appoint a fifth member, who then serves as chairman for a five-year term. The commission has legal authority to investigate sworn allegations of election law violations, particularly those dealing with campaign finance regulations. The commission also has power to subpoena records and witnesses, issue fines, and even recommend civil or criminal prosecution.

As the Democratic and Republican parties jointly control the state electoral commission and county boards of election and staff all polling places, they are expected to conduct and oversee elections in a bipartisan manner. While this ensures an honest contest between Republicans and Democrats, it is less than ideal for those parties lacking official recognition. They must rely upon the goodwill and evenhandedness of their established and far stronger adversaries to secure approval of their ballot access petitions, certification of their candidates' election petitions, and fair hearings for any objections or appeals they may raise. Ballot access has not always been subject to state regulation or major party generosity. Until the end of the nineteenth century, the parties produced their own ballots, and voters registered their choices by selecting their own ballots (or combinations of ballots). While these ballots were hardly secret—each party used a distinctive color, thereby ensuring the delivery of those votes they had bought and paid for—the process was undeniably democratic. The highest levels of voter turnout in U.S. history occurred in the late nineteenth century, even when due allowance is made for widespread vote fraud.[12]

The Progressive Era reforms of the late nineteenth and early twentieth centuries attacked the abuses that such a wide-open system allowed. Government maintenance of a permanent registration list made multiple voting more difficult, while use of the Australian ballot (a uniform ballot that the voter marked in private) largely eliminated ballot box stuffing. But these reforms exacted a toll on minor parties: if the state now prepares the ballot and keeps track of who is eligible to vote, then the state also sets the rules by which parties get on the ballot and voters get registered. All of this makes it harder for new parties to gain access to the ballot. When Democratic and Republican legislators write these rules, they have a natural tendency to favor the interests of their own parties and of the political status quo.

Given the role Ohio's major parties play in writing and enforcing election laws, it is scarcely surprising that the state's ballot access requirements have always been among the most restrictive in the nation. In fact, Ohio was the only state whose ballot laws George Wallace was unable to satisfy when he ran for president in 1968. His electors were placed on the Ohio ballot only after he prevailed in a U.S. Supreme Court case.[13]

While the state subsequently eased some of its ballot access requirements, minor parties still find it difficult to gain ballot status. For example, nonrecognized parties (such as the Libertarians) can place candidates on the general election ballot by filing nominating petitions prior to the primary election, but their party affiliation will not be identified on the ballot. Also, a party aspiring to formal ballot status must obtain it for the entire state. Unlike in Illinois, for example, a party cannot petition for ballot status that is limited to selected districts, counties, or localities. Finally, state law requires the counting of write-in votes only when the candidate has filed a formal declaration at least forty days prior to the general election.

Whatever hopes for political success a minor party may still harbor after dealing with these restrictive ballot access laws are apt to be snuffed out altogether by the "first-past-the-post" electoral system, which requires winners to finish first in a race for a given seat. By contrast, proportional representation, which is widely used in Europe, enables small parties to win representation in government even if they fail to carry a specific district. The almost complete absence of proportional representation in this country is often cited as one reason why our two-party system has endured for so long.[14]

The traditional power of parties in Ohio is rooted in two other prerogatives established by state law: to endorse in primary elections and to fill legislative, county, and municipal offices when vacancies occur between elections. These powers have much to do with making the state and county organizations important actors in Ohio politics. At least since the Progressive Era, party defenders and critics alike have understood that a party's ability to choose its candidates is central to its power. The Progressives, who sought to reduce the influence of parties and their leaders, succeeded in securing the adoption of the direct primary election for all Ohio partisan offices in 1913.[15] In some states (California, for instance) election laws went even further and barred official party organizations from attempting to influence the nominating process by endorsing candidates in contested primaries. In Ohio, however, both state and county parties have retained this privilege and do exercise it, frequently with great effect.

The amount of endorsing activity at the county level varies widely. Some central committees, including the Cuyahoga Democrats and the Hamilton Republicans, rarely issue formal endorsements in seriously contested primaries. Others use this power more aggressively and work hard to back up their endorsements with such support as slate mailers, financial support, use of the party's bulk-mail permit, and access to poll books, which identify those voters who regularly participate in the party's primaries.

Among the Democrats, Franklin, Lorain, Lucas, and Mahoning, as well as some of the smaller counties, enjoy reputations for serious and effective primary involvement. While relatively few Republican county committees (mostly in large counties) regularly make formal endorsements, those that do are likely to implement them vigorously. Perhaps the best example is Franklin County, which is prepared to deliver a strong primary vote for its endorsees through a large and well-disciplined precinct organization. Once bestowed, the party's nod is usually sufficient to drive other hopefuls from the race.

In some cases, the need for formal endorsing is precluded by effective slate-building beforehand, whether to fill a long list of judicial nominations (as with the Cuyahoga Republicans) or to minimize primary conflicts and craft the strongest possible ticket. Responsibility for slate-brokering rests chiefly with the county chair. An important recent example of slate-making at the state level occurred in early 1990 when the state Republican chairman's ability to force a strong candidate to switch races helped make possible the party's success in November. This application of political muscle struck one of us as akin to a Hollywood script.[16]

There is a scene in the film *The Godfather II* in which the calm consiglieri visits the mobster-turned-government informant who is being held in protective custody. The consiglieri wants to convey the godfather's wish that his former colleague in crime maintain a pledge of silence. In fact, the godfather wants him to commit suicide. The turncoat mobster gets the message, and he recalls for the consiglieri how defeated Roman generals would fall on their own swords rather than return home and face the wrath of a humiliated emperor. Despite being defeated on the battleground, these generals were always assured their families would be cared for after the self-inflicted deaths. The consiglieri as well heard that none-too-subtle request. A few days after that meeting, the government guards found the recalcitrant mobster in the bathtub, dead, his wrists sliced open and a contented look on his face.

That scene was fiction. What happened at the Hyatt Regency Hotel in Columbus on the evening of February 8, 1990, was real. In the ballroom, President George Bush was hosting a $1,000-per-person dinner for a few thousand of his Ohio supporters. However, the real political event, masterminded by the Republican party, was occurring downstairs, out of the way of the prying eyes of the press, out of sight of central Ohio's political bankrollers. Force was being applied in the basement meeting room, a type of force that was a specialty of the two political consiglieri attending this closed door meeting—Republican national chairman Lee Atwater and his Ohio counterpart, state party chairman Robert T. Bennett. With them in the room was Robert Taft II, scion of Ohio's most famous Republican family. Although Taft was a great-great-grandson of a founder of the Republican party in Ohio, Atwater and Bennett were more interested in discussing the facts of life than political history. Their goal was what Ohio political parties strive for but do not always achieve: the long view, the big picture.

At the time Taft was a candidate for the Republican nomination for governor, but these party leaders wanted this young star and his famous name to grace the Republican ticket by running for secretary of state. Atwater and Bennett told Taft that his political afterlife would be assured if only he would fall on his sword. To cushion the blow, Atwater added $100,000 to the $500,000 Bennett had already laid at the feet of Taft. All they wanted was for Taft to quit the race for governor. Run for secretary of state, they told him. We need you there. The party needs you there.

This generosity was driven by the surpassing need to regain Republican control of the Apportionment Board, which divides Ohio's population into 33 state Senate and 99 state House districts once every ten years. Party leaders know that whoever draws the lines is likely to enjoy a substantial electoral advantage throughout the following decade. Indeed, Democratic control of the 1971 and 1981 redistrictings had helped ensure that party's long-running House majority. Bennett and other Republican leaders therefore wanted mightily to avoid a hostile line-drawing for a third consecutive decade.[17]

The Republican party's plan to win control of the Apportionment Board in 1990 was based on the pragmatic conclusion that no Republican could beat incumbent state auditor Thomas E. Ferguson. Thus, control of the board came down to installing Republicans as governor and secretary of state. (The two remaining board seats were not at issue; state law provides that Democratic and Republican legislators appoint one member apiece). These were the stakes in 1990, and this was the topic uppermost on the minds of consiglieri Atwater and Bennett that cold evening in Columbus. Convincing Taft to abandon a hopeless quest to defeat Voinovich was the key to their strategy. And convince they did, thereby demonstrating that Ohio's party leaders are still capable of exerting great influence on the composition of their party's general election ticket.

Six days after his meeting with the GOP consiglieri, Taft announced he was abandoning his gubernatorial candidacy and would indeed run for secretary of state. That left George Voinovich unopposed in the Republican gubernatorial primary, and Taft, of course, was assured he would face no primary opposition that might threaten his new $600,000 gift from the party. This stack of cash later turned out to comprise one-fourth of Taft's entire campaign budget.

In fact, because of what Atwater and Bennett accomplished in that fifteen-minute meeting, no Republican statewide candidate faced primary opposition that year. Because Voinovich and Taft were able to save their campaign war chests for the general election campaign, they were able to spend their money wisely. Eleven months after that meeting in the Columbus hotel basement, Voinovich was governor, Taft was secretary of state, and the Republican party controlled the state's Apportionment Board. The party's money and its political interests had converged, and once again the party was alive in Ohio.

With Voinovich and Taft sitting on the 1991 Apportionment Board, Republicans drew district lines that enabled them to trim the Democrats' House majority from 23 to 7 seats in the 1992 election. Five Democrats won by fewer than 2,000 votes each, giving Republicans, for the first time in twenty years, real hope of capturing control of the House.

Parties can exert more direct influence on the course of Ohio government by using their legal authority to fill midterm vacancies for those offices won by their party in the previous election. Party caucuses in the General Assembly choose replacements for colleagues who leave before their terms expire, while county central committees are empowered to perform the same duty when a county government post falls open. This power does not extend to the U.S. Congress; as in other states, House vacancies are filled by special election, while the governor fills Senate openings.

A good example of the advantages this power confers on county parties is found in Cuyahoga County. Since 1970, Republicans have maintained a continuous presence on the three-member board of commissioners in this heavily Democratic county through a process akin to apostolic succession. When Commissioner George Voinovich was elected lieutenant governor in 1978, the party replaced him with Virgil

Brown, who was subsequently elected to three terms in his own right. When Brown was appointed state lottery director in early 1991 (by none other than his predecessor, Voinovich), the party filled his seat with former state representative James Petro, who was fresh off a strong race for state auditor. Having won a full commission term in 1992, Petro can again pursue statewide office (as he is doing in 1994 for auditor) secure in the knowledge that another Republican will replace him if he wins. Of course, the responsibility to fill highly prized positions carries with it the risk of offending those not chosen and may create (or aggravate) discord within the party.

Ohio's political parties have long cultivated and maintained power through such activities as grooming candidates and filling vacancies. Barring wholesale changes in state election law, those tasks will continue to be staples of party life. In other ways, however, Ohio's political parties have undergone important changes. Two changes deserving of closer examination are patronage and fund-raising.

Until at least the 1970s, the ability of state and county parties to obtain public employment for deserving party supporters was vast and largely unquestioned. The key actors were the county chairs, who tended to hold patronage matters close to their vests; apparently there was little in the way of such formal party structures as patronage committees. Even governors routinely deferred to county chairs when dispensing state jobs and favors. Perhaps the most notable example in recent decades was long-time Cuyahoga Republican leader Bob Hughes, who reputedly enjoyed carte blanche on state patronage matters in his county when his close friend Jim Rhodes was governor.

The gradual implementation of merit-based hiring and promotion policies by state and local governments has seriously diminished the parties' role in patronage matters. Some opportunities for patronage employment remain within the offices of county auditors, clerks of court, county engineers, and prosecuting attorneys. Even here, however, there is little necessary reason for officeholders to honor their party's recommendations. One observer says the patronage role of county parties has shifted from "power to influence," with most of the latter depending heavily on the political prestige of their chairs and the individual relationships they manage to cultivate with elected officials. Two who are reputed to carry great weight on patronage matters are Don Hanni, whose Mahoning County Democratic organization has been called "the last county machine"—that is, until reformers won control in the

May 1994 primary—and Summit County Republican chairman Alex Arshinkoff. At the state level, some pockets of opportunity remain; one example is seasonal unskilled work with the Ohio Department of Transportation. In general, however, state personnel reforms appear to have eliminated traditional opportunities for political appointees to work their way up the ladder from an entry-level position.

The 1980s also represented a transition for the financial environment in which Ohio's political parties operate. The establishment of competitive bidding for license bureau franchises (and the imposition of strict political contribution limits on bidders) removed a major source of party revenue. Formerly, franchise holders would return a percentage of deputy registrar's fees to the party (while continuing to make substantial personal contributions to the party and its candidates).[18] The blow of losing these funds was assuaged, though only partially, by the implementation of a public financing system in 1987. Ohio income tax filers can designate one dollar of their taxes to a pool that is divided among state and county party committees. The two state parties each receive one quarter of the funds, while the rest is allocated to the county parties in proportion to the share of fund donations that came from their county. (No provision exists for intermediate or minor parties to receive these funds.) In 1992, taxpayers designated $987,161 for party funding, a decline from 1987's $1.1 million. The state parties received $246,790 apiece in 1992, while the county shares ranged from $40,000 for Cuyahoga to $132 for Vinton.

Examination of party fundraising for 1990 reveals several patterns familiar to students of political finance in other states: Republicans have been more successful in developing an individual donor base; interparty transfers are an important source of funds for some party committees; and those currently in power find it much easier to raise funds than those who are not.[19] Considerable financial differences exist between the parties at the state level. During the 1989–90 election cycle, the Republican state committee outraised its Democratic counterpart $6.0 million to $3.5 million and relied heavily (63 percent) on individual donations, while 58 percent of Democratic revenues came from candidates and other party committees. Both parties devoted over half of their expenditures to candidate assistance activities.

Republicans enjoyed a comparable advantage at the county level ($3.7 million vs. $2.2 million), with individual contributions again leading the way (56 percent of all county committee revenues). While such donations were also important for county Democratic committees (41 percent), they were considerably more dependent than the Republicans on public funds (22 percent) and candidate donations and purchases (24 percent). Not surprisingly, county committee fund-raising in both parties was concentrated in the largest counties; the top eight county budgets accounted for three quarters of all county party funds. Voter contact was the leading category of county party expenditure (about 40 percent).

The committees controlled by party legislative caucuses are important forces in their own right. The parties already in control of a chamber fared far better ($2.4 million was raised by the Senate Republican caucus committee and $1.7 million by the House Democrats) than those out of power ($852,000 for the Senate Democrats and a paltry $339,000 for the House GOP). Although these committees are not eligible for public funds, they have been able to cultivate other sources; over 80 percent of caucus funds came from candidates (chiefly incumbent caucus members) and political action committees.

Political parties still play a major role in the state's political life. David Mayhew's comparative study of local parties in the 1960s and 1970s ranked Ohio as one of thirteen states with relatively powerful "traditional party organizations." Ohio's parties still measure up reasonably well against his criteria for "traditional" party activity. They are defined by well-established county organizations that enjoy substantial autonomy from state and national parties and from party-related organizations and interest groups; they maintain a hierarchical structure; they slate candidates in party primaries; and they offer material incentives and rewards for those who do organizational work to elect their candidates. Another indication of the relative strength and vitality of the state's parties comes from James L. Gibson, who ranked Ohio's local parties as seventh strongest in the country in the mid-1980s.[20]

Larger trends suggest that Ohio's parties are subject to many of the same challenges that have weakened parties elsewhere. The long-term erosion of party identification among Ohio voters suggests that the ability of parties to mobilize large blocs of reliable supporters is increasingly problematic, while the public's reliance on news media outlets, especially television, means that Ohio's parties have long since ceased to monopolize information about candidates and issues. Meanwhile, the parties' traditional role as organizers and managers of campaigns has been usurped by the emergence of self-employed campaign managers, consultants, and pollsters.

Ohio's parties must also contend with increased competition in setting the policy agenda. The state's many active and well-organized interest groups often exercise more influence in Columbus than the parties. Finally, the initiative process is always available for those who wish to bypass the parties altogether. As the 1992 general election ballot reminds us, this alternative can be used to promote both policy changes that affect Ohio's parties (term-limit proposals) and those that deal more directly with the particulars of government policy (as with an unsuccessful chemical labeling measure).[21]

❖

Notes

❖

1. OHIO POLITICS: A HISTORICAL PERSPECTIVE

1. Brand Whitlock, *Forty Years of It* (New York: D. Appleton and Company, 1925), 27.

2. John Fenton, *Midwest Politics* (New York: Holt, Rinehart, and Winston, 1966), quoted in Carl Lieberman, ed., *Government and Politics in Ohio* (Lanham, Md.: University Press of America, 1984), 31–32.

3. Detailed descriptions of ethnocultural diversity are found in George W. Knepper, "Flocking Toward a Promise: The Migration to Ohio" (Columbus: Ohio State Alumni Association, 1987); idem, "Essence of Ohio: Diversity, Balance, Conservatism," *Miami Valley History* 4 (1992): 4–20; Hubert G. H. Wilhem, *The Origin and Distribution of Settlement Groups: Ohio, 1850* (Athens: Ohio University, 1982).

4. Stephen C. Fox, *The Group Bases of Ohio Political Behavior, 1803–1848* (New York: Garland Publishing, 1989), 45, 106ff.

5. Philip D. Jordan, *Ohio Comes of Age 1873–1900* (Columbus: Ohio State Archaeological and Historical Society, 1943), chaps. 6, 9.

6. Other prominent Republicans such as Charles Foster and Calvin Brice influenced Ohio politics in this era, as did Democratic "boss" John R. McLean, a wealthy Cincinnati newspaper publisher. See ibid., chap. 6; and also Zane Miller, *Boss Cox's Cincinnati: Urban Politics in the Progressive Era* (New York: Oxford University Press, 1971); Eugene H. Roseboom and Francis Weisenburger, *A History of Ohio* (Columbus: Ohio Historical Society, 1964), 243–44.

7. Francis R. Aumann, "Ohio Government in the Twentieth Century: From Nash to White (1900–1931)," in Harlow Lindley, ed., *Ohio in the Twentieth Century, 1900–1938* (Columbus: Ohio State Archaeological and Historical Society, 1942), 6; Roseboom and Weisenburger, *History of Ohio*, 319; *Constitution of the State of Ohio: Annotated*, 1979 (Columbus: N.p., 1979), 322.

8. Hoyt Landon Warner's *Progressivism in Ohio, 1897–1917* (Columbus: Ohio State University Press, 1964) is useful throughout and is the best source for both general and detailed information.

9. Ibid. Delegates were elected on a nonpartisan ballot.

10. Roseboom and Weisenburger, *History of Ohio,* 347.

11. Ibid., 203–7, for the failed attempts to change the constitution's language. George W. Knepper, *Ohio and Its People* (Kent, Ohio: Kent State University Press, 1989), 335.

12 . Aumann in Lindley, *Ohio in the Twentieth Century,* 40–41.

13. The best overview of the depression's economic impact on Ohio is Raymond Boryczka and Lorin Lee Cary, *No Strength Without Union: An Illustrated History of Ohio Workers, 1803–1980* (Columbus: Ohio Historical Society, 1982), 158–219. Schools could not survive under minimal property tax assessments and limited state aid from the intangible property tax. Sixty percent of the new sales tax receipts were earmarked for schools. Larger amounts of state support were forthcoming after enactment in 1935 of the School Foundation Program Law. Aumann in Lindley, *Ohio in the Twentieth Century,* 63–64.

14. Fenton in Lieberman, *Government and Politics,* 41; Graham Hutton, *Midwest at Noon* (DeKalb: Northern Illinois University Press, 1990), 122.

15 . Fenton in Lieberman, *Government and Politics,* 47–49; Bernard Sternsher, "The Harding and Bricker Revolutions: Party Systems and Voter Behavior in Northwest Ohio, 1860–1982," *Northwest Ohio Quarterly* 50 (Summer 1987): 91–111.

16. These characteristics are discussed in a larger context in Knepper, *Ohio and Its People,* esp. 357–64. Immigrants from eastern and southern Europe helped swell Cleveland's population to 573,872 in 1910 and to 902,471 in 1930. In 1910 they constituted 36 percent of the population; in 1930 they were 33 percent. See John Grabowski, "Immigration and Migration," in David D. Van Tassel and John Grabowski, eds., *The Encyclopedia of Cleveland History* (Bloomington: Indiana University Press, 1987), 541–42.

17. Knepper, *Ohio and Its People,* 368.

18. Ibid., 371–72, 375–76; Karl B. Pauly, *Bricker of Ohio: The Man and His Record* (New York: G. Putnam's Sons, 1944), 83.

19. Pauly, *Bricker of Ohio,* 85, 91, 96, 100.

20. Neal R. Peirce and John Keefe, *The Great Lakes States of America: People, Politics, and Power in the Five Great Lakes States* (New York: W. W. Norton, 1980), 303–10.

21. DiSalle was the first governor to serve a four-year term.

22. Knepper, *Ohio and Its People,* 453–66.

23. One recalls the "Reagan Democrats" who returned to their party's fold in the 1992 presidential race and supported Bill Clinton.

24. *Akron Beacon Journal,* April 9, 1993.

2. THE LAUSCHE ERA, 1945–1957

1. Karl Schriftgiesser, "How to Survive a Landslide," *Collier's,* March 28, 1953, 80.

2. Sue Gorisek, "A Party of One," *Ohio Magazine,* August 1988, 64; Edward Gobetz, *Ohio's Lincoln* (Willoughby Hills, Ohio: Slovenian Research Center of America, 1985), 267.

3. Brent Larkin, "Frank Lausche: A Legend in Ohio Politics," *Plain Dealer Magazine,* November 10, 1985, 6.

4. "The Lonely One," *Time,* February 20, 1956, 21.

5. Gobetz, *Ohio's Lincoln,* 24.

6. John Gunther, *Inside U.S.A.* (New York: Harper and Brothers, 1947), 425.

7. "The Lonely One," 22.

8. Frederick S. Tisdale, "Strong Man of Columbus," *Saturday Evening Post,* July 7, 1945, 92.

9. Ibid.; Cleveland *Plain Dealer,* November 8, 1944.

10. *Springfield News,* October 11, 1946.

11. *Columbus Dispatch,* January 13, 1945; *Cincinnati Enquirer,* January 14, 1945; Gobetz, *Ohio's Lincoln,* 43.

12. Gunther, *Inside U.S.A.,* 428; Tisdale, "Strong Man of Columbus," 92; Gorisek, "A Party of One," 63.

13. Schriftgiesser, "How to Survive a Landslide," 79.

14. *Columbus Dispatch,* September 29, 1946.

15. Ibid.

16. Gobetz, *Ohio's Lincoln,* 46; *Cleveland Press,* October 15, 1946.

17. S. Winifred Smith, "Thomas J. Herbert," *The Governors of Ohio* (Columbus: Ohio Historical Society, 1969), 195.

18. George W. Knepper, *Ohio and Its People* (Kent, Ohio: Kent State University Press, 1989), 392; Neal R. Peirce and Jerry Hagstrom, *The Book of America* (New York: W. W. Norton, 1983), 297.

19. *Columbus Dispatch,* November 6, 1952.

20. Knepper, *Ohio and Its People,* 393.

21. Damaine Vonada, *Ohio Almanac, 1992–93* (Wilmington, Ohio: Orange Frazier Press, 1992), 155.

22. Knepper, *Ohio and Its People,* 412.

23. Vonada, *Ohio Almanac,* 155.

24. Larkin, "Frank Lausche," 25.

25. *Columbus Dispatch,* December 8, 1948.

26. Ibid., May 11, 1949.

27. Ibid., March 1, 1951.

28. Governor's letter to General Assembly Leadership, February 3, 1955, Frank J. Lausche Collection, Ohio Historical Society, Columbus.

29. *Columbus Dispatch,* June 22, 1949; ibid., July 12, 1951.

30. Governor's Message to General Assembly, January 13, 1953, Lausche Collection.

31. *Columbus Dispatch,* October 6, 1954.

32. Albert Woldman, "Frank J. Lausche," *The Governors of Ohio,* 192.

33. Ibid.

34. *Columbus Dispatch,* July 30, 1953; ibid., October 24, 1954.

35. Governor's Veto Message, July 30, 1953, Lausche Collection.

36. *Columbus Dispatch,* November 1, 1954.

37. Ibid., October 14, 1954.

38. *Plain Dealer,* September 7, 1974.

39. Governor's letter to Vice President Nixon, January 8, 1957, and Nixon reply letter, January 25, 1957, John W. Brown Collection, Ohio Historical Society.

40. *Plain Dealer,* September 7, 1974.

41. Ibid., February 5, 1964.

42. Gobetz, *Ohio's Lincoln,* 52, 58.

43. *Columbus Dispatch,* April 22, 1990.

3. THE O'NEILL-DISALLE YEARS, 1957–1963

1. John W. Brown press release, May 1, 1956, C. William O' Neill Collection, Ohio Historical Society, Columbus.

2. O'Neill remarks to the 1956 Republican State Convention in Columbus on September 12, 1956, O'Neill Collection.

3. Report of the Ohio Commission on Education Beyond the High School, June 1958, pp. 17–66, O'Neill Collection; Gongwer News Service Report, September 26, 1962, Gongwer News Service Inc. files, 175 S. Third St., Columbus, Ohio, 43215.

4. U.S. Federal Highway Administration, *Highway Statistics* (Washington, D.C.: Government Printing Office, 1960).

5. O'Neill remarks to the Cincinnati Transportation Club, October 16, 1956, O'Neill Collection.

6. DiSalle speech of April 3, 1956 at Toledo's Commodore Perry Hotel, Michael V. DiSalle Collection, Ohio Historical Society.

7. O'Neill press release of October 7, 1956, O'Neill Collection; *Ohio State Journal,* October 8, 1956.

8. *The New Republic,* May 28, 1951, 11–15.

9. *Ohio Taxation* (Columbus: Ohio Legal Center Institute, 1967), 316.

10. Keith McNamara, interviewed by the author, July 8, 1992, Columbus.

11. Gongwer News Service Report, February 26, 1957.

12. John C. Mahaney Jr., interviewed by the author, April 29, 1992, Columbus.

13. O'Neill speech to the Ohio Chamber of Commerce board of directors, September 30, 1958, O'Neill Collection.

14. O'Neill televised speech, October 23, 1958, ibid.; letter to O'Neill from Roger C. Brown of Waynesville, Ohio, October 27, 1958, ibid.; letter to O'Neill from Robert L. Kelley of Cincinnatti, Ohio, October 8, 1958, ibid.

15. Bureau of Unemployment Compensation, "Ohio Labor Market Information Report, August 15, 1959."

16. O'Neill letter to a Canton woman, November 15, 1958, O'Neill Collection.

17. John J. Gargan and James G. Coke, eds., *Political Behavior and Public Issues in Ohio* (Kent, Ohio: Kent State University Press, 1972); U.S. Department of Health, Education, and Welfare, *Biennial Survey of Education in the United States, 1956–58* (Washington, D.C.: Government Printing Office, 1962), 73.

18. Gongwer News Service Report, January 27, 1959.

19. Ibid., February 25, 1959; ibid., March 3, 1959.

20. *Cincinnati Enquirer,* April 15, 1961.

21. DiSalle letter to the Toledo *Blade,* April 21, 1961, DiSalle Collection.

22. Michael V. DiSalle and Lawrence G. Blochman, *The Power of Life or Death* (New York: Random House, 1965).

23. Canton *Repository,* November 23, 1961; *Troy Daily News,* September 30, 1961.

24. Mahaney, interview.

25. Gongwer News Service Report, November 7, 1962; *Columbus Evening Dispatch*, November 7, 1962.

4. RHODES'S FIRST EIGHT YEARS, 1963–1971

1. R. Dean Jauchius, "Gubernatorial Roles: An Assessment By Five Ohio Governors" (Ph.D. diss., Ohio State University, 1971). Jauchius was a long-time Rhodes staff member and coauthor of Rhodes's historical novels published while he was state auditor. He depended heavily on Rhodes's personal recollections of his early life, some details of which were not always consistent with Rhodes's own retellings nor always verifiable. "Sifting legend from fact is some job," Jauchius, working on Rhodes's biography, told the author during a July 25, 1992, interview in Columbus.

2. Jauchius, "Gubernatorial Roles."

3. Charles Fox, interviewed by the author, October 1962, Springfield, Ohio. Fox apparently chose not to recall that Rhodes was suspended from high school for calling a coach a "son of a bitch," according to Jauchius ("Gubernatorial Roles").

4. Cleveland *Plain Dealer*, October 26, 1969. The *Plain Dealer* was the main source for Rhodes's daily activity throughout this chapter. During his first two terms it became Ohio's largest newspaper. Editorially it usually supported Rhodes, except for endorsing his opponent in the 1970 senatorial primary. The paper's stable of Statehouse and political reporters—which included Sanford Watzman, James Naughton, William Barnard, Ray Dorsey, and, for the last three years of Rhodes's term, the author—was generally considered "tough but honest," to use former Cleveland mayor Carl Stokes's phrase.

5. The allegation that Rhodes once was charged with accepting policy slips was contained in an investigative report prepared for incumbent governor Michael DiSalle, Rhodes's 1962 gubernatorial opponent. Apparently DiSalle or his supporters hired a former FBI agent to probe Rhodes's activities during his early years, continuing through his terms as Columbus mayor and state auditor. DiSalle quietly circulated the report to a few Statehouse reporters on the condition that they check out the allegations without revealing the source of original tips. Reporters mostly demurred, finding many of the allegations too inferential, unprovable, old, or, in some cases, personal. Besides, according to published contemporary sources, being "arrested" in Columbus on low-level gambling charges in the 1930s and early 1940s was considered so common and so minor that violators were not even required to appear in court; their fines were simply deducted from funds posted in advance by the gambling operators. See Kenneth Meckstroth in the *Ohio State Journal*, circa 1943.

6. Carl B. Stokes, *Promises of Power* (New York: Simon and Schuster, 1973), 66.

7. This story, or some form of it, has been told so often that it is impossible to trace its original source. True or not, it fit the image many voters had of Ferguson.

8. The existence of many such "flower funds" (the origin of the term comes from the fact that politicians like to say the fund is just to buy funerary flowers) was an acknowledged fact around the Statehouse. But details as to sources, disbursement, and amounts remained guarded. Elected officials normally can get away with maintaining

such funds even between campaigns if (1) only appointed employees are tapped and those under civil service protection are not too heavily leaned on to make contributions and (2) the funds are used strictly for political purposes. The Internal Revenue Service frowns on such funds being converted to personal use and not reported as income for tax purposes.

9. Stanley Aronoff and Vernal G. Riffe, Jr., *James A. Rhodes at Eighty*, (Columbus: Privately printed, 1989), 25. This ninety-page paperback was "produced" by Aronoff, a Republican and Ohio Senate president, and Riffe, a Democrat and speaker of the Ohio House, for distribution at Rhodes's eightieth birthday party. It was compiled by Thomas H. Dudgeon, a long-time Columbus lobbyist and political operative. While the paperback makes no claim at being comprehensive or balanced, it offers a convenient reference for dates, statistics, and quotes. Since Rhodes so often repeated himself both in public and private, sometimes with slight variations, the booklet often was turned to as the authority for the exact form of a well-worn quote. Other oft-repeated Rhodes quotes are based on the author's recollection and notes from the endless hours he spent with Rhodes, and no attempt was made in all cases to pin them down as to a specific date, interview, or casual conversation.

10. Stokes, *Promises of Power*, 65–66.

11. George W. Knepper, *Ohio and Its People* (Kent, Ohio: Kent State University Press, 1989), 402.

12. Richard Krabach, telephone interview by the author, July 29, 1992, Cincinnati.

13. *Plain Dealer*, September 28, 1962. After the election, at a press party held at the Governor's Mansion, the only bourbon available was the newly listed Waterfill and Frazier. "Best we could get you fellows," Rhodes said, grinning. It was later again delisted for low sales.

14. Ibid., October 5, 1962. Rhodes claimed IRS information had been handed DiSalle by a friendly Democratic administration in Washington. DiSalle said his information had come from a "disgruntled" former auditor's employee.

15. Ibid., November 4, 1962.

16. *Columbus Dispatch*, January 25, 1963.

17. *Plain Dealer*, April 21, 1963.

18. Ibid., June 16, 1963.

19. Aronoff and Riffe, *Rhodes at Eighty*, 42. Like many of Rhodes's statistics, especially those involving industrial development, these figures are not verifiable and probably were made up out of whole cloth.

20. Ibid., 44; Knepper, *Ohio and Its People*, 403.

21. Theodore Gray, telephone interview by the author, August 11, 1992, Columbus; Charles Kurfess, telephone interview by the author, August 13, 1992, Bowling Green, Ohio.

22. Stokes, *Promises of Power*, 65–67.

23. Gray and Kurfess, interviews.

24. Krabach, interview.

25. *Plain Dealer*, April 23, 1967.

26. Aronoff and Riffe, *Rhodes at Eighty*, 29.

27. Ibid., 40.

28. Ibid., 39.

29. John Andrews, interviewed by the author, July 30, 1992, Washington, D.C.

30. Kurfess, interview.

31. *San Francisco Chronicle*, July 10, 1964.

32. Aronoff and Riffe, *Rhodes at Eighty*, 48.

33. *Life*, May 2, 1969.

34. Joe Eszterhas and Michael D. Roberts, *13 Seconds* (New York: Dodd, Mead, 1970), 143.

35. Aronoff and Riffe, *Rhodes at Eighty*, 31; Eszterhas and Roberts, *13 Seconds*, 111.

36. *Plain Dealer*, May 5, 1970.

37. Kurfess, interview.

38. Ohio Bureau of Labor statistics for the period 1960–70 show that while the Ohio labor force grew by 867,000, the number actually employed increased by only 804,000. So while it could be claimed that more than 800,000 jobs were created, there were in 1970 63,000 more unemployed persons than in 1960. An Ohio State University study, reported by the *Plain Dealer* on December 28, 1969, showed that Rhodes's policies, while maybe not creating quite enough jobs to keep up with the growth of the labor pool, were nevertheless "arresting a decline in the state's economy." Given the decline of the economies of other "rust belt" states, this in itself was no mean feat.

5. THE GILLIGAN INTERLUDE, 1971–1975

1. Hugh C. McDiarmid, "Jack Gilligan: The Taming of the Shrew," *Cleveland Magazine*, October 1974. From 1970 to 1975 the author was the Columbus correspondent for the now-defunct *Journal Herald*, a morning paper in Dayton, and a frequent contributor to *Cleveland Magazine*. A portion of the material in this chapter is drawn from stories that appeared under his byline in those years and from my personal files.

2. The others being James M. Cox, 1913–15 and 1917–21, and Michael V. DiSalle, 1959–63.

3. R. Dean Jauchius and Thomas H. Dudgeon, *Jim Rhodes' Big Win: The Making of an Upset* (Columbus: Privately published, 1978), 15.

4. *Journal Herald*, October 28, 1974.

5. John J. Gilligan, interviewed by the author, August 8, 1974, Columbus.

6. David R. Larson, "Ohio's Fighting Liberal: A Political Biography of John J. Gilligan" (Ph.D. diss., Ohio State University, 1982), 22. The Larson dissertation, available through University Microfilms International (83053225 DAI 4310A), was an invaluable source for this chapter. Larson, former archives and library division chief with the Ohio Historical Society, conducted 323 hours of tape-recorded oral history interviews with Gilligan and others involved with the administration, including the author, from 1969 to 1975. The tapes and the John J. Gilligan Manuscripts Collection are at the Ohio Historical Society in Columbus. Much of the material is restricted, and access requires prior approval.

7. Gilligan, interview; McDiarmid, "Taming of the Shrew"; *New York Times Magazine*, December 12, 1965. Gilligan beat Rich 74,525 to 69,114. Gilligan described his upset this way: "What started out as a sacrifice bunt turned into a home run" (interview).

8. *New York Times Magazine*, December 12, 1965.

9. Taft beat Gilligan 70,366 to 62,580; *Wall Street Journal*, September 19, 1968.

10. Kraft, now deceased, came to Ohio in the fall to write about the governor's race. He included the remark in one of his preelection syndicated columns, and it was picked up by various Ohio media.

11. *Journal Herald,* November 24, 1971. This lengthy article provided much of the background for this section on the legislative fight to secure new income taxes.

12. A May 20, 1974, *Journal Herald* article described King: "Frank King was ubiquitous. He stalked prey in the House, sat in caucus with Senate Democrats, held court with newsmen in the hallways and in general flexed his IOUs and union muscles all through the Statehouse. When he didn't act on his own, he used Calabrese, an aging and crafty ally as his mouthpiece. The result was havoc with much of the administration's legislative program and near disaster for its critical new state income tax on which everything else depended. Frank loved every minute of it, particularly the agony it was causing the governor, his only real rival for power among Ohio's historically disorganized Democrats." Two years later, at a stormy 1974 state convention in Cleveland, King was dumped as president of the Ohio AFL-CIO.

13. For these quotes, see *Journal Herald,* November 24, 1971.

14. *New York Times,* November 24, 1971.

15. Larson, "Ohio's Fighting Liberal," 196.

16. Ibid. Jauchius and Dudgeon, *Jim Rhodes' Big Win,* 16. The authors, who had been close to Rhodes for years and were key figures in his 1974 campaign (and who acknowledge a pro-Rhodes bias in their book's preface), write that one result of the Hansan coup was "the establishment, under new chief of staff Hansan, of a palace guard of overly defensive sycophants."

17. *Cleveland Magazine,* October 1974. Also, Larson reveals that it was a phone call from Gilligan to McGovern, not vice versa, as was reported at the time, that resulted in Gilligan's decision to visit the convention after all. And, of course, it was that visit that touched off the "Gilligan for vice president" flurry ("Ohio's Fighting Liberal," 187–88).

18. "Jack's Jalopy," *Cleveland Magazine,* November 1972.

19. *New York Times,* April 21, 1974.

20. *Journal Herald,* September 19, 1974. The full text of Glenn's statement is in the author's possession.

21. Jauchius and Dudgeon, *Jim Rhodes' Big Win,* 35. The authors also write that "Gilligan's action not only infuriated the Glenn forces but many other Democrats as well and a number of Republicans."

22. *OU* (Ohio University) *Post,* October 24, 1974.

23. Larson, "Ohio's Fighting Liberal," 256.

24. Jauchius and Dudgeon, *Jim Rhodes' Big Win,* 83.

25. Larson, "Ohio's Fighting Liberal," 236; *Journal Herald,* January 1974. Also of interest is a story recounted by Richard G. Zimmerman, who, as Columbus correspondent of the Cleveland *Plain Dealer* in the late 1960s, uncovered evidence that Calabrese had ordered up an Ohio Air National Guard plane to fly him back to Cleveland on personal business. Confronted by Zimmerman, Calabrese pleaded innocent and said he thought the lettering on the wing referred to "OANG" airlines.

26. *Cleveland Magazine,* October 1974.

27. Larson, "Ohio's Fighting Liberal," 233–34. Also see a private postelection memo written by Gilligan, dated November 10, 1974, copy in author's possession.

28. *Journal Herald,* October 28, 1974.

29. Larson writes, "Because Rhodes had no field campaign, the relative staff situations of the two campaigns was striking. While Gilligan had a campaign staff of 40 full-time people and 80 part-time aides, the Rhodes campaign operated out of his development firm offices in Columbus, had six full-time and two part-time employes. The Rhodes weekly payroll was only about one-fifth of Gilligan's" ("Ohio's Fighting Liberal," 241). For details of the concession episode, see Jauchius and Dudgeon, *Jim Rhodes' Big Win,* 125–30.

30. Larson, "Ohio's Fighting Liberal," 245.

31. The full memo, a copy of which is in the author's possession, went on for two, legal-sized, typewritten pages.

32. *Dayton Daily News,* November 11, 1974; Larson, "Ohio's Fighting Liberal," 246.

33. Thomas Suddes, then the editorial page editor of the Ohio State University newspaper the *Lantern* (and now a Cleveland *Plain Dealer* Columbus correspondent and author of chapter 8 in this book), offered one of the most insightful descriptions of Gilligan: "A man of decent and humane instincts with strong political ambitions somehow oddly compounded with a distance from others that he no doubt considers dignified but which others interpret as arrogant" (*Lantern,* June 6, 1975). *Cleveland Magazine,* October 1974.

34. *Plain Dealer,* June 21, 1975.

35. John J. Gilligan, telephone interviews by the author, August 13, 1992, July 27, 1993, and February 21, 1994.

6. RHODES'S SECOND EIGHT YEARS, 1975–1983

1. James A. Rhodes, interviewed by the author, January 12, 1993, Columbus; Eugene P. O'Grady, interviewed by the author, January 11, 1993, Columbus.

2. O'Grady, interview; Brian Usher, "A Study in Survival—Jim Rhodes' Magic Touch in the Statehouse," *Akron Beacon Journal Sunday Magazine,* January 17, 1985; Rhodes, interview.

3. *Akron Beacon Journal,* January 17, 1985; Rhodes, interview.

4. United Press International, January 10, 1975. Unless otherwise cited, all quotations in this chapter are from United Press International dispatches. The author was chief of the UPI Statehouse bureau during Governor Rhodes's third and fourth terms and draws extensively on his wire service files throughout the chapter.

5. "Rhodes vs. the Media: 'A Certain Souring,' " *Beacon Journal,* December 28, 1975.

6. Rhodes, interview.

7. Incidentally, many of the "repealed" features were part of the so-called motor-voter bill adopted by the U.S. Congress and signed into law by President Clinton in 1993.

8. Cleveland *Plain Dealer,* September 10, 1989.

9. Associated Press dispatch from Cincinnati, May 16, 1978.

10. Lee Leonard, "How Rhodes Hung On," *Columbus Monthly,* December 1978.

11. "The Rhodes Era: The Huckster," *Beacon Journal,* January 2, 1983.

12. Lee Leonard, UPI "Ohio Politics" dispatch, January 24, 1982.

13. Rhodes had outdistanced all but a handful of colonial governors and one postrevolutionary governor, George Clinton of New York, who served for twenty-one years in the late 1700s. After the Constitution was ratified in 1789, no governor served longer than Rhodes. Researched by the author for United Press International; *Biographical Directory of the Governors of the United States, 1789–1978* (Westport, Conn.: Meckler, 1978).

7. THE CELESTE ERA, 1983–1991

1. *Dayton Daily News,* January 9, 1991.

2. Ibid., October 1, 1978. The article draws on a 1978 interview with Richard F. Celeste conducted by Jim Ripley in Columbus.

3. *Dayton Daily News,* January 9, 1991.

4. Eugene P. O'Grady, interviewed by the author, January 5, 1993, Columbus.

5. *Akron Beacon Journal,* October 3, 1978.

6. Tim Hagan, telephone interview by the author, January 10, 1985.

7. Richard F. Celeste, interviewed by the author, January 10, 1985, Columbus.

8. C. J. McLin, interviewed by the author, August 1, 1988, Columbus.

9. Gerald Austin, interviewed by the author, February 14, 1988, Columbus.

10. Celeste, interviewed by the author, August 14, 1982, Columbus.

11. *Dayton Daily News,* October 17, 1982.

12. Cleveland *Plain Dealer,* February 19, 1983.

13. Ibid.

14. Ibid., March 24, 1984.

15. *Dayton Daily News,* March 2, 1986.

16. Ibid.

17. Ibid.

18. David Hobson, interviewed by the author, October 20, 1985, Columbus.

19. Celeste, interviewed by the author, June 20, 1986, Columbus.

20. *Beacon Journal,* September 9, 1986; *Columbus Dispatch,* September 7, 1986.

21. As of this writing, the cases were still pending in court.

22. Stanley Aronoff, interviewed by the author, January 9, 1991, Columbus.

23. Gerald Austin, interviewed by the author, March 10, 1993, Columbus; William Batchelder, interviewed by the author, January 9, 1991, Columbus.

24. Celeste, interviewed by the author, December 1990, Columbus.

8. PANORAMA OF OHIO POLITICS IN THE VOINOVICH ERA, 1991–

1. Voinovich was only the third mayor of Cleveland to become governor of Ohio. The others were Republican Harry L. Davis, mayor from 1916 to 1920 and 1933 to 1935 and governor from 1921 to 1923, and Democrat Frank J. Lausche, mayor from 1941 to 1944 and governor from 1945 to 1947 and from 1949 to 1957.

2. A similar image had helped another Cleveland mayor, Frank J. Lausche, rise to the governorship. "In the industrial cities, [Lausche] praised [Franklin] Roosevelt highly; in the rural communities, he never even mentioned Roosevelt's name—particularly in the America First belt of Ohio, in the western tier of counties—and so was accused of opportunism and equivocation. In fact, when you analyze it, everyone in the state was altogether dubious about Lausche—except 1,603,809 voters [in 1944] . . . . I heard someone say, 'Everyone is crazy about [Lausche]—and wonders why.' I heard someone else say, 'Was he really a good mayor? No one knows. But he'd be elected again anytime he ran.' I heard a third friend say, 'You can get so mad at him you'll call him every name in the world, and five minutes later be the best of friends. The guy who knocks him most says, He's mine!' " John Gunther, *Inside U.S.A.* (New York: Harper and Brothers, 1947), 427, 429.

3. See, for example, the "poverty indicators" regularly published by the Council for Economic Opportunities in Greater Cleveland. "Mayoral Administration of George V. Voinovich (1979–)," in David D. Van Tassel and John J. Grabowski, eds., *The Encyclopedia of Cleveland History* (Bloomington: Indiana University Press, 1987), 670.

4. Steve Luttner and Jim Underwood, "Celebrezze's Trail Was Plagued with Potholes," Cleveland *Plain Dealer*, November 7, 1990.

5. Mary Beth Lane, "Inaugural Blends Austerity, Optimism," ibid., January 15, 1991.

6. William J. Shkurti and John R. Bartle, eds., *Benchmark Ohio 1991* (Columbus: Ohio State University Press, 1991). Ohio ranked third in censuses from 1840 through 1880 and was fourth through the 1940 census, though in 1940 it barely outranked California. In absolute numbers, Ohio's high-water mark in the U.S. House was during the 1930s, then during the mid-1960s, when the state was allocated 24 U.S. representatives. Now Ohio has 19 seats, and California, the most populous state, has 52.

7. Mary Beth Lane, "Voinovich To Trim State Government with State Diet," *Plain Dealer*, March 6, 1991.

8. Ibid.

9. Thomas Suddes, "Voinovich Proposes 26.8 Billion Budget," ibid., March 19, 1991.

10. Ronald Mucha, Ohio Department of Taxation, telephone interview by the author, August 24, 1992; *Ohio's Taxes: A Brief Summary of Major State and Local Taxes in Ohio 1992* (Columbus: Ohio Department of Taxation, 1992), 26; *Pension Facts* (Columbus: Ohio Retirement Study Commission, 1991).

11. Shkurti and Bartle, *Benchmark Ohio*, 121, 126.

12. Ohio Public Expenditure Council, "Tax Facts: Report 92-4," May 1992; *The 1975/1977 Budget Act for the State of Ohio* (Columbus: Ohio Legislative Budget Office, 1975), 32; *Senate-House Conference Report on Amended Substitute House Bill 298 of the 119th General Assembly*, July 11, 1991; *Pension Facts*.

13. *Ohio House of Representatives Membership Directory*.

14. Mary Beth Lane, "Governor Calls for Limiting of Terms," *Plain Dealer*, October 22, 1991; Thomas Suddes, "Hypocrisy, Snorts Riffe, After Dig From Voinovich," ibid., October 23, 1991.

15. "Speaker urges drive to repeal term limits," Gongwer News Service, March 10, 1993.

16. "Voinovich vows to go to the people to loosen special interests' grip on State-house," ibid., July 31, 1992. For example, in April 1991 Voinovich flatly pledged to campaign statewide for a bottle bill. "I feel strongly enough about this that I will go around and campaign for this legislation statewide," Voinovich told reporters. (But if he did, he spoke in secret.) Thomas Suddes, "Voinovich Pledges Crusade To Pass Bottle-Deposit Law," *Plain Dealer*, April 24, 1991; Mary Anne Sharkey, "Ohio Democrat to Drop Niceness," ibid., March 3, 1993.

17. Thomas Suddes, "Nader Column Blasts Riffe as Political Tyrant," ibid., January 13, 1987; Thomas Suddes, "Nader Enters Riffe's Den, Takes Aim at his Power," ibid., March 4, 1988; ibid., May 30, 1987; Mary Anne Sharkey, "Keeping an Orderly House," *Plain Dealer Magazine*, August 26, 1984.

18. Thomas Suddes, "Fund-Raising by Riffe Vulgar, Also Awesome," *Plain Dealer*, June 26, 1991.

19. Idem, "Riffe's Bash Also Tribute to Rural Politics," ibid., July 3, 1991.

20. The biographical details are taken from *A Tribute to Vern Riffe, Speaker of the House*, a commemorative booklet published in 1983 by the Portsmouth Area Recognition Society.

21. *Plain Dealer Magazine*, August 26, 1984.

22. "Speaker Sets Sight on Ohio Governorship," *Plain Dealer*, February 2, 1975; "Riffe, Warner Announce as Gubernatorial Tag-Team," ibid., January 12, 1982.

23. One magisterial work suggests interesting analogies: L. B. Namier, *The Structure of Politics at the Accession of George III* (London, 1929).

24. All campaign finance data are from *Ohio 1990 Campaign Finance Facts* (Columbus: Ohio Secretary of State, 1990).

25. *Report of the Debates and Proceedings, Ohio Constitutional Convention, 1850–1851*, vol. 2 (Columbus, 1851), 225.

26. Total employment grew 25.6 percent in Columbus and 19.6 percent in Cincinnati from 1979 to 1989 but only by 1.7 percent in Cleveland. Shkurti and Bartle, *Benchmark Ohio*, 37. Though not explicitly stated, Central Ohio's nonunion environment was almost certainly a contributing factor to the location of Japanese auto assembly and parts plant in rural Ohio (e.g., the Honda plant near Marysville). Ohio Urban University Program, *Suburbanization of Ohio Metropolitan Areas 1980–2000* (Cleveland: Cleveland State University, 1990), 14–15.

27. Thomas Suddes, "Voinovich: Looking Beyond Lean Times," *Plain Dealer*, January 15, 1992.

28. Ibid.

29. The chronology and statistics are from "Bipartisan Budget-Balancing Proposal," a December 1992 press release by the Ohio Office of Budget and Management.

30. Thomas Suddes and Mary Beth Lane, "$315.7 Million Hacked Out of State's Budget," *Plain Dealer*, July 2, 1992. After all the hurly-burly of the spending cuts and the December 1992 tax hikes, the state ended up with a surplus of about $110 million on that date.

31. Jim Underwood and Thomas Suddes, "Governor May Be Taking 1-Term Road," ibid., July 5, 1992.

32. "Statement of Gov. George V. Voinovich," Governor's Communications Office press release, December 17, 1992.

33. Governor's Communications Office press statement, February 4, 1993.

34. Thomas Suddes and Mary Beth Lane, "Budget Maybe Start of Campaign," *Plain Dealer,* February 7, 1993.

35. Thomas Suddes, "Budget Bill Tour de Force for Speaker," ibid., December 23, 1992.

36. Mary Beth Lane, "Voinovich Sets Sights on Reforms," ibid., January 27, 1993.

37. Joe Hallett and Ann Fisher, "Voinovich's Unfulfilled Pledges," Toledo *Blade,* January 31, 1993.

38. Thomas Suddes, "Budget Awaits Scrutiny, Surgery by Voinovich," *Plain Dealer,* July 1, 1993.

39. Vindu P. Goel, "Ohio Ethics Bill OK'd, Forces Officials to Bare All Income," ibid., January 27, 1994.

40. Representative Vernon F. Sykes (D-Akron), president of Black Elected Democrats of Ohio, quoted in Thomas Suddes, "Riffe Says He Intends to Bow Out," ibid., January 15, 1994.

41. Mary Beth Lane, "Voinovich Ticket Mate Is Woman," ibid., January 21, 1994.

42. Thomas Suddes, "Shaker's Jones Ready for the Fight," ibid., February 12, 1994.

9. THE NEWS MEDIA AND OHIO POLITICS

1. Thomas Suddes, interviewed by Peter F. O'Connell, August 5, 1992, Columbus. Assistance in research and interviewing for this chapter was provided by Peter F. O'Connell, a graduate student at the School of Journalism at The Ohio State University.

2. David Adams, interviewed by Peter F. O'Connell, August 5, 1992, Columbus.

3. Mike Curtin, interviewed by Peter F. O'Connell, August 3, 1992, Columbus.

4. Sandy Theis, interviewed by Peter F. O'Connell, August 15, 1992, Columbus. After George Voinovich had been governor for just more than a year, Theis wrote a story called "The Governor and God," about how Voinovich has been affected in his policymaking and personnel appointments by his strong religious beliefs. Voinovich, for example, named as his state health director a former head of the Right to Life organization from Cleveland who had no public-health experience.

5. Lee Leonard, interviewed by Peter F. O'Connell, August 13, 1992, Columbus.

6. Curtin, interview.

7. Theis, interview.

8. Adams, interview; Mary Beth Lane, interviewed by Peter F. O'Connell, August 5, 1992, Columbus.

9. Robert Bennett, interviewed by the author, September 2, 1992, Columbus.

10. Gene Branstool, interviewed by the author, August 11, 1992, Columbus.

11. Robert H. Bohle, "Negativism as News Selection Predictor," *Journalism Quarterly* (Winter 1986): 789–96. While Branstool is frustrated with much of what the media do, he notes that coverage of his own political life improved dramatically when the local paper, the *Newark Advocate,* was purchased by the Thomson Newspapers chain. When the paper was owned by the Spencer family, he recalls, it was against policy to print the names of Democrats, "so, I didn't have any squawks about the Thomson chain."

12. W. T. Gomley, Jr., "Coverage of State Government in the Mass Media," *State Government* (Spring 1979): 46–51; Malcolm E. Jewell, "The Neglected World of State Politics," *Journal of Politics* (1982): 638–56.

13. Richard F. Celeste, interviewed by the author, August 26, 1992, Columbus.

14. Curt Steiner, interviewed by the author, August 14, 1992, Columbus.

15. Jim Otte, interviewed by the author, August 24, 1992, Columbus.

16. Deborah Countiss, interviewed by the author, November 16, 1992, Columbus.

17. Bill Cohen, interviewed by the author, August 24, 1992, Columbus.

10. OHIO IN WASHINGTON: THE CONGRESSIONAL DELEGATION

1. "The Ten Most Obscure Members," *Roll Call*, June 21, 1990.

2. *National Association of Watch and Clock Collectors Bulletin*, June 1988

3. Byron H. Walker, interviewed by the author, August 7, 1992, Columbus. For more on Senator Taft, see James T. Patterson, *Mr. Republican: A Biography of Robert A. Taft* (Boston: Houghton Mifflin, 1972).

4. Robert A. Taft II, telephone interview by the author, August 17, 1992.

5. Walker, interview.

6. John Morgan, interviewed by the author, September 2, 1992, Washington, D.C.

7. Randall Ripley, telephone interview by the author, September 2, 1992.

8. Thomas L. Ashley, interviewed by the author, August 7, 1992, Washington, D.C.; Charles A. Vanik, interviewed by the author, August 4, 1992, Washington, D.C.

9. Ashley, interview.

10. *Plain Dealer Sunday Magazine*, November 10, 1985.

11. Luane Tananbaum, *The Bricker Amendment Controversy: A Test of Eisenhower's Political Leadership.* (Ithaca, N.Y.: Cornell University Press, 1988). For more on Senator Bricker, see Richard O. Davies, *Defender of the Old Guard: John Bricker in American Politics* (Columbus: Ohio State University Press, 1992). Walter LaFeber, *The American Age* (New York: W. W. Norton, 1989).

12. Howard M. Metzenbaum, interviewed by the author, August 12, 1992, Washington, D.C.

13. Robert E. Miller, Associated Press, interviewed by the author, September 1, 1976, Columbus; Neal R. Peirce and Jerry Hagstrom, *The Book of America* (New York: W. W. Norton, 1983), 306.

14. Jim Hart, a former Hays staff aide, interviewed by the author, August 18, 1992, Washington, D.C.; Vanik, interview.

15. Ashley, interview.

16. Vanik, interview.

17. Robert F. Kennedy, *In His Own Words: The Unpublished Recollections of the Kennedy Years* (New York: Bantam, 1988).

18. Cleveland *Plain Dealer*, October 30, 1962.

19. *New York Times*, November 10, 1966.

20. Ibid.

21. Clarence J. Brown, Jr., interviewed by the author, August 17, 1992, Washington, D.C.

22. *Plain Dealer,* February 23, 1980.

23. *New York Times,* November 14, 1966.

24. *Plain Dealer Sunday Magazine,* November 10, 1985; William Saxbe, telephone interview by the author, September 2, 1992.

25. Peirce and Hagstrom, *The Book of America,* 304–5.

26. Vanik, interview.

27. Anonymous interview with the author, February 1992.

28. John H. Glenn, Jr., interviewed by the author, February 25, 1992, Washington, D.C.

29. Metzenbaum, interview.

30. *Plain Dealer,* August 25, 1985; Steve Avakian, telephone interview by the author, March 1, 1992.

31. Robert A. Taft, Jr., telephone interview by the author, September 1, 1992; Clarence "Bud" Brown, interview.

32. Anonymous interview with the author, February 1992.

33. *Plain Dealer Sunday Magazine,* November 2, 1986.

34. *Plain Dealer,* December 18, 1988.

35. *Congressional Quarterly Almanac,* 94th Cong., 2d sess., 1976, vol. 32.

36. Douglas Applegate, interviewed by the author, August 17, 1992, Washington, D.C.; Vanik, interview.

37. Vanik, interview.

38. Suzanne Garment, *Scandal: The Culture of Mistrust in American Politics* (New York: Random House, 1992).

39. Ibid.; *Congressional Quarterly Almanac,* 1976, vol. 32.

40. Jim Hart, interviewed by the author, August 18, 1992, Washington, D.C.

41. Vanik, interview.

42. Steve Kovacik, telephone interview by the author, February 25, 1992.

43. James E. Betts, telephone interview by the author, February 19, 1992. Poor Betts, a starting forward in basketball in the 1950s at Ohio University, had a boyish smile, ruddy complexion, and balding noggin. He was often mistaken for Glenn. "I just grabbed onto it and tried to make light of it," he said. "Somebody was sure to say that 'did anyone tell you you look like your opponent?' There is not much worse than that."

44. Anonymous interview with the author, February 1992.

45. Avakian, interview.

46. Pease statement regarding his noncandidacy, October 3, 1991, in author's possession.

47. As Pease put it, "I think the root of all evil is not money, but television." Donald J. Pease, interviewed by the author, August 21, 1992, Washington, D.C.

48. *Plain Dealer,* October 22, 1987; Gradison statement on ethics reform and pay increase, November 16, 1989, in author's possession.

49. Colbert letter, February 28, 1989, in author's possession.

50. John L. Jackley, *Hill Rat: Blowing the Lid off Congress* (Washington, D.C.: Regnery Gateway, 1992).

51. *Plain Dealer,* August 14, 1992.

52. Ibid., December 26, 1992.

53. *Congressional Record,* 103d Cong., 1st sess., June 29, 1993, vol. 139, no. 93; Glenn, interview.

54. Saxbe, interview.

55. Vanik, interview.

56. *Plain Dealer,* October 1, 1967.

57. Unpublished interview with a *Plain Dealer* reporter, June 1989.

58. Clarence "Bud" Brown, interview.

59. Michael Barone and Grant Ujifusa, eds., *The Almanac of American Politics* (Washington: National Journal, 1991); Northeast-Midwest Coalition report, September 1, 1992, Northeast-Midwest Congressional Coalition, Washington, D.C.

60. John Kessel, telephone interview by author, August 31, 1992.

61. Barone and Ujifusa, eds., *The Almanac of American Politics.*

62. Clarence "Bud" Brown, interview.

11. LEGISLATIVE POLITICS IN OHIO

Stephan V. Quinlan, a Ph.D. student in political science at The Ohio State University and a research associate at The Ohio State University Center for Human Resource Research, provided helpful assistance in preparing the data for this chapter. Valuable comments and suggestions were made by Representative Mike Stinziano (D-Columbus).

1. See Samuel C. Patterson, Randall B. Ripley, and Stephen V. Quinlan, "Citizens' Orientations Toward Legislatures: Congress and the State Legislature," *Western Political Quarterly* 45 (June 1992): 315–38.

2. Alan Rosenthal, "The Legislative Institution—In Transition and at Risk," in Carl E. Van Horn, ed., *The State of the States,* 2d ed. (Washington: Congressional Quarterly Press, 1993), 115.

3. Rosenthal, "The Legislative Institution," 116. Also, see idem, *Legislative Life: People, Process, and Performance in the States* (New York: Harper and Row, 1981), and Samuel C. Patterson, "State Legislators and the Legislatures," in Virginia Gray, Herbert Jacob, and Robert B. Albritton, eds., *Politics in the American States* (Glenview, Ill.: Scott, Foresman, 1990), 161–200.

4. William J. Keefe, "The Functions and Powers of the State Legislature," in Alexander Heard, ed., *State Legislatures in American Politics* (Englewood Cliffs, N.J.: Prentice-Hall, 1966), 37.

5. See Lucille Griffith, *The Virginia House of Burgesses, 1750–1774* (University: University of Alabama Press, 1968).

6. Daniel J. Ryan, *History of Ohio: The Rise and Progress of an American State* (New York: Century, 1912), 37–38.

7. See Beverley W. Bond, Jr., *The Foundations of Ohio* (Columbus: Ohio State Archaeological and Historical Society, 1941), 437–76; Andrew R. L. Cayton, *The Frontier Republic: Ideology and Politics in the Ohio Country, 1780–1825* (Kent, Ohio: Kent State University Press, 1986), 68–80; and George W. Knepper, *Ohio and Its People* (Kent, Ohio: Kent State University Press, 1989), 89–97.

8. Thomas A. Flinn, "The Ohio General Assembly: A Developmental Analysis," in James A. Robinson, ed., *State Legislative Innovation* (New York: Praeger, 1973), 233.

9. Lawrence Baum and Samuel C. Patterson, "Ohio: Party Change without Realignment," in Maureen Moakley, ed., *Party Realignment and State Politics* (Columbus: Ohio State University Press, 1992), 203–4.

10. The results of the 1957 interviews are reported in John C. Wahlke, Heinz Eulau, William Buchanan, and Leroy C. Ferguson, *The Legislative System: Explorations in Legislative Behavior* (New York: Wiley, 1962). In 1988, almost all members of the 117th General Assembly were interviewed as part of the Ohio Legislative Research Project at Ohio State University.

11. See Flinn, "The Ohio General Assembly," 237–44; and idem, "An Evaluation of Legislative Performance: The State Legislature of Ohio," in John J. Gargan and James G. Coke, eds., *Political Behavior and Public Issues in Ohio* (Kent, Ohio: Kent State University Press, 1972), 153–63.

12. For data on Ohio legislators' role orientations in the 1960s, see Flinn, "The Ohio General Assembly," 249–55.

13. See Wahlke et al., *The Legislative System*, 237–431.

14. Ibid., 281.

15. Newspaper and magazine articles featuring the speaker appeared regularly. The following are particularly useful: Lee Leonard, "Power at the Statehouse: The Riffe Reign," *Columbus Monthly*, August 1989, 54–59; idem, "Pro Among Pros," *State Legislatures*, November/December 1989, 13–15; Cliff Treyens, "Mr. Speaker," *Capitol: The Dispatch Magazine*, May 17, 1987, 6–15.

16. Richard G. Sheridan, *Governing Ohio: The State Legislature* (Cleveland: Federation for Community Planning, 1989), 27, 29.

17. Charles Funderburk, "Effectiveness in the Ohio Legislature: The Case of Representative C. J. McLin, Jr.," *Miami Valley History: A Journal of the Montgomery County Historical Society* 4 (1992): 24–38. Also see Margaret J. Simms Maddox, "The Development of the Black Elected Democrats of Ohio (BEDO) Into a Viable State Legislative Caucus" (Ph.D. diss., Ohio State University, 1991).

18. Legislative leadership political action committees (PACs) and caucus campaign committees like those in Ohio exist in thirty-four other states, as well. See Anthony Gierzynski, *Legislative Party Campaign Committees in the American States* (Lexington: University Press of Kentucky, 1992). Also see Rodney A. Anderson, "The Role of Caucus Campaign Committees in 1988 Ohio General Assembly Elections" (unpublished paper, Department of Political Science, Ohio State University, 1989).

19. Treyens, "Mr. Speaker," 9.

20. See Thomas H. Little, "The Role of the Minority Leadership in the Ohio Senate: Leadership to Majority Status" (unpublished paper, Department of Political Science, Ohio State University, 1987).

21. Flinn, "An Evaluation of Legislative Performance," 169.

22. Flinn, "The Ohio General Assembly," 272–74.

23. Wahlke et al., *The Legislative System*, 426; William A. Spratley, "An Analysis of General Assembly Voting on Ohio Constitutional Issues, 1941–1970," in Gargan and Coke, eds., *Political Behavior and Public Issues in Ohio*, 348–51.

24. Lance T. Leloup, "Policy, Party, and Voting in U. S. State Legislatures," *Legislative Studies Quarterly* 1 (1976): 213–30. Research on the nature of legislative party voting in Ohio is far from conclusive. But, see the suggestive findings and interpretations of Linda L. M. Bennett, *Symbolic State Politics: Education Funding in Ohio, 1970–1980* (New York: Peter Lang, 1983), 128–30; and Marie Hojnacki, "Voting Patterns in the Ohio House of Representatives: The Role of Party and Interpersonal Ties" (paper presented to the Southern Political Science Association, 1990, Atlanta).

25. Woodrow Wilson, *Congressional Government* (1885; reprint, New York: Meridian, 1956), 69.

26. See William J. Napier, "Committees in the Ohio House of Representatives: An Examination and Comparative Analysis" (Ph.D. diss., Ohio State University, 1982), 53–83. More generally, see Ronald D. Hedlund and Samuel C. Patterson, "The Electoral Antecedents of State Legislative Committee Assignments," *Legislative Studies Quarterly* 17 (November 1992): 539–59.

27. Napier, "Committees in the Ohio House of Representatives," 85–100.

28. On lobbying the Ohio legislature, see Barbara Bolt Lewis, "Ohio Lobbying" (Ph.D. diss., Ohio State University, 1992).

12. THE OHIO EXECUTIVE BRANCH

1. Thad L. Beyle, "Being Governor," in Carl E. Van Horn, ed., *The State of the States* (Washington: Congressional Quarterly Press, 1993), 98.

2. David Osborne, *Laboratories of Democracy* (Boston: Harvard Business School Press, 1988).

3. Beyle, "Being Governor," 101–6.

4. Larry Sabato, *Goodbye to Good-Time Charlie: The American Governorship Transformed* (Washington: Congressional Quarterly Press, 1983). On the topic of state governmental reform and reorganization, see James K. Conant, "In the Shadow of Wilson and Brownlow: Executive Branch Reorganization in the States, 1965 to 1987," *Public Administration Review* 48 (September/October 1988): 892–902; Keon S. Chi, "Trends in Executive Reorganization," *Journal of State Government* 65 (April/June 1992): 33–40; and Barry Bozeman and Michael Crow, "Organization Theory and State Government Structure: Are There Lessons Worth Learning?" *State Government* 58 (1986): 144–51.

5. Thad Beyle, "Governors," in Virginia Gray, Herbert Jacob, and Robert B. Albritton, eds., *Politics in the American States* (Glenview, Ill.: Scott, Foresman, 1990), 203–8.

6. Ibid., 207.

7. John H. Fenton, *Midwest Politics* (New York: Holt, Rinehart and Winston, 1966). On political developments in Ohio during the 1980s, see Lawrence Baum and Samuel C. Patterson, "Ohio: Party Change without Realignment," in Maureen Moakley, ed., *Party Realignment and State Politics* (Columbus: Ohio State University Press, 1992), 192–209. Among many examples, see Keith McKnight, "How Money Talks in Ohio," *Akron Beacon Journal*, December 27, 1992. Incidentally, even the state's Supreme Court elections are often interpreted in terms of the effects of changing court alignments on the interests of labor and business. See Mark Tatge and Jim Underwood, "Justice Andy Douglas—The Supreme Court's Supreme Pain," Cleveland *Plain Dealer*, October 25, 1992.

8. Conant, "In the Shadow of Wilson and Brownlow," 893. A prominent political scientist, Herbert Kaufman, has argued persuasively that throughout American history three values—executive leadership, neutral competence, and representation—have competed for dominance in politics and public administration. At the state level, governors, their offices, and their staffs are generally expected to maximize the value of executive leadership. Career service employees and the executive branch as an institution seek to maximize neutral competence. Legislators, as individuals and as members of party caucuses, and the legislature maximize representation. See Herbert Kaufman, "Emerging Conflicts in the Doctrines of Public Administration," *American Political Science Review* 50 (December 1956): 1057–73.

9. Andrew R. L. Cayton, *The Frontier Republic Ideology and Politics in the Ohio Country, 1780–1825* (Kent, Ohio: Kent State University Press, 1986), 77; George W. Knepper, *Ohio and Its People* (Kent, Ohio: Kent State University Press, 1989), 213.

10. The formal powers of governors are considered in detail in Beyle, "Governors," 215–30. In addition to Beyle, two primary sources on the office of governor and the relevance of formal powers to gubernatorial performance are Sabato, *Goodbye to Good-Time Charlie,* and Coleman B. Ransone, Jr., *The American Governorship* (Westport, Conn.: Greenwood Press, 1982). The National Governors' Association's composite index is assessed in appendix B of Gray, Jacob, and Albritton, eds., *Politics in the American States,* 568–74. All quoted material in the discussion of the formal powers of Ohio governors is from their appendix B.

11. Richard G. Sheridan, *Governing Ohio: Administration and Judiciary* (Cleveland: Federation for Community Planning, 1990), 134.

12. H. Edward Flentje, "Clarifying Purpose and Achieving Balance in Gubernatorial Administration" *The Journal of State Government* 62 (July/August 1989): 161–67.

13. William T. Gormley, Jr., "Accountability Battles in State Administration," in Van Horn, ed., *The State of the States,* 171–91. See also, Richard C. Elling, "Bureaucracy," in Gray, Jacob, and Albritton, eds., *Politics in the American States,* 287–329.

14. Interviews with a number of individuals knowledgeable about Ohio government and politics were conducted in late 1992 and early 1993. Since most of the individuals continue to be involved in the state's government and politics, they were assured that they would not be identified by name.

15. Thomas Suddes, "Ohio Government Detoured through Home State's Doors," *Plain Dealer,* December 29, 1985; Mary Beth Lane, "Conrad Shifted to New Position," ibid., January 9, 1993.

16. *Plain Dealer,* December 29, 1985; ibid., July 8, 1989.

17. Ibid., August 29, 1992.

18. *Beacon Journal,* October 31, 1992.

19. Robert D. Lee, "Developments in State Budgeting: Trends of Two Decades" *Public Administration Review* 51 (May/June 1991): 254–62; Sheridan, *Governing Ohio: Administration and Judiciary,* 135.

20. For a brief discussion of the Office of Budget and Management, see *Official Roster of Federal, State & County Officers & Departmental Information for 1991–1992* (Columbus: Ohio Secretary of State, 1991), 161; and Richard G. Sheridan, *State Budgeting in Ohio* (Columbus: Ohio Legislative Budget Office, 1978).

21. Wayne W. Hall, Jr., "Developments In State Administration and Management," in *The Book of the States: 1990–91 Edition* (Lexington, Ky.: Council of State Governments, 1990), 340–44.

22. Advisory Commission on Intergovernmental Relations, *The Question of State Government Capability* (Washington, D.C.: Government Printing Office, 1985), 177.

23. Sheridan, *Governing Ohio: Administration and Judiciary*, 112; James G. Coke, *Ohio's Urban Policy: A Non-Intervention Approach* (Washington, D.C.: Government Printing Office, 1980), 12.

24. See comments by Governor Richard Thornburg regarding the importance of strategic planning in "Panel on the Office of Governor: Problems and Possibilities," in Alan Rosenthal, ed., *The Governor and the Legislature: Eagleton's 1987 Symposium on the State of the States* (New Brunswick, N.J.: Eagleton Institute of Politics, 1988), 31.

25. These are the headings used in all of the plans. See Richard F. Celeste, *Toward a Working Ohio: A Strategic Plan for the Eighties and Beyond, Ohio's Natural and Physical Environments* (Columbus: Office of the Governor, June, 1985). For a very useful discussion of strategic planning in Ohio, see Barton Wechsler and Robert W. Backoff, "The Dynamics of Strategy in Public Organizations," *Journal of the American Planning Association* 53 (Winter 1987): 34–43.

26. The quoted material is from the November 1991 letter to the governor accompanying the report *Ohio's Best Bringing Out the Best in Ohio* (Columbus: Operations Improvement Task Force, 1991).

27. The quote is from *Securing the Future of Higher Education in Ohio* (Columbus: Ohio Board of Regents, 1992). The report was a response to recommendations by the Managing for the Future Task Force, "Managing For The Future: Challenges and Opportunities for Higher Education in Ohio," July 1992.

28. Among the amendments adopted in 1992 was one that changed Article 3, section 2, of the Ohio Constitution to limit persons holding the offices of lieutenant governor, secretary of state, attorney general, treasurer of state, and auditor of state to two successive four-year terms. Data on the number of employees were obtained from the Department of Administrative Services. Here, and throughout this chapter, the budgetary figures discussed are general revenue fund (GRF) data. An agency typically uses several different funds (general services fund, federal special revenue fund, state special revenue fund, etc.). Reliance on GRF data, therefore, underreports, in some instances, total agency spending. However, since GRF funds are subject to discretionary control by the governor and legislature, they provide an indication of state political priorities.

29. Knepper, *Ohio and Its People*, 403; Robert H. Snyder, "2,3,4,5 Defeat Is Judged Win for Opponent Celeste," *Plain Dealer*, November 5, 1975.

30. Joseph D. Rice, "Ferguson Wants Governorship Next Time," ibid., November 6, 1986. In 1993, Ferguson announced he would not seek reelection as auditor in 1994; Fisher said he would run for reelection as attorney general in 1994 rather than seek the state's top job; and Withrow was named treasurer of the United States by President Bill Clinton in 1994.

31. *An Assessment of Boards and Commissions Within the State of Ohio* (Columbus: Operations Improvement Task Force, 1992); Sheridan, *Governing Ohio: Administration and Judiciary*, 138.

32. U.S. Bureau of the Census, *Public Employment: 1991, Series GE-91-1* (Washington, D.C.: Government Printing Office, 1992).

33. For a discussion of the changes that shaped the context of Ohio politics throughout the 1980s, see John J. Gargan, "Urban Revitalization and Vitalization: Testing Ohio's State and Local Government Capacity," in William O. Reichert and Steven O. Ludd, eds., *Outlook on Ohio: Prospects and Priorities in Public Policy* (Palisades Park, N.J.: Commonwealth Books, 1983). For the effects of this "double bind" in other states, see Thad Beyle, ed., *Governors and Hard Times* (Washington, D.C.: Congressional Quarterly Press, 1992); and Marshall Kaplan and Sue O'Brien, *The Governors and the New Federalism* (Boulder, Colo.: Westview Press, 1991).

34. This is apparent in the remarks of governors at the Eagleton Institute's 1987 Symposium. See, for example, Governor James R. Thompson, "Keynote Address on the Governor," in Rosenthal, ed., *The Governor and the Legislature*, 5–16. Keon S. Chi and Dennis O. Grady, "Innovators in State Governments: Their Organizational and Professional Environment," in *The Book of the States: 1990–91 Edition* (Lexington, Ky.: The Council of State Governments, 1990), 382–404.

35. Steven D. Gold, "The Federal Role in State Fiscal Stress," *Publius* 22 (Summer 1992): 33–47.

36. The fiscal trends discussed in this section are based on data in the Legislative Budget Office report, "Update of the Forecast of Revenues and Human Services Expenditures for the 1991–1993 Biennium," March 19, 1992.

37. On the campaigning style of Governor Rhodes, see Abe S. Zaidan, " 'The Wonderful World' of Governor Rhodes," *The Reporter*, October 6, 1966, 44–46.

13. THE OHIO JUDICIARY

1. We appreciate Kathleen Barber's comments on an earlier draft of this chapter, James Leonard's assistance in our use of his study of the Ohio Supreme Court, and Roger Snell's providing us with copies of his articles about the Supreme Court.

2. Court Statistics Project, *State Court Caseload Statistics: Annual Report 1990* (Williamsburg, Va.: National Center for State Courts, 1992), 113, 140.

3. Adrienne Bosworth, "Why Everybody's Nice to Dick Metcalf," *Columbus Monthly*, November 1978, 58, 60. See also Sue Gorisek, "Probate Court: The Facts of Life . . . and Death," *Ohio Magazine*, March 1981, 70–72.

4. Frederic P. White, "The Cleveland Housing Court Act: New Answer to an Old Problem," *Cleveland State Law Review* 30 (1981): 41–56; Randall Edwards, "Here Comes the Environmental Judge," *Columbus Dispatch*, October 20, 1991.

5. *Ward v. Village of Monroeville*, 409 U.S. 57 (1972).

6. Arnold S. White, "Goodbye to Judge Roy Bean: A Study of Ohio's Mayor's Courts," *Ohio Bar* 54 (May 11, 1991): 877–84; Terry Holthaus, "Mayors' Courts Bring Bucks to Cities," Cleveland *Plain Dealer*, August 17, 1986.

7. On appellate court jurisdiction, see Alba L. Whiteside, *Ohio Appellate Practice* (Cleveland: Banks-Baldwin, 1991).

8. Court Statistics Project, *State Court Caseload Statistics: Annual Report 1990*, 77.

9. Charles W. Grau and Arlene Sheskin, "Ruling Out Delay: The Impact of Ohio's Rules of Superintendence," *Judicature* 66 (September–October 1982): 121.

10. Francis R. Aumann, "The Selection, Tenure, Retirement, and Compensation of Judges in Ohio," *University of Cincinnati Law Review* 5 (November 1931): 408–28: Hoyt Landon Warner, *Progressivism in Ohio 1897–1917* (Columbus: Ohio State University Press, 1964), 196, 252, 272–82. The term "semi-partisan" was applied to the Ohio system in Kathleen Barber, "Ohio Judicial Elections—Nonpartisan Premises with Partisan Results," *Ohio State Law Journal* 32 (1971): 762–89.

11. The decision was *Chisom v. Roemer*, 115 L. Ed. 2d 348 (1991). On Cincinnati redistricting after that decision, see John Hopkins, "Municipal Court Elections Restructured," *Cincinnati Enquirer*, July 18, 1992.

12. Howard L. Barkdull, "Analysis of Ohio Vote on Appointive Judiciary," *Journal of the American Judicature Society* 22 (February 1939): 197–98; Mary Grace Poidomani, "Merit Selection Doomed at Start," *Akron Beacon Journal*, November 8, 1987; John D. Felice and John C. Kilwein, "Strike One, Strike Two . . . : The History of and Prospect for Judicial Reform in Ohio," *Judicature* 75 (December–January 1992): 193–200.

13. Felice and Kilwein, "Strike One, Strike Two."

14. See, for instance, Mary Yost, "Brown's Departure Leaves Democrats in Lurch for '92," *Columbus Dispatch*, September 14, 1991.

15. Kathleen L. Barber, "Judicial Politics in Ohio," in Carl Lieberman, ed., *Government and Politics in Ohio* (Lanham, Md.: University Press of America, 1984), 89–133; idem, "Selection of Ohio Appellate Judges: A Case Study in Invisible Politics," in John J. Gargan and James G. Coke, eds., *Political Behavior and Public Issues in Ohio* (Kent, Ohio: Kent State University Press, 1972), 175–230; idem, "Ohio Judicial Elections"; Lawrence Baum, "The Electoral Fates of Incumbent Judges in the Ohio Court of Common Pleas," *Judicature* 66 (April 1983): 420–30. In the discussion that follows, data on the courts of appeals for the 1960–80 period are taken from the Barber articles; data on incumbent common pleas judges in 1962–80 are taken from Baum, "The Electoral Fate of Incumbent Judges."

16. These figures actually underestimate the impact of party strength, since the minority party is more likely to run a candidate when the majority-party candidate seems vulnerable.

17. Supreme Court elections prior to the 1980s are analyzed by Barber in "Ohio Judicial Elections," "Judicial Politics in Ohio," and "Selection of Ohio Appellate Judges." Ohio has had a long tradition of competitive elections to the Supreme Court. See Kermit L. Hall, "Progressive Reform and the Decline of Democratic Accountability: The Popular Election of State Supreme Court Judges, 1850–1920," *American Bar Foundation Research Journal* (Spring 1984): 354–65.

18. Barber, "Judicial Politics in Ohio," 117.

19. Barber, "Selection of Ohio Appellate Judges," 207–11; Phillip L. Dubois, *From Ballot to Bench: Judicial Elections and the Quest for Accountability* (Austin: University of Texas Press, 1980), 81–84.

20. Each candidate named Brown in each election is counted. The name was also common in nonjudicial contests. In 1966, for instance, Browns ran in both of the Supreme Court contests as well as in the races for lieutenant governor, secretary of state, and treasurer.

21. See G. Alan Tarr and Mary Cornelia Aldis Porter, *State Supreme Courts in State and Nation* (New Haven: Yale University Press, 1988), chap. 4.

22. Herb Cook, Jr., and Sharon Crook West, "Ohio Lawyers Ask: Is This Any Way to Run the Supreme Court? Frank Celebrezze Answers: Damn Right!" *Columbus Monthly,* July 1983, 51–56, 121–24; Rory O'Connor, "The Siege of Fort Celebrezze," *Cleveland Magazine,* September 1986, 81–83, 112–19.

23. For data on participation in appellate court elections in an earlier period, though measured in a slightly different way, see Barber, "Selection of Ohio Appellate Court Judges," 198–203.

24. Marie Hojnacki and Lawrence Baum, "Choosing Judicial Candidates: How Voters Explain Their Decisions," *Judicature* 75 (April–May 1992): 300–309; idem, " 'New-Style' Judicial Campaigns and the Voters: Economic Issues and Union Members in Ohio," *Western Political Quarterly* 45 (December 1992): 921–48; Lawrence Baum, "Explaining the Vote in Judicial Elections: The 1984 Ohio Supreme Court Elections," *Western Political Quarterly* 40 (June 1987): 361–71: idem, "Information and Party Voting in 'Semipartisan' Judicial Elections," *Political Behavior* 9 (1987): 62–74; idem, "Partisan Considerations and Voting Decisions in Nonpartisan Judicial Elections" (paper presented at the American Political Science Association, 1990, San Francisco).

25. Baum, "Partisan Considerations and Voting Decisions."

26. Idem, "Explaining the Vote"; Hojnacki and Baum, "Choosing Judicial Candidates."

27. Hojnacki and Baum, " 'New-Style' Judicial Campaigns."

28. Idem, "Choosing Judicial Candidates."

29. Baum, "Explaining the Vote"; Hojnacki and Baum, "Choosing Judicial Candidates."

30. Baum, "Electoral Fates of Incumbent Judges," 424–25; Barber, "Judicial Politics in Ohio," 93.

31. See *Newman v. Voinovich,* 789 F. Supp. 1410, 1413–14 (S.D. Ohio 1992).

32. Barber, "Judicial Politics in Ohio," 94; Dubois, *From Ballot to Bench,* 123–28. On the 1852-1968 period, see Barber, "Selection of Ohio Appellate Judges," 195. This record is striking because there were no appointments to the Supreme Court in the ten years from 1983 to 1992; appointees were vulnerable even in a time when campaigns were smaller in scale.

33. See Henry R. Glick and Craig F. Emmert, "Stability and Change: Characteristics of State Supreme Court Judges," *Judicature* 70 (August–September 1986): 107–12.

34. This discussion of the justices' backgrounds is based primarily on various editions of *Who's Who in American Law* and *Who's Who in America* (Chicago and Wilmette, Ill.: Marquis Who's Who). These sources were supplemented by "The Ohio Supreme Court Justices: A Biographical Sketch," *Ohio Northern University Law Review* 14 (1987): 561–63, and by newspaper articles. It should be noted that *Who's Who* entries often are incomplete and typically provide little information about political activities.

35. Court Statistics Project, *State Court Caseload Statistics 1990,* 77. On the selection of cases, see Ralph S. Locher , "A Supreme Court Justice's Perspective on Discretionary Appeals," *Ohio Northern University Law Review* 12 (1985): 301–5.

36. See James Leonard, "Ideology and Judicial Behavior: A Statistical Study of the Ohio Supreme Court: 1970, 1975, 1980, and 1985 Terms," *University of Cincinnati Law Review* 57 (1989): 974–77.

37. This figure and others concerning the court's decisions in 1990 and 1991 are based on the full set of cases that the court decided on the merits, whether with full opinions or through summary decisions.

38. This responsibility has been the source of some controversies and conflicts. One example is the court's supervision of the bar examination, particularly when it was charged that scores of a few favored applicants had been altered upward in 1986. See Michael L. Mahoney, "Bar Exam Controversies Continue to Test Top Court," *Plain Dealer*, January 28, 1991; and T. C. Brown, "5 Whose Scores Were Changed Lose Law Licenses," ibid., May 18, 1991.

39. Stuart S. Nagel, "Political Party Affiliation and Judges' Decisions," *American Political Science Review* 55 (1961): 844–50; Sheldon Goldman, "Voting Behavior on the United States Courts of Appeals Revisited," ibid. 69 (1975): 491–506: Dubois, *From Ballot to Bench*, chaps. 5–7; C. Neil Tate and Roger Handberg, "Time Binding and Theory Building in Personal Attribute Models of Supreme Court Voting Behavior, 1916–88," *American Journal of Political Science* 35 (May 1991): 460–80.

40. Tarr and Porter, *State Supreme Courts in State and Nation*, 127.

41. Robert E. Keeton, *Venturing to Do Justice: Reforming the Private Law* (Cambridge, Mass.: Harvard University Press, 1969).

42. Bradley C. Canon and Lawrence Baum, "Patterns of Adoption of Tort Law Innovations: An Application of Diffusion Theory to Judicial Doctrines," *American Political Science Review* 75 (December 1981): 975–87.

43. See Patricia C. Cecil, "The Role of the Ohio Supreme Court in Opening the Courtroom Doors to Tort Victims," *University of Cincinnati Law Review* 55 (Fall 1986): 477–500.

44. Frank D. Celebrezze, "Ohioans Gain Rights: The Supreme Court of Ohio," *Ohio Northern University Law Review* 9 (October 1982): 559–62. Another Democrat on the court lauded liberal doctrinal changes in Clifford F. Brown, "The Trend of Workers' Compensation in Ohio: Ohio Puts the Worker Back into Workers' Compensation," *Capital University Law Review* 13 (1984): 521–32.

45. Richard Greene, "The Hanging Judges of Business," *Forbes*, April 7, 1986, 62–64. The key decision was *Blankenship v. Cincinnati Milacron Chemicals, Inc.*, 433 N.E.2d 572 (Ohio 1982).

46. See Ronald K. L. Collins, Peter J. Galie, and John Kincaid, "State High Courts, State Constitutions, and Individual Rights Litigation Since 1980: A Judicial Survey," *Publius* 16 (Summer 1986): 141–61.

47. Leonard, "Ideology and Judicial Behavior," 964–73. The criteria for liberal and conservative decisions used by Leonard and in our analysis of 1990–91 decisions are those described in Stuart Nagel, "Political Party Affiliation and Judges' Decisions," *American Political Science Review* 55 (1961): 843–50. On the court's conservatism in civil liberties, see also Mary Cornelia Porter and G. Alan Tarr, "The New Judicial Federalism and the Ohio Supreme Court: Anatomy of a Failure," *Ohio State Law Journal* 45 (1984): 143–59. Also of interest is the finding that between 1981 and 1985 Ohio ranked low in both the number of laws challenged as unconstitutional in the state's Supreme Court

and the number and proportion of successful challenges. See Craig F. Emmert, "Judicial Review in State Supreme Courts: Opportunity and Activism" (paper presented at the Midwest Political Science Association, 1988, Chicago).

48. For the 1970–85 period, see Leonard, "Ideology and Judicial Behavior," 964–73.

49. In some significant cases, the three Democrats and Douglas have formed a majority for liberal doctrinal positions. See *Greeley v. Miami Valley Maintenance Contractors,* 551 N.E.2d 459 (Ohio 1990); *State, ex rel. Drum Service, v. Industrial Commission,* 556 N.E.2d 459 (Ohio 1990); and *Elek v. Huntington National Bank,* 573 N.E.2d 1056 (Ohio 1991).

50. Mark C. Miller, "Court-Legislative Relations: The Policy Role of the Courts in Three American Governmental Systems" (paper presented at the Midwest Political Science Association, 1992, Chicago), 9–13.

51. There has been considerable evidence of such responses in the legislative redistricting cases of the early 1990s. See, for instance, Edward Walsh, "Reagan-Appointed Judges Approve Illinois Redistricting Favoring GOP," *Washington Post,* November 8, 1991; Robert Suro, "Texas, in Redistricting Conflict, Seeks Delay in State Senate Vote," *New York Times,* February 14, 1992; and Vlae Kershner, "Top State Court OKs Redistricting—Demo Plea Fails," *San Francisco Chronicle,* January 28, 1992.

52. *State, ex rel. Rhodes, v. Brown,* 296 N.E.2d 538 (Ohio 1973); *State, ex rel. Carter, v. Celebrezze,* 410 N.E.2d 1249 (Ohio 1980); *State, ex. rel. Morrison, v. Franklin Board of Elections,* 410 N.E.2d 764 (Ohio 1980).

53. *Tschantz v. Ferguson,* 556 N.E.2d 655 (Ohio 1991).

54. *Voinovich v. Ferguson,* 586 N.E.2d 1020 (Ohio 1992); a Republican court of appeals judge sat in for Republican justice Wright and voted for the Republican plan. Later, the case did go to federal court, and a three-judge federal district court overturned the Republican plan by a 2-to-1 vote—with two Democrats in the majority and a Republican dissenting. On appeal, the U.S. Supreme Court issued a stay of that decision. It thereby allowed the Republican plan to go into effect, pending the court's own ruling on it. Ultimately, the court unanimously upheld the Republican plan. *Voinovich v. Quilter,* 118 L.Ed.2d 382 (1992), 122 L.Ed.2d 500 (1993). See Thomas Suddes and Jim Underwood, "Assembly Primary September 8," *Plain Dealer,* April 1, 1992; and Steve Hoffman, "Supreme Court to Hear Redistricting Debate," *Beacon Journal,* June 2, 1992. On redistricting litigation in the 1960s, see Kathleen Barber, "Partisan Values in Lower Courts: Reapportionment in Ohio and Michigan," *Case Western Reserve Law Review* 20 (February 1969): 401–21.

55. In *re Election of November 6, 1990 for the Office of Attorney General of Ohio,* 569 N.E.2d 447 (Ohio 1991).

56. The first case was *Brachman v. Limbach,* 556 N.E.2d 146 (Ohio 1990); see Michael L. Mahoney, "2 High-Court Judges in Knot Over Candidate's Tax Case," *Plain Dealer,* April 15, 1990. The second case was *State v. Conrad,* 552 N.E.2d 214 (Ohio 1990); see Mary Yost, "Democrats' Conrad Wins in High Court," *Columbus Dispatch,* March 22, 1990.

57. See Marie Hojnacki and Bill Swinford, "Interest Group Activity in the Courts, Legislature, and Executive Branch: Understanding the Participation Choice" (paper presented at the American Political Science Association, 1992, Chicago).

58. Mary Grace Poidomani, "Insurance Lobby Dug Deep for Moyer," *Beacon Journal,* June 14, 1987; Poidomani, "Separating the Judiciary From Big Money," ibid., June 15, 1987.

59. See "Ohio Supreme Court Contributions," *Columbus Dispatch*, February 9, 1992.

60. See Mary Grace Poidomani, "Moyer Grants Retrials to 5 Campaign Givers," *Beacon Journal*, March 4, 1987; Roger Snell, "AFL-CIO's Role in High Court Action Questioned," ibid., October 13, 1991; and *Episcopal Retirement Homes v. Ohio Department of Industrial Relations*, 582 N.E.2d 606 (Ohio 1991).

61. Roy A. Schotland, "Elective Judges' Campaign Financing: Are State Judges' Robes the Emperor's Clothes of American Democracy?" *Journal of Law and Politics* 2 (Spring 1985): 57–167; and Patrick M. McFadden, *Electing Justice: The Law and Ethics of Judicial Election Campaigns* (Chicago: American Judicature Society, 1990), 23–66.

62. Henry R. Glick and George W. Pruet, Jr., "Dissent in State Supreme Courts: Patterns and Correlates of Conflict," in Sheldon Goldman and Charles M. Lamb, eds., *Judicial Conflict and Consensus: Behavioral Studies of American Appellate Courts* (Lexington: University Press of Kentucky, 1986), 202–3. For the 1850–1920 period, see Hall, "Progressive Reform," 367; figures for some recent years are in Tarr and Porter, *State Supreme Courts in State and Nation*, 139; and Leonard, "Ideology and Judicial Behavior," 979.

63. Other Democrats also may have been involved in the conflict. See Justice Clifford Brown's response to a speech by Andy Douglas in "Re: Ohio Supreme Court," *Plain Dealer*, March 17, 1985.

64. *Blankenship v. Cincinnati Milacron*, at 617; *State v. Mowery*, 438 N.E.2d 897, 900 (Ohio 1982).

65. Lee Leonard, "Slugging it Out at the Ohio Supreme Court," *Columbus Monthly*, November 1985, 147. See also Mary Grace Poidomani, "The Little War in Ohio's Top Court," *Beacon Journal*, January 5, 1986.

66. Mary Anne Sharkey, "Discipline Ruling Angers Celebrezze," *Plain Dealer*, July 4, 1985.

67. Ken Myers, "Feud Erupts Among Ohio Justices," *National Law Journal*, July 29, 1985.

68. "Battling Supremes' Show Could Harm the Bystanders," *Dayton Daily News*, July 21, 1985. After the 1991 scuffle between Andy Douglas and Craig Wright, discussed below, the *Daily News* published an editorial cartoon in which two unidentified justices were depicted as professional wrestlers.

69. Mary Anne Sharkey, "Where Is New, Improved Court Headed?" *Plain Dealer*, April 26, 1987.

70. Roger Snell, "No Order in the Court," *Beacon Journal*, November 7, 1991. An earlier episode involving alleged leaks is described in Michael L. Mahoney, "Ohio High Court Blasts Leaks, Drops Action Against Douglas," *Plain Dealer*, June 20, 1990.

71. Mark Tatge and Jim Underwood, "The Supreme Court's Supreme Pain," *Plain Dealer*, October 25, 1992; Roger Snell, "Candidates for Court Won't Get There Alone," *Beacon Journal*, January 2, 1992.

72. Roger Snell, "Moyer Denies Colleague's Charge," *Beacon Journal*, January 3, 1992; idem, "Disciplinary Counsel Needed to Settle Fights, Justice Says," ibid., June 18, 1992; idem, "2nd Ohio High Court Justice Says She's Target of Chief," ibid., September 27, 1992; Tatge and Underwood, "The Supreme Court's Supreme Pain."

73. Mary Yost, "Ohio's Justices Weigh Campaign Contributions," *Columbus Dispatch*, February 9, 1992.

74. Tarr and Porter, *State Supreme Courts in State and Nation*, 139–43.

75. See, respectively, Preble Stolz, *Judging Judges: The Investigation of Rose Bird and the California Supreme Court* (New York: Free Press, 1981); Michael W. Bowers, "Personality and Judicial Politics in Nevada," *State Constitutional Commentaries and Notes* 2 (Summer 1991): 7–10; Paul Wenske, "Dissension Rocks Missouri Justices," *National Law Journal,* May 27, 1985; Jim Ludwick, "Volleys Fly in the Battle Over Montana's High Court," ibid., May 18, 1992; and Joseph A Slobodzian, "Infighting Rips Pa. High Court," ibid., December 14, 1992.

76. See Edward N. Beiser, "The Rhode Island Supreme Court: A Well-Integrated Political System," *Law and Society Review* 8 (1974): 167–86.

77. On the experience in Missouri, see Richard A. Watson and Rondal G. Downing, *The Politics of the Bench and the Bar: Judicial Selection Under the Missouri Nonpartisan Court System* (New York: John Wiley, 1969).

14. INTEREST GROUPS IN OHIO POLITICS

1. E. E. Schattschneider, *The Semi-Sovereign People* (Hinsdale, Ill.: The Dryden Press, 1979), 34.

2. Burdett A. Loomis and Allan J. Cigler, "The Changing Nature of Interest Group Politics," in Allan J. Cigler and Burdett A. Loomis, eds., *Interest Group Politics,* 2d ed. (Washington, D.C.: Congressional Quarterly Press, 1986), 1.

3. *Power in the States: The Changing Face of Politics Across America* (Washington, D.C.: Congressional Quarterly Press, 1984), 74.

4. See Lester Milbrath, *The Washington Lobbyists* (Chicago: Rand McNally, 1963); David B. Truman, *The Government Process,* 2d ed. (New York: Alfred A. Knopf, 1971); and Alan Rosenthal, *The Third House: Lobbyists and Lobbying in the States* (Washington, D.C.: Congressional Quarterly Press, 1992).

5. Cynthia Opheim, "Explaining the Difference in State Lobbying Regulation" *Western Political Quarterly* 44 (June 1991): 405–18.

6. *Dayton Daily News,* September 16, 1992.

7. Ibid., March 17, 1987; ibid., February 28, 1986.

8. References in this chapter to statutory regulations, definitions, and other requirements of Ohio law pertaining to lobbying are from the *Ohio Lobbying Handbook,* published annually by the Joint Committee in Agency Rule Review of the Ohio General Assembly.

9. *Dayton Daily News,* March 18, 1987.

10. Ibid.

11. Several articles and editorials on the "Jones affair" appeared in the *Daily News,* October–January 1993–94.

12. Official Report of Campaign Committee Contributions filed by Representative Vernal Riffe and Senator Stanley Arnoff, July 1, 1992, Office of the Secretary of State, Columbus.

13. Organizations Represented by Legislative Agents and Executive Agent Lobbyists, Joint Committee on Agency Rule Review, Ohio General Assembly, July 28, 1992, Office of the Joint Committee on Agency Rule Review, Columbus.

14. See Charles Funderburk, "Effectiveness in the Ohio Legislature: The Case of Representative C. J. McLin, Jr.," *Miami Valley History* 4 (1992): 24–38.

15. OHIO ELECTIONS AND POLITICAL PARTIES IN THE 1990S

1. For an excellent overview of Ohio electoral change, see Lawrence Baum and Samuel C. Patterson, "Ohio: Party Change without Realignment," in Maureen Moakley, ed., *Party Realignment and State Politics* (Columbus: Ohio State University Press, 1992).

2. Mike DeWine, interviewed by David E. Sturrock, October 15, 1992, Canton. The *Akron Beacon Journal*'s samplings of October 26–31 showed Clinton ahead of Bush 42 percent to 36 percent, with 18 percent for Perot. The *Columbus Dispatch*'s unorthodox but reliable mail poll, taken October 26–29, placed the candidates at 41 percent, 40 percent, and 19 percent, respectively.

3. This description is drawn from the Ohio Poll of October 28–November 1, which was conducted by the University of Cincinnati and the *Cincinnati Post*. The correlation coefficient was 0.97, which indicates that relative Democratic strength in Ohio's eighty-eight counties was nearly identical in 1988 and 1992, even though Bill Clinton actually trailed Michael Dukakis by four percentage points in the state. Jessica Haller and Florencio Yuzon, "Ohio Democratic Voting Patterns Since 1960" (unpublished paper, 1992, Department of Political Science, Case Western Reserve University).

4. Michael Barone and Grant Ujifusa, *The Almanac of American Politics 1994* (Washington: National Journal, 1993), 986. There is a strong county-level statistical relationship between Perot's support and the 1988–92 decline in Bush's strength. Perot ran best in suburban areas, northeast Ohio (outside of Cuyahoga County), and portions of rural southeast, northern, and western Ohio. His weakest showings came in counties that supported Michael Dukakis in 1988, urban areas generally, and in southern Ohio. Also the Ohio Poll conducted October 28–November 1 indicated that the demographic profile of likely Perot voters more closely resembled Bush's supporters than Clinton's.

5. *Ohio Election Statistics* 1989–90 (Columbus: Ohio Secretary of State, 1991).

6. Alan Ehrenhalt , *The United States of Ambition* (New York: Times Books, 1991).

7. *Page's Ohio Revised Code Annotated,* (Cincinnati: Anderson, 1988), Section 3517.01.

8. In most cases the same individual serves as chairman of both the central and executive committees. When the offices are held separately, the term "county chairman" is usually applied to the head of the executive committee.

9. Sitting judges and judicial candidates are excluded. See *Ohio Revised Code,* Section 3513.11.

10. The most recent party to join the Democrats and Republicans on the ballot in Ohio was the American Independent party, which qualified for intermediate status because George Wallace's elector slate received 12 percent in 1968. The party conducted primaries for state, congressional, and some county offices in 1970 and 1972 but lost its ballot status when it failed to meet even the minor party threshold of 5 percent in either the 1970 gubernatorial or 1972 presidential contests.

11. Technically, the lists are submitted by the state central committee chairmen of "the two political parties having the highest total vote cast at the previous election for the office of governor." *Ohio Revised Code*, Section 3517.14.

12. Janet Jordan, *Know Your Ohio Government* (Columbus: League of Women Voters Ohio Educational Fund, 1987), 99–100. See Walter Dean Burnham, *Critical Elections and the Mainsprings of American Politics* (New York: Norton, 1970), chap. 4; and Joel H. Silbey, *The American Political Nation, 1838–1893* (Stanford, Calif.: Stanford University Press, 1991).

13. *Williams v. Rhodes*, 393 U.S. 23 (1968).

14. See Paul Allen Beck and Frank J. Sorauf, *Party Politics in America* (New York: Harper Collins, 1992), 41–42, 308–9. An important exception to the rule of two-party domination exists in Cincinnati, where municipal elections have for many years featured three-way races between Republicans, Democrats, and the Cincinnati Charter Committee. The Charterites, whose roots trace back to the Progressive movement, were greatly advantaged by the use of proportional representation for council elections from 1925 to 1957; their strength has declined since the city switched to at-large elections. See Ralph A. Straetz, *PR Politics in Cincinnati* (New York: New York University Press, 1958); and Kenneth E. Gray, *A Report on Politics in Cincinnati* (Cambridge, Mass.: MIT\Harvard Joint Center for Urban Studies, 1959).

15. George Knepper, *Ohio and Its People* (Kent, Ohio: Kent State University Press, 1989), 333–40. Most of the information presented here about party endorsing and patronage activity comes from interviews conducted by David E. Sturrock in March 1993 with David Duffy, political director of the Ohio Democratic Party; Jeffrey Hastings, executive director of the Cuyahoga County Republican Party; David Payne, political director of the Ohio Republican Party; and Michael Thomas, executive director of the Cuyahoga County Democratic Party.

16. Robert T. Bennett, interviewed by Dick Kimmins, February 1993, Columbus; Robert Taft, interviewed by Dick Kimmins, February 1993, Columbus.

17. The importance Ohio party leaders attach to control of the redistricting process cannot be overemphasized. For example, consider the case of Earl T. Barnes, Ohio Republican chairman from 1977 to 1982, as he sat in his Cincinnati office on the morning of November 8, 1978. The day before, James A. Rhodes had won a record fourth term as governor by defeating Democrat Richard F. Celeste by a scant 48,000 votes (or less than 2 percent). A caller would have thought that Barnes would be happy. In fact, Barnes was inconsolate, near tears. "Goddamnit, oh, just Goddamnit. We lost it again," he said over and over. The party got to stay in the governor's office for four more years, Barnes knew, but once again was relegated to the political outhouse for another decade, since Democrats had won the auditor's and secretary of state's offices and with them control of the Apportionment Board through 1990. Earl T. Barnes, telephone interview by Dick Kimmins, November 8, 1978.

18. The parties' demise as franchise brokers has also diminished the ability of county chairmen to serve on a full-time basis. Until the 1980s, it was routine (and perfectly legal) for chairmen to use deputy registrar fees for personal use. While many are still able to underwrite their party service by drawing part-time salaries as members of county boards of election, most must continue their previous nonpolitical careers. As a result, about a dozen county committees in each party now rely on full-time paid staff to conduct the party's day-to-day operations.

19. The figures used here were compiled from official party campaign finance reports by the University of Akron's Ray C. Bliss Institute of Applied Politics. They include all

private and public funds raised by party committees in 1990 and those carried over from 1989. (Parties usually build up odd-year surpluses for use during the even-year campaign season.) Transfers between state and county parties can take different forms. For example, up to one half of the funds raised by the state Republican party in a given county will be disbursed to that county's GOP organization if it participates in state party programs. In other cases (especially in the Democratic party), county committees reimburse the state party for such services as printing and mailings.

20. David R. Mayhew, *Placing Parties in American Politics* (Princeton, N.J.: Princeton University Press, 1986). Mayhew's other traditional party organization states are Connecticut, Delaware, Illinois, Indiana, Kentucky, Maryland, Missouri, New Jersey, New York, Pennsylvania, Rhode Island, and West Virginia. James L. Gibson, "Whither the Local Parties?" *American Journal of Political Science* 29 (February 1985): 139–60.

21. The proposed chemical label law, officially designated Issue 5, qualified for the ballot after Citizen Action, a consumer and environmental group, gathered 352,000 petition signatures. The measure called for the labeling of products containing chemicals known or suspected to cause disease or birth defects and for firms whose operations emitted dangerous levels of such chemicals to notify those living nearby. Its opponents, a well-financed coalition of business, labor, and farm organizations, succeeded in tagging the proposal as anti-jobs, and it was defeated by a 78-to-22-percent margin. John F. Hagan, "Voters Incinerate Chemical Label Law," *Plain Dealer,* November 4, 1992.

❖

Bibliographical Essay

❖

JOHN J. GARGAN & ALEXANDER P. LAMIS

❖ The literature devoted exclusively to Ohio politics and government is quite limited. No comprehensive survey of the state's political system exists, and, in fact, this gap stimulated the production of the present volume.

There are, however, several multiauthored volumes that deal with selected aspects of Ohio's political system. *Government and Politics in Ohio* (Lanham, Md.: University Press of America, 1984), edited by Carl Lieberman of the University of Akron, reprints articles and book chapters previously published and also contains original chapters on the Ohio legislature and judiciary plus various aspects of local politics.

Two other edited books approach state politics from a primarily public-policy perspective. *Outlook on Ohio: Prospects and Priorities in Public Policy,* edited by William O. Reichert and Steven O. Ludd of Bowling Green State University (Palisades Park, N.J.: Commonwealth Books, 1983), contains chapters on sociocultural groups in Ohio as well as the dynamics of policymaking in areas as diverse as economic development, urban revitalization, land use, and prison construction. *Political Behavior and Public Issues in Ohio,* edited by John J. Gargan and James G. Coke of Kent State University (Kent, Ohio: Kent State University Press, 1972), deals with a potpourri of institutional and policy subjects: taxation and finance, legislative performance, judicial selection, public higher education, state policy toward urban areas, and constitutional revision. The forty-page introductory essay, entitled "An Overview of the Ohio Political System," still provides a serviceable starting point for examining politics in the Buckeye State.

Some of the most insightful comments on Ohio politics are contained in books in which Ohio is one of several states analyzed. The classic work in this tradition is John Fenton's chapter on Ohio in his seminal work *Midwest Politics* (New York: Holt, Rinehart and Winston, 1966). Fenton characterized politics in six key Midwestern states as either "issue-oriented" (Michigan, Wisconsin, and Minnesota) or "job-oriented" (Ohio, Indiana, and Illinois). Fenton's Ohio chapter, entitled "Issueless Politics in Ohio," zeroed in on what he viewed as a paradox: "Why did upper-income people in Ohio seemingly vote in terms of their economic self-interest, while low-income people failed to associate their economic problems with their votes?" (150). He found that the explanation lies in the legacy of potent historical events mixed with persistent conservative cultural patterns re-inforced by a pervasive lack of information salient to the working man or woman. The ongoing influence of Fenton's Ohio chapter is reflected in its all-but-universal citation in contemporary references to the state's politics.

Another widely cited chapter-length treatment of Ohio politics is found in the work of Neal R. Peirce, a distinguished national political journalist. Over twenty years ago, Peirce published the first volume in a series covering the politics of the American states, *The Megastates of America: People, Politics, and Power in the Ten Great States* (New York: W. W. Norton, 1972). The Ohio chapter, subtitled "The Middle-Class Society," portrays what Peirce terms the state's "neglectful" government from Frank J. Lausche to James A. Rhodes, profiles dominant political figures, and takes the reader on a tour of Ohio's major cities. Peirce also offers insightful summaries of the many changes that have occurred as Ohio's economy was transformed from one dominated by heavy manufacturing to one increasingly dependent on the service sector. Peirce and coauthor John Keefe expanded and updated the Ohio chapter in one of the regional volumes in the fifty-state series: *The Great Lakes States of America: People, Politics, and Power in the Five Great Lakes States* (New York: W. W. Norton, 1980). Four years later, Peirce along with another coauthor, Jerry Hagstrom, published a shorter update of this fine Ohio chapter in *The Book of America: Inside 50 States Today* (New York: Warner Books, 1984).

Two specialized book chapters deserve note. Contemporary developments in Ohio electoral politics are covered cogently in Lawrence Baum and Samuel C. Patterson, "Ohio: Party Change without Realignment," in Maureen Moakley, ed., *Party Realignment and State Politics* (Columbus: Ohio State University Press, 1992). Interest-group politics is treated in Fredric N. Bolotin, "Ohio: A Plethora of Pluralism," in Ronald J. Hrebenar and Clive S. Thomas, eds., *Interest Group Politics in the Midwestern States* (Ames: Iowa State University Press, 1993).

All but indispensable for those seeking detailed descriptions of the structures and processes of Ohio state government are two monographs written by Richard G. Sheridan, the founding director of the Ohio Legislative Budget Office and currently governmental affairs director of the Federation for Community Planning in Cleveland: *Governing Ohio: The State Legislature* (1989) and *Governing Ohio: Administration and Judiciary* (1990); both volumes were published by the Federation for Community Planning and are available through their offices at Suite 300, 614 Superior Avenue NW, Cleveland, Ohio, 44113-1306. Sheridan has also written extensively on state budgeting, welfare policy, and economic development.

Ohio government and politics ought not to be studied in isolation from developments in other states in the American federal system. Therefore, a comparative perspective is quite valuable. A fine source for insight into Ohio's comparative status is Virginia Gray, Herbert Jacob, and Robert B. Albritton, eds., *Politics in the American States: A Comparative Analysis*, 5th ed. (Glenview, Ill.: Scott, Foresman/Little Brown, 1990). Another useful comparative analysis is Daniel J. Elazar's *American Federalism: A View from the States*, 3d ed. (New York: Harper and Row, 1984), which is especially elucidating on the slippery topic of state political culture.

Comparison across time is just as vital as comparison across the federal system. Thus, full appreciation of the state's contemporary politics is enhanced by a thorough grounding in Ohio history. There is no better single treatment of Ohio history than George W. Knepper's excellent *Ohio and Its People* (Kent, Ohio: Kent State University Press, 1989), the indispensable starting place for exploring the state's rich past.

This bibliographic essay has focused almost exclusively on books or book chapters concerning Ohio politics. There are, however, many other sources available to researchers, including articles in scholarly journals, Ph.D. dissertations, and the impressive collections of the Ohio Historical Society. A number of these are cited in the notes to this book's fifteen chapters, making the note section a good starting place for further research.

Finally, to keep up with the daily give-and-take of Ohio political life, regular perusal of the state's seven major metropolitan newspapers is essential: *Akron Beacon Journal, Cincinnati Enquirer,* Cleveland *Plain Dealer, Columbus Dispatch, Dayton Daily News,* Toledo *Blade,* and Youngstown *Vindicator.* And, of course, complete coverage requires turning also to Ohio's many other fine newspapers published in the smaller cities and towns.

❖

Contributors

❖

ROBERT W. ADAMS is associate professor of political science and associate director of the Center for Urban and Public Affairs at Wright State University. He holds a B.A. and M.A. from Syracuse University and a Ph.D. from Ohio State University. A two-term chairman of Wright State University's Department of Political Science, he has written on Ohio's congressional redistricting as well as on urban education in the Buckeye State. Before joining the Wright State University faculty in 1965, he was an instructor at Ohio Wesleyan University and Miami University of Ohio.

LAWRENCE BAUM is professor of political science at Ohio State University. He holds a B.A. from San Francisco State College and an M.A. and Ph.D. from the University of Wisconsin. He is the author of *The Supreme Court* (1992) and *American Courts: Process and Policy* (1994) and has written several dozen articles and book chapters in the field of judicial politics, examining, among other topics, the U.S. Supreme Court, federal appeals courts, and state courts.

MIKE CURTIN is assistant managing editor for public affairs at the *Columbus Dispatch* and has been the *Dispatch*'s chief politics writer since 1985. He received a B.A. in journalism from Ohio State University in 1973 and joined the *Dispatch* that year as a general assignments reporter. He later covered Columbus city hall, Franklin County government, the Ohio legislature, and the state political scene generally. He has supervised the

Dispatch's Statehouse coverage since 1985, when he became head of the paper's public affairs section. He also directs the *Dispatch Poll.*

TOM DIEMER is a correspondent in the Washington bureau of the Cleveland *Plain Dealer*, covering Congress and national politics. A graduate of Ohio State University with a B.A. in history, he began his career in journalism by organizing the 1968 presidential vote count in New York State for CBS News; the following year he went to work for the New York bureau of the Associated Press. In 1978 he joined the *Plain Dealer* as a reporter and served as the paper's Columbus bureau chief for several years before taking his current Washington assignment in 1985.

CHARLES FUNDERBURK is professor of political science at Wright State University. He holds a B.A. and M.A. from the University of Florida and a Ph.D. from the University of Iowa. He is the author or coauthor of three books: *Presidents and Politics: The Limits of Power* (1982); *Political Ideologies: Left, Center, Rights* (1994, with Robert G. Thobaben); and *Issues in American Political Life: Money, Violence and Biology* (with Robert G. Thobaben and Donna M. Schlagheck). His articles include a study of C. J. McLin, Jr., the prominent black Ohio state legislator from Dayton. Before joining the Wright State University faculty in 1971, he was an instructor at Florida Atlantic University.

JOHN J. GARGAN is professor of political science at Kent State University. He holds a B.A., M.A., and Ph.D. from Syracuse University. The coeditor (with James G. Coke) of *Political Behavior and Public Issues in Ohio* (1972), he is the author or coauthor of several monographs and numerous articles and book chapters in the fields of public administration and public policy. Before joining the Kent State University faculty in 1967, he was a budget analyst for the New York State Legislature and an instructor at Union College.

JOHN C. GREEN is director of the Ray C. Bliss Institute of Applied Politics at the University of Akron and associate professor of political science at the university. He holds a B.A. in economics from the University of Colorado and a Ph.D. in political science from Cornell University. A specialist in political parties and interest groups, he has written extensively on the political activities of evangelical Christians and on other topics in the field of religion and politics. He is the editor of the recently published

Politics, Professionalism, and Power: Modern Party Development and the Legacy of Ray C. Bliss (1994) and coeditor of three other books, including *The Bible and the Ballot Box: Religion and Politics in the 1988 Election* (1991, with James L. Guth).

MARK KEMPER is a doctoral candidate in Department of Political Science at Ohio State University. He holds a B.A. in political science from Northern Illinois University. His specialization in graduate school is in the field of judicial politics.

DICK KIMMINS is Statehouse bureau chief for the *Cincinnati Enquirer.* He earned a B.A. in journalism from the University of Kentucky. Before coming to Columbus in 1975 as a Statehouse reporter for United Press International, he was a Statehouse reporter for UPI in Frankfort, Kentucky. From 1978 to 1984, he was a Statehouse reporter for the Scripps-Howard chain's Ohio newspapers—the *Cincinnati Post,* the *Cleveland Press,* and the *Columbus Citizen-Journal.* Before taking his present position, he was a senior reporter for *Business First* in Columbus from 1984 to 1987.

GEORGE W. KNEPPER is distinguished professor of history emeritus and university historian at the University of Akron. Following three years of service in the U.S. Navy during World War II, he completed his undergraduate degree in history at the University of Akron and later received an M.A. and Ph.D. in history from the University of Michigan. A faculty member of the University of Akron since 1954 and a former Fulbright Scholar at the University of London, he is the author of seven books and numerous articles dealing with aspects of Ohio. One of his recent books, *Ohio and Its People* (1989), is the first comprehensive history of the state written in this generation. His book *Akron: City at the Summit* was judged the best book on Ohio local history in 1982. He has served as president and trustee of the Ohio Historical Society, the Ohio Academy of History, and the Summit County Historical Society.

ALEXANDER P. LAMIS is associate professor of political science at Case Western Reserve University. He holds a B.A. in history from the College of Charleston, an M.A. and Ph.D. in political science from Vanderbilt University, and a J.D. from the University of Maryland Law School. A specialist on elections and political parties, he is the author of *The*

Two Party South (1990) and several articles and book chapters. Before joining the faculty of Case Western Reserve University in 1988, he taught at the University of North Florida and the University of Mississippi and worked as a research assistant at the Brookings Institution in Washington.

LEE LEONARD is a Statehouse reporter and columnist for the Columbus *Dispatch*. Before joining the *Dispatch* in late 1990, he was the manager of the Columbus Statehouse bureau of United Press International from 1969 to 1990. A graduate of Cornell University, he began his journalism career with UPI in 1962 in Boise, Idaho, and spent six years in Harrisburg, Pennsylvania, covering state government for the wire service before moving to Columbus. He was voted one of UPI's most respected bylines in a national survey of subscribing editors and is known to his Statehouse colleagues as the dean of Ohio political writers.

HUGH C. McDIARMID is a political columnist and former Lansing bureau chief for the *Detroit Free Press*. A graduate of Princeton University with an A.B. in politics, he was a reporter and editor at the Dayton *Journal Herald* from 1960 through 1975, with the exception of a two-year stint at the Washington *Post* in the late 1960s. He covered politics in Columbus for the *Journal Herald* from 1970 to 1975.

MICHAEL MARGOLIS is professor of political science and head of the Department of Political Science at the University of Cincinnati. He holds an A.B. from Oberlin College and an M.A. and Ph.D. from the University of Michigan. He is the author of *Viable Democracy* (1979) and coauthor of *Manipulating Public Opinion: Essays on Public Opinion as a Dependent Variable* (1989, with Gary A. Mauser) and has published a score of articles and book chapters, including several on political party organization. He joined the University of Pittsburgh faculty in 1967 as an instructor and reached the rank of professor in 1985, five years before leaving Pittsburgh to take his present position at the University of Cincinnati.

TIM MILLER is Statehouse bureau chief of the *Dayton Daily News*. After earning a B.A. at Ohio University, he began his journalism career at the *Newark Advocate*, where he was assistant managing editor, city editor, and chief political reporter. He next worked for ten years in Columbus for United Press International as a Statehouse reporter, Columbus bureau chief, and state editor, leaving UPI in 1985 to take his current position with the *Daily News*. In 1992 he became the first journalist to receive the Distinguished Alumnus Award from Ohio University's Department of Political Science.

SAMUEL C. PATTERSON is professor of political science at Ohio State University. He holds a B.A. from the University of South Dakota and an M.S. and Ph.D. from the University of Wisconsin. A former editor of the *American Political Science Review*, he is the author or editor of many books, including *The Legislative Process in the United States* (1986, with Malcolm E. Jewell), *Comparing Legislatures* (1979, with Gerhard Loewenberg), *American Legislative Behavior* (ed., 1968), *Midwest Legislative Politics* (ed., 1968), *Comparative Legislative Behavior: Frontiers of Research* (1972, edited with John C. Wahlke), *Handbook of Legislative Research* (1985, edited with Gerhard Loewenberg and Malcolm E. Jewell), and *Political Leadership in Democratic Societies* (1992, edited with Anthony Mugham)—plus scores of articles and book chapters. Before joining the Ohio State University faculty in 1986, he was a faculty member at the University of Iowa for twenty-five years, rising from assistant professor to Roy J. Carver Distinguished Professor.

MARY ANNE SHARKEY is the politics editor of the Cleveland *Plain Dealer*. After graduating from the University of Dayton in 1974 with a B.A. in English, she worked as a reporter for the Dayton *Journal Herald*, becoming the paper's Columbus bureau chief from 1978 to 1982. In 1983 she joined the *Plain Dealer* as a reporter in its Columbus bureau and served as the paper's Columbus bureau chief from 1984 to 1988. She moved to Cleveland to become director of the *Plain Dealer*'s editorial page from 1989 to 1990 after having served as deputy editorial page director briefly during the previous year. Before being named politics editor, she was the *Plain Dealer*'s assistant managing editor for metropolitan news from 1991 to 1992.

DAVID E. STURROCK is assistant professor of political science at the State University of New York at Brockport. He holds a B.S. and M.A. from San Jose State University and a Ph.D. from the University of California at Riverside. A specialist in political parties and comparative state politics, he has been a visiting assistant professor at Wittenberg University, the University of Georgia, Central College, and Case Western Reserve University, the latter during the 1992–93 academic year.

THOMAS SUDDES is the chief state legislative correspondent of the Cleveland *Plain Dealer*. A graduate of Ohio State University with a B.A. in journalism and a former editor of the *Ohio State Lantern*, he worked as a temporary editorial writer for the *Chicago Sun-Times* and *Des Moines Register and Tribune* in 1976 and 1977 and then became editorial page editor of *Foster's Daily Democrat* in Dover, New Hampshire, in 1978 and 1979. From 1979 to 1982 he was an editorial writer and editor at the Jackson, Mississippi, *Clarion-Ledger*. He joined the *Plain Dealer* in 1982, moving to the paper's Columbus bureau the following year. He was chief of the Columbus bureau in 1989 and 1990.

BRIAN T. USHER is president of Brian Usher Associates, a Columbus public relations firm. A graduate of Ball State University with a B.S. in journalism and American history, he earned an M.S. in journalism at Northwestern University. He was a reporter for the Dayton *Journal Herald* from 1969 to 1972 and a Statehouse correspondent for the Cleveland *Plain Dealer* from 1972 until 1975, when he joined the *Akron Beacon Journal*. He was the *Beacon Journal's* Columbus bureau chief from 1977 to 1981, the paper's chief politics writer from 1981 to 1983, and a national correspondent in the Knight Ridder Washington bureau from 1983 to 1984. He became press secretary to Governor Richard F. Celeste in 1984 and served until 1987, when he joined Paul Werth Associates in Columbus as director of media relations. He became director of communications for Columbia Gas Distribution Companies in Columbus in 1991 before opening his own business in 1992. In February 1993 he began *The Ohioan,* a lively biweekly publication devoted to covering Ohio state politics.

SHARON CROOK WEST is associate professor of journalism at Ohio State University. She holds a B.S. in education and an M.A. in journalism, both from Ohio State University. Before entering university teaching in 1982, she was Statehouse bureau chief for the Horvitz chain of newspapers from 1980 to 1982. She worked as a reporter for the *Mansfield News-Journal* from 1977 to 1980 and for the *Ashland Times-Gazette* from 1974 to 1977. She taught American literature and composition at Tippecanoe High School in Tipp City from 1970 to 1973.

RICHARD G. ZIMMERMAN is a Washington writer. He was the former senior national correspondent for the Cleveland *Plain Dealer* from 1978 to 1985 and was the *Plain Dealer*'s Washington bureau chief from 1972 to 1977. A graduate of Wittenberg University, he holds an M.A. from American University's School of Government and Public Administration. He was Statehouse correspondent in Columbus for the Horvitz chain of Ohio newspapers from 1962 to 1964, state legislative reporter for the Dayton *Journal Herald* from 1964 to 1967, and Statehouse bureau chief for the *Plain Dealer* from 1967 to 1971.

Index

Nursing homes, 113, 121, 148, 161
Nye, George D., 32

Oakar, Mary Rose, 212, 223; Hoke vs.,
171, 224, 228; House Bank fiasco and,
220; nominations of, 208, 335
Ocasek, Oliver: on bond proposals, 107;
J. W. Brown and, 104; Medicaid issue
and, 113–14; Meshel and, 130; on real
estate tax proposal, 109, 110; Senate
presidency of, 126
Occupation-related state boards, 274–75
Office of Appalachia, 180
Office of Budget and Management, 147,
268, 269, 270
Office of the Governor, 266–67
Office of the Legislative Inspector
General, 314, 317
O'Grady, Eugene P., 94, 95, 102, 140
Ohio and Its People (Knepper), ix, 381
Ohioans for Right to Work, 48
Ohioans for the Preservation of Honest
Elections, 121
Ohio Bar Association, 286, 294, 308
Ohio Bond Commission (proposed),
73–74, 75, 88
Ohio Chamber of Commerce, 9,
16, 48, 165
Ohio Citizen Action, 322
Ohio Clock, 197
Ohio Conference of Teamsters, 102
Ohio Council of Churches, 49, 107
Ohio Council of Retail Merchants, 48, 56
Ohio Deposit Guarantee Fund, 150
Ohio Development Center, 115–16
Ohio Education Association: lobbying
by, 305, 318, 321, 327, 330; Rhodes
and, 69, 107
Ohio Endowment for the Arts, 318
Ohio Historical Society, 39, 355*n*6
Ohio Hospital Association, 306, 321
Ohio Legal Rights Service, 147
Ohio Legislative Correspondents Asso-
ciation, 108, 126
Ohio Legislative Research Project,
250, 365*n*10
Ohio Manufacturers' Association, 9, 16,
48, 189, 321
Ohio Newspaper Association, 29
Ohio Poll, 376*nn*3, 4

Ohio Public Interest Campaign, 129
Ohio Public Radio/Public TV, 193–94
Ohio Reclamation Association, 92
Ohio Revised Code, 274
Ohio Right to Life Society, 167
Ohio River, 3, 82, 105, 118, 204
Ohio Scholarship Endowment Fund, 51
Ohio State Journal, 45
Ohio State Penitentiary, 35, 54, 105
Ohio State University, 60–61, 65, 149,
182–83, 355*n*38
—Ohio Legislative Research Project,
250, 365*n*10
—Polimetrics Laboratory, 242
Ohio Turnpike, 45
Oil embargo. *See* Energy crises
O'Neill, C. William, xii, 42–58, 64, 260;
J. W. Brown and, 38–39; parsimony
of, 12, 82; Supreme Court service of,
50, 285, 294
O'Neill, Thomas P. ("Tip"), 213, 219,
223, 246
Ontario, 69
Operation Crime Alert, 108
Operations Improvement Task Force,
271, 274
Opinion polls, 192, 292, 376*n*2, 376*n*3
Oral voting, 15
Organized crime. *See* Racketeering
Organized labor. *See* Labor unions
Orlett, Edward J., 310
Otte, Jim, 193, 194
"Our Merchant Marine Hymn," 222
Oxford University, 137, 138
Oxley, Michael G., 227

Pacific atolls, 25
Parks, 91. *See also* Cuyahoga Valley
National Recreation Area
Parties, xviii, 331–48; judicial elections
and, 287, 290, 292, 301; legislator atti-
tudes toward, 249–52; lobbyist access
to, 309–10; minority status of, 247–48;
Ohio Supreme Court and, 297, 298.
See also Campaign finance
PASSPORT program, 147–48
Patronage, 11, 345–46. *See also*
State employees
Patterson, Samuel C., 381
Payer, William, 107–8

❖

was composed in 9.7-point Palatino on a Macintosh using Quark XPress with Agfa Accuset output by BookMasters, Inc.; printed by sheet-fed offset on 50-pound Glatfelter Supple Opaque Natural stock (an acid-free recycled stock) with halftones printed on 70-pound acid-free enamel stock, notch bound over binder's boards in Holliston Kingston Natural cloth, and wrapped with dustjackets printed in three colors on 100-pound enamel stock with film lamination; also notch bound with paper covers printed in three colors on 12-point coated-one-side stock with film lamination by Edwards Brothers, Inc.; designed by Will Underwood; and published by

THE KENT STATE UNIVERSITY PRESS
KENT, OHIO 44242

❖